For Whom the Stars Came Out At Night

To

Ashley

With Very Best

Wishes

George Lawrence

2003

For Whom the Stars Came Out At Night

George Savva

BOULEVARD
Publishing

First Published in the U.K. in 2003 by
BOULEVARD PUBLISHING UK
16 Limetrees
Llangattock
Crickhowell, Powys NP8 1LB
01873 812363
e-mail Silvergb@aol.com

A CIP catalogue record of this book is available from the British Library
and the National Library of Wales.

ISBN 0-9545511-0-9

Printed and bound in Wales
By Creative Print and Design Wales
Ebbw Vale NP23 5SD

Dedications

My sincere thanks to Mary Lewis for the long hours she spent at her computer converting my hand written offerings into an ensemble of written words.

My wife, Pam, who suffered alone the 18 months of isolation whilst I set about the task of writing this book.

Finally, I dedicate this book to friends and colleagues...
Les Dawson, Lonnie Donnegan, Frankie Vaughan, Tommy Cooper and others who – whilst writing this book – sadly passed on to the big theatre in the sky. I will remember them always with great affection, and above all to Bob Herbert. His untimely death in a car crash was, without doubt, the loss I found most difficult to cope with.

"When you mention George Savva to the many great Stars from all over the world you have mentioned the man who brought theatre and style to the greatest clubs all over the world.

Like a champion racehorse nobody does it like 'George'. "

Danny La Rue 2003

"To know George Savva is to have one's life enriched with kindness, loyalty and laughter. I have had that pleasure for many years. George and his wonderful wife Pam are godparents to my son Blake.

George Savva's book is the definitive inside history of show business at its peak as well as the stars that were fortunate to work with George. I was one of the most fortunate."

Iris Williams 2003

George Savva is a legend in the world of 'clubland'. During his many years as one of the most important and colourful characters in showbusiness he has skillfully trodden the precarious and rocky road of diplomacy, dealing with greats and not so greats of our profession whilst trying to avoid either killing himself or them in the process. Not an easy task.

If there is a tale to tell he is the one to do it and I know we are all in for a treat as he regales us with his fascinating memories of the talented, the famous and the apalling. I am not sure quite where we, The Seekers, fit in amongst those descriptions but we are proud and privileged to have paraded our tiny talent on many a stage managed by George Savva.

With affection and gratitude

Frank Allen
on behalf of The Seekers.

"The super showman of Britains dazzling cabaret era, George could pick up a phone and summon the greatest entertainers to star in his glamorous night spots, not just because they trust him utterly, but because we all love him. His personal warmth, his professional excellence and his wicked wit are all on grand display in this captivating book, chocfull of fascinating insights, saucy anecdotes and unashamed name dropping!"

I loved it!

Bob Monkhouse OBE

"I had given up 'doing' clubs until George Savva approached me. Blazers in Windsor and Savva's in Usk became a part of my calendar. They provided wonderful memories which remain untarnished!

Many Thanks George

Sir Cliff Richard 2003

"Wherever George worked you could relax and know that you were in good hands.

I have never actually seen him throw anyone out of a club, but with me he was always trying to throw people in!"

Bruce Forsyth OBE

"I have known 'Sav' for many years. If anyone could be called
Mr Showbusiness it's him!

A very genuine person and someone I am proud to call a friend!"

Vince Hill

I ESCAPE THE BLITZ
NINE MAIDENS WORTH A MILLION
THE FIRST CHRISTMAS
TRESWITHIAN WELCOMES A GREEK
I BECOME THE MARATHON BOY

Fifteen years of age. Six feet two inches tall, slight of frame, but big of heart and very, very excited. I stood on the platform of Redruth Station that bright summer morning of 1955 and heard clearly the shrill whistle of the approaching train in the distance.

"Won't be long now," my Mother said. She was there by my side. "I'll put you on the train" she had said, finally facing up to the inevitability of my departure. "You're not going to that station on your own, I won't hear of it".

"There really is no need Mum," said I, "I've been to London before, I know the drill and after all I am fifteen now".

My protestations were in vain. My wonderful fat, cuddly Irish Mother, the woman who meant the world to me insisted

"I'll have no more argument, this is your big day and I'll be seeing you off to be sure. I'm putting you on the train".

I smile now when I remember that remark. Unwanted aliens, refugees, cattle, milk, fish and the post were all items that were 'put on trains' in those days. Now it seemed I was to be added to the list. The big day had arrived. My giant leap from the comparative obscurity of a small Cornish village, from school and school chums, from all the experiences of growing up in a country environment were at an end. I was heading into a new chapter in my life, to new experiences. I was going to work. To work in the great metropolis called London.

It was fate and the fortunes of war that brought me to Cornwell in the first place. 1941 was not a good year for many people for many reasons, one of which was the war. For me it was certainly not a good year to be born. I was conceived in London. The result of a passionate wartime relationship between my mother and a Greek-Cypriot restaurateur. The dark clouds of war had settled over the whole of Europe and Britain was struggling to come to terms with a daily and nightly bombing blitz by the German Luftwaffe which was causing great suffering and many casualties amongst civilians. One protective measure taken was the transportation of pregnant women away from the blitz, to safer havens in the country to produce their offspring, and so my very pregnant Mother was – you guessed it 'put on a train'.

Her labour pains, so the story goes, began just outside Slough and became much worse by the time the train had reached Reading. By the time the train reached Didcot the situation was desperate and a few miles down the line at Swindon my Mother was duly unloaded, from both the train and the strain of carrying me any longer or further. It was at Swindon therefore that I saw my first light of day. Alas, there was little time to dwell. It seemed we were deemed to be still in the line of fire. Neither the British War Cabinet nor the German High Command could wait to get rid of us and four days later, mother and child continued their journey to the peace, tranquillity and relative safety of deepest Cornwell.

Mother never returned to London or my Greek-Cypriot father. I gather that the relationship had more or less broken down anyway. It was certainly on its last legs before her unscheduled and speedy departure. My father was a married man and his wife and family as well as the Greek Orthodox Church were putting him under considerable pressure. My mother, because she was a Roman Catholic, was totally disowned by her large Irish family and excommunicated by the Catholic Church. Therefore, there seemed little point in her returning to London. Mother eventually met and married Frederick Gay, a Cornishman. He was a wonderful stepfather to me and took the place of my 'real' father throughout my early years. The marriage may well have been blessed in Heaven, but certainly not on Earth. My mother, an excommunicated Catholic with an illegitimate child, was shunned by the Gay clan (if you can pardon the expression). Four Lanes, the ex tin mining village near Redruth where we settled, was a small village, full of small-minded people.

Fred's Methodist Vicar became another member of an increasing number of aggravated clerics and flatly refused to have anything to do with a church wedding for Fred, the general consensus was that my mother was the 'Irish sinner from Hell'. Despite all this Fred, with great courage, stuck to his guns and went ahead with the marriage which took place at Redruth Registry Office. I was four years old and I suppose sitting there at the back of the room scratching myself, whilst watching my Mother marry, defines me as the original 'lousy bastard'. Herr Hitler, Mr Churchill and Comrade Stalin, were obviously unaware of the other war raging in the south west of England. The principal players. Three large families, Irish, Greek and Cornish; not to mention their respective religious representatives namely two Priests and a Vicar. Our very own three, (not so wise), men and a cast of several. Such were the times and the attitudes of the day. Mercifully, times change and with them attitudes. The close community of our village gradually accepted us; particularly when, a year after the marriage, Albert my Stepbrother was born. His birth helped to repair the rifts within the family, as well as with neighbours and other villagers. Fred was overjoyed at the arrival of his new son but, throughout my childhood and upbringing, he treated both of us with the same love and affection: Always.

Post-war Britain was a cocktail of pride and joy, hardship and deprivation. The nation rejoiced that the war was over at last and we had defeated the enemy. The bloodshed and the killing had ended and the nation faced the task of rebuilding not only towns and cities but also smashed and broken relationships and shattered lives. Hard times and deprivation were the order of the day and rationing seemed to last for ever. As a young boy, a dreamer, my life was a fantasy. In Post-war Britain for years after the war, newspapers and comics radio and the cinema, continued an outpouring of post-war propaganda, which for me, was manna from Heaven. I could imagine battles fought and won; heroic struggle and great sacrifice. In my vivid imagination it was easy for me to drift from one great event to another. I was not a child but the commander of a highly sophisticated, well-armed and courageous army. From Pengelli heights I could survey all the territory that my gallant forces had liberated. I drove the enemy from Eva's Downs to Carne Cai, from Penstruthiel to Stithians. No enemy survived the onslaught of my advancing army. Disused tin mines became former German cities I had destroyed the day before yesterday. The old quarry at Carne Cai, became a major Nazi military base which my forces overran after Sunday school. Tomorrow, I will set about taking Carne Brea and its hilltop castle. I might have tried today, but its teatime and my Mum will be waiting. Everywhere I go flag waving crowds line the roads chanting my name. Without doubt the mood environment and atmosphere of the late forties fuelled my fantasies. I was totally carried away. I imagined that because of my military genius I had joined the great names of British history. Clive of India, Gordon of Khartoum, Lawrence of Arabia, and now, Savva of Cornwell.

These halcyon days were seldom interrupted by the pressure of education. Nine Maidens Country Primary School was a typical four class

Cornish granite mausoleum situated roughly three miles outside our village. So named from the legend of the nine maidens who, despite being forbidden to dance by their elders, did so, and for their disobedience were turned to stone. 'Never mind girls, that's showbiz!' Nothing much has changed. At least you have the consolation of outlasting us all; and without the need to worry about 'Eyes, Tits and Teeth'. To this day the circle of nine large granite stones can be seen standing in a field quite close to the school. Nine Maidens School could hardly be described as a great hall of learning or centre of academic excellence but to be fair, Messrs. North, Lord, Timmings and of course headmaster Flann, did their best to point us in the right direction. Primary Education was pretty basic, at least they gave us a greater understanding of the world around us and gave us a foundation of knowledge on which to build. I should tell you at this point that I was a dunce and good at practically nothing except English Composition and History. The teachers never gave up on me, but despite the continuous blustering, shouting and cajoling, I felt they came to accept my academic limitations. Oh how I longed to surprise all and emerge from the pack to win recognition through achievement. I'm convinced that fate took a hand one dreary Thursday afternoon.

Each Thursday, headmaster Flann took us for Mathematics. The subject was a mystery to me. Let's face it, I was hopeless at Maths and for that reason I hated it and I think it hated me. At least until that fateful Thursday afternoon. Following the lunch break, we sat at our desks in readiness for the, boring Maths lesson, with the possible exception of old 'clever clogs' Osborne, who actually enjoyed the subject. The door of the classroom was suddenly flung open and the Mighty Flann entered. He was a hulk of a man, weighing between 20 to 22 stone. He had a ruddy face, a great shock of reddish hair and hands as big as shovels. I always believed him to be of Irish descent, not only because he looked Irish but I was sure he had shortened his name to Flann from the more humorous sounding Flannigan. However, he had no trace of an Irish accent and I never found out if my theory was correct. Surveying the terrified class with his usual intimidating glare, I could not help thinking of those nine maidens of stone and how they must have felt at the moment of petrifaction. Mr Flann was ready to ask us a question. He always started the lesson by asking a question.

"Can anyone tell me? What is a million?" he boomed. The classroom remained silent.

Reed and Roberts stared at the floor, Eathorne and Hale gazed out of the huge windows, but nobody received a sign from the god of education..

The other pupils stared blankly into space. Even 'know all' Osborne, usually the first with his hand in the air, remained totally silent and motionless.

Unbelievable as it may seem, I knew what a million was. The only person that knew less about Maths than me was my mother. Yet one day out of the blue she said

"I'll tell you how to remember a million. Not that anyone around here is likely to ever come into contact with such a sum", she said with a disapproving glance at Fred, who was unemployed at the time.

She conveyed her pearl of wisdom to me and I was so impressed that I actually remembered it. Now here was I, the only one in the whole class who knew the answer and yet I was frozen, too terrified to speak. I knew the answer. I knew it was right. Why should I hang back? My chance to make an impression, to make a name for myself. With adrenalin pumping and a sudden mega blush, I put my hand in the air. Mr Flann, who was by now beginning to despair, looked at me in total disbelief.

"Yes Savva", he growled.

All eyes turned to me. The shocked and disbelieving faces of my friends surrounded me. The moment of truth had arrived. I knew my destiny was sealed. I rose to my feet and speaking quite clearly said, "A million is a one and six noughts".

After a slight pause, Mr Flann said "Very good Savva" and "tell me," he continued, "Are you sure of this?"

"Oh Yes Sir" I replied "The numbers and the letters are the same sir, so it is easy to remember".

"I don't quite follow you," he said with a frown.

"Well Sir" said I, now growing in confidence "A million has seven numbers and also seven letters".

There was a gasp from my classmates and a look of astonishment from Mr Flann. Quickly gathering himself he asked me to come forward.

"Kindly show the class what you mean Savva," he instructed, handing me a piece of chalk with a smile.

I have no idea how my skinny legs carried me to the front of the class and further to the front of the blackboard, but there I was and with a trembling hand I wrote 1,000,000 and MILLION. I turned to face the class, in the shadow of the towering frame of Mr Flann. At that moment I knew just how Oliver Twist must have felt – God, he must have had balls of steel to actually 'ask for more'. I'll say one thing for Mr Flann, he owned up. He was not really an owning up type; but, taking me by the shoulders and gesticulating towards me the blackboard and the class, he uttered the words

"I confess, I didn't realise that. Again you see a perfect example of word and number association. How many times have I told you –all of you – you are never too old to learn. This is a classic example. I know how to spell a million and how to write a million numerically, but did not realise the obvious, as young Savva did. Well done Savva." He concluded.

I returned to my seat with head held high and a sense of great achievement. I was for once, the centre of everyone's attention. Not least the now smiling headmaster.

From that moment on Maths lessons were never quite the same. Coaxing and encouragement replaced rage and despair. From that moment on Mr Flann helped me to cope with the continuing saga of the Maths and me. He never asked me how I had worked out or acquired my little letter number scenario and I never volunteered the information. That little gift of wisdom from my Mother became a life-saving and treasured family heirloom. As if to prove that the stroke of 'mathematical genius' was not a flash in the pan and realising the benefit that single act had produced, I set out to improve even further. I even worked somewhat harder, according to my teachers, which goes to prove that shouting and terror seldom produce the best results.

I was a dreamer with a vivid imagination and a desire to impress; and it was probably this to desire to impress still further, combined with an ability with the written word, that encouraged me to write a play. The inspiration presented itself at Christmas in 1953. Each year during the festive season it was the tradition of the school to stage a nativity play. We were appointed to fulfil various roles each according to ability. Needless to say, because of my acting skills or should I say the lack of them, I was usually part of the large gathering of shepherd's or local Bethlehem onlookers. In short an 'extra'. The large cast of extras simply embellished the 'Top of the Bill', Mary, Joseph and the 'fully booked' Innkeeper, who was able to let his stable as well (lucky sod). Not only was he packed to the gunnels, but think of the publicity he received when his newborn distinguished guest arrived. The pupils chosen for the leading roles had to be extremely good at acting and remembering their lines. We 'also- rans' had very little to do or say.

A shopkeeper's son, a farmer's daughter and the son of a civil servant usually filled the top slots. They could strut their stuff and deliver their lines word perfect. Looking back I see clearly now that some of the kids from a middle class background had the edge on us. As the sons and daughters of the petite-bourgeois they had a considerably more stable economic and home life which, I suppose, gave them the confidence to reach the commanding heights of our Xmas presentation.

I enjoyed the annual ritual despite the fact that I was usually just an angel or shepherd. Even as I neared adolescences, I still enjoyed the razzmatazz and buzz of a school play presentation. Indeed all the pupils seemed to enjoy it, irrespective of age. After all, what kid would miss the chance to dress up and prance about on stage? Miss North was both Director and Producer. She was a kindly soul and very precise in everything she did.

She used to throw herself into the production and get quite carried away with it all. I'm sure that at times she thought she was at the London Palladium – bless her. The costumes were the usual combination of cardboard, crepe paper, tinsel, rags, cast offs and pieces of cloth, all donated by the supportive mums and dads who were unlikely to see the result of their donations until the Gala Night presentation at the Village Hall. All were invited.

I remember taking the part of the Angel Gabriel this particular Christmas. Not just any old angel, but the top dog, numero-uno. I had a big cloak, and much larger wings than the rest of the cherubs, and I could boss them about. This was a full supporting role with quite a lot to say and do, but let's face it I was not very good at this sort of thing. I was never going to be a Sir Lawrence Olivier or a Sir Alec Guinness. During rehearsal one day, I missed my cue, came in late and stumbled awkwardly through my lines.

"Oh come along Savva" Miss North called. "Pull yourself together".

Many years later I still find the remark amusing. Unbeknown to Miss North my Gabriel's cloak was made from an old pair of my mother's curtains.

Because of my greater involvement with the production, I had to work and think much more than usual. I realised that, year in year out, we would perform the same play with little variation. The set was invariably a stable in which much coming and going took place. Each year a different author, but pretty much the same set up. The idea came to me in a flash. I would write a Nativity Play with three acts instead of one:

Act 1. The home of Mary and Joseph.
Act 2. On the road to Bethlehem and
Act 3. The Birth of Christ.

By the time the school had reassembled in January after the Christmas break I had finished my play.

It was a 40-minute, Three Act play, I named 'The First Christmas'. Adding two five minute breaks between Act's One and Two and Two and Three, would bring the full time span to 50 minutes – perfect. In an addendum to the work, I outlined my ideas for three simple sets easily changeable.

Allowing time for other activities that always took place on the Gala night, I wrote in my exercise book:-

7.00.p.m. Carol Singing

7.10.p.m. The Lesson (read by teacher)

7.15.p.m. The First Christmas

8.05.p.m. Mr Flann's Speech

8.15.p.m. W.I. Tea and mince pies.

8.30.p.m. Onwards. Good Night and a Merry Christmas.

One cold sharp January morning, I sought and found Miss North gliding toward her classroom from Assembly.

"Excuse me Miss," I said, "may I give you this", handing her the exercise book containing the completed work.

"The First Christmas" she said, reading the label I'd stuck on the front of the book.

"What is it Savva?" she asked.

"It's a play miss" I replied. "A Nativity Play I have written during the school holidays".

"Thank you" she said, with a look of surprise and a smile as, clutching the play, she strode away to her classroom. The facilities at Nine Maidens Primary were quite sparse. The headmaster's study doubled as a teacher's common room, and it was to the common room that I was summoned that afternoon. I tapped on the door and entered, with some misgiving I might add.

"Ah Savva" said the headmaster loudly. "There you are. Miss North has shown us your play and we've all had a read".

The headmaster sat at his large desk, upon which sat my exercise book. Miss North, Miss Lord and Mr Timmings occupied chesterfield type chairs dotted about the room. The headmaster continued.

"Don't look so nervous boy; we think it an excellent piece of work. In fact with a few corrections and adjustments, we think it worthy of presenting next Christmas".

"What inspired you to write it?" asked Miss Lord.

"I don't know really Miss. I just had time on my hands and decided to have a go".   "Your composition work has always been very good," she said "but this piece of work is excellent. Well done" she concluded. Miss North was next to comment.

"I like the proposed sets" she said. "In Act Two you have Mary resting on a milestone which declares in bold writing, Bethlehem Four Miles. Most original".

After several other complementary remarks and some very agreeable backslapping I left the common room. Never in my wildest dreams did I ever imagine that I could impress my elders with my work. My feelings and my emotions were indescribable. To my mates I had become an icon. their number one person, their unelected leader. I suppose I've always strived to be the best at what I did and for sure, I've always been a bit of a poseur.

As if all this was not enough, my Greek Father began to take a renewed interest in my well being and I was quite regularly invited to join him in London during school holidays. From the moment I first met him I found him to be a fascinating person. He was a very serious man and very proud. He was fiercely defensive of his heritage and of his Greek background. He taught me much about the Greek civilisation without realising it. I'm sure he had no idea how perceptive I was. I hung on his every word and I remember he gave me a beautiful book on the Greek civilisation and its culture. I read every word. After all to a dreamer like me, ancient Greek culture, legend and mythology were the stuff that dreams are made of.

My Father was unaware that with his help I had become fascinated with the glorious past of my Greek and Greek Cypriot ancestors. My continuing love of history was given a real boost by these visits. On returning to school I was besieged by friends who wanted to hear stories from the great capital. I was never one to hang back and I related my many experiences in great detail and, on occasion, with a full measure of exaggeration and embellishment. Eventually I was made Head Boy of Nine Maidens and achieved all, indeed more, than I could have wished for from my days at the little Cornish country school. Sadly, I never got to see my play enacted as later that year we were moved on. Our entire class was allocated to new schools as part of the freshly introduced Comprehensive Education System decreed by the Government of the day. Of the thirty or so pupils in my class half were sent to the Redruth Comprehensive and the rest of us to Treswithian Comprehensive at Camborne. In the autumn of my final year I arrived with my fellow students and other small groups of pupils from other village primaries, to fill the sixty or so places within the six hundred capacity of Treswithian Comprehensive.

I'd never seen anything quite like it. The massive, fairly new, concrete, glass and steel building, surrounded by playgrounds and playing fields, occupied more ground than our entire village. On entering the gates, I quickly realised we had reached a type of Hell on earth. From the very outset, the five hundred and forty town students that already occupied the building, and had done so for the whole of the previous term, decided to make the arrival of the small group of new pupils as uncomfortable as possible. To walk to the cloakroom was, in effect, to run a gauntlet. Abuse was hurled at us from all sides. Taunts of 'country yokels, village idiots, country bumpkins, pigs, goats' and much worse filled the air. Treswithian was my Armageddon.

During the first few days we were subjected to the most miserable and unrelenting verbal, and some times physical, abuse. One or two of my more hot-tempered friends retaliated and got into fights. For the life of me I could not think why, the odds were obviously stacked against them. Being a devout coward I managed to avoid any fighting or physical contact, but day after day I longed for the cosiness of Nine Maidens and those wonderful days when I ruled supreme. I found myself utterly submerged in a swirling mass of pupils. I felt I had almost totally lost my identity, sunk without trace. The new arrivals were allocated to various classes according to ability and academic record, but my mates and I were no match for the townies and lagged behind in most subjects. We were considered by the others to be not very bright, which in itself provided additional ammunition for the bullies. What I found interesting and totally new was the moving about from classroom to classroom. English for example, was taken by one teacher, History by another and Maths yet another. Each teacher had their own classroom and specialised in a particular subject. We travelled from room to room, subject to subject. By the end of the first week I had reached an all time low. It seemed that we would never to be accepted by the town pupils and I felt isolated and depressed as I headed toward my History lesson. Two of my friends and I were running late. We had made the mistake of asking an enemy pupil for directions to a classroom and were of course sent in the wrong direction. Arriving a little late for our lesson we entered rather timidly to find the class in progress,

"Ah Welcome Gentlemen" said the teacher. "Better late than never!". That brought an outburst of laughter.

"Sorry Sir" said one of my mates. "We were given the wrong directions". Hoots of laughter followed the statement, as we made our way to some desks at the back of the room.

"Settle down now" said the History teacher, calling the class to order. "Well now" he continued, addressing his remarks in our direction. "We are currently dealing with Greek Mythology and my question, to which no one seems to know the answer is, who's face launched a thousand ships? Perhaps one of you new chaps could help me out".

This brought further sniggers from around the room. Without hesitation and without the customary hand in the air, I immediately clearly and quite sharply answered

"Helen of Troy, Sir".

The History teacher was clearly pleasantly surprised. The class fell into a stunned silence and I felt all eyes now turned in my direction. "Correct" came the eventual reply from the teacher,

"What school are you from?" he asked.

"Nine Maidens Sir" I replied.

"Ah yes" he said with a smile, "as far as I recall from the notes, you had not reached this stage at the primary schools, or had you?"

"No Sir" I replied, "we had not".

"Well you certainly knew the answer," he said with a puzzled look.

"Yes Sir" I said, "because I am a Greek". This, you will realise, was a bit over the top but it had the desired effect. It drew gasps from around the room and a look of incredulity from the teacher.

"Really" he said "and do you possess further knowledge of the Greeks and their mythology?"

"Yes Sir" I said. "My Father has told me many things and I have books on the subject". The teacher was now completely fascinated and said,

"What is your name young man?"

"Savvas, Georgiou Hadji-Savva Sir" I immediately replied. For the first time in my young life I used my full name. I had sensed that I was now the centre of attention and I was not about to let this position slip away. I was milking it for all it was worth.

"My word" said the teacher. "That certainly is a very Greek name, a real mouthful" he chuckled. This brought light laughter from the rest of the class. "You must forgive us young Savva" he continued "we don't get to see many Greeks around here". This brought more laughter, but not mocking or menacing. I sensed a change of mood, a sudden friendly atmosphere and laughter that was with me rather than at me. The mood of my adversaries had completely changed, not just because I answered the question but because I was different. I looked the same and sounded the same but I was a Greek, they had never seen a Greek before.

A combination of my declaration and the fact that the teacher was obviously a Grecophile made me a minor celebrity, particularly as the class had been learning about Ancient Greece all through the second half of the previous term and on into this. Little wonder they found me interesting. I neither specified the Cypriot origin of my father nor mentioned my Irish mother. Both my mates and I quickly became accepted by our former enemies. No need, I thought, to elaborate. Savva the Great from Greece sounded infinitely better than George the half Greek from Swindon. Shortly after this, further integration progress was made on the sports field. I had no idea how good a runner I was. I used to win most of the longer races at my previous school, but frankly, largely because of the lack of any serious competition.

Athletics at Treswithian were quite another matter. There were sufficient numbers of pupils for every track and field event to make the competition formidable. My introduction to the Sports master was somewhat amusing. He like everyone else had heard I was of Greek origin. He was a very fit and active man, totally dedicated to the success of the school over all others in all events. He obviously assumed that I had arrived, complete with an Olympic birthright. After studying my file, he looked up and said

"What are you good at Savva, what is your sport?"

"Well Sir" I began, "I don't really know, we did little at our previous school".

"Yes I can see that" he retorted, "but there must have been one field or track event you enjoyed and did quite well in" he enquired irritably.

"I was quite good at running Sir," I said. "Longish sort of distances".

"Ah I thought so," he said with a note of triumph in his voice. "You've got the lanky wiry build for it. I'm putting together some trials this afternoon so I'll try you in the half miler and we'll see if any of your forefathers' Olympic heritages rubbed off on you".

There were fourteen participants including myself for the half-mile trial, which took place later that day. The Sports Master trundled up to the start, complete with a large timepiece and a gun. 'Christ' I thought, he's going to shoot the losers. That's carrying sports too far. The weapon turned out to be a starting pistol, yet another giant leap forward from Primary to Comprehensive Secondary Education. The replacement of a teacher's bellowed 'Go', by a crack of a staring pistol. Ah! I thought, progress is a wonderful thing. The sporting landscape had also changed from twice round the playing field to a clearly defined multi laned track with distance markers every 200 yards or so. I have to say I loved the innovations and I was enjoying the newness and quantities of equipment to be found in every department and every classroom, in this my new environment.

'On your marks, set, bang' and we were off. I strode out with a deal of urgency over the first two hundred yards using my long legs and wiry slim frame, to the utmost, but without much success. I soon realised that most of the field were either ahead of me or pressing me to get ahead. I was clearly being left behind.

You may be familiar with the story of the Tortoise and the Hare; well they have nothing to do with the race I now found myself in. I suppose it would be fair to say I'm a plodder in life. I've never given up on any task;

instead, I've always worked my way to a conclusion, usually a successful one. The half-mile was to take us two and a half times around the track and by the half distance I was last. Suddenly I was amazed that I began from this point on, first to catch and then pass my fellow athletes. I had not speeded up, that for me was impossible, but the others were tiring and I retained the same relentless pace that I began with. By the time I reached the last bend I lay second and was closing on the leader who, incidentally, was Treswithian's Head Boy, Tom Elliot, later to become a very close friend of mine. We flashed across the finishing line together and without the aid of a camera it was impossible to separate us.

"I think you won," said Tom sportingly. Feeling thankful that I'd finished at all, let alone in the first two, I graciously suggested to Tom that I thought he'd got it 'by a nose'. Opinions from onlookers - fellow students, divided into three camps, Tom's, the Dead heaters and mine. The Sports Master came over to us positively gushing with pride.

"Well done boys" said he. "I don't know which of you won and I don't much care" he exclaimed.

"It was an excellent trial", and brandishing his timepiece, "an excellent time". He continued.

"We've come to expect good things from Tom, he trains a great deal, but you appear to be a bit of a find young Savva. When do you train?"

"I don't Sir" I replied.

"I knew it," he said. "A natural. I could tell from your tactics and your style. Imagine what you could achieve with some training". I could see he was now reading a lot more into the trial result than was really there and the reason soon became obvious.

"Tell me" he enquired, "you seemed full of running at the end of the trial, could you have run further?"

"Oh yes Sir" I replied.

"I knew it, a long distance runner, our very own marathon boy," he added excitedly. "I assume you know from whence the marathon originated?" he asked.

"Yes Sir, Ancient Greece".

"Yes indeed, maybe one of your forbears could have been a great Olympic athlete all those years ago" he said. "Who knows?" he concluded. How lucky can you get I thought. Another Grecophile.

I soon realised that these early term achievements, both in the classroom and on the sports field not only broke down the barriers between the new arrivals and the other Treswithian pupils but also got me noticed by the headmaster, who was obviously kept informed by his colleagues. Eventually, and I realised later inevitably, I was summoned to his study and installed as Deputy Head Boy. He had noted my early progress and was impressed with my previous school activities as provided in my file forwarded by Mr Flann.

"In making you Deputy Head Boy, I am also seeking to a bridge a divide between two sets of pupils. I am aware of some divisions and resentment and I've noted from your file that you were Head Boy at your previous school. You also seem to already enjoy a measure of popularity among both sets of pupils" he concluded.

In the twilight of my very modest education I spent an eventful and enjoyable final year. A year in which I made many new friends, many of whom I still remember and recall with affection.

The train whistle sounded again, much nearer. I stood with my Mother near the start of the platform because the guard was always situated at the rear of the train and it was in his safe keeping I was to be placed for my journey to London. At last I could see it as it crossed the Penventon Viaduct. The morning sunlight glistened on the green and black steel engine and carriages of yellow and brown, all smoke, steam and noise. Through my young eyes she was both awesome and beautiful. The Cornish Riviera Express. A grand title for a grand train that thundered into the station. Gradually the passing carriages slowed and with a screeching of metal she came to a halt. The hissing steam seemed to almost envelop the train as great gushes poured out from below the carriages and up between the doors and the platform edge. My mother guided me to the open door and the uniformed guard who stood by it. A few words and gestures between the guard and my mother were exchanged then turning to me she said

"This gentleman will keep an eye on you and your Father will meet you at Paddington. Look after yourself; write as often as you can. Look after your money and be a good boy" she was very tearfull.

"Don't cry Mum," I said. "You know I've been to London many times before. I know this time is different, but I'll write and visit. Remember London is only eleven hours away". She brushed away a tear.

"You're right," she said. She knew I always hated it when she cried.

I boarded the train with a half empty suitcase and a ten-shilling note. For security I had neatly folded the note and placed it in the breast pocket of my jacket. I completed the security arrangements by placing my white handkerchief also in my breast pocket, with a little showing out of the top. An ingenious disguise I thought. No one will ever think that beneath the hanky lay hidden treasure. The half empty suitcase and the ten-shilling note were the grand total of my finances and property.

The Guard seated me by a window in the compartment adjacent to his own tiny quarters at the rear of the train. The whistle blew a short blast, there was a shudder, a quiver and the train began to move off. I waved vigorously to my mother until her face was lost amongst the smoke and sea of other faces waving goodbye to their loved ones. The train slid into the tunnel that would take it under the east end of the town, soon emerging into the bright sunlight, as it gathered speed. We passed through Scorrier and I remember the vivid display of rhododendrons in full bloom that lined the railway embankment. I see them now as I saw them then. It is a memory that will never fade because at that moment the reality of my situation came home to me. I was on my way to a new life, new friends and new relationships in the big city.

What would the future have in store for me? What life would I make for myself? What was to be my destiny?

Little did I know then that I would soar like an eagle through the marble halls of fame. That I would walk amongst the stars. That I would experience joy, pride and prestige and that I would suffer the depths of despair. A vast landscape of incredible experiences stretched out before me. Now to be recalled and remembered. Like the rhododendrons that glided by the carriage window all those years ago.

2

I ARRIVE IN LONDON

I MEET THE FAMILY

MY VISION OF THE CAPITAL

I ENTER CATERING

QUASIMODO THE WAITER

SAVVA THE RED

I MARRY AND DIVORCE

MY DECADE OF PLEASURE

My previous visits to London had been during school holidays and were both short and sweet. This time I had come to stay and as a fifteen year old from the backwaters of the countryside I marvelled at all the wonders of city life. I new from previous visits that I already loved London, but now my love affair intensified. I simply adored this great capital city. I enjoyed each and every moment as if it were my last. The hustle and bustle of the people, the buzz of the traffic and above all the amazing choice of places to visit and things to do were exhilarating. I used to explore the city taking bus, trolleybus and tube to a variety of destinations in the heart of the capital and its suburbs. Shops, restaurants, theatres, cinemas and museums beckoned. I felt so at home, secure; and ready to take full advantage of any opportunities that might come my way. As far as I was concerned I was at the centre of the universe. There was no better place on earth to realise your dreams and to work, earn and play.

I threw myself wholeheartedly into employment seeking situations that required neither qualifications nor previous experience. Inevitably I arrived at the 'gates' of the catering industry, the very bottom. After peeling spuds and washing up I soon graduated to the 'stillroom'. Several thousand teas and coffees later I progressed to the 'floor' first as a 'comis' and then a short time later as a fully-fledged waiter. The work throughout the various departments was hard and the hours long, but the rewards were excellent. Real money was available to any experienced waiter who had speed, style, a pleasant personality and an ability to smile all day long. My progress in the industry took me from one location to another as I worked for a number of first class caterers. From Goodge Street to Hammersmith; Victoria to Balham; inevitably I arrived at London's great West End, the hub of the catering world. I had worked my apprenticeship at various suburban establishments and felt ready to take my place in the West End where the big money was to be earned. I took a waiter's position with the Forte Organisation - who else - Forte virtually owned the entire West End in those days.

The work was really tough, the pay very poor, but Oh Boy, tips a plenty. Income tax was almost non-existent, unless of course you were stupid enough to declare your tips. I learnt early on never to change your tips at work. No one should ever know the amount of your undeclared income. I remember waiting with my fellow waiters and colleagues for the night bus to take us to the suburbs and homes. How successful or not a day had been was easily measured by the degree of 'waiters tilt' caused by the weight of yet uncounted coins, gathered and transported in the earner's jacket pocket. As often as not I appeared to have done better than most. I always seemed to have a more severe tilt than my fellow waiters, who were quick to label me 'Quassie' for some reason. They often referred to the handicap of my heavily laden jacket, and therefore tilt, as comparable to a hunchback out for a nightly stroll. I felt the nickname they had bestowed upon me, a little misplaced. After all, Quasimodo's hump was on his back, not in the right hand pocket of his jacket.

I also recall a particularly bad day when the customers were virtually all 'stiffs', (a waiter's term for non-tipper). I arrived at the bus stop to be greeted with remarks of 'Quassie has had a bad day' etc.

"Oh no I haven't" I replied haughtily. "No coins today – all notes!" O.K. So I lied.

Throughout these early years of employment in London, my 'luxurious accommodation' consisted of a variety of bed-sits in upmarket areas such as Camden Town, Stoke Newington, Tottenham, Victoria and Tooting. It was also during this time that I was drawn closer to the Greek side of my family. I met and got to know my many uncles, aunts and cousins, as well as my four beloved step-brothers and sisters. Nick and Agathy, (the children of my Father's marriage), and Louis and Zitsa, the children of another of my Father's relationships, this time with an English lady called Vera Blake. Methinks Dad was a bit of a lad. Many London based Greek Cypriots were in catering in those days, and still are.

Many members of my family were in the trade and I found myself working with them on many occasions during my pre-Forte days. It was at this time I learnt to speak Greek fluently. This pleased and surprised everybody, including me.

In the early 60's I visited Cyprus with my Father and immediately fell in love with the 'Jewel of the eastern Mediterranean'. Throughout the early sixties I travelled quite extensively and visited France, Denmark, Sweden, Finland and the Soviet Union. I enjoyed travel and I'm sure it helped broaden my outlook. My thirst for knowledge increased dramatically and during 'off' periods of my split shift catering duties, I visited the great museums of the Capital. I also took on two correspondence courses through Wolsey Hall at Oxford. My most popular pastime was movies and every chance that came my way to wedge a movie in between work and other activities, I took. I can't say I had any favourite movie or movie stars, but visually, I consumed every celluloid moving image with the avarice of a locust.

As active as my life may have been, a young man's instinct had to surface and at the tender age of seventeen I became obsessed by the urge for female company. The ritual began. The dance halls of the West End, the numerous Jazz clubs, the Hoot Nanny Blues evenings at various locations. All were added to my already overloaded schedule. The boy meets girl scenarios of these haunts are obvious, but the music and companionship were also very welcome. A seemingly unending list of girl friends began as I entered into a series of relationships. I was no oil painting, but I could 'pull'. The attractive or the not so attractive, all were welcome.

Because of my hard work I had no financial problems and despite sending money to my family in Cornwall to improve their living standards I still had sufficient funds to pay my way and have a good time. I was a 'man about town' and in company I could always stand my corner. Meanwhile I certainly played the field. Miss Posh of Kensington, Miss Hideous of Peckham, Miss Horrendous of Walthamstow and Miss Perfect of Watford, were all part of a long list of acquaintances, some purely platonic, some deeply sensual and sexual. Economic liberation meant freedom and opportunity. Freedom to do and go when and where I liked and the opportunity to wine, dine, dance and ultimately charm and seduce. At this juncture I should mention that I would not wish the reader to imagine I was a young man whose only interest had become money and women, a person driven by greed and an insatiable sexual appetite. I was never a 'Hooray Henry'.

In 1961 Albert my Cornish stepbrother came to London and shared my flat at Victoria. He soon found work and settled in really well. A few years later

I brought my mother and Fred to London, settling them into accommodation at Muswell Hill and later at Highbury. There was little work in Cornwell. Fred soon found that London had much more to offer and landed the position of head chef at the National Children's Home, Highbury. The other more serious side of my life at that time, which I called my 'red period', was my introduction to the various political movements of the day. During this period I found myself more and more to the Left of centre politically, partly because it was fashionable, but mainly because so many of my friends and colleagues were of socialist persuasion. They, my friends, all seemed to be rebelling about one thing or another. The Anti Colonialist Movement, The Anti Apartheid Organisation, The Campaign for Nuclear Disarmament, The Young Socialists and The Young Communist League were the major organisations of the time. I think it would be fair to say I supported all of them and was an active member of most.

I married and divorced during this period. Roberta Herron was a cocktail waitress originally from Northern Ireland. She was both glamorous and beautiful, but had the voice of Ian Paisley – only louder. The marriage lasted three years. There were no children. Reflecting now on the decade from leaving school to settling and working in the metropolis, I must confess I am amazed I did and achieved so much – or did I. Admittedly, I learnt to work, to be self-sufficient and to stand on my own two feet. I mastered a second language and formed a whole of new friendships and relationships. I broadened my outlook through travel and study and I was much more aware of the world around me. I experienced passion and pleasure and deepest love; won and lost. I had crossed the abyss from adolescence to manhood, but had I really progressed? What was my ultimate goal and was I progressing toward it or did my achievements have the ring of 'dead end' about them?
Just when my life began to settle into a routine, a pattern, there was to be a major change in my fortune.

During the late part of 65 and into 66 I was a West End flyer. I was popular with everyone, customers, fellow waiters and even the management of the Forte Empire. I had firmly established my credentials as a hard working, excellent waiter who, above all else, was reliable. I was much in demand by many of the Forte establishments and was moved from place to place, as was the system in those days, mainly because of the unreliability of many members of the Forte workforce. One particular day, I was despatched to the Prime Cut at Cranbourne Street, an upmarket eatery next door to the famous Talk of the Town. Little did I know as I entered the fairly new restaurant, that my life was soon to change dramatically and that one-day I would by challenging the 'Talk' next door for supremacy in the field of entertainment and leisure.

Furthermore, I had no idea that the petite, immaculately dressed Frenchman who managed the Prime Cut and to whom I now introduced myself, was to be instrumental in bringing about a career change that would span the next thirty years. Monsieur Gelineau welcomed me and guided me through the operation before handing me over to his assistant Geoff Udeen. The Indian assistant manager completed my introduction to the restaurant and its staff. My fellow members of staff included an Italian, a Portuguese, a Spaniard, a Chinese, a Turk and a Palestinian; a veritable League of Nations. I enjoyed the Prime Cut and settled in very quickly. The tips were excellent and my multinational colleagues were great to work with.

I became very popular with the management, principally because I was so damn reliable. My colleagues often missed days and/or nights, but I never did. In fact as often or not I'd be brought in to cover someone's absence or served two stations instead of just one. That was fine by me – double the work but also double the tips. Although Monsieur Gelineau was not liked by the staff, this was natural enough, what manager was? His attitude towards me was one of friendliness and kindness, probably because I worked hard and was totally dependable. Gelineau, Jeff and myself enjoyed an excellent relationship. Trade was excellent and following a fulsome day we enjoyed a great night trade from Talk of the Town revellers who would pop in for late night pasta or smorgasbord before heading home. My first real contact with showbiz was to welcome and serve the many directors, artistes and dancers who took the opportunity during rehearsal breaks to 'grab a bite and a glass'. I enjoyed looking after Tony Hancock on several occasions during this time. Like millions of others I was a great fan of his humour, but I also remember how sad he seemed as he sat with his black coffee and equally black sunglasses.

One day, on arriving at work, I found the Forte's Area Manager sitting in Gelineau's chair. I knew the A.M. quite well. He always had a friendly word for me during his periodic visits. The A.M. looked quite grim.

"Savva" he said, "Monsieur Gelineau and his assistant are no longer with us. I'm here to tell you that this will not in any way alter the operation here. Indeed a replacement manager is on his way".

"Very well Sir" I replied, wondering what could possibly have happened, as of course did the other members of staff who were arriving and receiving the same news.

Taking me to one side the A.M. reminded me that I had not given him an answer vis-à-vis, would I like to train for management within the organisation? Rather flatteringly, he often pressed me to enter management and, not wishing to offend, I again stalled him with the answer,

"Sorry Sir, I've not made up my mind yet, but I will within the next seven days, I promise".

"O.K." he said, "I'll phone you next week". I had made up my mind at almost the same moment the offer came from his mouth. It was 'No Way'. The hours were just as long, the pay not too good and the tips non-existent. For me it would have been financial suicide. I really must tell the old sod soon I thought, but up to now I had not had the bottle to do so. A few days went by, perhaps a week.

"Savva" called Canel Pie Sung the Chinese, "the A.M. on phone, he want talk to you".

Oh no I thought, he probably wants my answer. As I reached for the phone, I was thinking how best to break the news of my decision. He was the first to speak.

"Savva" he shouted down the phone. "We have a bit of a crisis at the Criterion Grill Room". I gave a silent sigh of relief. The A.M. Continued, "Could you get yourself down there at once and ask for the Manager Mr Figarus, he's Spanish, I want you to help them out until further notice".

"O.K. Sir" I answered. "I'm on my way".

"Good man" he replied and hung up.

The Criterion dominates almost a whole side of Piccadilly Circus. For any waiter it was the hub of the Forte Empire. Serving in the Grill Room was a prize assignment. It was the haunt of prominent businessmen and American tourist, which of course meant mega tips. I reported to Mr Figarus. He was an affable, albeit aggravated man, thick set with massive shoulders. His bushy eyebrows, together with large protruding cheekbones, gave him the facial appearance of a bull.

"It's the chef here," he said mournfully. "He causes me all the problems. He's a good chef and he knows it and he also knows that in this establishment, he is more important than anyone, even me. Our reputation depends on his kitchen. He upsets the waiting staff and now another two walked out. Take my advice, do your job and don't let him upset you and you will be fine".

Once in my uniform, I decided to introduce myself to the Chef.

"Savva, what kind of name is that" he demanded.

"Greek" I said.

"Oh another bloody foreigner" he retaliated. "I suppose you've met the Spanish Bull".

"Yes" I replied and I thought I knew I was right (Mr Figarus) really did look like a bull. "Well do your job and keep out of my way and we will get on fine" he said, not that I believed him.

The fact is we actually did get on great – he hurled volleys of abuse at all of us, particularly when under pressure, but I rode it out. I let it go over my head. Nothing was going to interfere with my capacity to earn and earn and I certainly did. The notes began to fly – Ten Shilling notes, One Pound notes, even the occasional fiver. I loved every minute of my time at the Crit and I guess it showed as I danced around the customers who were neither slow nor mean in showing their gratitude.

My economic base was now so strong; I made a point of discreetly pressing some notes into Chef's hands on a regular basis. "I've done well again. Have a drink Chef," I'd whisper. A gesture, despite the abuse I received, that became standard procedure. Beneath it all however, I got better and faster service from the kitchen and this enhanced my popularity still further in front of house. I was adored by the business community, loved by the Americans and despite his blustering, abusive rudeness; I think the chef was in love with me too. During my many years in catering I came into contact with many chefs and almost all had an attitude problem. They were all very ill tempered, fiery and very macho. I've always believed that almost every chef suffers an identity crisis. Their sub-conscious tells them that they are men doing what is regarded as a woman's job – cooking- and I believe this forces them to be macho and rebellious. This is the Savva 'men wearing aprons' theory.

One night, on returning to my flat at Tottenham, I opened the door to hear the phone ringing. It was two in the morning. Who was ringing me at this hour I thought, as I lifted the receiver.

"Hello Savva" said the voice at the other end. "This is Gelineau", I recognised his Satcha Distell type accent immediately.

"My dear Sir" I gushed "how nice to hear from you. How are you?" I asked.

"I am well thank you and also very exited. I have set up a fantastic operation called Caesars Palace, which has just opened. The building houses a Casino, a Bowling Alley and a giant Dining Room with Cabaret and Dancing. A three in one operation and it is Magnifique".

"Wow" I said.

After a slight pause he continued. "I have much to tell you and show you, but in a nutshell I need a Maitre D'Hotel to organise the massive catering operation here and I believe you are the man. The room is made for you".

"Well" I stuttered "I'm at the Crit at the moment and it is very good".

"Yes I know you are "he interrupted. "That's why I phoned so late, but why don't you come down tomorrow night after work. We work late here. It is after all a nightclub. I know you will love this place. Ask the Bull (yes he remembered him too) to let you off a little earlier and come down".

"O.K. Mr Gelineau" I said. "I will".

"Very good, I'll see you tomorrow", he said with a note of satisfaction in his voice.

"Where is it?" I asked.

"Luton" he said with a hint of apology. In his excitement, he almost forgot to give me the location. "Luton; when you get to the town just ask for Caesars. Everybody knows where it is". After a pause "Well until tomorrow" he said.

"Yes" I replied. "Tomorrow" and hung up.

I paused for a moment and pondered the extraordinary phone call, and then I thought, where the bloody hell is Luton? I was completely unaware that fate had once again taken me by the hand. The wheel of fortune was in motion. I was about to embark on the Good Ship Discovery for my very own new world. Little did I know my decade in London was coming to an end? Ten wonderful years! Could any offer prise me out of the Capital? I was about to find out.

CAESARS PALACE

I ARRIVE AT LUTON

I THINK NO BUT SAY YES

I MEET THE STAFF

XMAS EVE A DISASTER

NEW YEAR'S EVE 1966

WAKEY! WAKEY!

GELINEAU DEPARTS AGAIN

It is said that if you seek chapter and verse on any subject, particularly a local subject, ask a taxi driver. The driver who collected me from Luton station on that misty and miserable night in October 1966 was, when questioned about Caesars, a positive mine of information.

"Won't last long" he said.

"Lutonians don't support anything for any length of time. It will be a one day wonder".

Charming I thought. The black Morris Oxford taxi wound its way through Luton's dreary streets.

"So what exactly is this Caesars Palace place?" I continued to enquire.

"Don't know for sure," he said. "I think its some kind of big pub with gambling. Too many pubs in Luton already".

"I hear it's getting some good local support" I lied in a desperate attempt to extract one morsel of good news from 'kiss of death' at the wheel.

"Maybe, maybe" he replied. "But its only novelty value. It will probably wear off soon". It therefore followed that my statement "I'm thinking of taking a job there" seemed totally ridiculous, given the depressing background information emanating from the front of the taxi.

"Well good luck to you" he said "and I think you are going to need it", he added, as we turned into Caesars brightly lit entrance. The car park was absolutely full and there seemed to be a real 'buzz' about the place as I approached the reception desk and asked for Mr Gelineau.

"Your name Sir?" asked the very pleasant young receptionist. "Savva" I replied. "Oh yes Sir, Mr Gelineau is expecting you." She immediately led me through to the back office and on through it to a door at the rear which led to the Manager's inner sanctum. She knocked and opened the door with almost with the same movement; ushering me in.

"Ah Savva" greeted Mr Gelineau. "Welcome to Caesars Palace". Rising from his desk he shook me warmly by the hand. "May I introduce you to the owners? Mr Ivor Arbiter and Mr Ivan Weston".

Ivor had light almost blonde hair and an equally fair complexion. Ivan was much darker with black hair and an almost mulatto complexion. Both were quite young – late 30's early 40's at a guess and were very down to earth sort of people. They spoke with a very definite London accent and were evidently self-made men. After handshakes, Gelineau spoke.   "I've told them all about you"

"And you sound like just the chap we are looking for" interrupted Ivor. "Mr Gelineau speaks very highly of you, he reckons you're the business and around here what he says goes".

Ivan entered the conversation. "I hear you've had plenty of experience in the catering game" he said.

"Yes Sir" I replied. About ten years. As a matter of fact I've come directly from work tonight; I am currently at the Criterion Grill Room".

"So I see," said Ivan, eyeing me up and down. Many years later both Ivor and Ivan admitted that the night I visited them at Caesars, after a hectic day at the Criterion, I looked scruffy, greasy and smelt like a mobile kitchen and that, had it been up to them, I would never have got the job.

"The restaurant is the problem," said Ivan. "It needs someone who can take charge and build up a regular clientele of satisfied punters. The catering is the weak link in the chain," he added. "We can't seem to get it right".

"I see Sir," I said, not really knowing what to say`. After a few pleasantries, both Ivan and Ivor left the office and made their way to the Casino. Mr Gelineau invited me on a guided tour of the Palace. Little did Mr Gelineau or Messrs Arbiter and Weston realise, but I had already made up my mind to turn down their offer of Maitre D'Hotel or Restaurant Manager. To begin with, Luton seemed so far from the capital. In addition, I had no previous experience in Management at any level and I also had the feeling that the owners were not over impressed with me. On top of all this; the taxi driver's adverse comments were still very fresh in my mind.

Gelineau and I descended a very wide staircase, at the foot of which, on our left, through an arch was Caesars Casino. We passed the arch and continued towards two sets of double doors, flanked on both sides by at least a dozen one-armed bandits. Pushing open one of the doors, Mr Gelineau invited me to walk in. I cannot describe my feelings as I took my first steps into the Caesar Palace Cabaret/Dining Room. I saw a magnificent auditorium, with two tiers of diners, stretching before me. The atmosphere and ambience were overwhelming. I could not think of one single eatery, one restaurant or any other place that equalled it. Every table, every seat was taken by a 550 capacity audience. Dining was over as it was after 11.30 at night, but the tables were laden with glasses and bottles as the audience relaxed and enjoyed the cabaret of stars. There was a feeling of intimacy, even in such a large room further enhanced by the lighting, now dimmed, so that the bright stage lighting could have maximum effect and be the focal point of the room for cabaret. The raised proscenium was situated at the far end of the auditorium, offering a perfect view for all. The layout, ambience, atmosphere and indeed the whole aspect of the cabaret room were pure magic.

The top of the bill was none other than the amazing comedian and raconteur Bob Monkhouse. The audience was enthralled. They not only hung on his every word, but laughed as one and applauded as one as they enjoyed their very, very funny journey with Bob. 550 individuals had become 'legion like' as they gave a united response. I was so impressed, so taken by what I saw that I knew I had to make this room, this club, my own. I performed a mental u-turn and decided there and then that, despite all the obstacles, I would take the job at Caesars. Throughout my career in show business I have never been star struck, but in this instance I was 'people struck'. The room seemed to beckon to me; to challenge me to a glorious duel. I accepted and, eventually, I won.

When I took the job at Caesars I also took a major cut in wages. My pay was £25 per week. Admittedly this was three times as much as my Forte's pay but the tips were virtually non-existent. This is the way with employment in catering management. I was however, very happy to meet the challenge and, hopefully, justify Gelineau's confidence in my abilities.
Although the cabaret club had only opened a few weeks prior to my arrival, I inherited a full compliment of staff in every department. The restaurant staff were supervised by a lady called Margaret. In the absence of a restaurant manager, she had taken her responsibilities well beyond her brief. My arrival therefore, was not welcomed by Maggie the Tabby who's time in charge and responsibilities were about to be curtailed. The bar was well organised by none

other than Geoff Udeen, the Indian lad from the Prime Cut; and the kitchen was headed by Monsieur Lucien Bernard, an Escofier trained chef from Paris. He actually had his own private secretary called Connie, whose daily and nightly role was to follow Monsieur Bernard about the kitchen armed with pen and clipboard. She was quickly christened 'Clipboard Connie'. The Second Chef, who did all the work, was an Italian named Peter Torterella. Peter had a club foot but despite his disablement, caused by a motor car accident some years earlier in his native Italy, he still managed to limp about at an alarming rate of knots and was the real powerhouse in the kitchen.

The stage personnel included Geoff Walker as musical director. He led a nine-piece orchestra and a trio. Between the two music combinations Geoff covered all the club's musical requirements, both for dancing and musical backing for the cabaret. The show was hosted and compared by Anthony Wager. He was always immaculately dressed and oozed class and style, a perfect presenter; prior to his arrival at Caesars he had been an actor. His claim to fame was his role as 'Pip the Child', in the first film production of the Dickens's classic 'Great Expectations'. The club secretary, Rita Eastham, was a most efficient lady and provided first class professional back up, much needed in an operation of this size. Michael Black was Caesars entertainment booker and worked from his office in London. The larger than life agent visited the club almost every night in those days, occasionally taking the job of compeer himself. He was a total extrovert, but wonderfully charismatic. He always gave me the impression that the whole showbiz world revolved around him and I liked that idea. We became great friends. It took me a few weeks to get my feet firmly under the table, during which time I met and established a friendly rapport with, Monsieur Rene of the Casino and Ron Atkinson, who not only ran the 20 lane bowling alley on the first floor but also held a watching brief over the whole of the Caesars operation on behalf of Messrs Arbiter and Weston. The three in one operation was unique in the South of England. This bold concept of a family entertainment complex was new; we were sailing in unchartered waters.

From the outset I got amongst the customers, greeting and seating them. My memory for names and faces was very useful and I made a good impression with everyone. However, the friendly welcome, atmosphere and excellent entertainment did not compensate for the overall disappointment of our dining customers because of our failure to provide a good catering service for such large numbers of people. During the run up to Christmas we presented a galaxy of star entertainers including the Barron Knights, Tommy Cooper, Matt Munroe and Tony Hatch and Jackie Trent; but we also presented cold meals and slow service. I began to dread each evening, yet there seemed little that could be done about it. Our executive Parisian Chef and Clipboard Connie were not up to mass catering. Neither was Maggie the Tabby and I was getting very fed up with the three of them. We seemed to struggle from the moment a person ordered a meal until it was delivered and because of my inexperience in management I held back from making my feelings and criticisms known, Christmas was upon us and I thought it best not to rock the boat at this time. Dinner was optional and because of our track record the numbers of diners were decreasing. We were becoming famous as much for our poor catering as our excellent entertainment. Despite this, Guy Gelineau and Lucien Bernard, (the French connection), decided to stage a Gala Night on Christmas Eve. Tickets for the auspicious occasion were sold in advance at three guineas each inclusive of dinner, dance and cabaret. Dining therefore, was compulsory and the Gala Dinner was to be a sumptuous five course affair, silver served rather than plated, with extra equipment hired so that the special service could be carried out by our staff with a touch of style and class.

The evening was a total sell-out. 550 Christmas revellers were duly seated and all determined to have a great time. I had grave misgivings about the evening from the moment the idea was first put forward. How the hell were we going to cope with 550 diners when we were struggling and seriously falling down dealing with numbers much less? I made my feelings known to both Gelineau and Bernard but the French connection swept my fears aside. Xmas Eve 1966 was a total and complete catastrophe. Our attempts to silver serve the gathered audience was a disaster. A third got some food, a further third got no food at all and most of the remaining third got their food over them rather than served to them. I recall a very irate punter complaining bitterly when a terrine of soup had been spilt over his dinner suit. "I came to eat the food not wear it" he yelled.

Complaints were soon flowing from all parts of the room in a rising cacophony of noise as exasperated punters demanded to see management. Margo Henderson, our star cabaret for the evening, arrived on stage and made an effort to entertain. She was an excellent act, but no match for an angry audience that was turning into an ugly mob. She soon gave up and left the stage tearfully, unable to perform, unable to be heard above the noise. It was like opening day at Crufts. Abuse was hurled in all directions. I am sure food would have been hurled as well, if anyone had any to hurl. I think the riot started after one rather kindly and normally placid regular customer finally snapped and became a snarling psychopath before our very eyes. He lunged at one of the waiters and this seemed to spark off acts of violence in various parts of the room.

The situation soon got completely out of control. Gelineau was over the far side of the auditorium dealing with a complaint on table 37, a large party of people who had travelled down from London. I signalled my Sound Engineer to give maximum volume to our background music system in the hope that the sounds of Herb Albert and the Tihuana Brass would help soothe the forthcoming rebellion. Gelineau had retired to his inner sanctum for a breather; he did not spend much time with table 37. (It appeared they only wanted to meet him to hang him). Nothing it seemed could calm the swirling mass of aggravated punters. They were beside themselves with fury, until at last Messrs Arbiter and Weston stepped into the turmoil and through our compare announced a full refund for everyone by way of a voucher that could be used on any date in the future. The distraught owners were right on cue with their timely intervention. The evening ended in disarray as furious punters left the premises clutching vouchers. The saying 'egg on your face' was probably born that very evening in a nightclub in Luton. The inevitable post mortem followed.

The Head Chef along with Clipboard Connie had taken the easy way out by slipping away quietly, during a lull in the fighting. Maggie the Tabby was too stressed to attend and left the premises disguised as a cloakroom attendant. The meeting took place in the auditorium itself as there were too many of us to fit into the manager's inner sanctum and in any event it was deemed more appropriate to hold the meeting at the scene of the crime, as some joker put it. Present were Messrs Gelineau, Udeen, Arbiter, Weston, Michael Black, Geoff Walker, Anthony Wager, Peter (the foot) Torterella and yours truly. Ron Atkinson dropped in later. Looking back I often wonder why I did not feel threatened by the events of the evening, after all I was in charge of the dining room. I put it down to the fact that we were all so inexperienced at running a nightclub of this magnitude and catering for such large numbers of people. I believe everyone felt a certain responsibility for the failures as well as the successes at that time. Ivan was the first to state the obvious.

"What a balls up" he said, "it's not enough that we already have a poor reputation for our catering, but to bugger up people's Christmas, that really takes the biscuit".

Gelineau acknowledged that the silver service was a mistake. Geoff Walker felt that the serving staff lacked training and many needed replacing. Peter Torterella laid his cards firmly on the table.

"Ees no good, the Chef is no good. You gotta geta rid of him. I make a good chef and you geta me one good boy to a work with me", he rambled on, "then I show you".

"He might be right Ivan," said Michael Black. "After all tonight was just another night when the catering let the people down; albeit on a grander scale but what's new?".

Anthony Wager wondered why we bothered with food at all. "Why not have a show and drinks only policy".

The breast beating, suggestions and accusations went on for some time. Both Udeen and I remained silent but not detached from the sometimes heated discussion, until Ivor Arbiter suddenly entered the fray and addressed his question directly at me.

"When is the next big night for dining?"

"New Years Eve Sir" I replied. "It's Five Guineas per person and it's sold out as well".

"I told you that would be a sell out Ivor" interrupted Michael Black. "What a great show. I've put in the Billy Cotton Band – bloody marvellous. He'll bring the house down".   "The punters will do that before he comes on unless we get it right out front" retorted Ivor Arbiter.

"If you don't mind me saying so" I said, "I think our whole catering concept is wrong. If we are expecting to fill this room nightly, we must appeal to the general working population and not a wealthy minority. Our menu and our whole approach is more in keeping with your friendly upmarket neighbourhood restaurant of forty seats or so; not a massive operation like this".

"What is your point Savva?" asked Mr Gelineau.

"Well Sir as you know, ninety per cent of our punters are working people. They come here to have a good night out, a good meal and an equally good drink, followed by cabaret and dancing. In my opinion, as far as the meal is concerned, what's needed is a simple Table de Hote limited choice meal, hot, wholesome with a speedy plate service delivery. This would permit the rest of the evening to roll along. I believe" I continued, "that our whole concept makes the meal the main event, whereas in reality it is ancillary to everything else. We make a rod for our own backs on a nightly basis".

"The man has a point," said Michael. "I mean, look how they do things up north. Fish and chips, bingo, a show, dancing and booze".

"Maybe, maybe" said Ivor. "But this is not a working men's club".

"With respect Sir, it is" I said. "Admittedly with a deal more sophistication, which is fine. The inclusion of gaming and bowling as added attractions also gives our business an added value. Nevertheless, in my opinion, remembering the large numbers we are aiming at, our market is to be found on the factory floor, not the boardroom".

Gelineau, sensing that the conversation was beginning to get away from him, nodded with approval.

"I think Savva has a point. We could reconstruct the nightly menu, including the New Year's Eve Gala Bill of Fare and see if this works. We may upset one or two of our wealthier clients, but if we satisfy the majority we will have succeeded".

The meeting ended with a mild blast from Ron Atkinson, who had stepped into the meeting while I was talking.

"Well something has got to be done for sure. As you all know, I am Luton born and bred and have lived here all my life and I can tell you there are some pretty nasty things being said by the local population. In my opinion, if we don't put matters right quickly, we will lose the operation completely".

Ron's timely footnote to the post mortem was not only accurate but a potent warning. The writing was clearly on the wall. During the few days between Christmas Eve and New Year's Eve, the Caesars Palace backroom became a hive of activity. The new concept was discussed in great detail. New menus were put together and an altogether new approach was fashioned.

There were of course many arguments; the new arrangements did not sit well with everyone. Lucien Bernard was present at most of our discussions but reduced, almost, to the role of observer. Guy Gelineau and I presented him with a fait accompli and he was not happy. He vigorously protested that we were downgrading our catering from high class cuisine to a grill and griddle type operation with canteen style plate service to match. The whole point forcibly put by myself and others, that in catering for such large numbers, we had to move toward a 'conveyor belt' type arrangement was totally missed by Bernard. The Escoffier trained chef, could not even contemplate the reasoning behind our proposals. All the aggravation, complaints and disasters of the early days at the Palace seemed to have gone over his head. He continued to stress that his method was the best and we should stick with it as eventually it would all come right. He was the eternal optimist. I always thought that if he had been the Captain of the Titanic he would have told the passengers that he had only stopped to take on ice. Lucien Bernard was becoming a liability. Lets face it, anyone who struts about his kitchen shouting instructions, but never cooks, and employs a full time private secretary, could have no place in our organisation. I made my feelings known to Gelineau but he chose to ignore them. Although no love was lost between the two Frenchmen, the French connection closed ranks, at least for the moment.

New Year's Eve was upon us. An excellent, but simple five-course set menu was put in place and a plate service to go with it. Maggie the Tabby was another difficult person to convince. Like the chef, she seemed to want to block my every move involving the staff and their presentation, as well as the three M's; method, mode and motivation. Maggie's reluctance to cooperate surprised me somewhat. I thought that, following our horrendous Christmas Eve, she would have welcomed a change of direction. Perhaps she failed to grasp the full consequences of that evening which is surprising; after all, although in the firing line for only a short while, she spent most of the rest of the evening in the foyer surrounded by angry punters, some of whom tried repeatedly to grab her by the throat. However, with the room dressed to perfection, bunting, balloons and all, table novelties, party hats and blowers in abundance on every table; with our menu, service and staff all rehearsed and organised, we were ready to welcome the guests, the New Year's Eve revellers, for the night of their lives. (And ours).

The evening was a triumph from start to finish, everything went like clockwork. Following the excellent meal and service; which took a mere one and half hours to complete, the audience were treated to a wonderful night of dancing and entertainment. The punters dug deep. The champagne flowed like a river. Billy Cotton and his band were sensational. With his cry of 'Wakey- wakey' he burst on to the stage and produced a non-stop hour and forty minutes of music, songs and laughter. The act was a perfect choice for a raucous occasion. To most of the punters the popular combo were just voices on a radio that they listened to avidly every week. But now they were live on stage, Billy, the man himself, Alan Breeze, Kathy Kay and of course the great band. At midnight the room erupted into a blaze of light and colour, the dance floor packed. The crowd danced in the aisles, on the tables anywhere that a tiny space could be found. In complete contrast to Christmas Eve compliments were heaped upon us by grateful and very happy people.

The reader could be forgiven for assuming that Caesars Palace entered 1967 enjoying prestige, pride and confidence; far from it. From the October opening, the run up to the festive season as well as Christmas Eve itself, severe damage had been done. Despite our new efficient food and service policy, hundreds, no, thousands of disappointed customers were both unforgiving and unforgetting. Gelineau believed that the punters would come back in droves as news spread of our success. I had my doubts. I was after all at the grass roots of the business and therefore had my ear closer to the ground. The punters gave me an insight; it was to me that they related stories of friends and colleagues who would never return to the club. I am sure good news travels, but it travels with nothing like the speed of bad news. The business had been seriously damaged and it would be some time before we could expect to recover.

We continued our line up of top stars including Lulu, Max Bygraves, Bruce Forsythe, Frankie Vaughan, Helen Shapiro and Mike and Bernie Winters. Michael Black went into overdrive to arrange star 'heavyweights' for our programme, but many people still gave us a wide berth. Of the week long cabaret attractions, many found it heavy going during the early part of the week, but at least the weekends, (Fridays and Saturdays), were sell-outs.

What was becoming clear was the serious financial situation of the company. For each week to be viable, we needed a sell-out of at least three nights, preferably four. This was not happening and there were rumblings of real financial problems. Bills were not being paid.

During the spring of 1967 I arrived at the club to find Ivor and Ivan occupying the inner sanctum. I always popped my head in to say hello to Guy.

"Oh I'm sorry Sir," I said. "I did not realise you were in here in conference".

"No, come in," said Ivan. "We want to see you". I entered. "Mr Gelineau is no longer with us," Ivan continued. Not again I thought. I wondered why this time. I never did find out. "A new manager will arrive shortly. I hope you will work with him as well as you did for Gelineau".

"Certainly Sir" I said.

Mr Smith the new manager, a middle-aged English gentleman, found himself completely out of his depth in the world of late night cabaret and left after one week. I was appointed Acting General Manager until further notice. Little did I know that I would hold the post of General Manger for the next ten years! The sudden departure of Mr Gelineau left me bemused. He was responsible for my entry into show business and a career that would span some 30 years. I never saw him again. Mr Smith's arrival and speedy departure was so short as to be insignificant, but my elevation to Acting General Manager was, by contrast, extremely significant. Fate had once again thrust opportunity before me. I was not about to let it escape.

GOODBYE TO THIRTY

HELLO TO THOUSANDS

I POACH FROM GREENSHIELDS STAMPS

WE GO TO SEVEN DAYS

MATT MONROE – LOCAL KING

INSTANT STARDOM FOR DAVE ALLEN

TOMMY COOPER BECOMES A WAITER

THE ULTIMATE DUCK

The Caesars Palace I inherited as acting general manager was a very different place to the one I had joined some months earlier as restaurant manager. The food, service, and entertainment were now second to none. Our reputation for a great night out and excellent value for money was spreading. We were receiving compliments by phone and letter on a daily basis and a mark of our progress was the increase in repeat business, so important for any entertainment complex, particularly one in the sticks. However, the headway achieved still left us a long way from being solvent; there were still many problems to be solved. Now I held the reins of power, albeit on a temporary basis, I was determined not to let go. A quotation comes to mind: 'History seldom truly records the achievements of a man unless he writes it himself': I made up my mind to write my own history.

Whilst at the Prime Cut, an Arab waiter gave me a few driving lessons in his little Renault Dauphine. I quite enjoyed the experience but did not pursue further lessons; but now I needed to drive as a matter of urgency. I was simply too busy to spend valuable hours travelling on trains. I was also determined to continue living in London. I bought a Mini for £75 and with a provisional driving licence, but without L-plates or a qualified driver as a passenger, I taught myself to drive by driving each day between Tottenham and Luton and back. I intended to take a couple of lessons and the Test, but it took me two years to get around to doing just that. Meanwhile, I progressed from the Mini, (which eventually conked out and was dumped where it had fallen apart, in a field at South Mimms), to a Ford Anglia, then to an Austin Cambridge and then to my pride and joy; a beautiful two-tone Austin Westminster super-de-luxe. Two years had gone by and I was still driving illegally. This would not do I thought. I was becoming fairly high profile now and the thought of being stopped by the police took on a new significance. I arranged a couple of lessons and eventually passed my test at the second attempt. Strange as it may seem, during two years of illegal driving, the Police never stopped me, but no sooner had I acquired my full licence than I was promptly stopped for speeding. What a relief. 'It's a good job you didn't stop me last week'. 'Sorry Sir, what did you say?' 'Oh nothing officer, nothing'.

To sum up my approach and attitude at that time is very easy. Firstly, I loved Caesars Palace and everything it stood for, I enjoyed every moment I worked there. Secondly, to me Caesars was the greatest place in the world to visit and I knew that I was very much Mr Average Man; I therefore felt that, given the opportunity, everyone would want to visit. We just needed to get the message across. Thirdly, I believed that if I could get people to visit the premises just once, they would become regular customers and perhaps even join as members. Fourthly, I would start to tackle the financial situation by cutting the overheads and reduce the enormous costs that the Palace had to shoulder on a weekly basis.

After arriving at these various conclusions, I set in motion a package of measures that if successful, would bring Caesars out of its financial doldrums for once and for all. I know now that had I failed, it would have meant a total collapse of the club and my immediate exit from show business. Strangely enough, I never considered failure as an option. Arbiter and Weston was a substantially wealthy company with gaming and leisure interests in other parts of the country. But quite rightly in my view, the owners were adamant that each unit, each operation, had to stand on its own feet. The Company would not tolerate the subsidising of one part of the business by another. I knew that I had to make Caesars Palace Cabaret Club viable for all our sakes, or it would be closed, so now came a period of upheaval and reorganisation. I had to increase numbers of customers while at the same time cut costs, but before the marketing could begin there had to be a considerable degree of bloodletting. The major item of expense was staff costs which were altogether top heavy. My hands on style of management meant I knew the areas that were overstaffed and under producing. I had learnt quickly and was no longer an inexperienced member of the management staff. I unashamedly set myself up as a supreme being, ready to crush anyone who stood in the way of the Club's progress.

Without instructions from my employers and executing my own agenda, I called a meeting of all staff. Geoff Udeen, whom I had elevated to assistant, unofficially of course, came to advise me they had gathered in the main cabaret room and awaited my presence. I arrived in the room clutching a sheet of paper and trying my best to look the part of 'Acting General Manager'. I was after all only 25 years of age and quite young to be in this situation. Although I say it myself I had lots of bottle. I addressed the staff.

"As you all probably know" I commenced, "I have been appointed Acting General Manager. Many of you will also know that Caesars has not being doing well and has been losing money. This cannot go on. Costs have to be cut. Part of these costs is the enormous wage bill and I'm afraid we simply cannot go on carrying the number of staff that we presently employ. It is therefore with regret that I have to say goodbye to some of you. On this sheet of paper I have a list of names which I will now read. If your name is not on it, then I'm sad to say you are no longer an employee of Caesars Palace".

One may be forgiven in thinking that this was a harsh almost callous way of doing things. The fact of the matter was that there were far too many names on the payroll that had to go. Caesars had become an overweight gravy train and there were too many that were not justifying their employment. Also, however much 'bottle' I had, I did not fancy a long drawn out programme of dismissals, personally seeing each individual on a one to one basis.

Dismissal is a terrible thing, but I think the blow is softened when one is part of a group of departees rather than on one's own. In any event, I took comfort in the knowledge that most, indeed all, would probably find work very easily. These were the flying 60's. There was certainly plenty of work about.

Reading the list went reasonably well and at the end there was little comment. A few gasps of surprise perhaps, but looking back I believe that for many the signs may have been there anyway. You did not have to be a genius to work out that something had to give if Caesars was to survive. Notable departures included Lucien Bernard, Clipboard Connie and Maggie the Tabby. Not only did I make a great saving in payroll terms, but also exacted my revenge for their continuous arguments and resistance to my policies. A considerable number of catering, reception and ancillary staff also had to go. I kept only my most dedicated and efficient body of workers. I appointed Peter Torterella, my club-footed Italian cook, as Head Chef. He delivered. He headed the kitchen with efficiency and hard work. Although at times abrasive, slightly mad and over the top as chefs often are Peter became renowned as the most successful mass-catering chef in club land.

I set about organising a programme of cabaret to cover the month of October 1967. I visited Michael Black's office in London and asked him to book four-star attractions to cover the four-week period. Popular 'names', not too expensive so that free admission could be offered from Monday to Thursday of each week in celebration of our first anniversary and by way of an introduction to potential new customers. Also to thank those who had supported us throughout the first year. After much haggling and a fair amount of persuasion, seven days later Michael Black phoned me and presented me with four of the best. The amazing and hugely popular Dickie Valentine, The Beverley Sisters, Lionel Blair and his dancers and of course the local band who were fast becoming top stars the Barron Knights. Each attraction complete with a supporting artiste was to play a week (six nights).

A first anniversary programme was produced and free admission invitations were printed. Leading a team of staff including my assistant Geoff Udeen and various waiters and bar staff, we distributed our 'invitations' far and wide; taking them beyond the boundaries of Luton and Dunstable to as far away destinations such as Bedford, Hemel Hempstead, Hitchin, Watford, North London, Stevenage and Northampton.

Dining remained an option, but as well as a four course Table De Hote meal for seventeen shilling and sixpence, I also installed a simple one course 'bar menu' for those punters that fancied a bite without getting too involved with expense. The average price of a bar meal was approximately five shillings. The shedding of thirty per cent of the staff, together with my other activities, had not gone unnoticed by my employers. They were clearly pleased so far and I began to get the feeling they were watching me very closely. I was probably considered either a genius or completely mad. The jury however was still out. One thing was sure; they had made no attempt to bring in a new general manager.

How can I describe the October 'First Anniversary' promotion? It was reformation, restoration and rejuvenation rolled into one. New punters came in droves from all over the Home Counties. Some had heard bad reports about the place, others had heard good and many had never heard of us at all. Taking advantage of the special free invitations, they flocked to visit us, to give us a try. A tidal wave of punters hit us night after night filling every seat so that I had to hire additional chairs and we were seating up to 620 at tables. In addition I permitted seating on staircases and in every nook and corner. Standing room at the 60ft long bar helped push the numbers up still further. I exceeded my fire limits by at least 250 people each night. Once in and settled the people loved the place, as I knew they would. The packed conditions seemed to increase the atmosphere and raise expectations. As a result, the wining, dining, dancing and show brought new heights of enjoyment to the visiting crowds. Our hydraulically lifted stage brought gasps of amazement to the huge gathering of first time visitors. The entertainment was the icing on the cake.

Dickie Valentine sent the ladies' hearts fluttering. Immaculately dressed, the good looking heart throb of radio and television was a huge success, earning a standing ovation that went on and on. He took five curtain calls, as did the Bev's during their week at the Palace. The girls who dressed the same, as well as looking the same, presented vocal harmony at its absolute best. They were also great fun on stage, with both well-rehearsed and ad-lib patter, which brought great enjoyment to the appreciative audience.

Lionel and his wonderful dancers were show stoppers as always. He was at the peak of his craft at that time. The colour, class, style and humour of his excellent show was a once seen, never to be forgotten experience. The punters marvelled at the speed of the show and adored Lionel's skill at a huge variety of dance. He was a great star.

The Barron Knights were playing the venue for a second time. They were local boys, living within walking distance of the twin towns of Luton and Dunstable. Their careers were taking off in a big way; radio, television and the charts. The act consisted of five lads, Barron, Duke, Peanut, Butch and Dave. They all played musical instruments. They sang, but above all it was the humour, mainly provided by Butch Baker, and the group's ability to impersonate other bands and send them up that was to make them famous internationally. Toni Avern managed the multi-talented group. He also lived locally and became one of my life-long friends until his retirement into obscurity some years ago. Their week at the Palace was both sensational and historic in that they broke the house record for attendance. I cannot describe how full we were, except to say that if one threw a handful of sand in the air, none would have fallen on the floor. One night Udeen was advised by a person close by that a lady had fainted but was unable to fall down. It seemed she was suspended horizontally by the crush of people around her which was particularly dense in the bar standing area.

Ivor and Ivan arrived one evening during this period and having managed to park their car, which in itself was very difficult, they fought their way through to the reception area and down the steps into the auditorium. The place heaved at the seams. They were very impressed.

"The invitations are a great success," I told them. "No admission money, but the food and drink sales are incredible and people are joining the club at a guinea a time by the hundreds". I had to leave them at that point to show more people to their seats. By the time I returned my boss's had vanished, to the casino I thought, or upstairs to the bowling alley. I found them some time later; washing glasses behind the bar. They never knew the pleasure it gave me to see them there. For me it was a defining moment I knew I had to give them my best shot, give them a business to be proud of. From that moment, I had the utmost respect and affection for them. They were my kind of people. Our four 'Top of the bill' star attraction were slightly bemused, but well pleased by the huge crowds and great audiences. It is said that applause is food to an artiste. They each in turn thanked me profusely for the feast.

Although the food and drink receipts for the month were fantastic, more importantly, people were taking an ever increasing interest in our forthcoming attractions. The volume of bookings and reservations grew rapidly. Satisfied customers were rebooking. Repeat business on a large scale was being achieved at last. This represented for me the utmost significant breakthrough. Caesars was coming out of the doldrums and establishing itself as the top spot for a good night out. Shortly after the anniversary promotion Messrs Arbiter and Weston showed their appreciation and approval, by promoting me to General Manager and awarding an appropriate wage increase that went with the title. There followed two years of development that set Caesars Palace on a path to national and international recognition as the place to play and to be seen as an artiste, as well as the place to be seen as customer.

To me entertainment, a good night out, was like any other commodity; it had to be marketed. Marketing had become the in word in the late 60's and many successful companies gave credit for their success to their excellent marketing departments. I decided on my market strategy, seeking to promote our product amongst factories and offices. I sought to sell our club as the ideal place for the 'Party Night Out'. Membership of the club had passed the 20,000 mark and continued to grow. To break into the party market would be the greatest prize of all. I knew that coupled with our huge membership, the party booking business would secure Caesars future. A leading marketing and promotional company at that time was Green Shield Stamps. I unashamedly headhunted an excellent marketing executive from Green Shield and her brief was to market Caesars Palace among the surrounding industry. Her name was Diane Rowley.

Diane went to work with a tremendous skill and professionalism which soon brought results. It was not long before coaches were rolling into the car park and offloading their parties of revellers for a night out at the famous club. I continued, (even more so as general manager), to meet, greet and seat the incoming customers. We provided top class food, service and entertainment. We became known for our hospitality and high standards. I cared not whether I greeted a factory worker, a small shopkeeper, a business man or a flash tycoon. All were guests to be impressed and welcomed to our establishment and all were treated without favouritism by myself and my staff; the rich and famous rubbed shoulders with ordinary working people in perfect harmony.

The growth of Caesars Palace Cabaret Club provided another very important spin-off.

Prior to the 1970 Gaming Act, Entertainment and Gambling Casinos did not have to be separate entities, and visitors to a show could wander freely into the casino for a flutter at any time during their visit. In fact, at the end of a show the customers divided roughly into two with 50% staying on to dance and 50% opting for a visit to the casino. With the growth of the club came a growth in the numbers attending the casino, which obviously pleased Mr Rene and his colleagues. Ron Atkinson's bowling alley did not directly benefit from either club or casino, but Ron personally was delighted that the business and its reputation had been turned around. He was pleased to comment that the early mistake and disasters had at last become fading memories.

Caesars fame spread far and wide as the support grew. We enjoyed packed houses practically every night. Ivor and Ivan, who were both Jewish, decided to open on Sunday nights and make the operation a seven nighter. They were certain that opening on Sundays would attract a major Jewish following from North London where a great deal of the Jewish community were concentrated. Sundays were traditionally the main Jewish night out. The M1 motorway made motoring to Caesars from North London extremely easy and quick and the club was only a stone's throw from the M1 at junction eleven. The boys were absolutely right. Within a short while we were enjoying a regular Sunday night capacity audience from London – mainly Jewish. With an eye on this new Jewish support, Michael Black (also Jewish) delivered what might be determined ethnic favourites such as Ester and Abbey Ofarim, Frankie Vaughan, Helen Shapiro and a whole number of lesser-known Jewish acts. (I'm pleased to report that our Jewish friends also supported our Gentile performers).

Frankie Vaughan had an amazing following countrywide. All over the U.K. people flocked to see him, and he had one of the biggest fan clubs ever formed in Britain. His devoted fans supported him with incredible loyalty and his appearances at the club were both regular and successful. Another great favourite was the amazing Matt Munroe. Although short in stature, he was enormous in talent and towered above many of the great male vocalists of that era. Frank Sinatra made the comment that Matt possessed the finest voice ever to come out of Britain. On top of all this, Matt was a local Bedfordshire boy and before his meteoric rise to fame drove a bus in the Luton and Dunstable area. The locals loved him. Matt played the Palace on countless occasions with great success and Matt, me and our families became great friends.

Each show comprised a 'Top of the Bill' and supporting artistes. Occasionally, a talented supporting act would get noticed, be discovered and become 'Top of the Bill' stars in their own right. It was during another sell-out Matt Munroe week that such an event actually happened. In his wisdom, Michael Black arranged for an unknown Irish comedian to support Matt. "I've got just the man," he claimed. "A comedian who can provide the right kind of balance. And an Irishman to boot". He was right; and well aware of Luton's 26,000 Irish population. From opening night onward, the show was a gigantic success. Matt of course was as always on top form. But the supporting artiste was a show stopper. After opening night Matt called me backstage.

"Where did you get that Irish comic from?" he asked.

"Apparently he arrived from Australia where he's quite well known" I replied. "Wants to make a name for himself in Europe".

"He'll certainly do that," said Matt. "The man's a star. Give him a bit longer George if you can fit the rest of the week. Forty minutes is no good, give him an hour. I think he's great and so bloody funny. I'll take a couple of numbers out to give him a bit longer on the green".

"No need to do that Matt. I'll give him his extra time – no problem," I confirmed.

"I'm coming early tomorrow night to catch his full act from the back of the club," Matt said excitedly.

From the second night the Irish comedian/raconteur was to performed for an hour. In the space of one week his name was on everyone's lips. He was an 'overnight sensation'. His name was Dave Allen.

"I'll bet you want a bit more of Dave Allen," bubbled Michael Black.

"I sure do," I said without hesitation. "However did you get hold of him?" I asked.

"Georgie, Georgie I've told you before. Leave it to your Uncle Michael" he crowed and added; "You know I'll only get you the best".

Dave Allen's fee was £125 for the week. After a back stage confab between Dave, myself and Michael on his final night, it was agreed to replay Dave on a date three months later for a fee of £175 for a week. Ivan Weston was at the club that night and later met up with Michael and me in the office.

We told Ivan of the confirmed arrangement to bring Dave Allen back to top the bill.

"Very good move I'd say" he commented.

"Very good" Michael exclaimed, "Very good".

"It's more than that Ivan. The man will be a star. Ask George about the reaction this week. Even Matt thought he was great".

"I don't have to ask George. I've seen for myself," said Ivan calmly. "So what's the deal?" he enquired with a smile.

"He's back in thirteen weeks for £175 and he's topping". The smile very quickly disappeared from Ivan's face.

"A fifty quid increase" he yelled. "What's the matter? Wouldn't he settle for twenty-five? It had to be fifty already".

I was a spectator to a clash of the Jewish Titans. On the one hand Michael, larger than the world of dreams he represented; outgoing and flamboyant. On the other hand, the cool calculating businessman whose view of show business was altogether different and who couldn't care less for the personalities that inhabited it. For my part I excused myself, pretending I had to sort out a matter with a member of staff and left them to it.

I saw Michael a little later.

"Can you believe your Guvnor?" he moaned. "Any way we'll show him won't we mate"?

"Yes Michael" I said. "I'm sure we will". Between Dave Allen's first date at the club as support to Matt Munroe and his return thirteen weeks later, Dave had landed a series of guest spots as compare-comedian on the hugely popular T.V. show Sunday Night at the London Palladium. Our £175 top of the bill was already commanding a fee of £900 per week. Dave played Caesars on many occasions during my ten years as Manager. His fee increased in leaps and bounds as his popularity soared and he established superstar status. I remember a point being reached when Dave became almost unemployable. A deal was negotiated whereby Dave, who enjoyed playing the club immensely, would accept a guaranteed fee against a percentage of the box office receipts, whichever the greater. Following opening night, Dave's office was telephoned with the figures from the first night's box office receipts to enable them to calculate the percentage due to him. Sadly an incident took place which I can still vividly recall. Within thirty minutes Dave's office phoned back. Dave was not at all happy and claimed there were far more people in than the figures suggested. I assured the office that the figures were correct and therefore so was his percentage. A short while later the office phoned again, Dave was now insisting that extra chairs were put in to accommodate extra people. I agreed, but stressed that when business demanded, I often packed a few more in but if they (the office) checked, they would see that I had calculated Dave's percentage on the extras as well. The argument raged for most of the day with wild guesses at numbers by one side and rejections and counter claims by the other. The result was the adoption of my suggestion that Dave's office sent a representative to join my box office staff for the rest of the week so that numbers and figures could be verified.

The rest of a very successful week passed without any further problems but the incident left a bad taste in my mouth. I understood perfectly the obvious conclusion to be drawn from the row. I have never cheated an artiste and I felt very strongly about the whole affair. I suppose I took it personally because of the friendly relationship that had grown between Dave and I since that first date as a support to Matt. Although Dave played many further dates for me during the succeeding years, the incident was always in the back of my mind. I bumped into Dave many years later, long after my departure from Caesars and equally long after his retirement from working the clubs and cabaret. By strange irony we were both at a function – a memorial dinner to honour the life and times of Matt Munroe, who had died of cancer. Dave and I shook hands and exchanged some friendly if brief dialogue. He probably did not even remember the incident. I on the other hand knew the day it happened, all those years before, that I would never forget it completely.

Tommy Cooper was another of the hugely popular entertainers who regularly played the club. Tommy in fact, opened Caesars on the 6th October 1966. Tommy was unique. Physically a very big man, Tommy would rumble onto the stage like an oversize penguin wearing a fez. He would send the audience into hysterical laughter with his quick fire humour and ridiculous magic tricks. It was Tommy's timing that was so special. Every comedian needs good timing, but in Tommy's case, timing was as much part of him as his magical props. Tommy even invented a routine of off stage humour. Armed with a microphone and his wonderful timing he would have an audience rolling in the aisles, before his appearance on stage, by pretending to be lost in the dark between the dressing room and the wings. He was the ultimate clown; a comic genius. His manager was Miff (the voice) Ferrie, known as such because I had never met him or knew of anyone that had. He was merely a voice on the phone.
I played Tommy an average of three times a year for eighteen years without ever meeting Miff.

'The voice' however was always fair and reliable and once a deal was done 'the voice' could be relied on to deliver. I never asked Miff why he never visited us like most of the other artiste's managers or agents did, or why I never came across his name at any of the showbiz functions that so many of us attended. I always felt it was rude to pry and anyway, showbiz was full of odd people with odd ways and lifestyles. I did however mention the matter to Tommy one night during a chat after the show.

"I've never ever met Miff your manager," I said, making it sound like a passing remark.

"You haven't missed much. He's not a pretty sight and he doesn't get about much" replied Tommy. "In fact I've seen more movement in a tramp's vest" he concluded with a chuckle.

Tommy lived in Chiswick, West London, but whenever he accepted an engagement, even if it was only a few miles from his home, he always stayed in a hotel close to the venue. He also always relaxed at the venue after his show and to say he was never in a hurry to leave would be the understatement of the century. He loved to sit, drink and chat for hours. First in his dressing room, and later when everyone had gone, in the auditorium. As already mentioned, I was never a star struck individual and certainly never booked an artiste for personal pleasure. Box office, talent and reasonably priced fees were my guiding principles. Tommy Cooper fitted all the criteria, but with one exception. He was my hero, even before I entered the business and so I must own up and confess that I booked him as much for my pleasure as that of my customers. I always made sure I was in the room when Tommy came on and laughed and enjoyed him along with the audience.

Although his habit of all night confabs could be a bit tiresome, I still sat with him chewing the fat through the long nights often departing in daylight, to the sound of the dawn chorus. I found him a most fascinating person and we became close friends. During one of our all night sessions discussing situation comedy I told Tommy of some old black and white footage, American I think, that I had seen, which was hilarious. I was sure it could be adapted for one of the sketches in the T.V. series he was filming. The sitcom featured a restaurant with an aggravated chef, filled with rude and complaining customers. Situated in the centre of the restaurant was a circular room with six doors, making the room accessible from all sides of the restaurant. In the room seated at tables, were numbers of stuffed dummies and close by on a sideboard were a variety of items such as riding crops, whips, baseball bats etc. There was also a large mirror. The restaurant boasted an all smiling, always pleasant, non-stressed staff. Each time a customer or the chef gave the hard working staff aggravation; the staff member would pop into the room and vent his emotion, his anger or stress, pick up one of the items provided and beat the hell out of the nearest dummy. Tommy was absolutely fascinated by the story and insisted I continue with it.

"Well" I said, "the upshot of the whole thing was that as the restaurant reached rush hour, the aggravation and stress increased and so did the visits to the room by the staff. Once at full stretch the film was speeded up with all six entrances and exits in full swing and staff beating the dummies in all directions. It was very, very funny to watch," I concluded.

Tommy enthused, "I like the sound of this" he said. We discussed the sitcom at great length and I pointed out that for me the really funny part was that each time the aggravated waiter had beaten the stuffed dummy, he went to the mirror, straightened his bow tie and neatly folded his serving cloth over his arm, put a smile on his face and re-entered the restaurant.

"I'll mention the idea to my Producer". Said Tommy. To be honest I never thought he would.

Some time after the conversation, I watched one of Tommy's T.V. shows, I hardly ever missed them, and low and behold on came the sketch with Tommy playing the waiter. It was hilarious.

A steady stream of top talent and stars played the venue. Notable successes included Bruce Forsythe, Max Bygraves and Mike Yarwood. Our very large Irish following was catered for by appearances of Brendan Shine, Johnny McEvoy, Brendon Blake, Foster and Allen and The Witnesses Irish Showband. There was universal support for the sixties bands and groups and we certainly played many of them. Although strangely enough, the sixties music seems to have become more popular with the passing of time. I can only deduce that middle aged folk probably realise now what a great musical era the sixties were, particularly when old rockers like us are subjected to the hot pop, rap and rave of today's bands. I believe passionately that we took our great sixties bands for granted at that time and now realise how fortunate we were to have lived, loved, listened and danced to the Sixties Sound. Wales, the land of song, was certainly living up to its claim. Shirley Bassey was already reaching superstar status, creating a furore on and off stage wherever she went and there was also great excitement concerning another Welsh artiste – a valley boy known as Tom Jones.

We played them both back to back. First presenting Shirley for a week and immediately followed with a week of Tom. Incidentally and as a matter of record, the two-week gala season of Welsh heavyweights was followed by a week of Donald Peers, (Old Mister Babbling Brook). Perhaps I should not have said, 'followed by' because poor Donald's week was a disaster. Hardly anyone came to see his excellent show. If you had fired a cannon in the auditorium it would have been impossible to hit a single soul. Donald could definitely not follow the Welsh stars – but then who could?

In my opinion Shirley Bassey was temperamental, demanding and quite unreasonable. However, once setting foot on stage she transformed into a goddess, an absolute sensation. As a club manager my dislike of the lady grew each day, only to melt away each evening as she took The Palace by storm. On her arrival at the venue for afternoon band call I was summoned to her dressing room during a break in the rehearsals.

"Are you the Manager of this shit-house?" she asked.

"Yes Miss Bassey" I said timidly.

"Then do something about this dressing room. It needs decorating and I want a chaise lounge. Get this done by tonight or I won't appear".

Like a fool I rushed around the locality that Sunday afternoon and found a decorator who managed to acquire some rather nice gold embossed paper and a furniture shop owner, who lived above his shop, to lend me a chaise lounge in exchange for a couple of tickets for the show. The decorating was finished by eight that evening – a wallpaper job of excellent quality and the chaise lounge was in place. No paint was used, although the newly papered walls made the skirting and door paint look shabbier than ever. I was experienced enough to know that the smell and chemical emission from fresh paint is anathema to a vocalist and can seriously damage their vocal chords.

Bassey swept in complaining bitterly about having to be collected by a chauffeur driving a black Rolls and not a white one, as stipulated in her contract. Thank God the transport was Ivan's department. Ivan reacted totally different to me when Bassey's complaint had reached him Michael Black that evening. Ivan was purported to have said, "Tell her to take it or leave it" and hung up.

She went into her dressing room and I hid in the cleaner's closet behind the main reception cloakroom. No complaint, no thanks, no anything. This was a relief. An hour later, on stage in glittering gown and with a presence larger than a house, Shirley Bassey cast her spell over an ecstatic audience and I must say over an ecstatic club management as well. All was forgiven. There were other dramas as the weeks progressed and I remember one very bad incident in particular. Our supporting act for the Bassey show was the excellent ventriloquist John Boucher. John was probably one of the world's finest ventriloquists. During his act he would highlight the extent of his skill by reciting items of poetry and prose whilst smoking a cigarette. For example! 'Peter Piper picked a peck of pickled pepper etc,' All spoken through his dummy while he smoked a cigarette, a very clever part of his act.

Each evening I arranged for a stage flunky to sweep up during the intermission and ensure that all cigarette ends were removed, prior to Shirley's arrival on stage. One night, the cleaner was interrupted and consequently forgot to sweep up, leaving the broom near table twelve, a table very close to the stage. Bassey made her spectacular entrance, sang three numbers as usual, and then paused to chat as usual. Looking down at the cigarette ends she remarked,

"Look at the muck on here Ladies and Gentlemen". She was smiling and got a laugh from the audience for the remark. "Can't the management afford a cleaner?" she continued to more smiles and laughter.

Suddenly someone from Table twelve slid the broom onto the stage. I died a thousand deaths. To hoots of laughter Shirley picked up the broom and swept the stage. This brought the house down. What a performer, the audience loved it. Shirley bowed to the cheers and rapturous applause and I hid from the inevitable tantrum. As soon as she came off stage there was absolute mayhem. Luckily Michael Black was in that night and pacified her. I remained hidden in the closet until the storm had passed. All through the engagement I, like so many club managers, would be heard to utter 'never again'; but, as soon as her show run ended you found yourself on the phone looking for a return date. The guarantee of a sell-out was certainly a factor; great media exposure for your club was also guaranteed, but it was the sheer magnificence of her performance that was the key to forgiveness.

Tom Jones was a darling. Tom of course was on his way to super stardom but did not possess an armoury of complaints or tantrums. At this time, Tom was an easygoing artiste who I believe found it difficult to understand the excitement he was creating. Tom was probably the first great cabaret sex symbol. The audiences, mainly female, shrieked and screamed their way through his every show. And it is true; literally dozens of them threw their panties on to the stage during his performances. Many ladies fainted, others swooned. Others fell off the chairs on which they stood for a better view. Florence Nightingale would have been hard pressed to cope with a Tom Jones show. My staff and I were kept busy, but despite the problems, Tom Jones was good to work with and a real down to earth person.

Johnny Ray the legendary American singer was next to pay us a visit, making a six-night appearance at the club. Although Johnny was not the dashing guy he once was, he nevertheless pulled a big audience; and having got them there knew how to entertain them. He was with us at the same time that Judy Garland was appearing at the Talk of the Town. Johnny was a long time pal of Judy's; indeed I believe he stood as Best Man at Judy's latest wedding. I received a call from Judy's manager to say that she would be coming Caesars to pay Johnny a surprise visit and the emphasis was on the word surprise. I delayed the show that night by approximately thirty minutes by making some feasible excuse to Johnny about a stage lighting fault that needed correction. Johnny eventually went on at 11.30.p.m. and was about twenty minutes into his act when Judy arrived. I remember the huge black limo drawing gracefully up to our front doors and the great Judy Garland making her entrance.

Like so many people I was also a fan, hardly ever passing up an opportunity to catch one of her films. The person I met and welcomed to Caesars that night was, however, a small shadow of the great screen goddess I had admired over the years. I guess the ravages of her lifestyle had taken a toll. She was much smaller than I had envisaged, but also looked older than her years would suggest and although she still had a tinge of sparkle, I have to say there was something sad about the figure that I escorted quietly and without fuss to her table that night. Judy slipped me a carefully wrapped package and asked if I could get it to Johnny at an appropriate moment. That moment came when Johnny took his bow at `false tabs`, the name given to the period when an artiste actually seems to have ended his performance only to return on stage to perform another song or two.

Back onstage came Johnny Ray clutching the package which had clear instructions written on it that it should be opened on stage. This he proceeded to do.

"Ladies and gentlemen" he said. "I've been asked to open this on stage and so please forgive me for taking a moment of your time this evening". Having opened the package, he read from the enclosed card.

"Johnny. Thank you for lending me your sweater recently. I return it to you here, but with my apologies for having had it washed before returning it. It seems to have shrunk a little". Holding up the garment to show the audience, Johnny succumbed to screams of laughter; because the sweater was so tiny it was suitable for a three year old, not a fully grown man. The laughter eventually subsided and Johnny gave an explanation.

"Ladies and Gentlemen" he repeated. "The note and the package are from my dear friend Judy Garland, who I believe is here tonight".

At this the audience erupted with gasps of disbelief and thunderous applause followed. Then the chants from the audience, brought to their feet. "'We want Judy, we want Judy' over and over again.

Our star sensing the mood and the occasion called out "Come on up here Judy" and Judy Garland duly obliged. After some kisses and hugs and to the great delights of the audience, Judy and Johnny agreed to perform a duet together.

The number was a hearts and flowers type of song and it was by far the most awful performance of the song I've ever heard. Together, the two aging superstars sang out of tune, out of key and out of sync. Yet in their rendition of that song there was pure magic. At the end of the song the audience once again leapt to their feet and gave the duo a five-minute standing ovation. This memory is one of the most moving moments of my life. It certainly was a time when hairs on the back of my neck stood tall. Brian Conley, our publicist, was in the club that night and gave me some names and numbers to call in London.

"These are the guys – night editors that would be really interested in this story". He told me.

I called at least a half dozen of the listed contacts, all of whom took details of the surprise visit to Caesars by Judy Garland. The following day the story made three national newspapers and proved the value of having a permanent publicist.

Many great artistes graced our boards and we reached out for even greater; international artistes previously unseen in the U.K. In order to keep pace with the ever increasing demands of both the public and the artistes we needed to expand. Caesars had an official capacity of 550 seats; it was too small.

Vince Hill had a massive hit with his version of Edelweiss, a song from the popular movie `The Sound of Music`. At Caesars we were very lucky to play Vince at the same time as his hit settled comfortable into the number four spot of the top twenty charts. Vince, who already enjoyed a substantial following, found himself playing to capacity houses everywhere he went. We had to turn them away at Caesars.

The popularity of the New Vaudeville Band and Lonnie Donnegan was also a feature at this time. `The Vauds` combined their unusual sounds with a compliment of comedy that remained evergreen and guaranteed box office ability. For Lonnie the hits just kept coming. The King of Skiffle reigned supreme and he enjoyed an enormous following. Again we sold out and turned hundreds away.

Great Northern attractions beginning to break through in the South included Dukes and Lee, Roy Jay, Tony Sands, Mike Terry and many others too numerous to mention. All played their hearts out at Caesars. In fact, having achieved a contract for a coveted Caesars date, most performers seemed to put that little extra into their act. Caesars had become a much sought after date to many cabaret artistes. A jewel in the ever increasing and expanding cabaret circuit crown. We needed to grow. We needed to build an extension.

During this period I married a second time to Joanne Gabillet, a French waitress at Caesars; and as I did not allow husbands and wives to work together, Joanne had to leave. (She was a married woman when we met and not unnaturally our affair led to the failure of her marriage). I installed her in my flat at Tottenham. Once her divorce was absolute, we married and, following the birth of my first son George, we moved to Watford and bought a bungalow at Carpenters Park.

A period of consolidation would be the best way to describe this period at Caesars. Having grasped the nettle, everything seemed to be going extremely well. We were going from strength to strength. Our catering was faultless. Good wholesome meals, hot and quickly served, were a feature of our establishment. The increase in the numbers of diners bore witness to the satisfaction amongst our customers. I now had time to look around, survey the whole scene and plan ahead. Quite by chance a representative called one day, he worked for a company called Alverston Kitchens. I'd seen him before as he was a fairly regular customer of the club and as he settled into a chair opposite my desk and prattled on for what seemed like hours, I tried not to look bored and gave him the benefit of an occasional nod and smile of encouragement. He was, after all, also a customer.

"The bottom line is the choice of food," he stated. "This will open up a whole new range of products and enhances the choice you have to offer. You can be the first in your field to try it".

I sat up and started to take notice. I liked being ahead of the game at everything I did.

"Just run that past me again" I interrupted.

"It's a revolutionary new process called Boil in the Bag". He continued. "The dishes are produced by top chefs, cooked to perfection and then blast frozen into solid blocks and bagged. The speed of blast over the normal freezing process results in the flavour and taste being held in. To prepare, you simply place the polythene bag into boiling water, heat thoroughly and when ready place on a plate, add veg and serve" the rep concluded.

"What sort of dishes are we talking about?" I asked.

"Beef Bourgoine, Cock eu Vin, Duck a la Orange, Venison in Cherry". Came the reply

"I see, I see" I said "and you are telling me that with the numbers we cater for, we could put these dishes on the menu and serve them without hampering the service".

"For sure" he insisted, "in fact properly managed, your chef could produce one of these dishes faster than any steak, scampi or chicken dish. I mean, Mr S, lets face it, I love coming here myself and I'm always well pleased with my meal and service but sometimes it gets as bit monotonous. It's the same dishes all the time. You really need a bit more choice, if you don't mind me saying so". I acknowledged his point, and I was very impressed when he uttered the words,

"You'll be a cut above everyone else in club-land with these dishes on your menu".

I was always anxious that Caesars was the best and was seen to be the best. His point regarding choice was also a valid one. Just lately there had been one or two rumblings about lack of choice. I was further impressed when I visited his warehouse at Yardley Hastings in Northants, to look at the products. I remember entering an old Norman barn to find rows and rows of fridge-freezer cabinets, in which the polythene clad brickettes were housed. I elected to promote two dishes. The Coq eu Vin and the Duck as additional menu choices. Within a few days, both dishes were added to our main course selection and, although deep down I knew it to be wrong, my greed got the better of me and I placed a £1 surcharge on each of the new features. I did this despite the fact that steak for example was dearer to buy and produce and also one or two other items on the menu. I took the view that since the public were unaware of the price I was paying, a £1 surcharge was quite permissible. Both new dishes, printed in French, beckoned the diner seductively. Peter the chef had added Keith Yang, a young Liverpudlian, to his team at about this time and we felt our kitchen was now staffed and equipped to conquer the world.

One evening during our Harry Seccombe week, I was relaxing by my lectern when suddenly an elegant looking middle-aged lady in a black gown came striding over to me. She was very tall and seemed to tower over me. She looked both menacing and formidable.

"I understand you are the General Manager," she declared with perfect diction.

"Yes Madam" I answered.

"Well I'd like to have a word with you".

Oh dear I thought, this does not sound too good. "Please feel free Madam," I said timidly.

"This is my first visit to your establishment" she began. "I'm here with some guests from London – we are all great fans of Harry's. For my sins I am known as something of an authority on duck. Indeed I am currently writing a book of recipes almost entirely based on duck".

By was now beginning to panic. This was all I needed, a duck expert and a formidable one at that. I sensed her speech was leading to a major complaint.

"I've eaten duck all over the world" she continued. "You could say I've consumed duck across all five continents, cooked in a variety of different ways". As she pressed on with her universal guide of the duck world my mind raced ahead to the oncoming anticipated onslaught. By now I was smiling, but white. The blood had drained from my face. I knew disaster was at hand.

"I can honestly say without hesitation" she insisted, "that I know good duck from a bad one just by looking at it, let alone tasting it".

I was now desperately planning my defence. It would be no good telling her the truth; that the duck is prepared at some obscure destination, wrapped in polythene and frozen etc. I'll have to choose appeasement. An apology followed by a free bottle of wine perhaps. No that won't do, perhaps I'll offer her a return visit with discount. No, she did not strike me as a regular clubbing type. In the end, I considered that I may have to resort to the ultimate sacrifice – a full refund. Heaven forbid!!

She was reaching the final stage of her lecture and by now I was practically a whimpering wreck. She uttered the words that rang like bells of doom in my ears.

"I have eaten your Canard a la Orange here this evening".

Here it comes I thought. I winced.

"And I have to tell you, this was the finest dish I have ever tasted". I blinked. "The marriage of orange and fine herbs in the delicious sauce was a joy. The succulent breast of duck, obviously carefully chosen, was simply divine. I must tell you young man your duck is nothing short of a culinary triumph".

Desperately trying to regain my composure, I thanked Madam for her compliment. She instantly brushed my comments aside and, fingering her pearl necklace, smiled and said,

"I asked to see you to enquire whether it would be at all possible to secure a copy of the recipe. It would not only make an old lady very happy, but I would certainly ensure pride of place for it in my book, as well as full recognition for you, your club and your master chef".

Still somewhat stunned, I told madam that I would speak to the chef immediately and return with his answer. I trotted into the kitchen to find Peter and his staff winding down from another night of victory at the stoves. Spotting me through his small office window, he came hurrying out to meet me, a total mess as he normally was at this time of night.

"Everything O.K." he said.

"Yes fine Peter, but I have a lady a real dowager duchess type that enjoyed the duck so much she wants the recipe". Peter understandably gave me a puzzled look,

"Ees no recipe, youa just tell her thata I taka the bag froma the fridge and puta in the boiling water, thena I open the baga and I puta on the plate". I cut him short at this point.

"I know that" I said, "but I can't tell her that, but I have an idea and I think it may work".

I left Peter still puzzled and returned to the duck loving duchess who was waiting patiently for my return.

"Madam" I began, "I've had a word with Peter Torterella my Italian chef, who thanks you for your compliment, but apologises for being unable to provide you with the recipe. It seems Mr Torterella comes from a long line of Italian chefs. His family have cooked for Italian nobility down the years and it would be more than his life's worth to reveal any of the many secret recipes handed down from generation to generation. He and his brothers are all sworn to safeguard the families 'secrets de cuisine'".

"How amazing" gushed the duchess "How wonderful, how inspiring? I want you to know that my esteem for your chef has risen still further. I more than anyone in this packed room of yours understand and appreciate your chef's reasoning. His care to protect the precious and unique from over anxious commercial predators is an inspiration". Reaching into her bag she produced a one pound note. "Please be so good as to pass this to him with my good wishes. I hope he will have a drink with my compliments and please convey my thanks to him. When I publish my book I will see that he receives full recognition and I shall name Caesars Palace, Luton, the home of the ultimate duck".

Compliments like this from so called people of quality only confirmed that we were unable to put a foot wrong As I made my way to the kitchen clutching Peter's gratuity I could not help thinking how far we had travelled in such a short time. Little did I know that I was about to travel still further to new surroundings, new friends and new experiences.

5

I'M SENT TO GLASGOW

THE DAVE ALLEN RIOT

LULU AND ROGER WHITTAKER

THE PLATTERS AT LUTON

OAP'S AND KIDS

EARTHA KITT'S PAYDAY

WE SELL THE PIC

Louis Wise a Glaswegian gentleman and relative of Ivan Weston contacted Ivan in connection with a defunct Night Club operation called the Piccadilly Club. The club was situated at Sauchiehall Street in Glasgow has lost its liquor licence and was for sale. Jimmy Bell the previous owner had been trying to sell the premises for months but without luck. As in Scotland once a premises had lost its licence it was almost impossible to retrieve it. In those days Scottish licensing regulations were different from those in England. For example, no public drinking could continue in a club beyond the permitted pub hours unless a meal was taken. Whether you eat it or not was of no consequence. Also pubs were not permitted to trade on Sundays. The Holy Day laws restricted the Scottish imbiber to hotel drinking only. These were just two examples of a raft of peculiar drink laws which existed north of the border.

A club without a liquor license in Glasgow was as much use as a car without wheels. Little wonder Jimmy Bell was having problems selling the premises. In Louis Wise's view the place could be bought for a song and if the licence was regained the premises could be sold on and at a substantial profit. The 'if' was a big one. There was the obvious the risk of acquiring the Piccadilly but failing to acquire a license and being lumbered with an unwanted piece of real estate. Arbiter and Weston took a chance and bought the 'Pic', as it was affectionately called. They asked me to hot foot it to Glasgow and acquire the licence. If successful they would sell the whole premises as a going concern after a few months of trading. Through Jimmy Bell, several people had enquired and even applied for licensing but had received short shrift from the City Fathers. The Pic had a hideous reputation, so much so that its demise was welcomed by most of the City's officialdom. My brief was simple. Arrange for cleaning of the premises from top to bottom. Install a proposed menu, entertainment programme and a suggested modus operandi and of course, to apply for full licensing.

I departed for Glasgow with the satisfaction of knowing that Luton was ticking over nicely. I had installed Albert, my stepbrother, to oversee the bars and drink sales. Geoff Udeen and Rita Easton would easily run things at the front. Merle Humphries controlled and organised the vast dining arrangements to perfection and my new seater Sally Underwood was a brilliant worker who soaked up my ideas like sponge. Not only was she technically very good, but also had a wonderful helpful and unflappable personality. Orchestra, compeer, bars and kitchen were all functioning perfectly. My forthcoming attractions programme offered a selection of the finest entertainment to suit every age and taste and provided Diane Rowley with a perfect springboard from which to pitch her sales drives. I decided that I would visit Luton every third week to ensure all was well and of course to report the progress in Scotland to my superiors at H.Q.

Louis Wise was a short middle-aged very Jewish looking gentleman, with a 'no nonsense' attitude to business. He had a friendly and warm disposition, and from the time I met him at Glasgow airport until I left Glasgow several months later, we never had a cross word and worked very well together. The Pic was a cabaret club and casino situated on the top two floors of a city centre building in Sauchiehall Street, one of the main arteries of the city. There was a Chinese Restaurant on a floor below. The Piccadilly was at the commercial end of the street next to the Royal Hotel where I stayed for the time being. If I was successful in my attempt to gain a license, a company flat would be arranged at a later date. After checking into the Royal, Louis took me next door for my first look at the Pic. We entered through a small door sandwiched between two shop fronts, went down a passage and into a lift.

We ascended to the second floor, (passing the Chinese Restaurant on one) where, on leaving the lift, I found myself in a vestibule leading to a spacious floor area which, with the exception of a few pillars, was completely empty.

"This is earmarked for the Casino" Louis commented as we returned to the lift.

Louis told me that a short staircase would take us from the Casino to the third and final floor, but on this occasion we elected to use the lift. On reaching the top floor, we stepped out into a much larger foyer. Off this, through large double doors, was the cabaret and dining area. I was surprised at the size of the room. The Piccadilly had a 700-seater auditorium with a large raised platform at one end that doubled as a stage and dance floor. The first level seated approximately 550 with an additional 150 seats situated in two galleries that ran the entire length of the room on either side.

There was a fully equipped but small kitchen and two bars. Unlike the casino below, the cabaret room was fully furnished, and wandering between the tables and chairs left in the positions they were in the night the Pic closed its doors gave a feeling of eeriness to the place.
The overall design of the cabaret room reminded me of the Lyceum in London only smaller.

"As you can see a major cleaning job is needed before any application for licence can be lodged". Pointed out Louis.

I agreed; the whole area lay under a thick coating of dust and cobwebs. I soon had matters firmly in hand and, following the clean up, made licence applications for a cabaret club to be named Caesars Room at the Piccadilly. Tom Koneally printed our suggested menu and wine lists, using Roman and Greek lettering and numerals, and Michael Black sent me a list of stars that would appear at our Scottish operation if our application was successful. The list included Lulu, Roger Whittaker, Tommy Cooper, Dave Allen and a variety of sixties bands and comedy show groups including the Barron Knights and the Rockin Berries. Many of the club acts from around the U.K. that had never been seen in Scotland also committed to our proposed entertainment programme. I gave a news conference and issued every reporter with an information pack containing a Menu, Wine List and Entertainment Programme, as well as biographies of the people involved from our company. (Media hype was as important then as it is now). Casino information was supplied by Louis Wise and his team. Right up to the final meeting with the City Fathers I had to suffer the pessimistic comments of everyone I met. The general consensus was that the application would be turned down because the City Fathers were 'anti drink teetotallers'. I asked Louis one evening, just prior to my visit to City Hall, for his honest opinion of our chances.

"Well you've done everything right" said Louis "and the press have been kind; you never know" he sighed.

"But honestly Louis" I insisted, "What do you really think. You've lived here all your life. You must know better than anyone".

"When I suggested this, I really thought we had a chance of pulling it off" he said. "But having been on top of it these last couple of months, I think you've more chance of becoming the Archbishop of Canterbury than obtaining the license" he concluded with a sudden burst of honesty.

The City Fathers sat in a row along a top table. There were thirteen in attendance to hear my application although only the Chairman and one or two others had visited the premises to carry out the statutory inspection. They asked whether I was aware that Scotland had different Licensing Laws to those of England; I replied I was well aware of this and underlined it by answering, without hesitation, their questions concerning times of opening and closing etc. The Magistrates fondled their press packs, (entitled Caesars Room at the Piccadilly), that had been prepared specially for them and which they had studied with interest. The Chairman reminded me that the previous business at the Pic was a disaster; the place a veritable den of iniquity.

"Was I up to the job of handling and controlling this very big Town Centre operation". He asked.

"I operated as Licensee and General Manager at Caesars of Luton" I stated " and your worship may know that Caesars palace has become one of the most prestigious night clubs in Europe. I believe the same can be achieved here in Glasgow," I concluded.

My Solicitors filled in one or two other details and both the Fire Chief and the Police had no objections. Asked to come forward, I stood with hands behind my back gazing up at the line of elderly gentlemen who voted one by one yea or nay. I remember trying to count the nays on the fingers behind my back, but lost count as my nerves got the better of me. Finally the Chairman spoke.

"Mr Savva" he said, "this Licensing Committee grants you a License to sell alcohol by seven votes to six and we wish you good luck".

Louis, who had attended the hearing with me, rushed to phone Ivan in London. I just strolled out of the City Hall and sat on a nearby bench to wait for Louis while sampling the cold sharp air of the Scottish morning and thinking 'what a wonderful day it's going to be today'.

The re-opening of the Pic created a showcase for all the major cabaret stars as there were precious few cabaret venues in Scotland in those days, largely due to the ludicrous Licensing laws. The Pentland Club in Edinburgh catered for the needs of that city whilst the only competition we had in Glasgow was the Reo Stakis Chevalier Club and Casino Stakis who in the main kept clear of big star cabaret, concentrating on lesser names for their entertainment and placing greater emphasis on their casino operation. The lack of competition meant that we had a free run in the cabaret field and quickly established our credentials as the top spot for cabaret in Glasgow.

The confirmation of Dave Allen's dates at the Pic was a revelation in itself. Dave, who grew in popularity year on year, was more than just a superstar in Scotland, he was a God. I was blissfully unaware when announcing his forthcoming week at the club that I was letting loose a box office bashing hitherto unknown. I remember mentioning the rush for advance bookings to Louis who did not seem at all surprised.

"It's the Celtic connection" he started emphatically. "The Scots always identify with the Irish because both nations are Celtic origin. Your man is not only a star and the man of the moment but also a fellow Celt. "

I must say I hadn't thought of that. It's to be expected I suppose that people popping over the border from England to Scotland are surprised to find such a different world, one of nationalism and anti Anglo-Saxon feeling. Dave Allen's entire week sold out in a few days. Such was the demand for tickets that we could have filled the club ten times over every night. I asked Michael Black for any further dates available to accommodate some of the disappointed fans but no date was to be had on Dave that year or the next. Such was the popularity of the Irish star in Scotland that a local newspaper engaged Dave to write a daily column for the duration of his stay.

Dave's dates arrived and on opening night the situation in Sauchiehall Street was incredible. My doorman's task was to turn away anyone without a ticket; that itself was not difficult. However, the disappointed public knew that the star would arrive at the front entrance to take the lift to the club, most locals knew that few celebrities entered by the back entrance because of the unending stairs to the top floor. The crowds therefore waited to get a glimpse of their idol while ticket holders tried to get through to the entrance and enter the club.

The situation became so bad that the Police had to be called to prevent a near riot. Sauchiehall Street came to a standstill as the Police took control of the surging crowd. Dave arrived and eventually made it to his dressing room. The rest of the week he elected to either take the back entrance staircase or arrive early enough to take the lift and enter the building before the arrival of the punters.

The Dave Allen week established Caesars Room at the Piccadilly once and for all and we enjoyed a season of great success with cabaret appearances by Les Dawson, Lulu, Roger Whittaker and Tommy Cooper. I was personally delighted to welcome my dear friend to the club, but although we had a remarkably good week with Tommy, he was never as popular in Scotland as he was in the South. On my return from Scotland for one week per month, I was pleased to find everything and everyone working successfully and all going well.

Around this time I became involved with the promotion of an American black group called the Platters; not to be confused with a second group of Platters that were already touring Europe, known as Buck Ram's platters. The group deemed the 'Real Platters' were resident and working in Miami and along the Florida and East coast seaboard of the U.S.A.

This group of Platters were controlled by a shady character with reputed underworld connections. He was the Platters' agent and owner of a number of east Coast nightclubs including The Springer, under the Marco Polo Hotel Miami Beach, Lucifers, Flicks and The Sugar Shack. The Platters included Herb Reed, Nath Nelson, Regina Coko and Duke Daniels.

Raymond Murphy was an extremely good customer of mine at Luton both in the cabaret section where he often entertained large tables of friends and in the casino where he was known to be a fearless punter. It was first thought that he was a professional gambler but in actual fact he was a hugely successful importer of American cars. In his dealings with the United States he had come across the platters and was so impressed he got the hots to promote them in the U.K. Raymond Murphy, better known to his friends as Chic, was the Mr Big of the Home Counties. Not that he was at all shady but because he was so well connected all over the London area. Chic was no rough diamond. Sure, he had a cockney accent, was a snazzy dresser and was never without a beautiful girl, but above all else he was a real gentleman and became a life long friend.

"If you play them here at Caesars I will fill the place on opening night with all my friends" said chic. "And believe me they will be good punters".

I acknowledged his offer, but I was concerned that Caesars should take the unusual step of introducing a new act from America without some kind of advance publicity. Local newspaper reporter and good friend of the club, Eric Harris, wrote about Caesars and its activities from the very start. He had access to most of the stars that played the club and through interviews etc. came to know many of them well, even befriending some of them. Chic, Eric Harris and I discussed the Platter's scenario and naturally Eric thought it could make a really good story. Chic thought it would make a better story if we sent Eric to Miami to see the group at work and write a Platters' review prior to their arrival in the U.K. Chic of course was absolutely right. Eric was despatched to America, a Platters date was set for their Caesars and British debut, Chic set about ensuring a sell out for opening night and I returned to Glasgow for another three weeks. Cabaret engagements of the Barron Knights, Gerry and the Pacemakers and Frank Carson were arranged for Scotland and whilst business was quite good, the ridiculous licensing laws hampered the overall profitability of the venue.

Frank Carson was as bubbly as a bottle of pop. On stage and off he talked and told gags at a hundred miles an hour hardly stopping to draw a breath, Frank was Mr Comedy personified; a real bundle of fun. I remember his arrival at Luton. Peering into the dressing room for the first time Frank said,

"I see you've played Bassey" referring to the gold embossed wall covering.

His arrival in Glasgow was observed long before he reached the third floor club. We could hear him cracking jokes as he ascended in the lift. Spying the dressing room for the first time, he said

"I see you've not played Bassey then". The slightly drab surroundings were a dead give away.

Frank was a people's comic, I suppose because the masses identified with him. We became great friends and worked together over many years. His incredible energy was legendary. Without being crude or dirty he was able to entertain on or off the stage, he was a great guest as there was never a dull moment with Frank at the table. On one occasion Frank told me he had been elected to a high office in his hometown in Ireland and was asked to open and review a local art exhibition.

"I know nothing of art," said Frank to his wife "I'll have to bluff it".

"Don't worry," she said "I'll help you through it".

"You know less than me" said Frank.

"That's where you're wrong" she said. "I knew the Readers Digest subscription you gave me for my birthday would come in handy one day. I've been reading a series on art and what to look for, so I can be of some help".

Frank duly opened the exhibition and he and his wife walked through the gallery admiring the art. They stopped at a particularly large picture, the work of a local artist. The picture was a series of wavy, brownish, reddish lines topped off by a large yellow blob.

"What do you think of that then?" said his wife.

"Absolutely crap" replied Frank.

"But it's wonderful" argued his wife, "Can't you see the message it's conveying".

"Yes," taunted Frank "it's telling me its crap".

"No! Be serious Frank" she retorted. "Can't you see this is a picture of a breakfast? The wavy lines are obviously the bacon and of course we spot the yellow blob as the egg. The artist" she continued, "was probably hungry and longed for but could not afford a plate of eggs and bacon. In a melancholy moment he captured his emotion on canvas. That is what art is all about. Expressing one's feelings," she concluded.

The artist who had observed the Carson's from some distance away, made his way toward the couple.

"Mr and Mrs Carson" he exclaimed, "I'm rather flattered that you have spent some time at my picture".

"What is it?" asked Frank.

"Sunrise over Killarney" the artist replied.

Back at Luton, the Platters date drew nearer and Eric Harris returned from Miami full of praise for the group.

"They are simply sensational" he claimed and promptly wrote a story for the local newspaper in the same vein.

His excellent review was given prominence in the paper and helped to heighten local expectations. Eric also sent stories to the entertainment trade papers, but I'm not sure the story had any real impact in that quarter; I think it was taken more as a news item than a promotional article by the trade. The Platters opening night arrived and true to his word, Chic delivered a full house of the most amazing punters. There were many 'Faces' in the audience as well as the cream of West End business society. Every car dealer from Romford to the East and Ruislip to the West was there. Betty Baldwin the grand Duchess of Langley arrived with twenty-four guests. She was a friend of Chic and a great friend of mine. Making an entrance, as she always did, in a beaded evening gown and white mink boa, which seemed to be 200 metres long, she upstaged everybody. One of my drinks waiters rushed to her table. No shortage of service for Betty, a large tip was always guaranteed.

"It's very hot in here young man" she complained. "You'd better get me a drink".

"Would Madam like a glass of water?" offered the waiter.

"I wouldn't be seen dead drinking a glass of water" Betty replied. "Dom Perignon please you silly boy and make it quick".

The illustrious gathering ate and drank as if it was their last day on the planet. Bar takings hit an all time record. The audience were well heeled but slightly intimidating and became quite raucous until the Platters came on to capture their attention. Chic's Platters were sensational, and he made sure they performed a programme almost entirely made up of their hits.

"That's what people want to hear. That's what's made them known in Britain" he insisted.

Their renditions of, Only You, Smoke gets in your Eyes, Great Pretender, My Prayer, Twilight Time, Red Sails in the Sunset and other great classics brought the audience to its feet. Chic's promotion of the group totally was vindicated; Eric's exciting write-up absolutely correct, and a great night was had by one and all. A useful outcome of staging such a night was not immediately noticed but came to my attention soon afterwards. The bulk of the crowd had never been to Luton for a night out before; believing that, (a) Luton was too far away and (b) why go to Luton when there was so much choice in London.

Once again the Caesars atmosphere was all conquering, our line up of stars unequalled and the added attraction of our casino made Caesars irresistible and within easy reach of London. Many of the Platters audience became regular supporters of Caesars Palace. Bob Jones, Steve Broadbent, Kenny Tiler and other prominent London business people spent a lot of time and money visiting Caesars in a regular basis.

Betty Baldwin and husband Victor were already good customers long before the Platters date. She was a great character; a larger than life Cockney Queen. The Baldwin's made their money in Plant Hire, particularly cranes. During the sixties Victor imported the U.K.'s largest mobile crane and by doing so cornered the market for its uses. The Baldwin's remained great friends and loyal customers throughout my life in club land.

The Drifters, Tommy Hunt, Frankie Howard, Mike Reid, Roy Jay, Jonathan King, Terry Thomas, Nicholas Parsons, Des O'Connor with Jack Douglas and Dick Emery were just a few of the talented line up being offered at our prestigious Luton venue. The amazing Eartha Kitt took Caesars by storm and was every bit as sexy and sensual as advance publicity had suggested. Superb English comic Johnny Hachet, whom I played on countless occasions, was heard to say that Eartha could turn any place into a cabaret room, whether it was a modern leisure centre or a dimly lit café in Rhyl. I believe that summed up the lady.

Some artistes were paid by cheque on conclusion of their engagement, others preferred cash. Mr Bending, our company secretary and accountant, continually scolded me for not getting artistes' signatures when paying cash. The last run in I had with Bending, ended in me promising on my very life to mend my ways and get the required signature when needed. He had impressed upon me that a large expanding company must be seen to be doing things correctly. Eartha Kitt was one of the stars who preferred to have her fee in cash.

On Saturday night after the final performance of her engagement, I made my way to her dressing room armed with a substantial and correct wad of cash, a petty cash voucher book and a pen. As I tapped on the door, I distinctly heard the sound of squeaks, squeals and laughter coming from within. The unmistakable voice of Eartha asked "Who is it?"

"The manager Miss Kitt" I replied.

"Oh come in," she purred.

On entering, I found Eartha and one of her musicians, rolling about on the dressing room floor enjoying what I can only describe as horseplay. Nothing lewd or indecent was in progress, but as simulation goes not much was left to the imagination. The scene of arms and legs was enhanced by the stage gown that Eartha was wearing. The garment resembled a Brussels sprouts bag; all string and holes. Trying to look perfectly natural I advised Eartha that I had brought her fee in cash as requested.

"Oh pop it in my purse" she said. I found the silk beaded evening bag nearby and stuffed her money into it as instructed.

"Just one other thing Miss Kitt" I said apologetically. "I need your signature".

"OK sure" answered the sexy voice from somewhere beneath the mound of bodies. First an arm then another suddenly shot out from the mass. Crawling on all fours, I managed to place the voucher book in one protruding hand and the pen in the other and secured her signature. As I got to my feet I blurted out

"Thank you for a lovely week Miss Kitt" and promptly left the scene.

Geoff Walker my bandleader, with whom I discussed my experience, assured me that the activity was 'after show exercise' which apparently relieves stage performers of stress etc. "It's catching on real fast," said Geoff.

"Really" I replied sceptically.

Every possible avenue was explored to increase business. I introduced Sunday family lunchtime shows and whenever possible senior citizen lunch shows. Mother's day, Fathers day and Easter were all opportunities for extra shows. From being just a cabaret club we became a family entertainment centre as well.

Trevor Little a Balloon Doctor and Comedian would often be called upon to do two shows. This was termed a noon and night contract because the first show was for a senior citizens lunchtime gathering followed by supporting a top of the bill star in the evening. Other senior citizen attractions included Arthur Askey, Tommy Trinder and a whole number of variety shows involving lesser known performers. A successful entertainer for Sunday family lunch shows had to have the ability to entertain children. Some of the best at this were Poz, Rod Hull and Emu, The Rainbow Team and the PG Tips performing chimps. Magic acts too were very much in demand for Noon and Night bookings. Meanwhile in Scotland, Les Dawson was making a major impact topping the bill at the Pic. Les was incredibly funny and had an extremely successful week.

It is strange now to look back and see how much the comedy scene has changed. Live comedy up to 1975 was good clean fun. The names of that time got laughs without the need of blue material. Mike Reid, Tommy Cooper, Les Dawson, Frank Carson, Bob Monkhouse, Dave Allen, Bruce Forsythe, Little and Large, Larry Grayson and many many more were much sought after comedians. Listen closely and you may hear a risqué line or two but overall it was good clean comedy, visual or spoken, it was never vulgar or dirty. Two very good but lesser known comedians during this period were Roy (Kinell) Jay and Jimmy (Kinell) Jones. The word 'Kinell', you may have guessed, is the spoken shortened version of the words 'Fucking – hell' e.g. "Look at that tall girl over there. Kinell what a bird".

Each of the two comics claimed to have founded the word for stage use with each accusing the other of stealing the word. Frankly which comic used it first was irrelevant. What was relevant was that in Roy Jay's case the word was used as part of a fairly clean act. Whilst Jimmy Jones used the word frequently as part of his highly risqué, in fact, fairly blue act. As a result Roy Jay played for us at Luton and Glasgow, whilst we constantly turned down the overtures of Jimmy Jones' manager because Jimmy was deemed to be too blue. Five years later Roy had faded away and Jimmy Jones became a star, playing all the top cabaret spots in England, including Caesars. Comedy was changing colour.

After a string of successes in Scotland, as well as a few disappointments, the Pic was ready to sell as a good business and going concern. Louis Wise told me that representatives of an up and coming disco, dancehall group were very interested in acquiring the premises and I should show them around and generally look after them when they visited. I met the gentlemen on their arrival from London and after a morning coffee in my office I showed them over the premises. Turnover and various other figures were not discussed. I was advised by my bosses to leave that to those in London.

A further chat followed our tour and the main question was asked, "Why after such a short time of ownership is your company selling?" I had prepared myself for such a question and as usual my research was about to pay off.

"Glasgow, indeed Scotland are non starters as far as cabaret clubs are concerned" I replied.

"The Licensing laws are far too draconian to make the proposition viable. I believe you are in the disco and dance business, an operation not familiar to us. You have fewer overheads than those of a cabaret club," I continued. "Without the burden of artiste fees the loss of a couple of hours on the bars each evening is not so critical. The cabaret circuit is almost non-existent north of the border. Caesars at the Pic is a lot of work for a small return as a cabaret room. It is a bit of a white elephant," I concluded.

"What a marvellous name for our discotheque" they replied. "The White Elephant, Sauchiehall Street, Glasgow. We love it".

Asked by Louis for a progress report immediately after their departure, I told him to tell London. "I'm not sure if we have a confirmed buyer or not, but due to the fact that they had renamed the place already for their operation, I would say a deal was odds on".

The Pic was sold a short time later and became a Disco called the White Elephant. I returned to Luton to be congratulated for a job well done.

6

CESARS

WE DECIDE TO EXTEND

ALEC FYNE LEADS LARRY TO ME

ANYBODY NEED A WHEELBARROW

I RECEIVE A CAR AND TWO SONS

FREDDIE STARR AND DUKES AND LEE

THE C.C.F

DICKIE HENDERSON

I BECOME A HOTELIER

NAJINSKY NEVER DANCED FOR ME

LITTLE AND LARGE

TINY TIM

WE GO PUBLIC

CHANGES AT THE TOP

Master Builder Max Lomax built the Caesars Palace complex and by all accounts only just made the completion deadline. The story is that the carpet was being laid only an hour prior to the grand opening. Also, the gigantic perspex sign, so proudly situated above the main entrance, only just made it in time; it had been forgotten in the confusion. Ivan phoned Max to stress that he would not countenance an opening without the sign in place and furthermore warning Max of the financial penalties if the deadline was not met. Max, in his haste to resolve the matter, sent instructions to the sign manufacturers, but during the transfer of information between the two offices, a mistake occurred. With no time to view proofs (before the helpful fax machine was even thought of), the sign was made with the letter 'A' missing. The error was discovered in the afternoon prior to the opening night as the sign was being hoisted above the front doors. Those that could spell the word Caesars stood open mouthed as the word came into view. A decision was taken to leave well alone. The time had long passed for corrections to be made and in any case the chances were that few would notice the mistake. It was agreed to correct it after the club was up and running. The sign was never corrected and Cesars remained without an "A" for the decade of my stewardship and beyond.

Max Lomax had constructed a magnificent complex and his services were much sought after. Therefore, it was to Roy Laws a small and less illustrious local builder that we turned to for the construction of our first auditorium extension a few years later. Roy Laws was an amazing character in as much as once he had received the various official permissions to build he would go forward with the construction planning on a day-to-day basis. He seemed capable of achieving his objectives purely from memory and everything worked out well in the end. When asked a question about this or that his favourite expression was 'We'll cross that bridge when we come to it'.

The extension ran in an L shape across the front of the auditorium and down the right hand side, effectively adding a further tier. The new levels accommodated an extra 250 people, bringing our official capacity up to 800 or unofficially nearly a 1000 people. I named the new extension Mark Anthony in keeping with a Roman image.

By this time many quite important people of the entertainment industry were visiting the Palace, show business personalities, TV producers, agents and pop moguls. A well-known and much respected TV producer, named Alec Fyne, visited us regularly. He enjoyed coming to the club and often brought his charming wife so that they could enjoy a night out together and Alec could catch our cabaret at the same time; thus killing two birds with one stone. Because Cesars was situated so near the capital and close to the M1 motorway it was an easy cabaret venue to reach and Alec was quick to recognise this. He kept his ear close to the ground and his finger on the pulse by asking questions and picking up items of news of variety in club land. He could also see for himself less established performers and supporting acts which always featured as part of our cabaret make up at Cesars Palace. We became great friends and I always looked forward to his visits. One night whilst chatting with Alec over a drink, he enthused about a series of shows he was putting on called Saturday Varieties and in particular he was extremely excited about one of the performers, a fairly unknown comic called Larry Grayson.

"Ever heard of him?" he asked.

"Yes I think I have" I replied. "He's very camp I believe".

"That's him," said Alec. "Camp, and outrageous with it; I've just put him in the can. He is so good we are going to give him a regular spot as host and compere for the whole series. We are talking prime time TV for thirteen Saturday evenings. Take my tip, book him now. He is going to be Massive".

As we said our goodnights, Alec once again impressed on me to book Larry for a date for that coming autumn. I had heard of Larry Grayson, and recollected that he was the artiste that had been 'paid off yet again' from some club or other. News like that had a habit of getting around. Nevertheless I took Alec's advice and the following day I called Larry's agent.

A week in the autumn seemed a long way off to his agent and anyway it was pointed out that he had a TV series out in the autumn and anything could happen.

"Does he want to play Cesars or not" I demanded. I knew practically everyone wanted to headline at the Palace.

"Of course of course, don't get me wrong," pleaded the agent, "I just want to do the right thing for Larry".

After more discussion a deal was reached and although Larry was going out at £150 per week at that time, I agreed £500 for a week in the autumn, taking into account his TV appearance. The Mark Anthony construction was well under way and would be finished by Christmas. Sadly however, it was but a concrete shell when the Larry Grayson dates came round.

Alec Fyne was of course completely vindicated. Saturday Night Varieties with Larry as host was an overnight smash. Bookings went through the roof. It seemed that everyone wanted to see the camp comedian. I faced something of a dilemma at this point, in that I had sold out, whilst possessing a 250 seater, uninhabitable and unfinished concrete L shaped cavern.

"If I only had made the decision to build it one month earlier I could have filled it this week" I lamented.

"Tell me about it" replied Ray the builder.

All however, was not lost. I acquired one hundred and fifty extra chairs and tabling and not wishing to overcook the numbers, I placed the extra seating in the concrete shell. Everyone was so desperate to see the star that they did not hesitate to book for the extra seating, despite the fact that we advised them of the rather stark conditions before taking their reservations and their money. At the end of each night, I had the tables, chairs and polythene floor covering removed and stored so that the workmen, Fire Officer and Building Inspector would be none the wiser. The decision to put in the extra one hundred and fifty punters exposed my inability to say, "No, so sorry we are fully booked".

Workmen often leave items of equipment in various parts of a construction site and my staff had to tidy up the concrete shell before placing the extra seating each evening. I took a nightly walk about to ensure that all was in order and that every one of our extra customers was comfortable. During one of these walkabouts, I came across a middle-aged lady wearing a beautiful red velvet gown sitting on a cement bag, which itself was resting in a wheelbarrow parked in a very precarious and very unfinished part of the site, which provided a great view of the stage.

"I'm sorry Madam, you can't sit there. I'm afraid you must return to your seat," I said in the nicest possible manner.

"No I'm not going to," she stated forcibly.

"My seat is down there." She pointed to the lower levels.

"In the sardine tin, I can't see the stage and I'm uncomfortable. It may not be so glamorous up here, but I can see and hear everything perfectly, so I'm not moving".

"But your lovely gown" I implored. "It will be covered in cement dust".

"I don't care about the dress" she replied. "I came a long way to see Larry Grayson, he's my idol. I don't know who you are, but you can bugger off. I'm not moving". And she didn't – I did.

Larry's fee had already reached £6000 per week by the time of his Cesar's £500 weeklong engagement. Occasionally, when a coup of this nature occurs, the artiste can become upset or touchy about it or uptight with the club management or their agent. Larry on the other hand, was either touchy or uptight.

"You lucky boy" he said, greeting me backstage on his arrival. "You know George, we are both lucky, and we must count our blessings. I've been flogging around all these years, playing such eminent venues as the Greythorpe Miners welfare and the Cambridge Railway Sidings Club and now when I'd almost given up ever making it, I arrive at the famed Cesars Palace and have a top rated TV series. Good luck to you, good luck to me, lets have a cuppa".

Larry became a great favourite at Cesars. He also became a lifelong friend. Larry 'rewrote the book'. He popularised the hitherto frowned upon camp or gay type of humour, giving it respectability and by doing so changed for all time the public attitude on the subject. Larry had an act of only 20 to 25 minutes and therefore, strictly speaking, too short to top the bill. To overcome this problem I always built a show around him. For example, a speciality act, a female vocalist and perhaps a local sixties band with Larry hurrying on and off with his very funny stories and innuendos. The show filled a two-hour slot of excellent entertainment value.

In November 1971, Andrew my second son was born. Shortly after this we sold our bungalow at Carpenters Park and bought a house at Dunstable only a mile from Cesars Palace. This made a lot of sense, as the driving to Luton from Watford and back each day had become a pain. Also the magnificent second hand Austin Westminster was beginning to feel its age. Although it was still my pride and joy and had given me an age of service. One evening Ivan rang me and asked if I intended going to Head Office in the morning.

"Yes Sir" I replied. "I have to go tomorrow to pick up the cheques and wage slips, as I do every Thursday". It seemed Ivan's car, an Aston Martin DB8 was away for a service and he needed to get into town.

I arranged to pick him up from his home at Hendon and take him to Head Office at Golden Square in Central London. Making sure the giant Austin was spick and span I duly arrived to pick up the chairman of the Company. It was a lovely sunny morning and as we headed down the Hendon Way, I noticed out of the corner of my eye he was giving my machine the once over. I felt a certain pride as I weaved slowly through the heavy traffic around Swiss Cottage. Here I was I thought, the blue-eyed boy of the company, giving a lift to my Chairman, who was obviously admiring my car!

"You still driving this thing" said Ivan taking me completely by surprise.

"Yes Sir" I said. "She's still going strong".

"Still going strong" said Ivan. "You must be joking. It's a death trap. Why have you not got a company car?" he asked. Trying not to look shocked at the attack on my motor I replied,

"I've never been issued with one Sir".

"I'll soon put that right" Ivan stated fiercely "as soon as we get to HQ, if we get there in one piece".

We arrived at Golden Square, Ivan alighting with a look of relief.

"Leave the car on that meter George. I'll speak to Mr Bending (the Company Secretary). You're not to get back in that car" he concluded and stomped off.

At the bottom end of Regent Street, just before the entrance to the Café Royal, the Ford Motor Company had a magnificent showroom and each week one of their new models would be hoisted onto a turntable that rotated gracefully in the huge window. I often stopped and admired those beautiful machines when waiting for a Director to sign the cheques or the wages clerk to complete the pay slips. Last week the car on show had been a magnificent Ford Zodiac Executive, aubergine in colour with black leather interior. With my nose pressed against the windowpane, I remained a little longer than usual because the gently rotating car was the most beautiful I had ever seen. I opened the door and Bending fairly flew at me.

"What did you do to our illustrious leader?" he demanded.

"I gave him a lift into town" I said.

"Well he's really got the bit between his teeth, as if it's my fault you've not got a company car" moaned Bending. "He has to make the decision not me – you'd better go along to the wages clerk and deal with your other chores while I sort out your transport. By the way what did you pay for your jalopy?" he asked. Bloody cheek I thought.

"£550 a long time ago" I answered.

The rest of the day was like a dream. At around four p.m. Mr Bending whisked me around the corner to the Ford showroom. Passing through it to the back we met up with an salesman and a mechanic. A bag was handed to me containing the few personal items from my old car, which had already been collected. A cheque for £550 was handed to me. The official advised this was the amount negotiated by Bending re the part exchange deal and was due to me, because no employee could share ownership of a car with a company. The company must be the sole owner. We made our way to the back of the workshops, where plates were fixed to departing new cars.

"Well here she is" said the mechanic.

"I don't believe it," I cried. Like a dream come true there stood the magnificent Aubergine Ford Zodiac Six Executive in all its glory. I don't really recall what happened after that. Only that the drive to Luton was on a cushion of air. I sat at the wheel on the polythene-covered seats hoping that everyone was watching my progress up the M1. Brand new, with only eighteen miles on the clock. What an experience. What a day.

I thanked Ivan Weston profusely when next we met. He dismissed my gratefulness with the words

"We had to get rid of that Austin. It was a death trap".

Only after driving my new company car and experiencing the effect of the advance of modern technology did I realise he was right.

Cesars Palace continued to go from strength to strength. Our increased seating capacity enabled us to play some of the major acts of the day. I was however, conscious that to produce live entertainment fifty-two weeks a year, one had to be constantly on the look out for new exciting talent with star possibilities. Some of the memorable supporting artistes of those times that went on to major stardom included Cannon and Ball, Michael Barrymore, Little and Large, Freddie Starr, Dukes and Lee and Les Dawson.

Freddie first appeared at Cesars from his Northern Clubs base as Freddie Starr and the Delmont's. With his quick wit, humorous impressions and excellent singing voice, he was an instant hit with Cesars' customers. It was only a few weeks after that date that Freddie burst on to the stage at the London Palladium as part of the Royal Variety Show. Working solo, his band evidently dumped, he proceeded to steal the show. The very next year Ronnie Dukes and Rickie Lee, a family act based in the North of England, were headlining in most of the Northern clubs when they received overdue recognition by appearing at the Royal Variety Show and once again being the unknowns who stole the show. By doing so they broke in the South of England and the rest of the country as a major headliner. Ronnie, Rickie and their sons who formed their band became lifelong friends. Les Dawson, Michael Barrymore and Cannon and Ball all went on to stardom and stamped their own unique styles on the British comedy scene. It took a little longer for them to reach the top, but reach it they did. Cannon and Ball's 'Rock on Tommy' became the catchphrase of the nation as much as Les Dawson's mother-in-law gags and his out of tune piano playing became legendary.

Michael Barrymore's unique style was remarkable. His ability to order people out of the auditorium was hilarious. Not to mention his upside down phone call to Australia. Sid and Eddie who later became known as Little and Large were the perfect double act for all seasons. They played Cesars on several occasions as supporting artistes, or more usually sharing the top spot with other up and coming artistes. It was Jimmy Smith of London Management, who later became Caesar's house booker, who alerted us to the news that big things were beginning to happen for the double act. The story was that Little and Large were earmarked for some top TV slots and also involved a considerably amount of guesting on the top shows of the day.

It was during a weeklong engagement at Cesars that an agreement was reached to return them for a short season of 21 shows as part of Caesar's ongoing Christmas programme of entertainment. A fee of £2000 was arranged for 14 night and 7 lunch time shows to run for the period up to and including Christmas. The boys were delighted. It was the biggest pay packet they had secured so far and a very prestigious date as Cesars Palace was the number one cabaret spot in Britain.

Once again, by keeping abreast of the ever changing and developing cabaret scene and taking the excellent advice of Jimmy Smith, we had secured a coup. Little and Large became household names and a major cabaret attractions before their agreed time with us, we had another bargain.

During these first half dozen years or so, Cesars, and cabaret in general, had undergone tremendous growth and change. No longer was Cesars an isolated outpost of entertainment in the South of England. Other venues had opened and were offering a first class night out, but I liked to think that Cesars was still the first and best. One thing was sure; many of the prospective new operators came to look at our operation and took on board some of our ideas. I was never bothered about this, in fact I was flattered. The Club Double Diamond at Caerphilly, the Circus Tavern at Purfleet and the Lakeside at Camberley were among the one-thousand seater venues available at that time, along with the Webbington at Weston, and the Whitewheat at Maesteg in Wales. All these establishments and a whole host of smaller but equally important clubs mushroomed throughout the South. Of course the less sophisticated but extremely influential heart of club land still resided in the North. The Cabaret Club, Blighty's, Copperfields, the Golden Garter and the Talk of the North were just a few of the major clubs around the Manchester area, successful despite the antics of a Manchester Police Chief who seemed to want to close every club under his jurisdiction. Some of the other major venues in the North of England were Batley Variety Club, The Wakefield Theatre Club, the Fiesta at Sheffield and Jollies at Stoke on Trent. The Forte Organisation also opened the Night Out at Birmingham. Each and every one of these venues seated over a 1000. Batley boasted 1650 seats, Jollies was rated the biggest with 1725 seats. The Sheffield Fiesta offered 1500 seats, with a perfect view of the stage from each of its ten levels. It was constructed in the mode of a Greco/Roman Amphitheatre with carpet, tables and chairs.

The biggest club company at the time was the Bailey Organisation. Based at South Shields, the Bailey Group was wholly owned by the Henry Brothers, but organised and overseen by John Smith. There was hardly a major city or town in the North and North East that did not have a Bailey's club and, like so many at that time, entertainment and gaming were packaged together. Dining, dancing, entertainment and a flutter were the ingredients for a perfect night out. The sheer number of clubs and the huge volume of people frequenting them up bore witness to the fact that these were the best days of club land. The effects of the war and its aftermath had become faded memories. The country was on a high and the sixties and seventies really did swing. People worked, earned and spent as life was enjoyed to the full.

During the period just prior to the 1970 Gaming Act the Cabaret Club Federation was formed. Dereck Wright of the Club Chesterfield was one of the main instigators and Phyllis Clark was appointed Secretary. The organisation met regularly with venues taking turns to host. Matters of common interest were discussed and debated including Artiste fees, Performing Rights Society charges and both alcohol and gaming Licensing matters. With hindsight, I believe that many of the decisions taken and much of the advice given was good; I also believe that the monthly get together was much anticipated by all.

It was fashionable in those days for anyone with money to buy a club and at CCF's monthly meetings one met a variety of people from differing backgrounds. A successful stocks and shares chap or someone with a large inheritance; a successful barrow boy or a public school type born with a silver spoon in his mouth. I don't think for a moment any of us wished to share our financial secrets with one another, but many became good friends and I feel extremely privileged to have known and befriended John Smith, Arthur Evans, Joe Pullen, Alan Wells, the Lipthorpe Brothers, Jimmy Corrigan, Steve Bartle, Julian Beck, Bob Potter, Bob Wheatley, Paul Lilycrap, Peter Rue, Mike Massey, Tommy Barnes, Gino Rabiotti, Dereck Wright, Ted Hardwicke and others, all cabaret club Managers or Proprietors who's passion for the business made them the great entrepreneurs of that era.

Despite the wealth of homegrown British talent, we occasionally, when an opportunity presented itself, played an American star. Having played many of our British stars on numerous occasions and although Hughie Green's Opportunity Knocks and other TV and Radio shows were producing new names, we felt a need to get into the vast American talent pool to prevent staleness in an industry which constantly craves new images.

Michael Black, who, in the very early life of Cesars, had delivered Vicky Carr the singing, crying American star, produced a quite remarkable USA follow up; without doubt this was one of the strangest engagements ever undertaken. The artiste was Tiny Tim. He was known to the British as the person with a peculiar high pitched warble that sang his way into the charts with a song called 'Tiptoe Through the Tulips'. I'm not sure if Tiny Tim's record was 'released' or escaped. One thing was sure; T.T. would be either a box office disaster or a financial smash hit. I must say we were lucky. Most of the nation, having heard his record, was unsure whether he was male or female. Imagine therefore, the surprise when he announced his intention to marry a very pretty American girl. The news came just as he was about to leave America for England and the media attention on both sides of the Atlantic was enormous. Tiny Tim was heartbroken to leave his fiancée behind, declared most leading newspapers, which also carried pictures of fond and sad farewells at airports, etc.

The saga of the forthcoming marriage catapulted Tiny Tim to top personality status. Ticket sales for his week at Cesars Palace went crazy and were soon sold out. The curiosity of the public together with the timely media interest guaranteed this. During his stay at Cesars there were many calls for him via the Atlantic Telephone, both from his fiancée, which were accepted by the star, and from the American media, which were declined. One evening a call came through for me.

"As Manager of the establishment, can you tell me how Tiny is coping with his work while being so far away from his sweetheart?" asked the American reporter.

I found the interview quite exciting, given that it was not often one got the chance to talk to the USA in those days. In fact it was my very first international phone call. Like a true professional I lied brilliantly.

"Mr Tim is doing just fine," said I. "Each evening he puts his personal feelings to one side and proceeds to wow our sell-out English audience with a great display of song and humour. Everyone loves him".

In actual fact Tiny Tim's act was awful and the audience hated it. He died a death every night and having caught his act in its entirety on opening night I have to say it was absolute crap. Thank goodness I had the foresight of building a show around him that featured two excellent support acts thus confirming the old saying 'you are less likely to get wet if you wear a mac and carry an umbrella'.

The strange American artiste had two even stranger minders. Both looked as if they had just stepped out of a James Cagney or Edward G Robinson movie. They certainly kept the star of our show safely cocooned all week. It was whispered that the shady looking characters were ensuring that Tiny Tim stayed on the straight and narrow. (Apparently he had undertaken the tour to pay somebody off. Or so it was rumoured). In any event the two mysterious gentlemen had obviously left their violin cases in America.

Talking gangsters, I simply cannot let this moment pass without recalling the night that Ronnie and Reggie Kray visited Cesars Palace. Michael Black our booker, fresh from his Tiny Tim triumph, delivered another American singing star, Mr Black Magic himself Billy Daniels; called Mr. Black Magic because of his huge chart success with the song of the same name. We were half way through our Billy Daniels week, when Harry Bond a fairly important casino executive of the company, called by my office to advise me that Reggie and Ronnie Kray were planning to visit the club that evening for dinner and the show. It seemed that the Krays were very friendly with the Americans. I must admit that I was not terribly well versed in the who's who of London's underworld at that time and, much to Harry Bond's annoyance; I merely thanked him for the information and went about my business. My indifference to the news of the visit upset 'Casino Man'.

"The most notorious brothers in Britain are coming here and you don't even bat an eyelid" spluttered Harry.

To understand Harry's extreme disappointment at my attitude, one had to know the sort of man he was. A Cockney born and bred, he had an Edward g Robinson build and walked and talked like James Cagney. He portrayed a screen character to perfection and always wanted people around him to believe he was a bit of a wide boy, a 'Face'. Often, in conversation, he would relate stories that left one with the impression that he moved with consummate ease through the shady and powerful underworld society of the day. However, beneath the screen character, he was a decent chap, gentle and kind. He certainly would not, indeed could not, hurt anyone and I'm sure the only villainous act he ever committed was no more serious than posting a letter without a postage stamp.

"What would you have me do, Harry?" I replied seeing his exasperation.

"OK OK" he said sinking with a sigh into one of my office chairs. "I appreciate you are not familiar with the gangland scene in London. I concede that you are so bloody wrapped up in running this place that the world outside and beyond showbiz is passing you by. But all I'm saying is can you make them feel important. Give them a good table and good service for Christ sake. We don't want any cock ups".

I apologised for my earlier lack of enthusiasm, as I realised that for Harry to get so hot under the collar meant that these customers were obviously some sort of really heavy dudes. I found the reservation with a little help from Harry which, I must admit, did impress me - it was a table for ten in another name, but one which Harry was able to identify.

"Right" I said. "Leave it to me. I'll give them the real Savva treatment".

The party of well-heeled people arrived at about 9.30p.m and ate and drank aplenty. They were quick to show their appreciation for the table, in the front and central to the stage, by tipping me ten pounds. They were great to serve and to look after. At the table were five males with their five female partners and all seemed to be enjoying their night out? The star of the show came on stage promptly at 11.00p.m and it was obvious that he knew the

Krays were in, as he dedicated at least four of his numbers to various members of the illustrious party.

After the show, the ten went back stage and stayed with Billy in his dressing room until the club closed at two in the morning. A large quantity of champagne was ordered and served without delay. One of the brother's side kicks settled the substantial bill as the party, including our star, made its way through the foyer to cars. My staff and I received many compliments, underlined by more gratuities from the brothers and other members of the party. Shortly after the party had left, I visited Harry in the Casino where he had remained throughout the evening

"They had a great time Harry" I said, adding that I was sure they would visit us again.

"I hope not" he replied. "People with their reputation could get the place a bad name".

"That's a pity" I sighed. "They seemed such nice people and they were great spenders and tippers. They would be welcome back at any time".

"You'd sell your own mother for a tip" Harry remarked and stomped off.

I discovered afterwards that the Krays and Billy Daniels were part of what had become known as the 'George Raft set'; a combination of American Celeb's and underworld heavyweights from both sides of the Atlantic. Indeed it was rumoured that it was the Krays that had helped George Raft gain entrance to the Colony Club, a chic gambling establishment at Berkley Square in the heart of London's West End.

At this time, Arbiter and Weston as a company, undertook an expansion of their interests. The company bought the Lucky Seven Bingo group, a Midland and Northern chain of Bingo halls, and a hotel in Wakefield, Yorkshire. It seemed the company saw a future in the rapidly expanding hotel business and took on Wakefield as a pilot scheme to learn about the business and to ascertain its potential. Messrs Arbiter and Weston called me in and asked me to take a watching brief on the hotel, which had been renamed Caesar's Hotel.

Meanwhile at Luton, having grown weary of the constant battle against pilfering in the bars, I promoted Albert Gay, my stepbrother as bar manager; I felt a family member would ensure the security of the bar stocks and takings. Albert could also keep an eye on things during my absence. He kept me informed and also turned out to be an excellent bar manager. He met and married a pretty little Irish girl called Pauline and they eventually assisted me by running the hotel at Wakefield.

My visits to the hotel as company watchdog started quite badly. The manager turned out to be 100 per cent, pompous buffoon. He was a very slim Scotsman with a long pointed nose who had apparently made a name for himself running a pub on the Champs Elysee in Paris, I got the impression he thought he was still there. He made everyone uncomfortable by pretending he was a vastly superior human being capable of far greater things than running a hotel for the 'peasants' of Yorkshire. His attitude did not sit well with me, the hotel staff or the customers. He was to hotels what Myra Hindley was to childcare.

I trod carefully to begin with as I knew nothing of hotel management. Catering and bars are part of a hotel operation so I was off to a good start, but in my weekly tours of inspection and discussion I had to pretend I knew more about the hotel business than I really did. I learnt quickly and one thing was evident, we could not expect to make any progress while this Manager was in control, so once I had my feet under the table, I dismissed him. He really was quite dreadful.

I knew that dismissing him before finding a replacement would create a vacuum but I could take no more – he had to go. Although Albert was handling the bars operation at Cesars Luton with great efficiency and success, I was eventually forced to arrange for my stepbrother and Pauline to take charge of things at Wakefield. I saw no reason for a husband and wife not to work together running a hotel. It was quite different from working in a club. In fact having a husband and wife team at Wakefield proved to be advantageous.

The weekly visits to Wakefield, and back for opening time at Cesars soon became tedious. Motorway travel was both fast and efficient and I had a very comfortable motorcar, but the journey was monotonous. I remember listening to the radio on a Friday afternoon and getting totally hooked on a serialisation of well known past personalities. I was fortunate to catch the very first of a thirteen part series on the life story of Nijinsky the Great Russian dancer. The programme helped to pass the time away while driving from Wakefield to Luton. I was so taken with the series that each Friday I timed departure from Wakefield to coincide with the start of the next episode. A week or so after the end of the series I was thumbing through my newspaper and spotted the headline, 'Nijinsky for the Triple Crown'. A wonder horse bearing the name of the Russian dancer was thought capable of winning the 2000 guineas, the Derby and the St. Leger; all three of the greatest races in the English racing calendar.

I was not a betting man, but William Hill offered odds of 500 to 1 against the horse winning the Triple Crown it was a chance I could not let slip by. It was fate that brought me to listen to the Najinsky life story in thirteen weekly instalments and it was fate that made me read the newspaper headline and write up. I carefully cut the betting form from the paper, filled it in and invested a £5 note at 500 to 1. I asked Rita my secretary to address the envelope in which I placed £5 and the slip.

"£5 is a lot of money" Rita scolded. Ignoring her remarks, I placed the envelope inside my dinner jacket pocket ready for posting.

"I'll post it for you if you like" she offered.

"No thanks Rita" I replied "I'm taking no chances. I'll post this one myself".

Ivan Weston rang me later that evening and asked if I could arrange to have some casino paperwork dropped off at his house in the early hours of the morning.

"I'm sorry about this" he apologised. "But I need them for a meeting first thing in the morning".

"No problem Sir" I said. "I'll see to it". I had no intention of dispatching a minion to carry out this chore; I was fiercely protective of my privileged position with the owners.

It was three o'clock in the morning when I reached Ivan's house in Hendon. I pushed the casino papers through the door as quietly as I could and turned for home. Suddenly I realised that my fuel gauge was showing empty; the unscheduled journey had emptied my tank. What was worse was I had no money on me; I was still wearing my dinner suit and had not bothered to change. What was I going to do? It was then that I remembered the £5 note nestling in the envelope in my pocket. What a stroke of luck; I'll borrow it for fuel and replace it tomorrow and post it. The envelope remained in my pocket empty and forgotten. Each time I remembered it something came up and it was forgotten again. Nijinsky went on to win the Triple Crown and was hailed as one of the greatest racehorses of all time.

Michael, our house booker, continued to supply an amazing line up of talent including the comedienne and singer Joan Turner, whose impression of Ema Zumack was legendary, Cathy Kirby who I believe was slightly mad, Sandie (no shoes) Shaw and the wonderful Dickie Henderson. His send up of Frank Sinatra's (set em up Joe) Casablanca bar scene brought even the Royal box to its knees in hysterics at a famous Royal variety Club show. Dickie's attempt to smoke, drink and sing, all at the same time, whilst sitting on a bar stool, became a comedy classic.

By this time my second marriage was moving towards the rocks. Even before my visits to Wakefield started Joanne and I were not seeing eye to eye and were constantly fighting. Row after row caused the worst possible atmosphere for our sons to grow up in. The late nights, long hours and glamour of showbiz were not conducive to a happy marriage. Also, I was a philanderer.

At Wakefield I met a hotel customer, Mrs Jean Stanley and soon started a relationship with her. Jean was a young widow whose husband, an RAF officer, had been killed when his plane crashed in the Indian Ocean. Love had nothing to do with our relationship; it was purely physical; and having had a number of miscarriages during her marriage, she took no precautions and neither did I. She was assured that she could not bear children. But she could, and did, and gave birth to my son James. I continued to live with Joanne and the boys but provided Jean with a flat in Luton and kept the relationship and my illegitimate son a secret.

The 1970 Gaming Act effectively separated entertainment from gaming. All establishments that had both businesses under one roof had to separate the two activities by building separate entrances and exits and, in effect, create two separate clubs. If separation was not possible, the operator was forced to close one of the operations in favour of the other. The newly formed Gaming Board, under the Chairmanship of Sir Stanley Raymond, produced a list of approximately 30 areas that would be permitted to have gaming. If your premises were outside one of these designated areas you simply could not hold a Casino Licence. At Cesars, a separate entrance was built and a two Club Scenario created. Everything was done, at great expense, to ensure that Cesars conformed to the new regulations. Imagine the shock when we discovered that Luton was not on the Gaming Board list as a designated gaming area.

We enlisted the services of local politician Tom Koneally and mounted a massive campaign, including a petition with 10,000 signatures, which persuaded the gaming board to include Luton on the list of gaming areas. It was a triumph of common sense; the Luton and Dunstable population made it clear they had no wish to travel either to Northampton or London each time they fancied a flutter. Tom Koneally led the campaign brilliantly and although unable to receive a financial reward for his services, the small printing business he owned was given all Caesar's work as a gesture of appreciation.

The Gaming Act did not harm Cesars Palace, but it devastated clubs up and down the country. Many clubs were forced to close, particularly entertainment venues which depended on gaming as a subsidy. Of the 107 one thousand seater clubs open prior to the Gaming Act only 30% continued to operate after the Act became law. Some parts of the Gaming Act were quite sensible, but the Act in its entirety, put together by a group of non-professionals went too far and became an Act of extreme folly from which the entertainment business never really fully recovered.

My success at Luton, coupled with my triumphs in Glasgow and Wakefield, where the hotel was doing extremely well, resulted in my elevation to the post of Director of Sovereign Entertainments Ltd. A company newly formed as part of the reorganisation of the Arbiter and Weston Group, formed for the purpose of a flotation of the company on the London Stock market. I was also given five hundred shares.

I missed having Albert, my stepbrother, at Luton but I was determined to bring him back once I had secured a suitable replacement manager at the hotel. My wife Joanne, who at one time worked for Fullers Restaurant in London, told me of an excellent young man employed at Fullers as assistant manager. According to Joan he was extremely competent and in her opinion would make an excellent candidate for the Wakefield position. I decided to investigate and visited Fullers soon after receiving the information. The establishment was the classical ground floor and basement arrangement, as so many of the London Coffee Bars and restaurants were in those days. The ground level seating was completely full and so I descended to the basement area and managed to acquire a seat at a small corner table. It was there that I spotted Rodney Johnson helping with the service in this unlikely setting, under a pavement in Victoria Street. Poaching staff was quite acceptable in those days. I ordered some food and drink and as best as I could I told Rodney that I had a job offer for him. He muttered something about being rushed off his feet because of staff absenteeism. Nothing has changed I thought, and left my number for him to call when he was free. He called later that day and accepted my offer. Rodney, although lacking in hotel experience was quick to learn and being young and enthusiastic he was easy to mould into an excellent manager. After a short time at Luton he was sent to Wakefield, allowing Albert to return to Cesars.

Since the company flotation Michael Black seemed to have vanished, he no longer booked our cabaret and for some unknown reason had been dumped by our directors and replaced by Stanley Barnet. He was a nice enough person, but as an agent gave me the impression that he had none of the contacts of Michael and certainly none of the charisma. I was sad to see Michael go. Sadly I also lost Tony Wager at this time. Our excellent compere decided to depart for Australia.

During my visits to Wakefield I heard of an excellent compere at Jimmy Corrigan's Batley Variety Club; so I took in a show at the famous club one night in order to see the compere at work. His name was Gerry brooks.

I managed to get my calling card to him and later at the hotel I made him an offer he could not refuse, work-wise that is.

Gerry was a big man. In fact his signature tune was "Big Daddy's Alabama Bound". Big Daddy Gerry was larger than life. We had a Roman toga made to fit his bulk and a crown of golden laurels. He stamped his personality on Cesars and became as famous as the club itself. He reigned supreme for the duration of my management and beyond.

Life at the top of my profession was good. Such was our reputation we could most certainly claim to be the leaders of the industry. Cesars Palace was undoubtedly calling the shots. I felt the world was at my feet with a team of players second to none.

I was blissfully unaware of the dramatic changes soon to take place. I could never have imagined how an industrious and stable business activity could be so severely jolted, shocked and reorganised almost overnight by a furious attack from a most unlikely quarter.

7

WE CHANGE HANDS
JIMMY SMITH ARRIVES ON THE SCENE
I ATTEND THE COURT OF KING CYRIL
FRANKIE LAINE – MY HERO
I VISIT U.S.A.
JIMMY, ME AND THE MORMONS
ROY ORBISON ARRIVES
FANCY DRESS AND THE BURNING DOVE

It happened suddenly and without warning while I was on holiday with Joanne and the kids. We had driven to St. Agnes in Cornwell to stay at the Driftwood Spa Hotel. After the customary daily beach tea tray at about eleven in the morning we settled down to a full day of sun and beach. While relaxing in my deck chair, I thumbed casually through my morning paper, too relaxed to be bothered with the news that day. The city page looked as boring as ever, very much the usual. Gold up, silver down, oil steady. Coffee and sugar futures recommended etc. etc. I was about to turn the page when I caught sight of a sub-headline near the foot of the page which read; 'Arbiter and Weston take over by the Ladbroke Group confirmed'.

I read the brief article and sat for a moment riveted to my seat. After six wonderful years was I really going to be working for new employers? Indeed, was I going to be working at all? Maybe they have their own Ladbrokes people. I may be out of a job. Perhaps the betting and gaming giant only wanted Arbiter and Weston for its bingo and casino interests and will close the club down. Or perhaps Ivan and Ivor may still be the owners of the club and hotel. All these thoughts raced through my mind and I knew I could not continue the holiday but had to return to Luton immediately and find out for myself the exact situation.

I phoned Ivan's home from a Cornish phone kiosk. Marion, Ivan's wife answered. She told me that Ivan was out, but she did not know where.

I mentioned the newspaper article and she confirmed that the news was correct.

"I think it is a good idea to return to Luton," said Marion. "Ivan will no doubt fill you in with the details later".

I thanked her and set off immediately for the Palace. Albert Gay, Geoff Udeen and Rita Eastam were there but knew no more than me. Ron Atkinson and Monsieur Rene were able to tell me that the whole A and W group had been bought by Ladbrokes. It seemed that although the main target was indeed the very large bingo and gaming interests, when such bids take place the buyer often ends up with other businesses and properties that it may or may not want. Ivan came down from London in the evening and to all intents and purposes it was business as usual.

Roy Jay was topping a variety bill which included a blind Liverpudlian female vocalist called Annie and a superb speciality magic act called Victor Burnett and June. Roy Jay wanted me to catch a new gag he had introduced into his act. My mind was obviously on other matters but while I waited for Ivan to arrive I had time to oblige. The gag went as follows: - The shipwrecked man was washed up on a desert island. Once he had recovered he decided to explore, it was a small island and seemed uninhabited. His heart began to sink at the thought of being marooned all alone and miles from anywhere. All of a sudden a beautiful girl in a wet suit appeared from the undergrowth.

"Hello luv" he said in his finest Yorkshire accent.

"Well hello" she replied. "You must be the man I saw come ashore. Were you shipwrecked?"

"Yes" replied the man.

"Would you like to come to my hut for a cup of tea," she asked.

"I don't mind if I do" came the eager reply. As they walked back to her hut he noticed her incredible figure accentuated by her wet suit. She was 36-23-36 he thought. Shaped like an egg timer. They entered the hut and she reached for a fresh packet of PG Tips and made the tea. 'Kinnell' he thought; real tea.

"Would you like some cake?" she asked.

"You've not got cake?".

"Oh yes" she said, producing a Mr Kiplings walnut supreme. 'Kinnell' thought the man, real cake.

"Tell me; is there anyone else on this island?"

"No" she sighed. "We are quite alone. In fact you're the first man I've seen in three years". She gradually began to pull down the zip fastener that ran down the front of the wet suit to reveal her magnificent body. Looking at the man seductively she said, "Is there anything else you fancy?"

"Kinnell" he yelled, "You've got a chip pan as well, have you".

The gag was good and was well received. I told Roy and from then on he kept it in the act.

Ivan Weston arrived much later than usual and took me through to the inner sanctum. The company had been taken over and this would be his last visit. There should be no reason for panic as he did not believe Ladbrokes's had any intention of replacing staff.

"They will I'm sure keep everyone on at least for the time being," said Ivan.

He thanked me for my efforts on behalf of the company over the years. He gave me a small card on which was written the phone number of Jimmy Smith a London Management Booking Agent.

"You need to ring him to tie up a week of Frankie Vaughan. The date and fee is agreed but he was waiting for confirmation," said Ivan.

We shook hands and he was gone. Ivor Arbiter phoned his farewells the next day, thus bringing to an end an era in my life that I would long remember. Those wonderful fulfilling years with A & W established my credibility and prestige in club land. I had then and still have the greatest possible affection for Ivan, Norman and Lennie Weston and their families. Also Ivor Arbiter, Michael Black and Louis Wise and their respective families.

The time that followed was a period of limbo; nothing seemed to happen for a while as Ladbrokes got busy organising the vast gaming and bingo interests they had acquired. Mr bending our company secretary and accountant was around for a short while, but was soon swept away by the new regime. The wind of change took time to reach the club. I was advised by phone from Ganton House the Ladbrokes H.Q. in London to continue as normal until further notice. I rang Jimmy Smith's number and tied up the Frankie Vaughan contract.

"What's happening up there?" said Jimmy. "I'm hearing all sorts of rumours".

"We've been taken over by Ladbrokes" I replied.

"What about future artiste bookings. Do you have a house booker?" he asked.

"No" said I. "As you may know Michael Black used to book for us, then Stanley Barnett, but just before the takeover Ivan and I were doing the bookings ourselves".

"Maybe I can be of some help," offered Jimmy. "I am part of the London Management Booking Agency and I'm sure we can cope with all your needs".

"I'd like that" I said. "Perhaps we could meet and talk it through".

The following week I met the Mighty Smith for the first time, and after a full discussion and a lunch at Verry's in oxford Circus a deal was struck; Jimmy became my booker and remained so for the rest of my showbiz career. For Jimmy, the landing of Cesars Palace exclusive booking contract on a permanent basis was a prize indeed. For me, appointing Jimmy to be house booker for Cesars was probably one of the best decisions I'd ever made. Jimmy's office was at Regent House, Oxford Circus in the very centre of London and at the very heart of the entertainment world. The industry at that time seemed to revolve around London Management and associated agencies with the main man being Jimmy's boss, Billy 'Fagash' Marsh, so named because of his habit of chain smoking. A grateful artiste once commented that when he died he would like to be cremated and his ashes sprinkled over Billy Marsh's jacket. Through Jimmy's representation Cesars was able to scoop the very best of entertainment. The combined strength of Cesars Palace and London Management became a force so strong it took the club a stage higher in its development, from famous national to a truly international venue.

During the heady days of negotiations and deals the arrangement between Jimmy and I was perfect. Jimmy went after the attractions, discussed dates and fees and then once fixed would seek the ultimate yes or no from me. Jimmy always insisted that this was the only way to proceed. The final decision had to rest with the management of the venue. During this time, I met and came to know many well-known managements and agents who controlled the 'stables' of artistes and stars. Like club owners the agents also had their share of characters. I recall meeting Dave 'gravel voice' Forester, Eve 'the handbag' Taylor, Phyllis 'the hat' Rounce etc., some you loved, some you hated, some you loved to hate.

Across the road from the hub of the entertainment world, just a few yards down from the London Palladium were the offices of the Ladbrokes Group, Ganton House. After a fairly lengthy period of inactivity from that direction, I was summoned to attend the court of Cyril Stein, my new and illustrious chairman. On arrival I was directed firstly to the office of Dereck Sate, the Company Secretary. He was a smallish man with sharp pointed features who reminded me of a weasel, in both looks and movement. After a brief run down of my duties and the operation at Luton, I was advised that due to the complexity of the arrangements in securing artistes and the sometimes very substantial amounts of money involved, in future, contracts would be signed by a Director of the company and not by me. I was then taken along to meet Mr Stein. He was everything you imagined a high-powered executive of a huge company to be. A face chiselled from granite and a razor sharp mind undoubtedly lacking a sense of humour. The meeting was hurried, short and to the point.

"You come highly recommended as the best in the business of running clubs. Carry on the good work. Some new systems will be put in place but the less disruption the better. Report to Mr Sate on a regular basis and discuss anything you need with him. Nice to meet you. Goodbye".

A month or so went by and the feeling of isolation became quite acute. Visits from other Ladbrokes executives were few and far between. I got the distinct impression they (Ladbrokes) could not make up their mind whether they should keep the cabaret operation or sell it. Eventually it was decided to keep it, and a decision had to be taken as to which division of the group would be responsible for it; the Casino Group, Bingo Group or the betting Shop Group. We finally ended up as part of the Leisure Group, which comprised a hotel in Malta, a Holiday camp at Great Yarmouth and three other hotels under construction at Middlesborough, Leeds and Bristol. Cesar's Palace Luton and the Wakefield Cesars hotel were seconded to this group and because Ladbrokes had a specialised hotel set up, Rodney Johnson's services were no longer required and he returned to Luton.

Jimmy had secured a superb line up of stars for the forthcoming autumn season which included Freddie Starr, Gene Pitney, Frankie Laine, Des O'Connor and Bob Monkhouse. Freddie and the Dreamers shared a sixties bill with Marmalade, supported by comedian Dave Copperfield. During this period we welcomed for the first time to Cesars, The Three Degrees and Peters and Lee. One day, armed with a fistful of contracts, I arrived at Ganton House to arrange for a director to sign the documents so that our programme could proceed to advertising and sales. Calling on Dereck Sate, I went through the details of the autumn entertainment package. He was impressed with the line-up, but would not sign the contracts. "With that sort of money at stake you had better take them along to the Financial Director".

I visited the Financial Director, the Director of Operations and various other Directors present in the building that day, none were prepared to sign the contracts. I returned to Mr. Sate who was surprised that I was still on the premises.

"I cannot find anyone who will take the responsibility to sign the contracts" I said "and I really need them signed now, the deals and dates could drift away from us and be offered to other clubs".

Sate's eyes narrowed and his features sharpened still further. He seemed to look even more like a weasel. I realised he had backed himself into a corner.

"Perhaps I should take them to Mr Stein" I suggested tentatively.

"No no" said Sate emphatically. "You must not bother the chairman". After pausing for thought he said, "Sign them yourself. Perhaps we've been a little hasty. Maybe it's a little too soon to change the system after all. We will cancel my earlier instructions for the moment".

I signed them and countless others during my years with Ladbrokes. I learnt early that most executives working for a major public company spent half their time jockeying for position. Luckily, I was left pretty much alone to get on with the business of developing the club, and with Jimmy Smith and the enormous power of the London Management machine behind us, and being part of a very large and respected Corporation, no star was too bright to approach.

The need to build another extension was now pressing. We were in the enviable position of turning people away on a fairly regular basis, despite growing competition from a whole number of cabaret venues that had sprung up throughout the Home Counties. Ladbrokes agreed to a proposal to add another tier to the right hand side of the auditorium which would take our official capacity to a little over a thousand people. The services of Roy Laws were called upon once again.

During the first year of the Ladbrokes regime we had courtesy visits from various functionaries at head office. A major player was an American named Harley Watson, brought in by Cyril Stein to organise and oversee the development of the Hotel Group. His visit was much trumpeted, as he was considered top echelon. He had joined Ladbrokes from the Sheraton Hotel Group and by all accounts was rated very highly by all concerned. I was on hand at the front entrance to welcome the great man, who arrived in a fairly sizeable limo accompanied by a number of aides including Mr Felix Bentley, a man I eventually got to know quite well.

I shook hands and welcomed the party. Harley Watson was a big man, thick set and quite tall. He walked with the aid of a stick and had a serious limp. Typically American, he was loud, slightly intimidating and looked like John Foster Dulles, but was down to earth and easy to talk to. As we entered the packed auditorium Harley Watson was visibly taken by the size of the room, most first timers were as the club entrance disguised the vast space inside. I apologised to Mr. Watson for the shabbiness of the auditorium explaining that the club had not been decorated since its opening and that plans were in hand for a redecoration programme.

"Mr Savva" he replied, "Without doubt, the finest decoration in the world is wall to wall people. This you have. I need no apology".

It was at this time that my childhood hero, Frankie Laine, made his debut at the club. The American singer of a string of hits including Rawhide and Jezebel was a sensation. During his week at the club we received some very large bookings, not just from locals but from all over the U.K. Some were from members of (F.L.I.A.S.) The Frankie Laine International Appreciation Society. Following Frankie's opening night performance I asked him what he wished to do with reference to autographs. Some stars would accept a limited number of autograph books for signatures; others had signed photos to be handed out, and a minority did not want to be 'troubled' with autograph hunters or fans. Frankie Laine was refreshingly different. When I asked about autographs he, without hesitation, asked if it would be possible to have a table and chair in the auditorium near the backstage door, in order to meet fans and sign autographs as requested.

"But Mr Laine" I said, "There are close on a thousand people out front. You could be in for a long haul. They will probably all wish to meet you".

"I guess that's OK by me" Frankie replied. "The alternative is to look at the four walls of my hotel bedroom. These people bought my records and by doing so made me famous here in England. Now they have come to see me, the least I can do is to meet them and say Howdee and Thank you".

In a way I'd always longed for a star to utter those words, never for a moment believing that it would happen. Yet here was an international star, an idol with a huge following world wide who never forgot where he came from, or the people that made him a household name.

I asked Gerry my compeer, to announce over the house system that Frankie Laine would be signing autographs at a designated area, and inviting an orderly queue to form. After the show almost the entire audience formed a queue right around the club like a snake. It wound its way around the entire circumference of each level. Frankie Laine met everyone, signed autographs and had his photo taken with those that had cameras. For well over three hours he worked his magic with all. How they loved it. Word soon got around that the great Frankie Laine was meeting and greeting at Cesars. By the end of the week the public were fighting to get into an already overcrowded club.

"Thank you Mr Laine for a wonderful, wonderful week". I said, saying farewell to the great American.

"Thank you George for your kindness. It has been a real pleasure" he replied.

"I'm already negotiating for a return date," I said.

"Well I'd sure like to come back again," said Frankie. "By the way, I've heard that you've been one of my fans for many years".

"Oh yes" I said, slightly embarrassed. "For longer than you can imagine; long before I entered the business". He reached into his pocket and pulled out a small gift box.

"I want you to have these," he said, placing the box in my hand. I opened the box and inside lay a pair of the most exquisite cufflinks.

"Thank you Mr Laine. I shall really treasure these".

"It's just a small gift from an admirer. I've become 'your' number one fan this week. You see it works both ways. We both have a job to do. I've been watching you this week. Boy O Boy you are a master and by the way it's Frankie to my friends. No more Mr Laine please" he concluded with a grin.

Another American star that played the venue with great success was Gene Pitney. In conversation between me and associates he was known as, jokingly, 'Jack Pigley'. Gene, like so many American performers was utterly professional. The artistes from the other side of the Atlantic seemed to be far ahead of most of the Europeans in presentation, content and style.

Frankie Vaughan was the last contract arranged by Ivan Weston and signed by yours truly. This was a significant time as it was during this week that I noticed a very attractive lady in the audience, I had seen her before and taken more than a shine to her. Pamela Robinson was her name. I soon arranged to bump into her so to speak and the more I got to know her the more I liked her. Things were not at all good at home between Joanne and me and the affair between Jean and myself had grown cold so I was ready for a new relationship. I kicked over the traces and swept Pam off her feet. The love affair between us went on for some years and eventually ended in divorce for both of us. We set up home together and married some years later. Joanne never remarried, and Jean, tragically, died of cancer.

My life with Pam is for keeps. Pam's three children from her previous marriage, Steve, Jayne and Chris, and my three sons George, Andrew and James all got on just great and although my relationship with Pam caused some upheaval amongst our families at the time, Pam and I never ever walked away from our children or our joint responsibility towards them all.

Because of my involvement with more and more American stars, Jimmy thought it would be a good idea for both of us to travel to the U.S.A. for a working holiday, so we did. London Management, through its connections with the William Morris Agency, made arrangements for us to take in some entertainment and review some acts. We flew to New York and took in a cabaret at the Rainbow Room, thirty-five floors up a Manhattan skyscraper. Next was a comedy double act in a seedy dive called, The Copa' in Brooklyn; both shows were awful.

We flew down to Nashville and met Roy Orbison. Jimmy secured a U.K. tour from Roy and I of course secured some prime dates for Cesars. A two-week short season in fact. After a super dinner in a real Southern Steak House, contracts were duly signed and we flew on to Las Vegas, the showbiz centre of the world. My impression of America was a combination of awe and wonderment. Although in New York everyone was upbeat and professional, Las Vegas really opened our eyes.

We were met at the airport by Charles Mather, an Englishman who had settled in Vegas and booked acts for some of the leading hotel showrooms. The drive from the airport to the M.G.M. Grand Hotel took us down the entire length of the famous Strip and the size, glitz and glamour of this desert city was mind-boggling. Like a giant movie set hotels and casinos, each with its own fabulous showroom, drifted past the car window. The Desert inn, The Sands, The Golden Nugget, Cesars Palace, The Flamingo, The Hilton, The Dunes; I felt I had come home, to me Las Vegas was the Mecca of our industry.

We were guests of the M.G.M. Hotel President and his wife, Berni and Muriel Rothcopt. They were delightful hosts and invited Jimmy and I to join them on our first night in the fabulous town, dinner and a show featuring the Jackson Five. Little did I know then that the tiny lad that came off the stage to wander singing among the audience, with an afro hair style, silver suit and a radio microphone almost as big as him, would become one of the greatest rock stars of all time. Michael Jackson was a showstopper even way back then.

Muriel invited us to lunch at the Las Vegas Golf Club the following day. After some drinks at the bar we were taken to Debbie Reynolds's house for more drinks and by seven in the evening we had still not had lunch. The idea seemed to be lost in a sea of alcohol and conversation. On arrival back at the hotel, both Jimmy and I began to feel the effects of jet lag, alcohol and starvation; a sort of triple whammy. Reaching my room was quite a hike, not surprising as there were 4000 bedrooms. Once there I ordered a meal from room service but crashed out before it arrived and slept till late next morning.

This visit was the first of seventeen visits over the years and while I am, and probably always will be, a great fan of the place, I must admit that a lot has changed since the first visit, whether for better or worse depends on your point of view. The previous 'faces' were gradually moved out of Vegas and the town slowly became controlled by the big business corporations of America. In the old days the safety of the visitors was assured. I'm not so sure that the same could be said today, and above all, the touch of class always associated with Las Vegas is not as evident as it once was. The top class restaurants and lounges which were once so plentiful, have made way for plastic and chrome areas that serve fast food and drink without character and style. Bournemouth has become Blackpool and value for money no longer exists. In the era of 'Family' controlled casinos, the gaming subsidised the hotel rates, and practically everything else, now accountants ensure that every facet of the business makes a profit. For a non-gambler like me who once saw the world's greatest shows, wined, dined and stayed in the finest hotels, all for little cost, Las Vegas has become extremely expensive. While one realises that time moves on and that Las Vegas still offers entertainment and breathtaking innovations unavailable anywhere else in the world, perhaps the time has come to restore a human element into the profit margin and really balance the books.

Our visit to Vegas was short but I left with fond memories and we went to Los Angeles and San Francisco before returning to London. The Jumbo Jet was a new service and the huge carriers were still experiencing some in-flight service difficulties. To be blunt, getting a drink in flight reasonably quickly was almost impossible. However, the return trip was a revelation. We got the most amazing service; despite the plane being packed from cockpit to tail our glasses were continually recharged all the way across the Atlantic. On arrival in London we were somewhat the worse for wear. As we staggered off the plane we commented on the service received and congratulated the attendants. They in fact thanked us for being on the flight to keep at least some of them busy, we were the only two passengers imbibing. The rest of the four hundred travellers were total abstinence Mormons attending a conference in the U.K.

Cesars at Luton was as busy as ever but some of my team found working for Ladbrokes unattractive and left for pastures new, including Jeff Udeen and Rodney Johnson. To fill the void I advertised and eventually interviewed and appointed Mr Keith Broadhurst to be my number two. He was a smart young man with a pleasant manner who knew his way around the catering industry. He was completely reliable and not troubled by the peculiar hours we kept in club land. Albert remained, and looked after the bars. He did not care for the new regime but got on with his job and kept his head down. The new extension was completed and Ladbrokes' connection with Malta via The Dragonora Hotel led to the Dragonora sponsoring Miss Malta, a Miss World contestant to officially open it just prior to the finals in London.

The arrival of Roy Orbison in the U.K. was always headline news in entertainment circles, but his club tour, including a two-week engagement with us, was very special indeed. 'The Big O', as he was affectionately known, had a world following of millions and numerous hits. He also suffered unbelievable personal tragedy when robbed of his beloved family. The terrible accidents and resulting anguish in his life seemed to lend a deeper poignancy to his recordings. The Big O's trade mark was his mane of black hair and tinted shades. A totally professional entertainer, his act comprised himself and three musicians, with his drummer Terry Widlake doubling as Musical Director and the other half of the close harmony vocals. Eighteen numbers, most of which were his own personal golden hits, with no stage patter; the only words he spoke during his show were "How about a hand for the Boys in the band". He simply gave the audience what they wanted; his songs and his music and they loved him for it.

For the duration of his engagement we played a speciality dove act called 'The Great Santini'. He posed as an Italian Count and spoke with the appropriate accent. In actual fact he was from Pontefract and once worked for Lipton's tea. Peter my Italian chef soon rumbled Santini's false accent. "If he ees Italian, Ia show mya ass in the Vatican" he was heard to say. Santini wore a large black cloak on stage, for effect as well as to store a number of doves in inside pockets and pouches. Tall and lean he looked a dead ringer for Christopher Lee in one of his many Dracula roles. He was a great warm up man for the Big O and an excellent spec' act, producing doves from seemingly thin air and making whole cages of them disappear before one's very eyes. His finale was nothing short of spectacular.

"Ladies and Gentlemen" he would say. "Nowa for my piece-de-resistance. I will produce the dove from a burning flame a".

For this trick Santini took a frying pan and lid, after squirting lighter fuel into the pan he set it alight, then he placed the lid on to the pan and a few seconds later lifted the lid to reveal a beautiful white dove. The trick received thunderous applause from the audience and Santini departed the stage. After a brief intermission, Roy came on to complete the evening's entertainment. An excellent and entertaining evening to be had by all, until a dreadful Thursday night during Roy's first week when it all went horribly wrong.

I always maintained that the club was bigger than any artiste or star as it had to be remembered long after they had moved on to other venues, so with this in mind I would often arrange theme nights for no other reason than to promote the club. One such night was planned for the previously mentioned Thursday.

I'd always fancied a big fancy dress mid-summer ball with dinner and cabaret. Admission was by prepaid ticket with the added proviso that you had to attend in fancy dress to gain admittance. There were brewery-sponsored prizes for the best costumes and the night was a complete sell out. While helping to seat the guests that evening I was amazed at the trouble so many customers had taken, a parade of a thousand people in the most amazing costumes. I issued Roman mini togas for waitress and bar staff and a variety of costumes for the rest of us. Albert was Friar Tuck, Keith Broadhurst was a Butcher, I opted for a false goatee beard and black velvet plus fours with buckled shoes and a black velvet berry. I carried a book and I was to the entire world a perfect Shakespeare. The bouncers were Robin Hood and some of his merry men.

Dinner went well as usual and Gerry the compeer, dressed as Caesar, launched the cabaret with his usual gusto. The great Santini provided his stunning display of trickery and took his usual false bow, or as we say false tab. After much applause and shouts for more Santini returned and went straight into his frying pan routine, his piece-de-resistance. With a flourish he removed the lid but instead of a beautiful dove standing there, out of the frying pan flew a screaming, burning dove. It made two horrendous circuits of the stunned audience before burning out and crashing onto table forty-three, a large table of ten at the centre of Cleopatra's balcony where several large tables were situated back-to-back. The impact of the crashing dove on table forty three not only knocked over several bottles of spirits and mixers but, obviously, shocked the guests who quite naturally jumped back in their seats. Because the seats were so close together this caused the people on tables forty-two and forty-four to be knocked forward, thus spilling the drinks on both those tables as well. Accidents will happen, but of course people 'in drink' and from a part of London where 'agro' is fairly commonplace meant a situation began to develop which, if not handled correctly, could easily have got out of hand.

Having heard from one of my staff about the burning dove, I was making my way backstage when I was intercepted by a very irate Henry the Eighth demanding compensation for the loss of his drinks. He was from table forty-three and also demanded that I eject the people on tables forty-two and forty-four, as the people on both tables had been rude to him and his guests. I asked the King to bear with me as it was star time and the Big O was about to take the stage. I told him that I most certainly could not eject the other tables, but assured him that all would be sorted out to everyone's satisfaction after Mr Orbison's appearance.

The next hour was one of the worst I have ever experienced. I had to contend with the belligerence of people from three tables (approximately thirty people), and an audience who had turned from being a happy contented gathering into the jury at the Nuremberg trials. I realised at that moment that whatever you do on stage in England, never, never mistreat or kill, even accidentally, one of God's creatures. Either of these actions could probably get you a standing ovation in continental Europe, but not in England.

To say the audience were unhappy would be an understatement. Almost to a person they wanted to lynch the Great Santini which meant that their focus and concentration on our international top of the bill was a small percentage of what it should have been. Roy felt the coolness in the room and apparently turned to Terry his M.D. at one point in the show to check that his mind was not playing tricks on him. Terry told him about the dove fiasco and Roy plugged on, eventually winning over the audience.

At the end of the show I sent the Butcher, Keith Broadhurst, to ask representatives from the three aggrieved tables to come to the office so that grievances could be aired and, hopefully, bridges mended. I then waited at my desk, exhausted by the stress of the previous hour. Under the Shakespeare costume I sweated profusely and this had unhinged my goatee beard, which hung from my face by one corner. I removed the beard completely. Sod it I thought, I'll be Renoir instead.

Henry the Eighth was the first to enter the office, followed by Cardinal Wolsey, the Sheriff of Nottingham and Uri Gagarin. I asked the butcher, who had escorted the party, to fetch Albert from behind the bar so that spilled drinks could be replenished.

"I'm just not having this kind of treatment," said Henry the Eighth. "This man hurled abuse at my party". He pointed to Cardinal Wolsey.

"I never did," said the Cardinal. "I did complain at the behaviour of your table, but long before the dove dive-bombed you".

"You were bloody abusive mate," said Henry. "Isn't that right Charlie?" he asked, pointing to the Sheriff of Nottingham.

"I should say so, you should be asked to leave," stated the Sheriff.

Uri Gagarin chimed in, the representative from the third table in the fracas. Speaking through the mouthpiece of his space helmet, he had something of a conciliatory influence over the others at least momentarily.

"My table has come here for a good night out. You lot have been arguing all night. We've all paid good money. Let's enjoy the whole evening without ruining it for other people" he pleaded.

At last Friar Tuck (Albert) appeared from the bar and we set about listing the drinks.

"Let's get an order for each of the three tables" I suggested. "So at least that's sorted out". My remark, together with Uri Gagarin's point and Friar Tuck's diligent work on the list seemed to calm things down; but alas not for long. With the arrival of Ivanhoe all hell broke loose.

I heard the clanking of the armour as he made his way to the office. Suddenly he came through the open door and lunged at Henry the Eight.

"Hold up, hold up" I shouted. "Gentleman this is not on." But it was too late. Henry the Eight gave Ivanhoe a mighty shove and the huge pile of metal crashed to the floor unable to get up. The commotion in the office was heard by various members of the three parties waiting in the reception area nearby. It was only moments before a whole set of new players had entered the fray. Cardinal Wolsey immediately tangled with a Viking. Blows exchanged. The Sheriff of Nottingham managed to push his way past a Beefeater, only to be throttled by Napoleon. In the mayhem, a typewriter was hurled across the room narrowly missing Uri Gagarin. I sent Tuck and the Butcher to fetch my bouncers, who were taking care that the Big O was secure backstage. Meanwhile I retreated to the inner sanctum and continued to plead for calm through my open door. Without success. Fu-Man-Chu arrived along with Ulysses and two Arab sheikhs, I never knew who was with which party, but they all seemed to know which disguise to punch and which to support.

The female members of the parties, in various costumes, were desperately trying to part the warring factions, but with little success. At last Robin Hood and his merry men arrived. Little John, the biggest of the bouncers, looked totally ridiculous in his green costume, including hat with feather. He was at least 26 stone and built like a brick outhouse. Robin and the others were very strong and very fit merry men and they soon managed to separate the parties.

"You have two choices gents," said Robin Hood. "You can either wait for the Police or you can leave. Now!"

They opted for the latter and left the battlefield moaning and complaining about a ruined evening and compensation etc. Fu-Man-Chu, two Arab sheikhs and the Viking were particularly vicious, but for utter abuse, Cardinal Wosley took the biscuit. Turning to us as he left, in full regalia including black and crimson habit, he blasted;

"You're all a bunch of fucking wankers".

Charming I thought from a man of the cloth. It took me, Friar Tuck and the Butcher, together with the combined efforts of Robin Hood and his merry men to pick Ivanhoe up off the floor. In his fall the metal visor had stuck so the muffled comments from inside his helmet were almost inaudible. We had in mind to prise him open, but on reflection I took the view that since he had started the whole fracas he could go, and take his problems with him. I understand that on their way home, his transport broke their journey at Watford to call at the fire station. Eventually they managed to release the beleaguered knight.

The Great Santini completed the rest of his run but replaced the frying pan finale with another, safer, trick. A small stand on which was tied a balloon, which burst to reveal a beautiful dove standing where the balloon had been. A tiny radio signal to a device at the base of the balloon punctured it, and released the dove hidden beneath the plinth at the same time. The effect was spectacular and infinitely safer.

The Stylistics, the Three Degrees and Lovelace Watkins completed our season of American stars. The Big O did appear the following year for a week in our autumn programme, but Roy was rather prone to illness, particularly in extremes of temperatures, and leaving the heat of the club and being exposed to the cold October night air had a dramatic effect on him. By eight o'clock the following evening, after a whole day of medical treatment, his London doctor advised Roy not to perform. His glands had swollen badly and he was almost unable to speak, let alone sing.

The audience was already in place and dining, unaware of the drama unfolding in the office. I called Jimmy, who in turn called Billy Marsh. Roger Whittaker, by now a major star, was headlining at the London Palladium. Billy contacted him and Roger agreed to travel down to Luton after his show. The Palladium show ended at approximately 10.30p.m. Roger would be in Luton by 11.30p.m. with ease. Tony Dowling, Cesars excellent comic support act could do a little more time and after an intermission Roger could top the bill, albeit a little later than normal.

Gerry the compere, made the announcement, advising the audience of Roy's illness and the arranged replacement. There was natural disappointment amongst some sections of the audience, in particular four hundred members of the Roy Orbison fan club, and while replacing the irreplaceable is nigh on impossible I felt we had almost achieved the impossible that night. Roger Whittaker, a man with a guitar and a velvet voice, the replacement for a man with a guitar and golden voice, how lucky could I get?

Roger soon won over the most disappointed in the audience with his excellent and very entertaining act and received a standing ovation. He returned to Cesars to headline in his own right some six months later and one of the biggest group bookings during his sell out week was for 400, from the Roy Orbison fan club. A fine compliment for any artiste.

The new extension meant that Cesars was catering for huge numbers on a nightly basis, but was it going to be enough. Bigger and bigger attractions were about to come our way as well as two Royal events, The club of the year award and Neil Diamond and Danny La Rue.

8

JOHNNY MATHIS – DEREK BLOCK

AL JOLSON HAS A BREAD ROUND

WORLD BOXING AND NEIL DIAMOND

DEMIS ROUSSOS THE SINGING MOUNTAIN

THE HOLLIES RETURN TO THE CLUBS

BLUE MINK AND MADELINE BELL

H R H PRINCESS MARGARET

H R H PRINCE PHILLIP AND CLUB TROPHY

PETERS AND LEE THE GOLDEN TREBLE

TENNYSON FLOWERS – ANDY WILLIAMS

DANNY LA RUE

THE END AND BEGINNING OF AN ERA

Dereck Block was an obnoxious character who, because of his sole representation of an American superstar named Johnny Mathis, thought of himself as something special. He viewed club operators as a lower form of life and stated on numerous occasions that although Johnny often toured the United Kingdom he never played clubs, only theatres and despite numerous attempts to book him, Johnny Mathis was a very hot American star that I was finding impossible to deliver.

Over a period of years I continued to press the claim that Cesars played most of the world stars that came from, or visited Britain but received the same rude brush off from Block.

"Johnny Mathis does not do clubs. Johnny Mathis thinks clubs are trash-cans so he does theatres not, I repeat not, clubs". He would then generally add;

"In any case the tour is set so stop bothering us".

I could not move him from this unreasonable position, and believe me; I tried. Until one night, quite by chance I met a man at the bar who was to alter completely the circumstances surrounding Johnny Mathis and his agent Dereck Block.

One night while making my rounds, I noticed a man ordering a drink and remembered seeing him on several previous occasions. I smiled, nodded and said good evening and he responded.

"Hi good to see you". An American I thought.

"By your accent I'd say you're not from around here" I commented.

"That's right" he said, "The West coast of the U.S.A. is my manor, although I am English by birth. Mom and Dad emigrated to the States when I was very young".

"Really" I said "And are you here on holiday?"

"Yes" he replied. "But if I like it here I might stay a while and get a job".

"Are you staying locally?" I enquired.

"No, in London," he answered. "The fact is I'd heard about Cesars and popped down some weeks ago, I liked it so much I've made it a regular haunt. I guess it's because the style of evening here is similar to back home – there's nothing like this in London, except the Talk of the Town, but I find that place too stuffy and formal".

"What shows have you managed to catch so far?" I asked.

"Jack Jones, Dusty Springfield, Des O'Connor, Sandie Shaw and tonight, The Grumbleweeds. I must say I've enjoyed them all" he enthused.

"Well I've got some more great cabaret coming up" I proudly pointed out. "I hope we can continue to entertain you".

"I'm sure you will" he said, "but if you really want to make my day play Johnny Mathis".

"I wish I could, but he doesn't do clubs you know, only theatres" I said sadly.

"He does clubs in the States," replied the American. "Your room here is not unlike a Las Vegas room, or any other large cabaret room in the States. Johnny plays them, why not yours?"

"I was told clubs were a definite no no" I insisted.

"Did Frank Rio say that? I wonder why he would say such a thing".

"Hold on" I interrupted. "I'm talking about Derek Block".

"Derek who?" asked the American.

"Derek Block the English promoter of Johnny Mathis tours," I said. "I've never heard of Mr Rio".

"Well there's your problem. This English guy is not the man to talk to. You've got to talk to Frank Rio, Johnny's manager. He's the power behind the star," stated the American and went on to tell me that he had worked for Frank Rio's office whilst in Los Angeles and therefore spoke with some authority. I must admit I was more than a little sceptical and I think he sensed it.

"If you will let me use your phone, I'll call him now and give you an introduction". I agreed immediately and we disappeared into my office.

The ensuing fifteen minutes were quite amazing. Once the American had made the initial introductions the phone was passed to me, and I found myself talking to a very pleasant, well-mannered American about a Johnny Mathis date. Frank Rio pointed out that sadly the U.K. tour was now set, but perhaps I could be accommodated next time around. After a few more pleasantries the conversation ended and I thanked my American customer for the introduction, bought him a drink, and advised him that I would soon be going to the U.S. on business. He suggested I call on Frank at the 9000 building on Sunset Boulevard. I had lied about having to go to the States, but with the departing American's comments still ringing in my ears, decided I had to go.

The desire to play one of the world's greatest singing stars was only part of the driving force behind my decision to fly to the States; the other part was the rudeness and arrogance of Derek Block and my determination to defeat him and his attitude. On arriving in Los Angeles, I called Frank and told him I was in town in transit to Vegas, but would like to stop by and put a face to the voice. 'It would be a pleasure to meet you' was his reply. At the meeting in the famous 9000 building I told him about our huge corporation, Ladbrokes, that controlled Cesars Palace and I agreed a suggested fee for a six-night set of dates some time in the future.

I told him that The Stylistics, Gene Pitney, Roy Orbison, Frankie Laine, Vicky Carr and others had played the show room and that any of them could verify its suitability. In fact Jack Jones had played the club only a few weeks previously and enjoyed it. Frank Rio found all the information most interesting.

"Ropy Gerber, Jack Jones's Manager, has his office in this building and I know him well," said Frank. "But tell me" he continued, "have you spoken to Derek Block. After all he represents our interests in the U.K".

I pulled no punches. I told him of Block's rudeness and intransigence, the whole story. A prestige club date in the U.K., the fee agreed and payable in advance if required and guaranteed by one of Britain's biggest leisure corporations. Was there something wrong with our money? Was playing one of the most sought after dates in Europe such a problem etc. etc. Frank Rio was visibly bemused.

He thanked me for calling on him and asked when I was leaving Los Angeles. 'Tomorrow night' I answered. He asked for, and I gave him, my phone number at The Roosevelt. My phone rang at about 11a.m. the next morning.

"Good morning George" said the voice at the other end of the phone. "Listen" he continued. "We can do those dates you wanted. We will add them to the end of Johnny's upcoming tour".

"That's great Frank," I said.

"Tie up everything with Derek Block when you get back". I was immediately apprehensive.

"Are you sure the dates will be delivered".

"You bet," said Frank. "Derek Block has his instructions".

As I crossed the Atlantic I reflected on the chance meeting at the bar with a customer which led, ultimately, to the appearance of Johnny Mathis at Cesars; I was determined that he would be rewarded. I never saw that man again, and as I did not know his name I could not trace him.

On the other hand I saw and heard plenty from Derek Block. He was furious that I had dared to go over his head, literally, as I had flown to the States and spoken directly to Frank Rio. If nothing else endured, our dislike for each other lasted a lifetime.

Johnny Mathis broke all records at Cesars; audiences filled ever nook and cranny of the club, including the recently built extension, every night. I used a hilarious act called Lambert and Ross as the support for the Mathis show and they provided the perfect balance. Johnny Mathis was sensational and I had no choice but to turn away hundreds of people with a promise of tickets next time around, if there was one.

Among the many unable to get tickets was a man named Patterson Cowan, a very insistent millionaire, who pestered the very life out of me to no avail. I just did not have space left for a table of twelve. Known to his friends as Pat, Cowan had made a fortune as a property developer in Windsor and was a great friend of Des 'Connor with whom he shared the ownership of racehorses. Allan and Susan Blackburn were neighbours of the Cowan's. Allan was a theatrical agent and quite well known to me as his agency produced and presented shows from Margate to the Bahamas. Pat phoned me several times.

"I'm building a magnificent show room at Windsor on top of one of my new buildings" he said. "I shall be inviting you to run it," he continued. "Allan Blackburn and Des have told me you're the best".

"I'm flattered" I replied, but despite these compliments I was still unable to provide him with a table for Mathis. I did however, meet Pat some time later and worked for him for over a decade.

On closing night I presented Johnny with a beautiful English silver tea service as a record breaker's gift. He adored it so much that after he returned to the U.S. he telephoned to ask me to buy another as a gift for a friend of his.

Club entertainment nationwide was now at its most buoyant. The mid seventies saw a parade of some of the world's greatest stars gracing cabaret stages. Shirley Bassey at Batley, Dion Warwick at Sheffield, Jack Benny at the Talk of the South, and Morecambe and Wise at the Lakeside. The Helmaen at Usk in South Wales saw Tom Jones and Engelbert Humperdink appearing back to back. Cesars continued to offer programmes of top entertainers as well as entertainment for our ever-increasing pensioner following with more and more lunch time shows. Our Sunday lunch family shows also went from strength to strength.

At this time I began to promote other activities at the club, including Amateur and Professional Boxing and talent competitions. The TV show, Opportunity knocks produced new star talent on a regular basis and I believed that we could produce a kind of Op-knocks of our own so I advertised for applicants. We received literally hundreds of applications and decided to hold a series of daytime auditions to whittle down the mass of hopefuls to approximately thirty-six acts in six heats leading to a six act final.

On audition day, I joined my Assistant Keith and compeer Gerry and although we occasionally found various acts tedious, we also found others entertaining and often very amusing. On one particular occasion, everything was proceeding satisfactorily with the exception of Act No. 38; a Luton based man down to do an Al Jolson routine, who had failed to appear. Gerry suggested that we proceed to number 39 and so on, and if 38 turned up we could pop him on at the end. We were already running late thanks to Number 16, an escapologist from Harpenden who was chained and locked in a potato sack. He claimed the ability to completely escape his captivity in the time it took to play Land of Hope and Glory on a gramophone record. As there was no audience, the only independent person available to chain, lock and seal the unfortunate escapologist was a kitchen porter. The record finished and the sound of music was replaced by cries of help, followed by cries of panic from the trussed and suffocating occupant of the bag. We managed to cut open the sack and cut away the straight jacket and our resident electrician snapped open the chains using a metal cutter. First Aid was administered by a member of the bowling alley staff from upstairs, a part-time member of St. John's Ambulance brigade.

The concluding act of the auditions was number 52 the singing tea lady from the Vauxhall Motor Company, who sang while pushing the tea trolley around the stage. Once she had finished I made my way back stage with Gerry to confer and decide on the acts most likely to go through to the heats. As we discussed matters, the door suddenly flew open and standing there was Al Jolson, black face, white eyes and lips, in a sequined jacket and trousers, wearing a straw hat and carrying a banjo.

"Why have the musicians gone home," he demanded. "I've not been on yet".

"Number 38?" asked Gerry.

"Yes" replied Al.

"You're too late" I said. "You were called but you did not appear".

"Well I was delayed at work," he said angrily.

"Didn't you arrange time off to be here?" asked Gerry. "After all you've known about the audition long enough".

"I normally finish by midday, but today I was really delayed – sod's law," he said. "I don't have a set finishing time; it depends on the needs of my customers. I work for Wonderloaf you see. I have a bloody bread round". He sank despondently into a chair, resting the banjo against the wall.

"We've another set of auditions next week. I'll fit you in there" I said, feeling sorry for the fallen star, with his sagging white lips.

"Oh that's great, thanks a lot," he said, fairly leaping out of the chair. "You won't regret it. I do Mammy better than Al Jolson and I promise I won't be late. I'll take the day off work. Fuck the bread" he concluded and left. Gerry and I looked at each other and collapsed into fits of laughter.

Cesars was regarded as the originator of boxing in nightclubs and our promotions became legendary and were very good business even though the purists reckoned that boxing could not be successful in clubs because the ring had to be positioned on a stage and was surrounded by an audience on only three sides instead of four as was normal in boxing. Frankly it made no difference at all; the purists were proved wrong, boxing tournaments complete with dinner, drinks and after boxing entertainment became a big hit in clubs. Our Amateur Boxing needs were ably served by the Luton A.B.A. and our Professional Boxing was provided and promoted by Reg Young and George Igram, both local boxing pundits who had excellent connections with the boxing world. The well supported boxing evenings were packaged and marketed with dinner and a post boxing cabaret which usually featured fairly blue comedy provided by the likes of Bernard Manning, Lew Lewis, Roger De Courcey or Jimmy Jones.

This was the era of the open air concert. In America, a festival in a farmer's field at place called Woodstock attracted hundreds of thousands of people, and British imitations at places like the Isle of White, Reading and Glastonbury attracted huge numbers of people. Gradually an idea crystallised in my mind. Why not combine the two? Boxing and musical entertainment, one dynamic evening in front of fifty thousand people, a world first. My boxing guru's, Reg and George, were not impressed. They pointed out that pop was tainted by drugs; this would not sit comfortably with the reputations of either Cesars or boxing in general. I, on the other hand, was not thinking of pop as such, but popular, solid, middle of the road entertainment.

At the time the British champion was John Conteh and the World champion a South American named Galindez. I felt that Conteh versus Galindez for the World title, followed by a Neil Diamond type attraction would be a guaranteed success. The whole project could be presented by us and staged in the grounds of nearby Woburn Abbey. Woburn was the first of the country's great stately homes open to the public. The former owner, the Duke of Bedford, was a real entrepreneur and devised all sorts of schemes to attract the public to the abbey. The mantle then passed to his son, Robin Tavistock, who together with his wife Henrietta developed Woburn and began the world famous Animal Kingdom. I felt that the huge grounds and the sloping lawns that fronted the abbey would be an ideal setting for the boxing and the show that followed.

Both Reg and George were eventually won over to the idea once they realised that I had thought it through. They agreed to talk to Conteh's management as well as contacting Galindez's people in Latin America, while I went after Neil Diamond, Perry Como or Andy Williams. Some weeks went by before any answers were received and the first was a body blow. After convincing Conteh of the viability of the fight and securing an agreement, Galindez declined. To all intents and purposes that was the end of the matter. A week or so later I received word that Neil Diamond would be delighted to play the event and was ready to talk terms. I sent a telex advising of the cancellation of the boxing element of the evening. Back came the immediate reply that Neil was very happy to hear that the boxing was off and to tell me that his advisors would like to fly in and finalise arrangements for the open air event.

A fee of one hundred thousand pounds was sought by the great American singer in advance, or at least to be held in escrow and so armed with this information I went hotfoot to Ganton House and laid the plans for the open-air concert before Mr Stein for his consideration. After explaining the promotion to him, I asked for an up front payment of £100,000. Poor Cyril might as well have been clobbered by a baseball bat; he nearly fell out of his chair. Needless to say, the answer was a definite no, and that was that.

Rather sadly, I took the whole story to Robin and Henrietta Tavistock. I laid before them the Telex's, the letters of intent, the proposed contracts for seating, together with costs and dates etc.

"Ladbrokes will not undertake to promote the event either as the parent company or through its Cesars Palace subsidiary," I told them. "But I believe it would have been a great event, prestigious and profitable" and I left them with everything they needed to proceed or cancel.

To their credit, the Tavistock's proceeded with the event, funding it themselves. It was a massive success. On a summer day under a cloudless sky, an estimated one hundred thousand people turned up and spent an enjoyable day at Woburn which ended with a two hour concert of Neil Diamond at his best. I did not attend, I was gutted that our company had not seen fit to involve itself in such a unique event.

Through my family connections I heard of a fat Greek singer who wore a frock and sang in a high-pitched voice. His name was Demis Roussos and he was attracting attention throughout Europe. I asked Jimmy to make enquiries as I thought the artiste might break big in Britain as he was already getting a lot of radio airplay. Jimmy discovered that Robert Patterson was representing Demis in the U.K. and was open to offers. Negotiations got under way and eventually a deal was struck. However, a few weeks prior to the arrival of the Greek star, Robert called Jimmy to tell him that the deal struck between us some months earlier, contracted in good faith was now off. Demis had become a major European star and as such would be working much larger venues.

"Not on" said Jimmy.

"Sorry that's the way it is" came the reply. After some wrangling and much argument, Jimmy called me. While holding Robert on the other line he quickly outlined the problem, I could see that my coup would go clean out of the window unless I appeared to be strong.

"I'll sue the bastard," I screamed down the phone.

"Just one second Sav" answered Jimmy and went on to the other phone. "My client will take legal action," he told Robert diplomatically.

The argument rumbled on and on resulting in a visit to show biz lawyer Charles Neagus-Fancy, who looked at all the paperwork and declared that our case was watertight. If the agent continued to refuse to play the date, I, on behalf of Cesars could injunct the whole British tour.

After more negotiation and argument, a dinner in a Kensington restaurant, followed by an inspection tour of Cesars, then drinks, discussion and even more drinks, Robert became as drunk as a skunk and somehow managed to get locked into a toilet cubicle.

"I'm not letting you out until you agree to honour the contract," I shouted jokingly, being a little the worse for wear myself.

"OK, OK you win. Lets be friend, let me out, let me out" cried Robert.

Demis Roussos played the date and Robert became a good friend of Cesars, me and Jimmy.

Another major coup for Cesars was an appearance of The Hollies for a full week's engagement. The Hollies had stopped playing clubs many years prior to their appearance at Cesars because during a nightclub performance some years earlier a fight had broken out in the audience and at one point bottles were thrown, some of which landed on the stage. The Hollies left the scene in fear of their lives and vowed there and then that they would not play the clubs again. Ten years later it was put to the Hollies that Cesars Palace had hosted some of the world's greatest attractions without any major problems. The group were eventually persuaded to play the date as a trial run, if satisfied they would go ahead with a nationwide club tour.

I was also thrilled to play one of my favourites groups Blue Mink. Two of the group's leading lights, Roger Cook and Madeline Bell were amazing. I believe that the group were among the all time greats. It was a sad day when they split up and although it was thought that they would get back together, they never did. Maddy Bell distinguished herself as an excellent solo performer and became a life long friend.

The reader can be forgiven, in thinking that I had peaked and that there was no more that I could promote. Superstars, unknown artistes, ethnic evenings, boxing and wrestling events, Senior Citizens shows, Children's Sunday lunch events, Charity nights and Mayoral Banquets, Gentlemen only 'Smoking Concerts' complete with a full compliment of strippers, The Hurling and Irish Football finals direct by satellite from the Emerald Isle to the Cesars big screen. The list of activities goes on and on; but to our credit, now came two very special nights, which would give Cesars ultimate respectability and a prominent place in the history of club land.

I refer to two royal fund raising evenings; glittering events at which the guest of honour was a prominent member of the Royal family. The first was an evening on behalf of the Oxford and Cambridge Boat Race Committee. It seemed they were so strapped for cash, that unless money was raised and sponsorship found the Great Boat Race waould not be able to continue. Cesars Palace was chosen as the venue for the event as its location, Luton, was approximately midway between Oxford and Cambridge. I was approached and readily agreed to provide the facilities and put together a Gala night, dinner and show. I was advised that H.R.H. Princess Margaret would be Guest of Honour.

The story of the impending Royal visit to our club made big news locally. Former adversaries of the club were wrong-footed and found themselves having to praise the fund raising work the club had so often involved itself with. The local community as a whole spoke of Cesars with pride. As well as raising five thousand pounds for the fund raising committee, the event led to a second important result. Derek Sate officiated on behalf of Ladbrokes and confirmed sponsorship of the race for five years by our parent company Ladbrokes. I had written and spoken to both Stein and Sate regarding sponsorship, after all I argued, the race is steeped in history and is also a major sporting event. Ladbrokes were never a company to fight shy of sponsorship in sport and they delivered when needed.

In the month leading up to the Royal night there were many visits from various V.I.P.'s connected with the Royal household, security services, equerries and press etc. It was a month of memos and I was advised on every aspect of the impending visit from time of arrival and departure to the food and drinks likes and dislikes of the Princess. I arranged a first class show with American singing star Jack Jones as top of the bill. I had already played Jack and I knew his golden voice and striking good looks would be a winner with the audience, particularly the female members, Princess Margaret the principal.

In those days Jack Jones could be quite a rude and arrogant man off stage, but I ignored this unfortunate side of the man aside in favour of his talent. With only ten days to go a newspaper story accompanied by pictures revealed that our Royal guest of honour was romantically linked with one Roddy Llewellyn and the Caribbean island of Mystique. The media went berserk with Princess Margaret the centre of attention. Cesars was already sold out for the Royal event yet when the story broke I could have sold the tickets ten times over – demand was amazing. Upon her return to England her first official engagement was with us.

Such was the furore caused by her relationship with Roddy Llewellyn that I began to wonder if she would attend at all. A lesser person would certainly have opted for a hide away, but to her credit she stuck to her arranged schedule and carried out her first public appearance as guest of honour at our establishment.

As well as the thousand people inside Cesars, there must have been close on that number of press representatives outside. When it comes to publicity, the old adage is absolutely right. 'When it's good it's very good and when it's bad it's still good'. Money could not buy the vast amount of publicity that Cesars enjoyed that night.

Photographs were only permitted in the Royal receiving room taken by our own club photographer his brief as follows. H.R.H. will be introduced to various table sponsors and top table guests and while meeting and greeting is in progress she will occasionally put her glass and cigarette down. This action will be a signal for the club photographer to capture the event on film. Under no circumstances must he photograph H.R.H. whilst she has either a drink or cigarette in her hand.

H.R.H. mingled and chatted with all our honoured guests and was the perfect Guest of Honour. Throughout the entire pre-dinner reception she was completely relaxed and seemed unconcerned at the press attention of the previous week. She drank White Satin gin and smoked using a long stylish cigarette holder. My house photographer dutifully followed her every movement around the room waiting for the Princess to put her glass and cigarette holder to one side, in order to take some shots. Whether carried away by the ambience or just plain enjoying the evening I shall never know, I only know that H.R.H. hung on to both drink and fag. At a point towards the end of the reception she turned to the photographer and looking him straight in the eye said,

"Young man, are you ever going to use that camera? Because if you are you had better hurry. We will be going in to dinner soon".

Surprised and somewhat flummoxed he began snapping. Almost every shot was an excellent picture of a very photogenic Princess Margaret complete with drink and fag.

The dinner went extremely well. I went back stage and ran through the order with Jack Jones. Jack was in his usual condescending mood but took the info on board with the ease of a great professional. I had hired a special guest compeer for the night – the actor Patrick Cargill. The show flowed and built to the finale, the balance was perfect and the guest compeer added an essential touch of class. Jack came on to headline and at the end of his excellent performance received a standing ovation. One of the first on her feet was H.R.H. calling for more.

The timing that had worked out to perfection as per the memo dealing with the Royal schedule, was about to be forgotten. Patrick, who had come on stage to take Jack off, was now stranded unable to be heard over the applause for Jack and the calls for an unscheduled encore. I was standing beside Jack when Patrick called him back on stage. In that instant, Jack, who had stuck rigidly to his instructions on timing, looked to me for guidance.

"What should I do George?" he asked. For once he looked both lost and rather humble.

"You must go back on Jack," I said. "It's a Royal command". He did and rounded off a most perfect Royal night, our first at Cesars Palace.

I played Jack Jones on numerous occasions after that great night. Somehow the aloofness of those early years had vanished. He was, as far as our relationship was concerned, a perfectly charming gentleman and remained always a great professional.

Our second Royal night came via publicist Max Butterfield and Evening Standard columnist Richard Afton. I was approached by Max to stage a Royal charity night and told that Richard Afton would be able to provide a Royal Guest of Honour. Dickie, as he was known to his friends, was a big wheel at the Eccentric club in London and knew the Duke of Edinburgh quite well. Dickie, escorted by Max, visited Cesars and after viewing the facilities, was happy to proceed with arrangements. In the meantime I received the great news that Cesars had won the prestigious Club of the Year award for Britain and a date was requested for the trophy presentation. I decided to combine the two events.

Prior to his employment at the Evening Standard Dickie had been a fairly senior television producer. He retained excellent connections with the world of TV that enabled him to persuade Anglia Television to televise the event. This was not the first time that TV cameras had been at Cesars. We were the venue chosen to host 'The Colour Of Soul' TV series and the series 'George Hamilton the Fourth and Friends'. Both of these programmes sought the intimacy of a nightclub as a backdrop for their productions. Another time TV cameras were used at Cesars was the night that my dear friend Frankie Vaughan was ambushed on stage by Eamon Andrews for his "This Is Your Life" programme.

The Royal show comprised a number of first class acts supporting and a double top of the bill of The Drifters and Les Dawson, compered by Gerry Brooks. Each member of the Royal Family has their own personal standard, Dickie managed to obtain the Duke's standard and permission to fly it over the premises, the first time a Royal Standard has ever flown over a nightclub.

Following the excellent fund raising evening, I was honoured to accept the prestigious Club of the Year trophy and certificate from James Dowd of Club Mirror.

Hughie Green's Opportunity Knocks continued to produce a steady stream of 'people's stars' created by a studio audience and their 'clapometer'. Lennie Peters was a kind of white Stevie Wonder; a blind singer-pianist from the East End of London who had played Cesars' several times with great success. He teamed up with a young and very attractive blonde singer called Dianne Lee and, as Peters and Lee, they took Opportunity Knocks by storm. I was quick to recognise their potential while watching them perform their repertoire at Cesars, including their big hit of the time called 'Welcome Home'. I called Jimmy and said that having seen the act I felt they had durability and asked for further dates. Unfortunately I was too late; their diary was full for the rest of the year including a summer season at Blackpool.

However; I am not a man to give in easily. It was about this time that Ladbrokes asked me to provide Sunday entertainment for their newly acquired Caister Holiday camp near great Yarmouth. Organising a weekly Sunday evening show at Caister's Neptune Palace was simplicity itself; I simply included Neptune in Cesars weekly programme. With this in mind I got the idea for my Peters & Lee Golden treble. A three shows in one-day proposition, the day in question being Sunday, a day off for Peters and Lee.

The idea I put to Jimmy was to engage a small private plane and fly them from Blackpool to Luton for a lunchtime show, then on to Caister for the evening show, and then fly them back to Luton for our late cabaret spot. Amazingly Peters & Lee agreed to the proposal and arrangements were made. Even more amazing was the weather, the forecast was not good. We were having one of those typical English summers. In the week running up to the big day we had some of the worst summer weather ever recorded.

I telephoned Blackpool on the Saturday evening to be told that it was pouring with rain, but more importantly the gale force winds were so severe that waves that were crashing over the piers. I must say I turned in that night with a feeling of total helplessness. Even in Luton we were experiencing the most atrocious weather and I remember falling asleep to the sound of the howling wind well aware that three sell out shows on the morrow might have to be called off.

I awoke at 7.00a.m. to the sound of a large gathering of birds (the feathered kind) that used the tree in my garden as a perch, and stage. I went quickly to the window and greeted a perfect summer day. The morning sun shone from a cloudless azure sky. I made my way to Luton Airport as arranged and as I drove up Stopsley Hill, the approach road to the airport, I spotted a small single engine four-seater plane preparing to land and knew instinctively that it was Lennie and Di. The day was a triumph. All three shows presented and produced with professional proficiency and near perfect timing.

The couple stayed overnight at Luton and were flown back to Blackpool the following morning. The overnight stay due mainly because of their exhaustion, but partly because the pilot, who had been under pressure all day, got absolutely legless and had to be helped to bed. Jimmy, who had been sceptical when I first muted the idea but who had eventually agreed and even accompanied the stars to Caister and back was philosophic.

"I must say I had my doubts," he said. "But I've known you long enough to know that your enthusiasm and faith in a project know no bounds. Failure or problems do not enter your mind or your vocabulary".

A season of Monkhouse, Forsythe, Charlie Williams, Roy Castle, Tom O'Connor, Ronnie Corbett, Norman Vaughan and American's Andy Williams, The Inkspots and Gene Pitney continued an excellent programme of top entertainment. Comedian Freddie Starr, a very big name indeed also block-busted our Christmas arrangements and a succession of lovely ladies helped to make our programme glamorous as well as entertaining. We were delighted to present Lulu, Lena Martell, Cilla Black, Selena Jones, Ruby Murray, Joan Turner and the stunning Annie Anderson.

Black American groups had a big British following which grew steadily during the seventies. Three Degrees, Platters, Drifters, The Detroit Emeralds and Stylistics were all featured in our mid-seventies programmes, as well as black entertainers Ray Charles, Jack Hammer, Bill Fredericks and the amazing Lovelace Watkins who was undoubtedly the greatest showman of them all. I think it fair to say that Lovelace Watkins did not possess a particularly brilliant voice, in fact as far as male vocalist's go he was very average, but if you went seeking showmanship, stagecraft, presentation and charisma then look no further than him, he had them all. Lovelace's stage patter between numbers was legendary as was his immense sex appeal. He wooed ladies from the stage, and a considerable number backstage as well. It was his various relationships and some personal problems arising from them that lead to his rapid fall from grace.

Initially Lovelace was spotted at a northern club by Jess Yates who had his own TV programme at the time called "Stars on Sunday". The programme was a quasi religious and showbiz coming together type production and boasted a very large viewing audience. Lovelace's appearance on the show was an instant hit. By shear coincidence Pearl Bailey's appearance at the Talk of the

A gala evening with Her Royal Highness Princess
Anne, Iris Williams and Joe Longthorne.

Freddie was always a 'Starr' attraction.

Danny La Rue, a living legend and a dear friend.

Another sell out Blazers appearance for Lenny Henry.

Unlike Queen Victoria some royals are amused.

Lenny Peters of Peters and
Lee with Pam.

Comic genius 'Tarby' and
Petula Clark.

A magic moment with Tommy Cooper and his brother.

Town was interrupted when the star became ill, so Lovelace was invited to step in. He took to the great West End stage like the proverbial duck takes to water. The rest is history. Lovelace made such a massive impact that within days the media propelled him into superstar status and every club operator throughout the British Isles as well as concert promoters and agents were after him. I succeeded in securing his services for Luton and he took Cesars by storm.

Lovelace's rise to fame was spectacular, but sadly and after only a few years at the pinnacle of his success his fall from stardom back to obscurity was equally spectacular. Lovelace was busy conquering the rest of Europe when his troubles began. A story involving a beautiful German girl and his intention to marry her hit the headlines. Hot on the heels of this report came the story of a heavily pregnant Yorkshire lass who had been jilted by the American. The press fell upon the story with the avarice of a cloud of locusts. Pictures of the girl, heartbroken and cast aside walking up a street of drab terraced houses, big belly and all, shocked the nation. The cad! How could he have done this, how outrageous, etc.etc?

At this time the star featured on many forthcoming programmes including mine and as usual his week was sold out well in advance, but like avenging angels the public showed their wrath by cancelling their reservations. I remember the phones ringing non stop day and night as Lovelace's bookings melted away until there was hardly anyone left to support his appearance. The British Public deserted the star and consigned him to a dustbin of history. He was the end of one of the most amazing showmen I had ever seen but in those days stars were expected to set certain standards and although many scandals of one sort or another were tolerated by legions of British fans, Lovelace's was unforgivable and rightly so. In a sense it is sad to reflect that today such behaviour would have probably enhanced his star status.

We, along with other major venues around the country, continued to provide the best entertainment available from both sides of the Atlantic. The only incident I can recall that posed an unnecessary and unfortunate glitch along the way was the attitude and ultimate aggro between me and Tennyson Flowers, the American stage manager for Andy Williams.

Andy was booked for a one-night appearance at an enormous fee. Dinner and show inclusive tickets were sold out at twenty-five pounds per person, at least three times the normal amount charged for a night out at that time. I arrived early in the evening, just as the lighting and sound rig was being installed by Andy's crew. To my horror I found that my seating had been totally disregarded and a large section of prime seating removed. I called to my lighting and sound technician who acted as my stage manager to explain.

"I know what you are going to say Mr S, but their stage manager insisted on moving the bank of seating to make way for that huge sound consul". I grunted disapproval and moved on to find their Stage Manager.

"That's me." came the reply to my enquiries. "My name is Tennyson Flowers. What can I do for you?"

"Mr Flowers; you can remove your equipment so that my seating can be restored. There are a number pf places for your console to be positioned that would not affect the seating" I replied tartly.

"Sorry no can do" came back the American drawled reply.

"I must insist you do," I said sternly "and now".

"You don't seem to realise, unless I have this position for Andy's equipment he won't go on" said Flowers.

"No, you don't seem to realise that unless I have that seating, which incidentally is sold out, I won't want him to go on because I need every bit of income in order to be able to pay his record fee". I was seething, but tried to remain cool but strong.

"Well I'll have to call Andy and tell him the show is off," taunted the Stage Manager.

"No let me call" I interrupted him. "I'll tell him it's off and why. Where's he staying?" I said, calling the stage managers bluff.

"OK" he said. "Let's try and resolve this. Where do you want the equipment to be placed, we'll get it moved".

The mini crisis over, all was well, the show fantastic and Andy Williams sensational. After the show however, as my well heeled , twenty-five pounds per person audience were dancing, I suddenly spotted step ladders appearing in the middle of the dance floor and crew members proceeding to ascend the ladders to unbolt and de-rig Andy Williams lighting and sound set-up. I never ever allowed derigging to take place before the end of the evening and after the punters had left. I sent my security men in to remove the crew and their ladders and made my way backstage where I found Tennyson Flowers breathing fire and brimstone and Jimmy Smith trying to diplomatically calm the situation down by pointing out the rules of our club with regard to de-rigging. Catching sight of me Flowers lunged.

"Why you son of a bitch" he screamed. "I've had enough of you and your club".

I managed to avoid his lunge and, being a devout coward, I would normally have done a runner at this point but I was so obsessed by this moron's attitude that I let rip in reply, blasting him with a few chosen words of my own. I also lunged at him; to everyone's surprise, including my own. Jimmy pulled us apart and we eventually stomped off in different directions.

I tell this story because fate led me to meet Tennyson Flowers again some years later and as the reader will discover, he did me a huge favour for which I would always be grateful.

Another spectacular coup was achieved during this period. Jimmy called me one morning and asked if I'd be interested in playing Danny La Rue and his show at the Palace.

"I sure would" I replied without hesitation.

"There's just a possibility he might be persuaded to do the occasional club date," said Jimmy.

"I'll speak to Sonny or Anne Zhal, Danny's management and see if they will go for it."

Danny La Rue was unquestionably the biggest and most durable star in the West End of London. He'd been packing them in for years and was Mr Show Biz personified. To get tickets for one of his shows was a task and a half, for Cesars to present Danny would be a coup. Jimmy called me the next day and arranged a visit to the club for Sonny Zhal and himself that evening.

Sonny liked what he saw and approximately a week later the deal was done. A seven-night appearance arranged, signed and sealed. The show would be of two hours duration with an intermission after the first hour. Danny would be bringing a reduced cast of thirty-two people for the more limited facilities of a club engagement.

Club land at large greeted the news with jealousy, accompanied by comments of disbelief. 'You can't bring pure theatre into a club. In any case thirty-two performers on a small cabaret stage; La Rue and Savva will come unstuck'. 'It won't work' was a fairly common cry around club land.

I have always thought Danny to be the ultimate theatrical. He visited the premises incognito to reconnoitre the facilities and in an instant worked out exactly what he would do and how he would run the show.

"Mr Savva" he said when introduced to me by his tour manager and close friend Tony Hanson, "I'm going to give you the greatest club show on earth. Thirty-two very talented people in beautiful costumes, performing some wonderful numbers. And I am going to present the most elegant tart you've ever seen"

Much rehearsal took place to ensure the production fitted the venue and while it was a little cramped backstage, the intimacy of a club audience and a theatre show was a great plus. The club sold out completely. Even tables that had hitherto not existed were sold and once sold, were made.

On opening night Danny arrived at the front entrance, rather than the stage door, accompanied by Jack Hanson and Annie his dresser and wardrobe mistress. I had forty people in the foyer area dining from little tables of twos and fours that had been hastily put together, to cope with the extra 'chance' arrivals.

"Oh look" Jack whispered to Dan as he swept by. "What a kind person Mr Savva must be giving dinner to those people who have travelled down; but they cannot possibly see the show from there".

"Actually Mr La Rue, after dinner and just before you come on, I invite them to sit along the sixty foot bar counter which will be closed for the duration of your performance. From there they will see the whole show".

"What a wonderful idea" said Danny. "You are both kind and thoughtful".

"I charge them one pound less than the advertised price for the slight inconvenience" I replied. Danny looked at me gob smacked and again burst into laughter.

"I thought they were freebies" he said "silly old tart". "But tell me" he asked as we proceeded to the dressing room. "Don't they ever complain?"

"No" I said "Not really. They are so pleased to get in. Only one person has ever made a sour comment; a lady who never reserves a seat and always turns up with her husband on the spur of the moment. She got a bit het up one night and asked me whether she looked like a toby jug.

"Quite the contrary Madam" I replied. "You look perfectly lovely."

"Then why do you keep putting me up on that shelf like some old toby jug?" Danny laughed.

Later when he came on stage he called out as he always did "Say Hello to Dan" and looking across at the bar now supporting a line of some forty people perched along it, legs dangling "and you too my little toby jugs, say Hello to Dan".

The show was a huge success and signalled the start of Dan's great love affair with club land. He played theatre tours and club tours with boundless energy. He brought glamour, style and class into the cabaret clubs of Britain. We worked many times together and became life long friends.

Since the Ladbrokes takeover of Cesars Palace, and although permitted to work with an amazing amount of freedom, I was never quite as happy as when I worked for Arbiter and Weston. My pay was good, as were my conditions, but I felt I lost as a person in the ever growing conglomerate. Recognition of achievement meant a lot to me, but unlike working for a smaller company, the proverbial slap on the back was seldom forthcoming.

Names became numbers on an ever-increasing list. Endless meetings at Ladbrokes H.Q. to discuss policy, corporate image and the like began to try my patience, added to which new challenges were being thrust in my direction and offers of work at any one of a number of venues were available to me.

It was therefore almost inevitable that I should tender my resignation to John Jarvis, our hotels division chairman, and depart from Cesars in the spring of 1977. It was the end of one era but the start of another, even more remarkable.

I AM INTRODUCED TO WALES

I MEET FRANK & JESSE JAMES

AN INCIDENT AT THE BLACKBIRDS, CWMBRAN

A SERIOUS MR CARSON

THE PG TIPS CHIMPS DON'T TALK

DEAD OR ALIVE – TERRY HALL

COWAN ARRIVES AT USK

I ARRIVE AT WINDSOR

THE JAMES GANG RIDE OFF INTO THE SUNSET

I BEAT A PATH TO WILLIAM STREET AND GLORY

During the period 1966 to 1977 I made a major discovery. Success breeds success and when you are riding high job offers with better pay become plentiful. Throughout the seventies, many such offers came my way but I did not place much credence in their viability. The reader may recall my reference to Pat Cowan and his scheme to put a night spot on top of one of his Windsor developments. At the time I thought this to be a pipe dream with his job offer due more to the appearance of Johnny Mathis than my ability.

My departure from Cesars Palace and Ladbrokes was not acrimonious, indeed we parted company on the friendliest of terms but I felt I had to follow my game plan. Through Max Butterfield the publicist, I was introduced to the owners of The Helmaen Club at Usk in Gwent, South Wales. A deal was negotiated and my management services were transferred to Usk where I was to continue my career in the cabaret and club world. The situation at the club was interesting to say the least. It seemed that the playing Tom Jones and Engelbert Humperdink back to back in a two-week gala extravaganza had been something of a financial disaster. The seating capacity at the fairly small

Usk venue meant that the ticket price asked for Super Star duo was clearly beyond the reach of many and therefore anticipated sales and income did not fulfil expectations. I was advised at an early stage by Max and others that the club had never quite recovered from this incredibly ill conceived booking. My job was to breathe new life into the place.

I settled in fairly quickly and from the very beginning fell in love with this Welsh nightspot. The club itself was way out in the sticks but within easy reach from a variety of directions. Its location was close to the Pontypool-Newport link road and the A449 Ross Spur an extension of the M50/M5 which runs through to the M4. In short, although situated in the most stunning countryside overlooking the Vale of Usk, we could be easily reached and serve the entertainment needs of major cities such as Bristol, Swindon, Cheltenham, Gloucester, Newport, Cardiff, Hereford and Ross. I renamed the club "The Stardust", installed a menu akin to the highly successful menu at Cesar's and using many of the tried and tested techniques of the Cesars Palace marketing operation I got down to serious work. Jimmy Smith remained my house booker and soon put together an excellent programme of entertainment to suit every age and taste.

The club was owned by Ron James and his son Tony and from the outset I sensed that Tony, an only child, fitted perfectly into that category of 'know it all disaster', who grew up cocooned in his parents over generous support. In short a spoiled brat. I had met Tony some years earlier at Cesar's Palace where he acquainted me with his club and its successes. He told me of a mega show he was putting together and which he hoped to be in a position to announce soon. Acknowledging my generosity that evening, a freebie, he hoped I would accept his invitation to attend the show as his guest. The double top of the bill was to be Shirley Bassey and Tom Jones. The support artiste Harry Seccombe and the Treorchy Male Voice Choir would open the extravaganza. Richard Burton would be flown in from his film location to compere. Not bad I thought, for a five hundred seater venue.

The all star, all Welsh show was certain to be a world-beater he enthused. No doubt about it I thought. I speculated that he probably went after Uri Gargarin the Russian cosmonaut to welcome the guests and show them to their tables, but had decided to dispense with the idea because there was not one Welsh ancestor to be found anywhere in Uri's family tree.

From that first meeting I deduced that Tony was a dreamer, but taking up the management reins of the very club his father owned I soon realised that my first impressions of James the Younger were the tip of the iceberg. The double week of Jones and Humperdink had brought the club to near disaster and was the last of a number of bad decisions by Tony. The father had gently moved him sideways into a butchery business to make way for a new club manager. Enter Savva into the middle of a family problem.

The son had already tried his hand at bookmaking, hairdressing and the transportation business, all apparently ending in disaster. Tony was ever present and obviously resented the decision to bring me in. I realised I had made a major error of judgement in accepting a position with the family, but nevertheless I was being well paid to do a job and I intended to do it to the best of my ability.

I loved the club and the setting. I found the staff very responsive and I soon realised that the Welsh people hungered for good entertainment and once won over, were to prove excellent punters and extremely loyal customers. The club soon showed signs of progress. Attendance and business were increasing. It was hard work made doubly difficult by having to temper my decisions and ideas with the owners because of the sensitivity of Tony. Since I determined the James's to be cowboys I secretly named them 'the James Gang', with Ron and Tony as 'Frank and Jessie' and the rest of the family and friends 'The Gang' It made life at Usk a little more amusing.

A procession of greats and not so greats proceeded to play the tiny Welsh venue and the club was really beginning to make its presence felt. Roy Hudd, Danny La Rue, Frank Carson, Roy Castle, The Rockin' Berries, Barron Knights, Des O'Connor and Les Dawson were just a few of the stars to play the Stardust in the early days. Steering a careful and diplomatic path between my management operation and the James Gang's sometimes odd attitudes, I was pleased to report that the Stardust was making a considerable impact. Throughout I tried, as much as possible, to promote the James's image, particularly Ron's, laying much of the credit for various club triumphs at Ron's door. I must say I felt sorry for Ron; he had a good heart and a reasonable disposition. Sadly he was constantly torn between family loyalty and the love of a son on the one hand, and business decisions and common sense on the other.

With my departure from Cesars palace, I naturally had to leave behind the trappings of my position, which included the company car. I bought a second-hand white Jag, which had, apparently, once had been a police car. It seemed extremely good value at the time, a real snip and I often wondered why a car of that size and model was so inexpensive. So called car experts came up with various reasons, the most common being the high insurance for this type of vehicle, or the fuel consumption, which made it expensive to run. Only one person told me that the motor would probably clap out and then 'You are in for major repair expense'.

One fateful summer day while out and about in Gwent leafleting and distributing programmes of Stardust forthcoming activities, I broke for lunch, a drink and a sandwich at the Blackbirds Inn, Cwmbran. It was a delightfully hot summer's day and the busy pub had opened every door and window in order to capture at least a small amount of summer breeze. As I sat there, the pub began to fill with smoke. Someone shouted that a car was on fire in the car park and the fumes were wafting through the pub's open windows and doors. A customer entering the pub shouted, 'It's a white jag'. Oh no I thought, it's got to be mine; it was.

One other memory of my short stay at Usk was another Frank Carson tale that he told me one early morning over a cup of coffee. I mention it because it was so unusual to find Frank in such a sombre mood. I've known him for twenty-five years but I can honestly say this was the only time I'd ever seen the sombre side of the effervescent and funny Irishman.

He told me of a Japanese farming family, Mum, Dad and son. Between the three of them they eked out a living from their small farm. Every so often they would load their cart with produce and take it to the city some distance away. Once there, they would sell their produce in the market.

One day, on one such a trip, the son was impatient to get to the market as quickly as possible. "If we get there early, we will have a chance to sell all our goods before our competitors arrive" he said.

"Slow down" replied his father, "You must learn to take each day as it comes and at a steady pace. Never run before you can walk my son. Remember patience is a virtue".

Along the way they came across a fellow Japanese farmer whose cart had shed its wheel. "We must stop and assist our compatriot," said the father. "He'll not manage to repair his cart alone".

"But father" implored the son, "this will make us later still. The delay could lose us customers. Let us leave the man and press on to the city".

"My son, you surprise me with such talk" scolded his father. "To help your fellow man is the most important thing to do in your life and it has its rewards. Of this you can be certain".

Reluctantly the son obeyed and together they repaired the wheel and the cart of the traveller, who thanked them and bid them farewell. By now it was nearly nightfall. "We can press on through the night," said the son "and make up for lost time".

"No" said his father. "We will camp here tonight, eat and rest, and proceed tomorrow". The son was not at all happy.

"We might as well," he said grumpily. "We've lost the initiative now. Everyone will get to the market before us. There will probably be no customers for us by the time we get there tomorrow".

"Patience my son, patience" said his father gently. "Come, eat and sleep. We have progressed well enough today and helped a fellow human being. Come and rest and sleep with the angels. Our patience and our actions are all measured elsewhere and we shall be rewarded". During the night, the couple were awakened by a distant rumble and they witnessed the night sky light up, over the hill in the direction of the city. They scrambled to the top of the hill for a better view of this wondrous sight, but when reaching the top gazed down in horror to see the city in the distance, in flames. The father took the son's hand and turned away. "Let us go home son," he said.

"Yes father" replied the son. Within a short while they packed their belongings, turned their cart and set out on the road home, leaving behind the burning city of Hiroshima.

Few people could ever claim to have been in Frank's company and catch him in a serious reflective mood. I was one of the fortunate ones and I must say he tells a very good story very well. It's probably 'the way he tells em'.

As time went on and I began to get grips with the operation at Usk the Stardust really began to draw the crowds which in turn drew the attention of the local Fire officers who repeatedly received reports about overcrowding at the venue and attempted to verify them by surprise visits etc. I'm pleased to I was never caught out.

Bryn Yemm became resident compere and distinguished himself at the club. I had met and played Bryn as a support artiste at Cesar's; he was an excellent entertainer and commanded a formidable following. He possessed boundless energy, and our success at the Stardust club was as much due to his input as mine. Rod Johnson, my erstwhile former assistant also joined me at this time and the Stardust cabaret shows became simply the best. A superb night out guaranteed by compere and host Bryn and the management team of Johnson and Steve Austwick our new restaurant manager. My marketing strategy began to bear fruit. More and more agency and coach company business was pouring in from across the borders from nearby England to compliment the growing following from the valleys, towns and cities of Wales.

Stardust agency representation was established with Del and Graham Dee's Three d promotions of Cheltenham and Gloucester, Yeoman's of Hereford, Barnes Coaches of Swindon, Peter Carol Tours of Bristol and so on. Professional representation in surrounding towns and cities was crucial to the club's development.

Despite the club's success and definite rise in the ratings, my relationship with the James Gang worsened. It became clear to me that, whilst my passion for the business continued to increase and my love of the club remained undiminished, going to Usk was a major mistake. There was never going to be unity between us. A good working relationship between owner and manger was essential for the process to continue to move forward. I became relentless in my efforts to build the business up and worked with increased energy, but deep down I think I always knew that the strained relationship would ultimately fail.

I introduced a whole number of extra activities including boxing, wrestling and Sunday family lunch shows. The staging of Sunday children's entertainment was new, novel and very successful. I recall one particular attraction that was extremely popular; the P.G. Tips chimps show. These were the chimpanzees that became famous as the talking monkeys that advertised the famous tea on TV. On one occasion following lunch, I was accosted by an irate mother from Tredegar who demanded a refund. She clutched a child in either hand, both crying. She verbally lashed at me accusing me of taking money under false pretences and ultimately upsetting the children and ruining their day. I implored her to calm down and asked her to be more specific.

"Was it the food or the service perhaps Madam?" I enquired.

"No that was OK" she replied. "It was the chimps. They never said a word". Put slightly off balance by this statement, I retorted as politely as possible.

"Madam Chimpanzees do not talk".

"I know that" she yelled her anger welling up again. "Do you think I'm stupid? But those chimps do. I've seen them on the telly".

That complaint was only topped by a drunken old soak that emerged from a Sunday lunch show involving Terry Hall and Lennie the Lion. "Settle an argument would you young man," said the soak. "Was that the Terry Hall who was killed on the M4 not so long ago or was that the other one!!"

Tommy Cooper week arrived and the master of comedy was as popular in Wales as he was in England, possibly more so as of course Tommy was Welsh, he was born in Caerphilly. During the Tommy Cooper week, my receptionist popped into the auditorium to let me know that a huge Rolls limousine carrying two men had just arrived in the car park. I arrived at reception just as the two gentlemen entered the premises. It was none other than Mr Pat Cowan and his architect Mr Geoffrey Woods.

"Mr Savva what a pleasure to see you again" said Cowan. "May I introduce my colleague Mr Geoffrey Woods" We shook hands and proceeded into the auditorium.

"What brings you to Wales Mr Cowan?" I asked, as we walked towards the back of the room to an empty table situated behind a couple of pillars which obstructed the view of the stage, the reason why the table was invariably empty.

"You of course" replied Cowan. "You are the reason why we're here. I had no idea you'd moved. They told me at Cesars where I could find you. Can we talk?" He continued, lowering his voice.

"Yes" I said. There appeared to be no one within earshot.

"Well I'm here to talk about Windsor" he stated with an air of triumph. My puzzled look prompted him to elaborate. "The club I told you about. It's nearing completion. You know; the club you promised to manage for me".

"Oh I don't know about that" I replied.

"But you promised" Pat said quite assertively. "In fact your very words were 'I'd be delighted to run it for you, let me know when it's ready to open'".

Slightly embarrassed, I told him that I was always flattered by the many job offers I had received many over the years, but that usually nothing came of them. I placed little credence in them and it was easier to say Yes to well meaning prospective club owners at the time. Pat Cowan was quite put out to hear this.

"But I am a man of my word and I expected you too be too" he said.

"You Sir" I replied "are the exception. I never for moment suspected that you did really mean to build a cabaret club in Windsor. As you can see I am wholly employed here and doing rather well and I really can't let people down".

"This is a really poor show," said Pat, who was quite upset.

"Look" I interrupted, "let me fix you some dinner and wine. The cabaret is about to begin and we will talk again later".

Throughout the next couple of hours, whilst the show was in progress, I turned over in my mind the problem at hand. True, I was not happy at Usk but I was successful and I loved the people and the premises; despite the cowboys that owned it. Much as I fancied the idea of escaping to Royal Windsor, which after all was just outside of my beloved London, I could not expect the enterprise to be anywhere near the required size in an area which boasted some of the highest overheads in the U.K. I felt that although his venue was probably 'up-market', it would probably be quite small and unable to compete with the mighty Lakeside Cesars or Circus Tavern, all within easy reach of London.

After weighing up the pros and cons and wrestling with my conscience, I formulated a policy that I hoped would get me out of trouble. After all the guy had come all the way from Windsor to see me and I was embarrassed beyond belief, how many people are genuine enough to make you a promise and deliver a couple of years later.

The show over I invited Pat and Geoff to step into the privacy of my office, so that we could talk without having to compete with the band that provided the after show dance music. Having settled in their chairs I began.

"Look Mr Cowan, I feel really embarrassed that I misled you with my answer some time ago".

"So you should be" interrupted Pat bluntly, but with a smile.

"For reasons which I've already explained, I did not take you seriously at the time. As you can see I am totally committed here and cannot contemplate moving again within such a short space of time. My long term of management at Cesars bears witness to the fact that I'm not a mover as such. However, if you wish, I am sure I can nominate someone who would be ideal to open and manage the venue for you and who would do an excellent job and who, perhaps as a gesture of goodwill; I could help and assist with the setting up of the club. My present employer would I'm sure have no objections, Windsor is a long way from Wales and can hardly be regarded as competition".

There followed a long silence. Pat was very put out by the whole visit; he looked about the office, towards the ceiling, then the floor. This was obviously his way of considering a response while cooling down. Suddenly he stood up and said,

"Well so be it. We'll be off now and I'll be in touch" and he started to move towards the door, clearly annoyed. "As I told you once before I want the best for my place. Everyone said you were it. I'm not for having second best. I don't operate like that".

As these parting remarks struck home, I felt quite ashamed. Geoffrey Woods who had remained fairly silent throughout got to his feet to leave.

"Mr Savva" he said. "I have the task of fitting together all the pieces for the club and having built the shell so to speak, would like some professional guidance on where to place the various areas, reception, toilets, kitchen, stage etc., from an experienced club operator such as yourself. Any chance you could pop up to Windsor and go over the plans with me?"

"I'll be glad to" I replied without hesitation, gaining some satisfaction on actually being able to oblige on at least one item of the evening requests. "I'm off next Thursday. Will that do?"

"Fine!" Replied Geoffrey.

We parted company and I gave a sigh of relief. Cowan was obviously an extraordinary person, direct and very tough. The James Gang who had been informed by one of their resident spies were very interested to know who the occupants of the chauffeur driven Rolls were were. I told them they were some acquaintances of mine who intended opening a small club and needed some advice on licensing. I don't think for a moment either Frank or Jessie believed me, after all, that advice could have been given over the phone.

On Thursday, I drove up the M4 to Windsor and to the Dedworth Road offices of Mr Cowan's property development empire. After coffee we were about to look at the plans when Pat suggested it would be a good idea to visit the site first as this would help me to relate to the plans. I readily agreed; I was quite hopeless at looking at plans anyway. The site was only a short drive away and on arriving at William Street we pulled up outside the unfinished entrance to the nightspot. I immediately felt vindicated. The club would be as I imagined, small but probably elegantly constructed, to cater for the Pat Cowan type's that lived all over the Royal County of Berkshire.

As we ascended the rather dreary staircase to the top floor, the lifts having yet to be installed, Pat asked me if I had found someone for the managerial position.

"I'm standing by to interview," I said. And told him I had one or two possible candidates in mind and that I was sure one of them would be available for an interview shortly.

At last we reached the top floor. The whole area was a hive of activity. Painters and decorators, roofing experts, electricians, plasterers and a whole army of other building workers and craftsmen actively pursued their tasks. The staircase brought us to a fairly large reception area and from here we entered the auditorium. It is difficult to describe my first impression, my utter surprise and amazement at what greeted my eyes as I entered. It was the total unexpected vastness of the auditorium that stretched out before me that took my breath away.

"What do you think then Georgie?" said Pat almost affectionately. He was obviously very proud of his creation.

"I am dumbfounded" I replied. "It is a magnificent room and so big. I had no idea".

Below this floor was a storage area and below that a supermarket, an office block and a bar and below all this an underground car park. The club auditorium straddled across the entire top of the multi purpose building enabling it to comfortably seat one thousand people minimum.

"Do you think your candidate will be able enough to take this on?" Pat asked.

"My candidate" said I. "Not a chance. There's only one person who's going to get a chance at managing this and that's me – if you'll still have me" I quickly qualified.

"You're a pain in the ass Georgie," said Pat. "I thought you'd never say yes. Welcome aboard".

The twinkle in Pat's eyes said it all. He knew all along that no self respecting club operator could ever walk away from that room and he was right.

On entering the auditorium the floor fell away to three levels thus offering an excellent view of proceedings from every angle. There were a couple of pillars but none to give any real problems. To the left was an outside balcony accessed through two huge sliding glass doors. This area offered an excellent view of Windsor castle which was only 300 yards away. The ceiling was very high and supported by massive metal girders.

On returning to the office we poured over the plans which from my point of view now meant something, having had an opportunity to walk the course. I suggested the best position for the bandstand and stage and Geoff Woods unveiled a drawing of a stage that effectively came out from the fixed proscenium like a drawer and then hydraulically lifted into position; an amazing piece of engineering. We placed the kitchen to the right hand side and a long bar at the back of the room, with an additional small bar by the windowed balcony.

Other items were sorted out such as the reception, shop and office and of course a back stage dressing room complex. I also advised that the lifts could never be expected to cope with the arrival of one thousand people and therefore the staircase needed to be glamorised. After a full days work with Pat and Geoff I hurried back to Wales a born again club manager. It was a magnificent creation that could quite easily become the greatest club in the land.

My unhappiness with my present employers had reached a high point and it seemed that fate had brought Pat Cowan to Usk that evening. I was off to Royal Windsor at the earliest opportunity. There was still quite a lot of work to be done at the new club and completion was not expected until the autumn six months away. I would need three months to set it up, so I must wind up my operations at Usk within three months. The James Gang did not take long to suspect that something was going on. The occasional phone call or carelessly dropped remark soon convinced them that I was on my way out. A day came along, almost inevitably, when I once again clashed with the son. The argument resulted in a full meeting the result of which was that we parted company, by mutual agreement, in July 1978.

Although there was no sadness attached to my departure I must say that I loved the Stardust and I had come to know many people and made many friends. The Stardust had a special place in my heart and I vowed that if I ever found myself in the position to buy my own club I would look no further than Usk.

My arrival at Windsor to take charge of the opening and management of Pat's new club was to be the start of one of the most exciting periods of my life. I was no longer fearful of what the future held. I was now well aware of my potential; I'd more than served my apprenticeship. I was proud of my record. I had eleven years of cabaret club experience under my belt and felt confident in my ability to make a success of the Windsor venue.

The venue itself was sensational. In my opinion, no one else could have put together such a scheme. Pat Cowan's ownership of the entire site, and for that matter many other building enterprises in the Windsor, Eton and slough area, made it possible for him to use the whole top floor of his William Street development to realise a dream. To his everlasting credit he did just that and by doing so became in my opinion one of the greatest cabaret entrepreneurs of our time.

I thought I'd done everything, seen everything and presented everything, but boy was I wrong. In the words of Al Jolson, *'you ain't seen nothing yet'.*

10

I MOVE TO WINDSOR

WE 'SET UP SHOP'

LAKESIDE BURNS TO THE GROUND

OPENING NIGHT – A BIT OF A DISASTER

THE PRUDENTIAL ASSURED OF NO FOOD

ARTHUR GETS THE WORKS

PAT COWAN A GENT OR A GENIUS OR BOTH

WE OPEN AGAIN

DANNY LA RUE AND TABLE 84

FREDDIE STARR GOES TO THE TOP

I suppose it would be true to say that from July 1978 to November of the same year, were five of the busiest months of my life. At first I thought that being employed on a full-time manager's salary some five months before the opening of the premises was a generous gesture by Pat Cowan to ensure I remained tied neatly to his future plans. Nothing could have been further from the truth. During those five months, I personally arranged to furnish, equip, staff, market and open the Windsor club. Each day I worked from 8.00a.m. till midnight seven day a weeks. As I had always been something of a workaholic the hours did not bother me in the least; in fact quite the contrary, I found setting up the Windsor operation exciting, exhilarating and stimulating. I can honestly say I enjoyed every minute of it. Pam and I eventually moved into a semi at Hayes Hill, Windsor on a one year lease. Pam and the kids moved to nearby Sunningdale where I negotiated another short term lease on a bungalow.

Pat Cowan was not the easiest person to work with, at least not at the beginning, but gradually as we became better acquainted we became an excellent team and worked extremely well together. Pat was often brash, even downright aggressive, but what I liked about him was his directness. There was no behind the back stuff with Pat; he called a spade a spade. He was a self-made, self assured man and absolutely honest.

At one of our meetings, quite early in our relationship, we discussed the matter of a name for the club. I suggested the Landmark or the Flamingo, two names plucked from the Las Vegas strip; Pat was not impressed.

"This is Royal Windsor. I think we have to come up with something more in keeping with that image," he said.

The Orb, Sceptre, Coronet, Crown and many other royal trappings were considered, but rejected. For a week or so Pat reflected on the matter. Then one day suddenly entered my office and triumphantly declared

"Blazers, that's what we're going to name it, Blazers". I thought for a moment and turned the word over in my mind. Blazers, Blazers.

"That Sir is brilliant. How did you think of it?" I asked.

"I'm involved in a large construction site at Eton as you know, and yesterday while walking over the bridge from Eaton back into Windsor I spotted some blazer clad guys rowing and punting on the river. A familiar scene in this part of the world and it came to me in a flash".

The name was registered, the licence granted and the various items of equipment ordered and delivered. By the middle of October we were well on our way towards the gala opening. Word got round that a magnificent nightspot was being opened and enquiries were being received at an ever-increasing rate. Jimmy Smith was to be our house booker and he began putting together a programme of entertainment containing most of the well-known and popular performers of the day. Staffing the operation was not a problem. A constant stream of applicants visited me seeking the various positions on offer.

Peter Torterella, ex-Caesars was engaged as Head Chef. Rod Johnson rejoined me from Wales to become Assistant Manager. Geoff Walker also formerly of Cesars Palace, became Orchestra leader and, for a short while, midlands singing personality Rickie Desoni became blazers resident compere. I cautioned Pat about the pitfalls of an opening and the early life of a club, and we decided to keep the numbers down to just four hundred people per night so that our staff could train on real customers on a ratio of one waitress per fifteen customers instead of double the number of customers as was the norm. The idea was to gradually increase numbers, reaching our capacity of one thousand by the middle of December, allowing every member of staff in every department to become fully conversant with their task and responsibilities.

With only three weeks to go I moved my office to Blazers. Once on site, I was able to personally oversee the completion and monitor the arrival of all the necessary equipment. Pat spared no expenses in furnishing the club; he even had the carpet especially woven with the initials BZ for Blazers. The investment he made to realise his dream was frightening and, although Pat was a millionaire, I became increasingly conscious of the costs and became determined to make sure Pat got a good return from his investment.

There was no doubt that Pat's property interests earned him a fortune and financed a lavish lifestyle. However, more important to him than his businesses and wealth, were his family; and he delighted in being able to secure for them the best of everything. He was a millionaire who enjoyed his money, and experienced great pleasure seeing family and friends enjoy themselves at his expense. Each summer he took his family to Cannes for a five or six week break at the Presidential Suite of the world famous Carlton Hotel. From here he kept in touch with all his business interests back home, particularly in the morning. After lunch he would join his family and friends for beach, sea, sun and rest. I was fortunate to be invited to join him during the Blazers pre-opening period to discuss and confirm items of policy. During my short stay I was treated as a member of the family and enjoyed all the best facilities Cannes had to offer.

During these early months Pat and I became very close friends. I was never a yes man, or too entrenched in my beliefs not to be prepared to listen to another's point of view. I would not always agree with Pat's methods, but never lost sight of the fact that he was the boss and it was his investment. Also I never addressed him as anything other than Sir; especially in company, although he often said, 'No need to call me Sir you know Georgie', I felt that deep down he liked it. For me it was a sign of respect for a man that I came to admire more with every passing day.

With just a few days to go to our opening night, Pam and I, together with other heads of department were busy de-crating, de-boxing, unwrapping and cleaning copious amounts of cutlery, crockery and associated dining items. The Bar manager and the Chef together with their people were also doing much the same thing for their respective departments. Steve Rawlins and Garry Hunt, our stage crew, were fitting and testing the stage lamps. Because of their newness the lamps gave off a burning smell as a consequence of heat reacting to the new paintwork, particularly on the Par Cans. Steve assured me that this was quite normal and that the burning fumes and smell would soon disappear. Suddenly the sound of fire engines could be heard all over the town and in neighbouring Slough.

"Are you sure we are not on fire?" I asked Steve slightly panicking.

"I can assure you Mr Savva it's not us. Anyway they are going away from us by the sounds of it, not towards us" he replied.

We thought no more of it until a taxi driver came up to reception to collect a member of our staff towards the end of our evening's work.

"I suppose your main competitor is the Lakeside Club at Camberley?" said the cabbie.

"Well yes I suppose it is," I said hesitantly. "But you know there is enough population around the area for everyone, so we do not regard the Lakeside as a threat".

"Well they are not any more," replied the cabbie. "because it's just burnt to the ground".

We sat staring at each other for a moment in stunned silence.

"The fire engines we heard earlier on," murmured Steve.

"The Brothers lee are on there this week" said Garry.

What an irrelevant thing to say at that moment I thought. Radio, TV and the press carried the full story the following morning and the pictures captured the full extent of the devastation which was nothing short of complete. Bob Potter, the owner, was pictured standing beside a pile of smouldering rubble and a background of bent and twisted girders. People began to think of two things. Firstly; how the fire started. Secondly; where would the huge amount of people with bookings at Lakeside go for their pre-Christmas entertainment?

With regard to the cause of the fire, both Bob and I came in for some stick from both the public at large and the comedians of the day. It was jokingly suggested that either Bob burnt it down to build a bigger and better one or George Savva burnt it down to wipe out the opposition before opening Blazers. One comic told the audience to ask George for a match if they needed a light as he always carries a box with him these days. Another told his audience that, without naming names, he had been told that a tall dark stranger wearing a 'blazer' was seen wandering around Camberley just before the fire trying to borrow a box of matches. Bob Potter always pursued a strict dress code and on balance I think the line that got the biggest laugh was

"The reason Lakeside burnt down was because Bob would not let the Fire Brigade on to the premises because they were not wearing collars and ties".

Another gag at that time went as follows. George Savva, on holiday in the Caribbean, bumps into Bob Potter.

"I used to have a club in England, but it burnt down," said Bob. "I await the insurance".

"I used to manage a club in England, it had a flood" replied George. "I too await the insurance".

"What an amazing coincidence" said Bob? "But tell me George how do you start a flood?"

The gags kept coming for some months after the fire, but I certainly did not mind and I don't think Bob did either. While various comics were getting their laughs at our expense, they were at least leaving some other poor sod alone.

The other problem created by the fire concerned the placement of thousands of people that were left stranded – all dressed up with nowhere to go so to speak. Needless to say, because we were close by, new and with availability, it was to Blazers they turned for their pre-Christmas night out, a night they had saved for all year. The coach booked, the evening paid for; there was no turning back for them. The evening had to go ahead.

They came clutching refund cheques and begging to be booked in for one of the nights on the forthcoming Blazers programme. I of course found it totally impossible to say no. My policy of holding down numbers to about fifty per cent of capacity until the operation was up and running went out the window. I not only allowed the numbers to climb to full capacity, but allowed them to drift upwards by at least another hundred over our limit so that from opening night on the twenty-sixth of November until new Years Day 1979, I had bookings of approximately eleven hundred people per night.

I felt the fire was an act of god, facilitating our ability to claw back some of the massive investment during those thirty-five evenings of business at a prime time of the year. Wrong! Opening the bookings to a full house from the very start was in fact a dreadful mistake and showed my immaturity.

To say the opening night was a disaster would be an understatement. Unlike Cesars, which was up and running when I was called in and with most of its technical problems already ironed out, at Blazers, everything that could possibly go wrong, did. The lifts kept sticking, trapping people between floors. The electric beer pumps kept breaking down. The chef had problems with cookers and fridges. The dishwasher packed up altogether. The stage stuck in an up position. The main Tabs closed, but would not reopen and then after cranking them manually open would not close. The catering was a catastrophe. The food was good, but only if you actually got any.

For ten days I suffered the most horrendous problems and the resultant complaints. I once read a book called the Ten Days That Shook the World, about the Russian Bolshevik revolution. Opening Blazers was Ten days that shook my world.

To those people that said first impressions are the most important and to those who say last impressions are the most important, I say we achieved both. People got a bad impression on arrival and a pretty bad one on departure. Even the bit in the middle left a lot to be desired. Blazers was a beautiful venue, but because absolutely everything was new many things simply did not work. The fact was that we should have tried and tested time and again before opening. Added to which trying to cater for maximum numbers from day one was a disastrous mistake.

Pat, being unfamiliar with the cut and thrust of an opening night and the inevitable complaints found the whole thing difficult to contemplate and was very unhappy to say the least. We clashed on a couple of occasions during this time, but I remember ending one such clash with the words

"Don't worry Sir, it will soon settle down and one day we will look back and laugh at all this" and we did. But that day was a long time coming.

The opening show starred Little and Large who had become a U.K. major attraction and apart from some limited trouble with the tabs and the stage, our opening night entertainment was well received. Our problems were service related. We had insufficient staff to cope with the numbers and of the staff we had, ninety per cent were inexperienced.

The fact that we had offered excellent discounts for the first few nights as part of an invitation to have a night out and 'guinea pig' for us at the same time seemed to have been forgotten by the recipients. A night out was a night out irrespective of the price and many of our hard pressed, inexperienced staff were given a hard time by the customers, despite the fact that the guinea pigs enjoyed incredible value for money at only four pounds per head, they were the worst complainers. They certainly took no prisoners. Some of the complaints have become amusing with the passing of time. For example, a letter that a lady sent to me following her opening night visit.

I have dined, she wrote, all over the world and occasionally experienced the odd incident. I've had dishes spilt over me, even a meal dropped on me during service, but to have twelve main course meals dropped on me must be some kind of record. It seemed the waitress passed by the writer's table carrying a stack of meals on rings, piled one on top of the other, lost her balance and all twelve meals ended in our complainants lap.

A greengrocer from Hounslow rang me to complain about his treatment by a waitress he described as a 'tyrant from the very start'.

"She behaved like a nazi officer," he claimed.

"What exactly happened?" I asked.

"After telling her to get a move on in the nicest possible way," he stated, "when she eventually arrived at our table with the meals all I said was, about time".

"What happened then?" I enquired reluctantly.

"She took offence to my remark" he said "and threw the meals at us with the words 'here get your own bloody food'; she stormed off never to be seen again".

"Oh yes that would have been Angela" I replied. "She did actually walk out". "Angela" shouted the man. "She should have been called Medusa".

A friend of mine brought a party of forty to the opening night, all from local branches of the Prudential Insurance Company. He remained mute throughout the night and indeed thereafter, until I happened to bump into him at the reception desk a week or so later. He was booking for a show in January and I was delighted to witness this first bit of repeat business.

"So it all went well with your party at Christmas then, Tim?" I said.

"No George not really. We did not complain about the service, because we did not actually get any. We did get a starter and a soup, but nothing else. In a nutshell, our service started slowly, and then petered out altogether. But what the hell you gave us great seats, the show was brill and we had a good drink and dance. Worth every penny of the four pound special rate".

One other extraordinary incident took place on opening night. A couple who decided to try the new venue, but understood fully there could be teething problems, were seated in an area serviced by our waitress Rita. Rita was unique. A type who never got ruffled and was the ultimate in politeness, but very one paced. She had a delightful personality and was a great favourite with the customers. Rita remained at Blazers for eight years and was as solid as a rock throughout. On opening night she was probably one of the calmest persons in the room. Nothing troubled her.

While looking after the couple, amongst others on her station, she accidentally upset the gentleman's prawn cocktail over his jacket. He arrived at reception displaying a dark suited shoulder, heavily soiled with a substantial dollop of pink prawn cocktail sauce. He was charming about the incident, citing the fact that after all it was opening night and accidents are bound to occur. Pam took his jacket and cleaned it as best she could.

On returning to his seat, he was just in time to receive his soup course, which Rita managed to spill on the other side of his already soiled jacket. This was a great pity. Not just because of the unfortunate accident but because Peter Torterella's minestrone was delicious; a 'culinary treat in a bowl' as someone once described it. Returning to reception still smiling and being very understanding, Pam once again cleaned the other part of the gentleman's jacket. Roughly twenty minutes later he was back at reception sporting a new stain; Rita had managed to drop an entire coq-au-vin into his lap.

The gentleman was beginning to turn a little ugly at this point. He was smiling or perhaps grimacing

"I know its opening night, but this is getting ridiculous and what's more the damn waitress is so nice, so polite and so apologetic," he concluded. He had to clean himself up on this occasion because of the position of his latest stain. Pam provided him with various items of damp cloths and sponges. Once again he returned to his seat. But not for long, he was soon back in reception wearing a trifle – down the front of his shirt. He now succumbed to a furious rage and lashed into me verbally as the Manager of a totally out of control dinner dance establishment which, if it carried on like this, would have no chance of success let alone survival.

We calmed him down as best we could offering him a return visit for any show as a freebie, plus free wine, free transport, the crown jewels and anything else I could think of at the time. He returned to his table by now quite damp from the various cleaning expeditions. Rita, apologising most profusely, offered coffee.

"Would Sir and Madam like coffee," she asked in her sweetest and most pleasant manner.

"No-no not for me" the man replied without hesitation. "Please don't bring me anything else".

"Now don't be like that Arthur" said his wife scolding her husband. "Accidents will happen".

"It's alright for you" he said angrily. "You've remained unscathed throughout, whilst I have been mugged by this waitress".

"Well there is no need to be like that about it" she retorted. "Any way I would love a coffee Miss please".

Rita fetched the lady's coffee, but in leaning across to serve her slipped, and spilt the entire contents of the pot over her husband. Arthur, the husband, at this point had sunk to the level of a traumatised catering refugee. He was understandably incensed. We could neither console nor pacify him.

"I'll write to the papers, the TV people, the radio," he shouted. "I'll tell the world about this place. People have been locked up for less than has happened to me tonight" he insisted.

Luckily he gave us one more try, using his freebie, a few weeks later and enjoyed everything during an accident free visit and any thought of bad publicity was forgotten. Both he and his wife became regular customers and always asked for Rita to serve them every time they visited Blazers, rewarding her on each occasion with a substantial tip to show their appreciation of her service.

After ten tumultuous days everything began to fall into place. The equipment and the service that had taken such a battering now began to work and became more efficient with the passing of each day. In short we had turned the corner and could look forward to a bright future for our venue.

Paul Daniels, The Barron Knights, Les Dawson, Jimmy Tarbuck working with Kenny Linch, Tommy Cooper and The Three Degrees were just a few of the stars that played Blazers during those early weeks, with great success. The demise of the Lakeside Club meant that we opened unopposed; the only entertainment venue of note west of the capital. I was conscious however; that we needed to be forward looking and innovative if we were to seize the lead in the Home Counties cabaret scene. The Talk of the Town, Baileys of Watford, The Circus Tavern at Purfleet, not to mention my old stomping ground Cesars Palace were all offering top class entertainment. With my reputation reasonably intact I set about making Blazers the Number One night spot in the area. Many of my Cesars customers were beginning to visit on a regular basis. Coach companies and even former customers of the Stardust were making the trip to Blazers. The motorway system meant that potential business was available from all points.

Pat Cowan, who had become reasonably supportive after the traumatic opening days also took a view with regard to the question as to whether his venue should want to play the same entertainment as the other cabaret clubs. He wanted Blazers operate on a higher level. I understood his point of view, but persuaded him that a balanced programme, a cushion of top British stars, studded with gems from international show business would be the best way forward.

Alan Blackburn, Pat's long time neighbour and friend, an entertainment agent of huge experience and incidentally the guy who nominated me to run Pat's new project, became a familiar face on the scene and was extremely helpful. His wife Susan, a former singer, who had headlined in many West End shows, became a very close friend of Pam, my wife. During the course of numerous dinner parties, the four of us often talked about the Boss and his amazing rise to fortune. Alan made me aware, not only of Pat's astuteness, but also his weaknesses. Pat it seemed, often yearned to play artistes that he liked but not necessarily artistes liked by the public and who could be a commercial disaster.

"You have to make money for Pat despite himself" said Alan and I understood what he meant, perfectly.

Pat felt that since he was richer and more powerful than most of the British cabaret stars they should feel a kind of subservience to him. There were times when Pat's arrogance towards the various people of show business was often embarrassing. Mercifully, he had little contact with the stars he employed and was not a back stage person. Neither was he in any way star struck.

On one occasion I was asked to set up a lunch with Peter Hepple editor of Stage and Television Today, our main trade paper and bible of our profession. The lunch at the Hinds Head at Bray was a simple get to know you affair, but Pat's attitude vis-à-vis all aspects of show business left Peter singularly unimpressed.

"I don't know for the life of me why you bothered to build and open a club if you find the business and the people in it so distasteful and insincere" he said.

"The only way to change showbiz is to first join it," replied Pat. It was all rhetoric really. Pat, I believed, sought recognition from the industry for his contribution to it; he had built and opened a club at a time when recession had closed many clubs in various parts of the U.K. Eventually he became recognised as the owner of Britain's leading nightspot.

As the last of the Christmas festivities concluded, Pat called me to the office to discuss a reopening. As far as he was concerned we had not really opened in the true sense of the word. Pat wanted headline grabbing personalities and distinguished well-known guests now the operation had settled down and was running well. The seventh of February 1979 was selected as the appropriate date for the star studded bash, two and a half months after Blazers had commenced trading.

The Mayor of Windsor and Maidenhead accepted an invitation to make the opening speech. Pat, through Alan Blackburn, arranged for his boyhood movie hero Douglas Fairbanks Junior to fly in from the States to cut the tape, officially opening the venue. Alan also secured the services of Petula Clarke to headline the cabaret. I asked Danny La Rue to come down to Blazers after his performance at the Palladium, to draw the charity raffle and generally join in the festivities as our honoured guest and he accepted the invitation. Pat's top table guests included a number of well-known personalities including Patrick Mower, Barbara Windsor and Teazy Weazy Raymond. But the guest that created the greatest press interest was Roddy Llewellyn. Even a couple of years after the story of his relationship with Princess Margaret had broken he was still the most talked about member of London Society.

Jimmy Tarbuck was our star host and compere for the evening and the vast audience comprised the cream of society and the core of show business, front and backstage. The evening was something of a non-event. It went splendidly well and was extremely well organised, but as far as press and publicity were concerned it only made the local Windsor and Slough Express and the "Stage". Pat had wanted the Nigel Dempster column, but it was not to be.

Despite the ongoing recession Blazers did better than most during this early period, trading seven nights a week and attracting good business thanks to an aggressive marketing regime and using my tried and tested contacts amongst the coach companies and ticket agent fraternity. Our artiste line up was essentially non-risk. A programme of solid stars such as Gene Pitney, Frankie Vaughan, The Searchers, The Platters and of course the Danny La Rue show, all contributed in the building of Blazers' reputation into a reliable venue for a great night out.

Since the start of Danny's club performances at Cesars Palace we had become great friends. I had played him on many occasions and his first three week run at Blazers was nothing short of spectacular. Blazers, unlike the Stardust or Cesars, had the facilities to make a difference. The magic of theatre could be captured on our club stage, unlike any other club venue of that era. During his Blazers run, an incident occurred that has entered the folklore of the night club scene. Dan sent for me one evening quite unexpectedly. As I made my way back stage to his dressing room I was more than a little apprehensive as I knew Dan would normally see no one whilst preparing for his stage appearance. He took almost two hours to make up – to turn himself into a glamorous woman – during which time interruptions were out of the question. To send for me now meant something was wrong.

I entered to find Dan in his fifty per cent mode, half woman and half man, with Anne his dresser assisting with his makeup. His Manager jack Hanson was present as was his hairdresser Robert.

"George" said Dan. "I've lost Margaret Thatcher, Marlene Dietrich, Dolly Parton and Shirley Temple. I can't even find Marilyn Monroe, Za Za Gabor or Mae West".

I stared at Dan dumbfounded, not understanding what he was talking about. He obviously sensed this straight away.

"My wigs love" he said slightly agitated. "My beautiful wigs which Robert here is waiting to comb and prepare – we can't find our wig skip anywhere". At last all was becoming clear to me.

"The skip" I said. "Is it a sort of fairly large basket with a lid?"

"Yes that's it," said the hairdresser somewhat excitedly. "I left it just outside the main dressing room last night, as I do every night, but it has disappeared".

"Ah" I replied rather hesitantly, "I know where that is". Dan gave me a strange look.

"What do you mean George you know where it is – what has happened. Has there been a fire, a flood, a burglary – what has happened to it". I sensed an air of desperation in Dan's voice and quickly moved to allay his anxiety.

"No I can assure you Dan its perfectly safe" I replied. But I still hesitated to tell him the truth.

Dan gave me another searching look and waited for news, as did Robert and jack. I knew I had to come clean and take the consequences. Would it be the end of my career I wondered? Would Dan fly into a rage at the news of my actions? The West End's greatest star would have my guts for garters at the very least I surmised. It would probably be the end of our wonderful friendship.

"I borrowed it," I blurted, cheeks flushing from embarrassment. "A party of four people had travelled up from Southampton for the show without a reservation. I did not have a table left in the place, a few chairs but no table, so I borrowed the skip, not realising it was full of wigs. I put a tablecloth over it and fitted it into a space on the top tier of the auditorium. The skip is table eighty-four".

There was a deafening silence for a moment, until Dan turned to Jack and uttered the memorable words.

"Did you hear that jack, is that not the most wonderful story. The man is a genius; those lovely people all the way from Southampton to see me. The whole thing is too wonderful for words".

I must say I was surprised at Dan's reaction, as well as heartily relieved, although I can't imagine why, after all I knew Dan well enough to know that his public came first in everything. A full house was well worth the temporary loss of his wig skip. Dan despatched Robert to Table eighty-four.

"Tell the good people Mr Savva and Mr La Rue send their compliments and their apologies for the intrusion, but could you remove the items from beneath the lid of their table in order that the show may proceed".

The story of my deed became legendary as Dan told it as his party piece at every social gathering he held, Pam and I were always invited. I remember vividly his beautiful home at Henley on Thames and a party of many of Dan's show business friends. He was such a wonderful host. My wife Pam, who fell in love with the huge riverside residence, was given a guided tour and Dan took great pleasure in acquainting her with his famous Capi D'Monte room. It was absolutely magnificent and the displays of Capi D'Monte pieces were the most beautiful and numerous she had ever seen.

Freddie Starr was another major attraction to play Blazers. Freddie was now a very big name indeed and commanded a hefty fee, but had a hefty following to go with it. Blazers was his local as he, like myself, lived in Windsor. He bought a mansion at St. Leonards Hill while my more modest abode was at Hayes Hill a quarter of a mile away. Prior to Blazers completion and filling my car with petrol one day at our neighbourhood filling station, in drove Freddie in his very flashy automobile with the same intention. We exchanged pleasantries and he enquired about the new club. I updated him with our progress and that we hoped to open soon. He wanted to know the size, layout and exact location of the club and so I invited him to come and take a look.

I remember it was a Sunday afternoon because the site was deserted and locked, but I had access from the rear of the building. After parking our cars we started the strenuous upward journey by the back stairs. On reaching the top, we had to climb over a scaffolding frame to gain entrance to the auditorium, I think that Freddie was about ready to retreat at this point, his designer clothes were becoming a trifle soiled by copious amounts of dust, not to mention the filthy condition of the scaffolding frame which he had to clamber over. On arrival at the top, Freddie got his first sight of the massive auditorium. The room was quite dim because of the lack of electric lighting and the only light came from the Castle end, way over the other side of the room. The huge glass windows allowed shafts of afternoon sunlight to throw huge rays of light and shadow across the area, making the auditorium even more beautiful and magnificent than ever. Like me some months before, Freddie stood amazed at what he saw.

"You'd never know all this was up here on top of this building would you?" he said.

Instantly he became a fan, a Blazerite. I did my best to give a guided tour of the establishment, at the end of which we stood in the dust and dirt of the unfinished club and did a deal for a week in the following spring. The first of many dates Freddie would do at Blazers.

I presented a season of black groups during the summer and early autumn, including the Four Tops, The Drifters and the Detroit Emeralds. Roy Orbison also made a welcome return to Britain and Jimmy Smith secured a date for Blazers. My dear friend Frankie Laine was also back on tour in Britain and was welcomed to Blazers. Our reputation for playing only the best in entertainment was established over this period. Despite our progress, Pat was not entirely happy. He felt that we were offering shows that could be seen at any club of similar size and capacity.

"Blazers at Royal Windsor has to be better than the rest. I have the money, you have the skill," he told me. "Let's go for it".

"Excuse me" said the woman. "Are you the Manager?"

"Yes Madam" I replied.

"Then tell me what film you are intending to show me this evening".

"Film Madam" I queried. "I'm sorry I'm not with you".

"You know" she continued slightly more aggressively, "a movie, what movie are you showing this evening?"

"But this is a live cabaret venue Madam, we don't show movies. Tonight our entertainment comprises comedian Bernie Clifton and the Four Tops from America".

"I know this" she retorted. "I'm not completely daft. I know the rest of the audience will be watching a top class show but since you've chosen to sit me facing a blank wall with no hope of seeing the stage, I presume you're going to show me a movie".

One or two complaints during our hectic Christmas season were to be expected. Jimmy Smith, Mark and Arthur Howes and myself had negotiated a unique contract with the British agents of the Four Tops whereby they had agreed to play not only twenty one night shows but also ten lunch time shows to accommodate the seasonal office parties. Pleasing around thirty-five thousand people over a three week period was always going to be difficult.

Blazers, now well established, was perfect for seasonal 'long run' presentations. As we were near to London and close to Europe's biggest motorway interchange, its accessibility made it possible to play an occasional long season a reality as there were more than enough people within easy reach of Windsor to support a number of stars for more than the customary one week only.

The Four Tops deal was put together many months previously and was well advertised in the run up to the festive season, this meant a complete sell-out. Billed as 'workers pre Christmas office and works parties' on our publicity handouts, we invited firms to book Blazers instead of the dreary traditional bash. Doors opened at 11.30 a.m. and following the traditional Xmas lunch, we offered cabaret starring the Four Tops, ending the afternoon with dancing until 5.00p.m leaving just enough time to 'turn the room around' for our evening functions.

I remember the faces of our lunch time customers as the curtain opened and the Four Tops came on. As they were paying half the price for the lunch time presentation as the evening show, most of the customers were expecting a reduced performance so seeing the full show of the Four Tops, including a twenty-piece backing orchestra, the afternoon entertainment was deemed outstanding value for money. Standards had been set, not just for this season, but for every season to follow. This was underlined by the fact that in following years as soon as arrangements were announced and tickets went on sale that a sell out, even of added dates, was guaranteed.

Pat called me to his mansion at Sunninghill following the Christmas rush and we discussed fully the implications of the completed season and, especially, the figures.

"Most satisfactory Georgie" he said. "You have really worked your ass off".

"Maybe Sir" I said "but what is most satisfying is the fact that we have come such a long way since the opening and in a fairly short space of time".

"That's a maybe" replied pat, "but at what price? You look bloody terrible".

"I'm a bit knackered Sir, but believe me I've really enjoyed the recent business. It's given me a great personal thrill".

"I'm sure it has" Pat chipped in, "but what are your plans now" he asked. I thought for a moment and then replied "We are closed for the first five days of January and we reopen with our Sounds of the Sixties shows".

This was a show comprising three sixties bands, Gerry and The Pacemakers, Freddie and The Dreamers and Marmalade.

"Well I want you to take a complete break from work for the five days. I don't want you to go near the place" Pat insisted.

He left the table and went through one of the doors leading from the huge reception room where we were seated. He returned clutching a carrier bag.

"Here take this and go right away for three days," he ordered. "If you stay in Windsor you'll be in and out of the club, the phone will ring and so on; you'll have no peace". Thrusting the bag in my hand he concluded. "Take this and bugger off on a holiday. I may not always be right but I'm always the boss".

"Yes Sir" I replied. Taking the bag I opened it and peered inside at a large number of banknotes.

"Three grand" said Pat. "Treat it as a bonus. Now take Pam and go".

"Thank you very much Sir," I mumbled; in shock. Three thousand pounds was an awesome amount of money.

I got home and after telling Pam the story phoned the club and told Rodney I'd be away for about a week and to take care of things. He could take a break when I got back.

We threw a few things in a suitcase and Pam, her daughter Jayne, and me, set out for nearby Heathrow not knowing where the hell we were going. On the departure board we saw a flight to Geneva, so we arranged tickets and changed a large sum of English currency into Swiss francs. This greatly increased the size of my 'wad' as there were six francs to the pound.

On arrival in Geneva I hired a car, a yellow Mercedes and Pam, Jayne and I took the road into the city of Geneva. We had never been there before which added to the excitement. Just outside the city centre I spotted the Hotel Intercontinental and made a beeline for its entrance and reception. It was only on entering the plush hotel that we became conscious of our scruffiness; in our haste to depart little thought was given to our personal appearances.

No wonder therefore that the reception manager eyed us over his brilliantly polished mahogany and marble counter with a look of disquiet.

"No monsieur, we have no rooms available" was the immediate answer to my question; I half expected the response. Just behind him on a card of royal blue with gold lettering I spotted the various rooms and the tariffs.

"Perhaps you have one of your suites available," I suggested. "How about the Louis the Sixteenth Presidential Suite" I added. I had taken a leaf clean out of Pat Cowan's book. He always told me how money and the ability to pay opened all doors with little care as to who you were or what you looked like.

"Monsieur, the Presidential Suite is twelve hundred francs per night" replied the Manager, his stiff white collar, tails and white gloves giving him the look of an overgrown penguin. "So I'm afraid we cannot help you monsieur," he concluded rather impatiently, fearing that other potential customers would enter his ornate temple and catch sight of the dishevelled Englanders.

"Oh of course, I do beg your pardon, you need payment in advance," I said catching him off guard. "I do apologise I was not thinking. This is our first time in Geneva you see".

I placed the carrier bag on the counter and extracted from it an enormous wad of Swiss francs.

"Four nights at twelve hundred, let me see – forty-eight hundred francs – I think that's right," I said " and here is a further one thousand francs deposit against our extra's account".

I thought the poor chap was going to pass out at the sights of the loot on the desk, quite apart from the amount that remained in the bag, which he obviously also saw; I made sure he did. He gathered himself quickly, almost leaping over the counter while mumbling something in Swiss or French to an assortment of flunkies who came rattling out from all corners of reception.

"No need to register now Monsieur. You must be tired. I will send my secretary to acquire your registration later" he gushed, shaking me by the hand and welcoming us to the hotel with a pat on the head for Jayne and a bow to Madame. "Your luggage Monsieur" he enquired.

"Only one case" I answered.

"Of course Monsieur, all the very best people travel light these days".

"You will find it in the boot of the yellow Mercedes just outside, which also needs parking" I instructed.

"Ah yes Monsieur, the Mercedes, ah yes of course".

Snapping his fingers to all and sundry, everything was dealt with efficiently and effectively. Pat Cowan was right; money did indeed speak all languages. One other incident happened during the wonderful, brief but sensational, holiday break.

On our way back to Geneva one evening after a day on the slopes of L'Huez and looking even more dishevelled than on our arrival, we stopped to eat in the dining room of the Grand Hotel at Malvern des Alps. The restaurant was empty, perhaps because we were early; we were cold, damp and very hungry. The head waiter was a toffee nosed catering prat who showed us, reluctantly and without courtesy, to a secluded table in a dimly lit corner of the restaurant. It was evident we were not welcome. Time I thought, to go into Pat Cowan mode.

"May we have a drink to begin with?" I asked, "While we consider the menu".

"Yes" came the curt reply. A wine and drinks list was produced and after ordering a Coca Cola for Jayne, Pam and I decided that we would share a bottle of wine.

The wine list was extensive as is the norm in this part of the world. I waded through its many pages and at last my eyes beheld the inevitable 'box'. This was the little window, the announcement of something special, something particular to this establishment. There in all its glory was advertised a Sauterne. Reading as best I could I deduced that the hotel proudly owned the six remaining bottles in the world, priced at a very reasonable £100 per bottle (or the Swiss Franc equivalent).

The waiter reappeared with Jayne's coke and I asked for a bottle of the unique Sauterne. "Which one Monsieur?" asked the waiter.

"This one" I replied without hesitation, pointing to the special page dedicated to the very special wine.

"It is a Sauterne which is essentially a desert wine and above all it is very expensive; perhaps a little beyond Monsieur's reach?"

"I fully appreciate what you say but my wife and I are very fond of Sauterne at anytime, before or after a meal" I lied. Reaching for my bag I plunged my hand in and extracted a huge bankroll, offering to pay for the wine in advance.

"To allay your concern about the price, allow me pay you in advance."

The poor headwaiter became seemingly demented on seeing such monetary resources and leaped into action. We were promptly moved to the centre of the restaurant where assistants removed our damp coats to be dried while we dined. The wine, duly served, was quite dreadful in as much as both Pam and I hated sweet wine, but it was a point well made and was pronounced delicious and worth every penny.

Following the excellent break it was back to Blazers refreshed and ready for action. Chic Murphy, who managed the Platters, now managed the talented Roy Jay. Roy had a habit of going off the rails at regular intervals, and had passed up the opportunity of a screen test by simply not showing up. The test had been arranged before some TV heavy weights, assembled by Ernest Maxime the TV guru. It was one of Roy's greatest mistakes and in my view cost him a glittering, mega star career.

Roy's drink and gambling habits were well known and it is sad to record that such a talented performer never made the big time due to his own stupid fault. If anyone could straighten him out it would be Chic. His down to earth, no nonsense methods, coupled with thinly disguised threats for anyone who stepped out of line might just do the trick. Sadly, it was not to be. A week at Blazers with Roy was seven days of genius and talent peppered with wild tantrums, unpunctuality and unreliability.

Chic also took over the management of the three Degrees from American Richard Barrett. This was good news for everyone who had dealings with the girls. Richard Barrett was much disliked, no, down right hated in British cabaret circles. He was a very rude, extremely arrogant, all round pain in the ass. No tears were shed when Chic stole the degrees from him.

Chic also moved to Windsor after buying Wintergarden House off Maidenhead Road. Pam and I bought a house in Bradshaw Close, just off the same Maidenhead Road and very near Chic Murphy's home. It was therefore, inevitable that our already strong friendship would continue to grow through both our business dealings and social contacts as neighbours.

Richie Disoni, our guest compere, completed his contract with us and was replaced by Del Derrick. Del, an immaculate, suave and sophisticated silver haired Midlander, was perfect for Royal Windsor and for the room. He remained compere at Blazers for over a decade.

Dionne Warwick, Howard Keel and Chris Christopherson were all played as one or two nighters and all did good business, but on the domestic front there was a definite lack of new talent coming through. Variety programmes which aimed new talent at huge TV audiences were no longer being screened. Even Opportunity Knocks, the number one vehicle for the projection of new talent was off the air and sadly missed. Mercifully a programme called 'New Faces' did help as a springboard from which a small number of artistes broke through although not many and by no means enough. Clubs like Blazers existed through a combination of replays of well known stars and an ever increasing flow of American and other foreign entertainers. I remember one three-month programme that included Charles Asnavour, Sister Sledge, Sacha Distell, Frankie Howard and Cannon and Ball; a real mixture of local and international talent.

The impact of Blazers on the area was evident and the activities of the huge penthouse nightclub a major talking point amongst local folk. It was not long before 'the house on the hill' (Windsor Castle) was in touch and discussions for a fund raising night taking place. Princess Anne was very involved with the Windsor Park three-day Horse Trials event and like her work for Children in Need and Riding for the Disabled she proved to be a tireless worker for any organisation that was fortunate enough to have her patronage. It was Princess Anne, through her representative Davina Cannon that set the pace for a fund raising Royal Dinner, Dance and Cabaret at Blazers. All protocol agreed, we proceeded to publicise the Gala Event selling tables of ten at £500 each inclusive of dinner and show. The presence of her Royal Highness and guests at the top table were as much a high point of sales as the star of the show, Neil Sedaka. Supporting and compering the show was a new up and coming comedian called Jim Davidson, who had been brought to my attention by Pat Cowan. He spotted Jim winning New Faces and was impressed with his performance.

"I think this young man is going to be a big star," said Pat.

I must say Jim brought a breath of fresh air to the business and a refreshing new style of comedy in the sense that it was in the Max Miller mould, but in the modern every day idiom. His fast talking cockney accent coupled with his unique stagecraft was a joy and he soon had audiences eating out of his hand, particularly his policeman routine, which earned him the nametag of Nic Nic. In my view 'Nic Nic' Davidson stole the show.

The first Blazers royal evening was a great success and the only slight problem was Neil Sedaka's shuffling of the top table name cards. It is well known, at least to us British, that the seating arrangements for a Royal Top Table are carefully worked and set out in conjunction with H.R.H. and her sides. At rehearsal and sound check on the day of the function Neil decided, quite unilaterally, to move his wife closer to him and by doing so altered the whole Top Table arrangement. Pat was furious and demanded an explanation. I diplomatically calmed everyone down and an altercation was averted. As a result of the success of our Royal night I did several more during my time at Blazers, mainly for Princess Anne whose fund raising night became an almost annual event. I also catered for Princess Alexandra and Prince Phillip.

I vividly remember the day my dear friend Joe Pullen came to Windsor to see me and to propose a Charity Night for Prince Phillip. Joe and the

Duke of Edinburgh were on the fund raising committee of the Horse Drawn Carriage Association or some such thing. Joe came huffing and puffing into my office one day apologising for being late.

"I got a bit lost," said Joe in his Manchurian accent.

Joe was from Eccles, a suburb of Manchester and as well as owning a hotel called the Wendover he also owned a nightclub called Talk of the North.

"I stopped to ask this chap for directions to Blazers" said Joe "and he looked at me rather puzzled and replied I've never heard of it. A night club in Windsor" I said.

"A night club in Windsor" he shouted "impossible" and walked on.

I laughed at this but Joe took a more serious view.

"It's alright for you to laugh but I find them all bloody peculiar round here. They all think they're royalty just because they live in Windsor. You know the types all clothes and no bloody money," said Joe.

Jim Davidson's introduction to Blazers was the start of a long and very pleasant association between Jim and the club and between Jim and myself. Jim lived in nearby Wentworth and a date at Blazers was, for him, a home date. Moreover Jim often popped in on his way home from a gig elsewhere for a nightcap and a chat. We became and remain close friends.

A few other new faces emerged at the time. One in particular was a fresh-faced youngster called Bobby Nankeville, later to be known as Bobby Davro. The Nankeville family lived at Virginia Water and were close enough to Windsor to use Blazers as the local for their nights out. They loved to visit the shows and presentations that were on offer at Blazers and later I realised that the family's interest in cabaret was probably due to young Bobby's desire for a stage career. One evening Mr. Nankeville asked me if I could find a spot for Bobby in one of our productions. They were such good customers and nice people that I was only too happy to oblige. After a discussion with Del Derrick my compere, I decided the best way forward was to offer Bobby a whole week's engagement as Assistant Compere. He could introduce some of the acts and throw in a couple of his excellent impressions. I felt this would give the young lad some stage experience and assist in his aspiration to become a cabaret comedian and impressionist. Bobby was a natural and took to the stage like a duck to water, gave an excellent account of himself and the audiences enjoyed his style and work. Bobby Davro was on his way to stardom of that there was no doubt in my mind.

Whilst on the subject of rising stars, I began to realise that as I grew in stature in the industry, I had employed, watched and even helped many of the young hopefuls of that era to go on and become household names. Michael Barrymore used to thank me from the stage at Blazers for assisting him with his career. At his debut all those years ago at Cesars Palace as a young comic supporting act I knew he'd be a star one-day, and told him so.

Little and Large, Les Dawson, Roger Whittaker, Cannon and Ball and others, all went on to superstardom with or without help from me, but by playing them at regular intervals meant that we built a special friendship and mutual respect between us.

At Blazers I was more imaginative and innovative. For instance, I introduced the credit card telephone hotline for customers wishing to make reservations, removing the need for prospective revellers to either visit the premises to pay for bookings or send a cheque in the post. It was clear to me that 'plastic' was becoming more and more the order of the day and I ensured that Blazers was in at the start. Other clubs were quick to follow.

Another inspired innovation was the formation of a gift shop or kiosk on the premises. I felt that with a captive audience of often a thousand people an opportunity was available for additional income from the sale of records by appearing artistes, gifts, cigarettes, souvenirs, cuddly toys, etc. I never imagined that so much additional income could be generated. The gift shop was a great success.

Only once did I misjudge a particular situation, but mercifully managed to rectify my mistake. John Perry my supplier of cuddly toys and other items for sale in the club shop had delivered some E.T.'s made of brown fur in the image of the film character which had just hit the cinemas with such an impact. The toy was extremely well made and invitingly cuddly. I bought them for four pounds and sold them for ten and as the emotions surrounding the movie reached fever pitch so did the sale of my cuddly look alike.

I rang John Perry and advised him of the impending Oscar's ceremony and that in my opinion E.T. would sweep the board. It had a number of nominations and I saw nothing strong enough to stand in its way, with the possible exception of Gandhi, but in my opinion E.T. was due to sweep the board.

"John I want four hundred E.T.'s as soon as possible" I demanded, "to meet the inevitable surge in sales when E.T. wins the Oscar's".

"It will take a bit of doing. The man that makes them works in a basement at Golders Green and is a one man band," explained John.

"Well tell him to take on staff" I said "and get a bigger basement or whatever – I need this order and I need it quickly".

The shipment of E.T.'s arrived and stored in an area below the main auditorium, ready to meet the anticipated demand. The Oscar ceremony was screened a short while later, but to my amazement Gandhi was the number one movie, leaving E.T. for dead. Disguising my disappointment I arranged for a large display of E.T.'s to be assembled in the shop hoping that the very fact that it had been nominated would increase interest. Alas it was not to be. The display of E.T.'s remained undisturbed.

What was I to do? I was knee deep in E.T.'s the boss would not be pleased. What a disaster. Suddenly I had a brainwave. I despatched Lizzie Ferguson my shop assistant to a nearby shop to buy a large quantity of white handkerchiefs. On her return, I set about unfolding the hankies and then wrapping them around the E.T.'s furry crutch to make them seem like loincloths. "There we are" I exclaimed with great satisfaction. "A cuddly toy Gandhi".

"You will never get away with it," said Rod Johnson.

"Why not?" I replied. "E.T. is a bald thin brown wizened creature with big eyes. Wearing a loincloth E.T. becomes Gandhi. It is the perfect foil provided the punters don't count its fingers," I said triumphantly.

They sold like proverbial hot cakes. Little and Large found out about the E.T.-Gandhi switch and told the rest of club land, news of my exploit was carried far and wide. For a long time visiting artistes would rib me about E.T.-Gandhi and shop sales. Club land had an amazing grapevine.

Pat called me to his house one afternoon, following an early morning discussion on upcoming attractions for our autumn programme. He was especially impressed with the recent Danny La Rue season giving it top marks for profitability and noting that Danny was not featured in any of our forthcoming plans and he queried this.

"No availability Sir" I said. "He (Danny) is in Australia at the moment and when he returns will have only two weeks available before opening in pantomime".

"Why don't you grab the two weeks?" asked Pat.

"It's not quite as easy as that" I replied. "The whole world and his dog wants those two weeks and Dan's management are non committal at the moment. Batley, Wakefield and the Diamond want him not to mention Bob's new Lakeside," I continued.

"But you're his friend" said Pat. "Surely that gives you an edge".

"Perhaps it does. I think we stand a good chance, but his return to the U.K. is a long way off and we shall have to wait and see"

"What are you doing for the rest of the week?" said Pat suddenly.

"Just normal working" I replied, somewhat startled by the question.

"Who's on at the moment? I've forgotten," said Pat.

"Ronnie Dukes and Richie Lee Sir" I answered.

"Well Johnson can handle the rest of the week. Go home, pack a case, grab Pam and fly to Australia and secure the two weeks of Danny La Rue for Blazers. If you walk in on him, he'll not deny you" said Pat with a flourish and I thought he was probably right.

Still reeling from the instructions, I was in the process of saying something stupid like "I'll do my best Sir" when Pat interrupted.

"Go via Los Angeles and see if you can arrange for Blazers to fly over Dean Martin for a ten night exclusive. I really fancy that".

"Very well Sir" I replied. "I'll keep in touch".

After leaving Pat's mansion, I went straight to the club and advised my secretary Shirley Hiller and Rod Johnson of my impending departure, after which I returned home.

"What are you doing this afternoon" I asked Pam.

"Well I've just done the washing and I'm going to pop to Tesco's before they close" she said.

"Could you pop to Tesco's via Australia," I asked. Pam looked at me suspiciously.

"I thought for a moment you said Australia," she said laughing.

"I did," I confirmed. "Pack a bag we're off".

Louis Berlin our pet travel agent had fixed two 'around the world' tickets, following my call to him from the office and a few hours later we were airborne on the first leg of our journey. Once in Los Angeles I phoned my long time friend Charles Mather for information on Dean Martin. I expected his management to be based somewhere in L.A. but Charles called back to tell me that Dean was appearing in Las Vegas at the MGM Grand and his Manager, Maude Viner, was with him. Pam and I spent the next day securing visas for Australia, which we had realised rather belatedly we needed in order to enter that country; the L.A. Australian Consulate obliged. We stayed at the Beverly Hills Hilton and from there enjoyed the briefest of visits to that great city. A stroll down Sunset, a visit to Rodeo Drive and dinner at the Scandia summed up our day and evening's activities before we flew on to Las Vegas.

Together with Charles, we attended the late night cocktail show of Dean Martin and met with Maude his Manager. I thought Maude to be a woman but Maude turned out to be a laid back, self-assured Negro gentleman. With a name like Maude I suppose you would need to be laid back and self-assured. I was eternally grateful to Charles for arranging the meeting. He had filled in Maude with the details of my visit, who I was, and who I represented.

Without this introduction I am certain I would never have to secured a one on one meeting with the inimitable Maude Viner.

"A ten day contract for a quarter of a million pounds might appeal to Dean," said Maude. "Plus airfares and accommodation for him, his musical director and at least four other people and the hotel accommodation has to be top class of course".

Maude slipped away during the break and returned to tell me that the deal was a possibility, but Dean would insist on flying Concorde to London. Apparently he disliked flying. He was aware that Concorde only flew from the east Coast of the United States, but that did not matter because Frank (Sinatra) would lend him his private jet to take him and his party to Washington or New York to connect with Concorde.

I told Maude Viner that I saw no problem in flying the Dean Martin entourage by Concorde to the U.K. and armed with this information, Maude slipped away again. I took this opportunity to call collect to Pat at Windsor and relayed the state of the negotiations so far. Pat was both pleased and surprised that such progress had been made. I returned to my table with the misguided feeling that all was going my way. Only to be completely shattered by the news from Viner who had once again returned. Dean was grateful for our agreement to fly his party over to London and back on Concorde, but needed to clarify that the plane would be solely for his party; private and without any other passengers.

"Let me get this straight" I said to Viner. "You want us to hire a Concorde from British Airways to fly to the United States, collect Dean and his party, bring them to London, accommodate everyone in a five star accommodation, and lay on transportation to Windsor and back to London for ten nights. You also want us to provide an orchestra of no less than twenty musicians at our expense, pay Dean a quarter of a million pounds, and at the end of it all return Dean and his party back to America on our privately hired Concorde".

"Yep, I guess you've covered everything as discussed and agreed," said Viner.

"Discussed yes, but not agreed" I replied. "The hire of Concorde is the deal buster," I declared. "There is no way we can meet that demand".

"In that case we cannot proceed," said Viner. "Dean was quite adamant with regard to the private Concorde for his party".

He thanked me for coming to see him and for my interest in his star for our U.K. dates. We shook hands and in his laid back style he stole away into the shadows of the MGM backstage area. Although I gave him my contact telephone numbers, I never heard or saw Maude Viner again.

Charles apologised for being unable to bring about a successful conclusion to the negotiations. Throughout my discussions with Maude Viner, Charles had injected some very useful 'backup'. He confirmed to Viner how beautiful Blazers was as a venue, probably the best in England, and what a prestigious date it would make for Dean's trip to the U.K. etc. etc. all to no avail.

"Don't worry Charles; I sensed the deal was not going to happen. In my opinion Maude Viner or his client or both were taking the piss" I concluded.

Two days later Pam and I were on the second leg of our journey to Australia. We received something of a shock to the system on arriving at a freezing cold Sydney from the heat of L.A. We stayed at the Wentworth Hotel and I immediately established that Dan was working in a theatre in Canberra. I decide to hire a car and drive down from Sydney this would give us an opportunity to see a little bit of rural Australia as we went.

Canberra was a lot further away than I thought and frankly the four hundred mile journey through rural Australia was about as interesting as watching paint dry. I was not impressed. The hotel at Sydney was beautiful but lacked service, the car hire staff were rude (sorry to have woken you up girls) and the policeman I stopped to ask directions was nothing short of an arrogant pig who told me to get a move on as I was holding up his precious traffic by asking stupid questions.

I must say in the space of a few hours I found Australia by far the worst place on earth. I was at a loss to understand why everyone seemed to be so bloody awful to us, after all our dear friends Rod Hull and Martyn St. James the comedy hypnotist, and Rolf Harris, were such nice people – perhaps that was the reason they all left Oz for foreign shores.

Canberra the capital of Australia was an absolutely brand new purpose built city. The small 'A' road from Sydney was little better than a 'B' road which suddenly opened up into an eight lane highway leading into an amazing steel and concrete tomb. There was no problem here with people being rude or ignorant towards us because there were no people. Not a soul; that's why I called it a tomb. Apparently everyone lived outside the city and poured in each morning to work and in the evening poured out again.

As my little car traversed the massive highway – the only car on it – making our way to the city centre theatre, one could not help feeling an eeriness to the place; a designer city. On arrival at the theatre I thought for a moment I had the wrong night. There was no sign of people or cars or anything resembling life. I discovered later that the theatre car park was tucked away like all the others in the city, above and below the establishments they served.

It was ten p.m. and having gained late entrance to the theatre I found Danny in full flow half way through the second half of his performance. I managed to bribe an official, pointing out that I'd flown across the world to be there and he admitted Pam and I to the stars receiving room backstage. We sat in the far corner and waited. The next party shown in was the Irish rugby squad who were touring Australia at the time and as a fellow Irishman, Danny was an essential part of their schedule.

Once the show ended and Dan had changed from an elegantly dressed lady to an immaculately dressed man, he entered the room accompanied by his colleague, Wayne King. As they went down the line shaking hands and exchanging niceties with the Irish rugby team, Dan glanced in our direction. Perhaps it was because we were unexpected, or perhaps because of our location, sitting patiently in the far corner of the sizable room, but we were not immediately recognised. As Dan said his goodbyes to the departing Irish party he turned to Wayne and said.

"Doesn't that couple resemble George and Pam Savva". Wayne looked over

"Yes you're right Dan" he replied. "The resemblance is remarkable". We stood and crossed the room to meet them.

"It is them," screamed Dan – "I don't believe it". Hugging us both he actually shed tears.

"Forgive me," he said. "I am so pleased to see you both."

After a great deal of chat and laughter we went for a late night supper at a restaurant called Bogart's. Over dinner we discussed many things, including Canberra the city without people.

"It's a great place for do it yourself mugging kits," said Dan. "I walked four miles from my hotel today and never met a single person".

"That's because it is Saturday," said Wayne. "No one comes into the city at the weekend, unless they have a reason to".

I brought the conversation around to the matter of the autumn fortnight and the contract.

"My dear man" said Dan without hesitation. "The contract is yours for Blazers. How could I refuse even if I wanted to, which I don't"?

Pam and I stayed at the Lakeside Hotel, Canberra that night and from there drove to Sydney Airport and took the first available flight home. Dan's autumn dates, the only club dates in the U.K. that year, were a total sell out and regarded in the business as a coup for Blazers. All credit to Pat Cowan, he was right. The extra effect of flying across the world was the clincher as he said it would be; the power of surprise.

People found it difficult to contemplate that I went to Australia for dinner! My stay in that country was a mere forty-eight hours in total. On arriving back at Sydney Airport from Canberra, I was asked to pay an airport tax and as was the norm the demand was made in a rude manner. I was tired of the way we had been treated so far and demanded to know why I needed to pay this tax as I held round the world tickets. Everyone has to pay airport tax when leaving Australia I was told.

"Suppose I did not have the money to pay, after all this has come as a surprise, I may not have budgeted for the extra expense. What would happen then"?

"You would be unable to leave Australia" came the uncompromising reply.

"In that case I'll pay it with pleasure" I said. I really did not like Australia one little bit and I was not sorry to be on my way home.

On arriving home and reported to Pat and settled down to the daily routine of organising Blazers programme of events, working as I always did, almost a year in advance. Jimmy Smith visited Windsor and together we discussed a number of possibilities for top-flight entertainment to meet the excellent and still growing demand. We put together a season of comedy show groups that were always a popular form of entertainment. Essentially they were 60's and 70's groups that maybe had a hit to their name but played excellent sixties music and vocals as well as performing great comedy routines. The season was immensely successful and featured The Barron Knights, The Rockin' Berries, The Black Abbotts, The Ivy League, Black Onyx and The Grumbleweeds. Each band played a full week, thus providing a six-week season of music, song and laughter. Pat however, was once again aiming higher and once again I was about to come under pressure to produce something spectacular. In addition, my friendship with Jim Davidson blossomed and was to lead to a whole variety of incidents. A Christmas season began to loom large but a surprise support act almost put a spanner in the works.

12

PAT WANTS TO BECOME A HUGHIE GREEN

WE MEET AN AUSTRALIAN IN VEGAS

TOM CHRISTIE EARMARKED FOR STARDOM

A SET BACK IN L.A.

FLORIDA COMES GOOD

TARBUCK AND LYNCH FOR CHRISTMAS

WHO IS WAYNE DOBSON

THE SWORD SWALLOWING CHICKEN

LES DAWSON AND DES

ANDY AND TENNYSON

It was perhaps inevitable that sooner or later Pat would start the process of star making; taking totally unknown artistes and promoting them, in-house, so to speak. If the artiste had talent, then this coupled with a financial investment and exposure could result in Blazers producing its very own homegrown star. If successful, the club could expect huge benefits not only from playing that 'Name' for modest wages, but also selling dates to other establishments for fees commensurate with the stars box office appeal.

I was sceptical as to the viability of the project. I made Pat aware of the huge financial commitment involved with no certainty of any return and also pointed out that there had been little or no success within the club industry from earlier attempts by club operators at realising the idea. One example of this was the promotion by the Talk of the Midlands in Derby, of Richie Disoni. The owners, Julian beck and Tommy Barnes, had spent an enormous amount of time and money in an attempt to make him a star.

Richie was Blazers compere during the first period of our Windsor operation and had all the qualities thought necessary for star status. He was extremely good looking, charismatic and had a golden singing voice, but for all his attributes, lacked that certain something that would take him to stardom. In addition, although a highly talented male vocalist, there simply was no niche at that time for such an artiste. Tom Jones and Engelbert Humperdink were just two of the new breed of male vocalist that were storming the commanding heights of the music and recording industry. My colleagues at Derby never really recovered from the drain on their resources.

Pat listened to my advice, but he still felt he knew better and was definite about his intentions. Pat argued that in his opinion, the reason that the idea had such a bad failure rate was because previous club owners sought talent only amongst the artistes of the home market. "It's to the United States that we should focus our attention, by bringing over half a dozen completely unknown American artistes, talented and with star potential".

I must say I was somewhat stunned by this suggestion and the possible costs involved, but despite my scepticism Pat was adamant that he wanted to try. Allan Blackburn, Pat's long time friend, had connections worldwide, especially in the United States, was asked to make the arrangements. Having done so Allan, Pam and myself set off for the U.S. to seek, through auditions, artistes with budding star qualities that could become 'Class A Names' for the U.K. market. It was our expertise and judgement that Pat Cowan relied upon to deliver the potential star.

Our first port of call was Las Vegas; where else. We arrived late due to airline timetable problems and when we entered our hotel, the Desert Inn, we discovered that the weekly talent show they presented had started. In fact we had missed fifty per cent. We left Pam to check in and Allan and I rushed to the showroom to catch the rest of the show with our old friend Charles Mather who was there to greet us. He had made the organisers aware that we were flying in to catch the week's talent production. Word had got around and we were told that the very best of local talent was performing that week. The show was run like a variety store with each artiste allocated between five and eight minutes to perform in front of an audience of club, hotel and restaurant owners as well as entertainment agents. Although suffering the early stages of jet lag, Allan and I sat through two hours of the four hour show and having seen nothing to excite us decided to call it a day just before the final act came on. Making our way out of the showroom we were approached by a charming girl who introduced herself as the wife of Billy Mayer the concluding act.

"Please stay and see my husband," she begged. "He's about to come on and he deliberately took the last spot because he heard you were delayed".

We could do no other than agree to stay on and by doing so acquired the first of our potential stars. Billy was, to our surprise, an Australian, who having failed to climb the showbiz ladder in Australia, had decided to give it a go in the U.S.A. However, having been in the States for some time he was not faring much better and had not even secured the services of an agent to represent him. His act was stylish and classy. He possessed a beautiful singing voice and a wonderful line in patter which, combined with his Australian accent, was totally different. He was a kind of Australian Matt Monroe, and we felt he had star quality.

The next day Charles alerted us to a boy who was currently a lounge attraction in Vegas, but who he [Charles] thought could be a big star with the right management and breaks. His name was Tom Christie. We went along to watch Tom at work and were impressed. An all American boy, he had stunning good looks and a voice to match. Tom, in his early twenties simply oozed sex appeal. At home, Gordon Mills was flying high with the success of his own two stars; Tom Jones and Engelbert Humperdink. Not only did they possess great singing ability, but also the other quality essential for success, sex appeal. Was it possible for one person to have the deep blue eyes of David Essex, the body of Tom Jones, the movement of Elvis and the voice of Engelbert? Yes it was; Tom Christie had the lot and, without hesitation, became our second potential star.

The second leg of our journey took us to Los Angeles, where Allan had prearranged a studio just off Sunset Boulevard for a six-hour audition. The man that was supposed to have organised everything for us was, without doubt, some kind of klutz. He advertised the audition as a 'happening' in the local media and we were subjected to the worst acts that Los Angeles had to offer. People were wandering in off the street to give us a turn in the bad sense of the word. It was worse than a Merthyr Tydfil karaoke on a bad night.

Needless to say we did not acquire any more potential stars. Indeed the highlight of the disastrous day came in the shape of a huge fat black lady with a bronchial problem aggravated by continuous smoking. She fell clean off the stage during a coughing fit in the middle of her presentation of 'New York, New York', the city that never sleeps. My last memory of her was a departure assisted by a team of paramedics. Another moment that lingers in my memory is of a scruffy looking individual who arrived clutching a guitar and asked to be forgiven for having to read the words of a brand new song he had discovered only the day before, thus not allowing enough time for him to memorise the lyrics.

Allan turned to me.

"It seems this guy not only makes his own clothes from left over bits of rags, but writes his own songs as well. We may have found a rare talent indeed," he concluded slightly sarcastically. The tramp started to play and sing, both quite badly.

"Morning has broken, like the first morning; blackbirds have spoken, like the first bird".

"Stop" shouted Allan somewhat exasperated by now. "Next please"

"But what about me?" cried the tramp "I had only just started".

"The song you found yesterday is 300 years old," replied Allan contemptuously.

"Next".

Fortunately, the flight to Miami was long enough for us to unwind from the disappointments of L.A. A days rest in the sun and a superb dinner that evening at Le Chevron prepared us for our final audition which had been arranged by an excellent contact of Allan's who had undoubtedly got his finger on the pulse of the business and had understood completely our requirements. The whole production was the best in terms of talent. The participants had obviously been vetted and only the best permitted to audition. We managed to sign three potentials for a U.K. debut, talented artistes with star quality, chosen from a large number of top quality acts.

The chosen three were: Harry Bee; a harmonica player in the Larry Adler mould. He had a great line in chat and played both classical and pop music. He had played for two American Presidents at the White House but was still unable to reach star status.

The Amazing Balalaikas: An American song and dance combo with a Russian style act that excelled in colour and movement. The world situation at that time prevented an act like this progressing in the U.S. and it remained to be seen if the U.K. could forget the cold war and give them a chance of stardom

Gina Lopez: The third act that Allan and I earmarked for possible stardom was Hispanic; a very attractive girl with a voice like honey who sang in the style of Selena Jones. A great deal of her material was refreshingly original and she had clearly made a heavy investment into her well planned singing career. We discovered that unlike many of the participants at our auditions, Gina was a woman of 'means'. She had made a very good living as a semi-pro golfer.

I spent a further day in the sun on Miami Beach while Allan visited some past contacts and colleagues. We then wrapped up the legal details with our selected five acts and took a flight back to England.

On my return to Windsor I reported to Pat on both the trip and artistes secured for appearance at Blazers. Lawyers were instructed to contract the five acts to Adengrove Productions, trading as Blazers of Royal Windsor, as sole representatives of the artistes outside the United States. A special five-week season of the 'New for You' Americans was set out on our forthcoming attraction programme and with much trumpeting and media advertising we opened the season with Harry Bee and his harmonica.

Harry was well received and had excellent stagecraft but after just a few nights it became clear that any star quality we had spotted during auditions was not making the slightest impact on British audiences. For Harry, the highlight of his week was his Thursday night appearance before H.R.H. Princess Anne, who was attending another fund raising event.

The date just happened to be slap in the middle of Harry's week and although we had to secure additional artistes and a top of the bill for the special night, we decided to include Harry as part of the show. When he found out that he would be performing in a Royal show and meeting the princess, he flew his wife in at his own expense to be with him. To an American, meeting a junior member of the Royal family was a major experience.

The seven-day appearance of The Amazing Balalaikas was an amazing flop. Their show was of its usual top quality but nobody came to see them. The U.K. market decided to give them a miss and as a consequence Blazers recorded one of the worst week's business since its opening.

The Billy Mayer week was only marginally better. We tried pushing Billy's week and dished out thousands of free admission invitations; but to no avail. Billy Mayer and his golden voice was a non-starter.

My luck now took a turn for the better. A telegram was received advising me that Gina Lopez, while playing a round of golf, had slipped into a bunker and broken her leg. With the recent poor returns the news was like manna from heaven. No alternative date was ever offered to the lady.

The final participant from the 'gang of five' was Tom Christie. Tom actually did quite well. Our billing concentrated on his striking good looks and sex appeal, and although not a show stopping week, we did at least hold our own from a business point of view.

My very good friend John Mills, who had a thriving Artiste Agency in the west Country visited Blazers during Tom Christie week and was so impressed with Tom that he offered him a Summer season of thirteen weeks at Bream Sands Holiday camp in Somerset. Hardly a superstar career move, from the M.G.M. Las Vegas to Bream Sands and Pontins, but at least it was a start.

One did not need to be a mathematician to realise that the attempt at star finding did not work for us. All we had achieved was to pluck some semi names from their cosy and comfortable environments, bring them to England and place them firmly on the road to complete obscurity. In the words of one of the acts.

"I started at the bottom and I like it here. Why don't you leave me alone?"

I quickly released the acts from any legal obligations to the company, with the exception of Tom Christie who was eventually released to join the John Mills Company. He played another summer season in the West Country and produced an album of his work.

After the great American experiment I was relieved to get back to organising our next Christmas presentation. Such was our reputation for a top Christmas night out that the public were already clamouring for news of our programme.

For some time negotiations had been taking place between Jimmy Smith, myself and Peter Pritchard who represented Jimmy Tarbuck and Kenny Lynch, for a four-week season covering the month of December, including Christmas and New Years Eve. With terms agreed and contracts signed, I was able to publish our entire autumn and winter programme; I am proud to say this was one of the best I had ever produced. In terms of entertainment there was something for everyone.

Jimmy Jones, Charlie Williams, Bob Monkhouse, Tommy Cooper, Jim Davidson and Freddie Starr were some of the comic attractions throughout the period. Sister Sledge, Jack Jones, Frankie Laine, Gene Pitney and Frankie Vaughan to name but a few, were part of our varied music programme along with a selection of top sixties groups. Sunday lunch time shows, boxing promotions, fashion shows and a host of other theme nights and days proved our ability to cater for almost all tastes.

With Tarbuck and Lynch headlining our Christmas presentation I recognised the need for a good support act. I felt I needed a speciality act that could handle the responsibility of opening the show every night for twenty-eight nights. The artiste would have to be top class because at least twenty thousand people would be visiting Blazers during this period. Without any searching, I managed to fill the Christmas vacancy by the most incredible stroke of luck.

Throughout my career I had always insisted on seeing all new or unknown acts perform before deciding to use the artiste in any of my shows; I never ever booked blind. My rule was well known throughout the business and because of it I received calls from managers and agents of unknown artistes seeking to promote their entertainers by inviting me to see them perform at various establishments around the country.

I would often be whisked away to some social club, pub, leisure centre or holiday camp to catch a budding star.

"Would you like Shirley Bassey for a week for two hundred and fifty quid" said a voice on the phone.

"For that money I'll take her for a fortnight" was my reply. The girl was being hailed as the new Shirley and was appearing as a support act in Fagin's in Manchester. I made the trip only to be subjected to the most hideous singing voice ever. I was not that astute a judge of talent, but I felt I knew enough to decide a yes or a no in those circumstances.

"Billy Connelly is the greatest raconteur that ever came out of Scotland," stated yet another caller.

"Billy who" said I.

"Billy Connolly" he said. "He's at the Town Hall in Kettering".

Off I went to Northamptonshire on a very cold foggy October evening. The weather conditions delayed my arrival, forcing me to slip quietly into the back of the auditorium. Billy was on stage. I watched him work for thirty minutes, and did not understand a word he said. The audience were in hysterics and lapped up his very Scottish humour, but sad to say I was left behind and made yet another wasted journey. I was very wrong about Billy and of course a few years later he became one of the great British raconteurs. These are just two more examples of talent spotting that did not work out for me, but many did and some amazingly talented artistes were discovered on other trips.

The Stage newspaper held an annual talent showcase as did other well known agencies or management organisations. These were the most productive vehicles for spotting fresh and entertaining new talent. As showcase could feature up to one hundred new attractions, one seldom came away from a showcase empty handed, with regard to artistes that is. However, I digress; I was still without my support act for Tarbuck and Lynch but not unduly worried as I still had time.

During the autumn fortnight of U.S. singing group Sister Sledge, the support act became ill and unable to fulfil the remainder of his contract. I alerted Jimmy Smith to the problem and a new comic support act was sought for the nine remaining days the contract had to run. Johnny Hackett, a wonderful Liverpudlian comedian who was a great favourite at Blazers and a personal friend of mine, was always the first to be contacted in this kind of emergency and always helped if available.

Johnny's wife told us that he had not yet arrived home from the previous night's gig at Southend. It became apparent while discussing the problem with Jimmy that we could hardly expect Johnny to arrive home in Liverpool from Southend and then ask him to drive all the way back down the motorway to Windsor. So we searched for another replacement. At five p.m. we were still without an act. It was one of those rare occasions when most artistes were either already committed or unreachable, and those that were available understood our dilemma and asked double or treble their normal fees. I refused to bow to blackmail. Johnny Hackett phoned at five fifteen.

"I've just got in George." said Johnny "Have you got fixed up yet?"

"No Johnny not yet" I said.

"O.K. I'm on my way; I should be there by ten o'clock".

Such was the depth of friendship between us that the distance was of no consequence to him and neither did he enquire as to the fee. For Johnny it was helping someone, that was all that mattered. Johnny opened the show Friday, Saturday and Sunday with his usual professional style and hilarious act, but was unable to remain with us for the remaining six shows due to a commitment in the North of England.

"You know George; this is the third time you've used me as someone's stand in. It seems the only way I get to play the mighty Blazers these days is due to someone else's misfortune," said Johnny smiling across the dressing room.

"You're right" I apologised. "I promise I will speak to Jimmy on Monday morning first thing and fix you a date in your own right".

"That's great" he replied. "In the meantime let's hope someone on your February programme drops dead or commits suicide; I've got very little work in that month".

With a few half-truths and downright lies I was able to shuffle a few acts about which resulted in dates for Johnny in February of the following year. Jimmy spent the weekend mulling over our problem and on Monday rang with a possible solution.

"Wayne Dobson would be perfect," said Jimmy "He's a comedy magician and comes highly recommended. Paul Lillycrap uses him a lot".

Paul managed the Night Out, a major cabaret club in Birmingham, and was adamant that Wayne Dobson was an excellent choice. I agreed to play him, thereby breaking my golden rule and permitted an artiste to set foot upon Blazers hallowed stage unseen. I 'booked blind' for the very first time.

At about nine thirty Monday evening Wayne Dobson arrived. As he stepped out of the lift I was confronted by a young lad with closely cropped hair. He was also very small. In his hand he held a carrier bag and it was easy to see that the bag contained very little.

"Wayne" I gushed insincerely. "How nice to meet you". We shook hands and he told me how he'd always wanted to play the fabled Blazers and was so grateful for the chance.

"You'll want a help up with your props," I stated.

"No I have them here" he said, gesticulating with the carrier bag.

"Oh I see," I said.

As Del the compere led him to the dressing room I had made up my mind that this unknown guy would be a disaster. Why, I asked myself, would Paul dupe Jimmy and me in this way? Perhaps it was a deliberate sabotage of Blazers' reputation. My paranoia about 'booking blind' was getting the better of me. As show time approached my fears grew. This young lad, this skinhead, would probably die a death on the stage. Although he was only the supporting artiste it was an embarrassment that I could not countenance. As Del announced Wayne Dobson, I hotfooted to the back storeroom of the main bar, taking sanctuary amongst the many bottles and cases.

From my bunker I could not see the stage, but I could hear the goings on. All was fairly quiet for a while but then I jumped with fright as the audience roared. I thought Dobson had fallen off stage and the punters had thought it part of the act. I was saved I thought, as I sat in the dim corner of the stores, the lad will have gone out with a bang. He's probably broken a leg or perhaps both, but at least got a laugh and tomorrow I'll get someone else. Hooray I'm saved.

But there were more roars of laughter and yet more, I was puzzled; what was the kid doing? I gingerly opened the storeroom door and peeped into the crowded auditorium. There on stage in full swing enthralling a full house with a combination of magic, voice transfer and jokes was the youngster. The act was refreshingly new and highly entertaining. Seldom had I seen such a universal appreciation for a support act. In a word, sensational. At the end of the evening the customers were still buzzing with praise for the support artiste.

"Where did you find such an excellent young man?" I was asked over and over again. My answer although untrue was obvious and simple.

"You know, I only bring the best for my customers at Blazers. No stone remains unturned in my quest for new talent"

"Was that alright for you Mr Savva" asked the polite young man when I visited his dressing room.

"Wayne" I replied. "That was first class".

I told him of my pre show worries, which he found very amusing. He told me again how he so wanted to appear at Blazers and how he had loved every minute of his time on stage. I offered him the month long Christmas season as the opening act to the Tarbuck and Lynch spectacular and he readily jumped at the opportunity. I knew, and I think Wayne did too that twenty eight thousand people at a venue considered the centre of club land, would be sufficient to send him on his way to eventual stardom and of course, we were right.

The Christmas season was a triumph, although off to a shaky start because of Jimmy Tarbuck's objections at the strength of the support act, Wayne Dobson. Jimmy felt that the excellent Dobson would detract from the top of the bill. Jimmy, in a way, had a point. In his view Wayne was overcooking them. I assured Jimmy his worries were unfounded. It was him the punters had come to see not an unknown support act. We overcame the problem by moving Wayne to an earlier time of nine thirty followed by thirty minutes of dancing and then bringing on top of the bill time with Tarbuck and Lynch creating a two-show scenario that worked well and kept everyone happy.

Once the last cracker had been pulled, the last streamer thrown and the last paper hat discarded, the success of the festive season soon made way for the post festive blues. I must say I was pleased to have had the foresight of not only instigating a programme of top quality entertainment, but also our very own star search talent competition, comprising twelve heats, two semi-finals and a grand final. I think the overwhelming response to our advert for local amateur or semi-professional talent brought home to me for the first time the popularity and standing of Blazers. In the early years of Blazers development I was so busy, so wrapped up putting the operation together that I failed to notice the rise and rise of the Windsor club.

Del and I sifted through thousands of applications from hopeful amateurs and semi-professionals for a competition designed not only to find new faces but as each participant had a body of support, or even fan clubs of their own, the exercise also helped the business by 'padding out' the audiences on dismal early or mid week evenings. Some notable failures will be forever etched on my memory including a husband and wife act that arrived by motorbike and sidecar from the Isle of Wight and had a domestic squabble on stage, disagreeing as to the correct running order of their three song offering. It was a pity really as they seemed to be doing well. He played the keyboard and sang; she played the guitar and sang. Their opening number 'Me and my Shadow' went well, but during his brief introduction of the second number his wife interrupted to claim he'd made a mistake.

"It's not With These Hands" she said. "That's to finish on. The second number is jailhouse Rock".

"No it's not" replied the husband. "We discussed this and agreed we'd finish on Jailhouse Rock and With These Hands would be the second number".

"I've bloody told you once you've got it wrong" she shouted angrily and so the argument went on, the couple completely oblivious to the fact that the audience were sitting patiently watching the conflict with an air of bemusement.

A magician from Reading, who claimed to posses the only sword swallowing chicken in the world, spoilt his chances of progressing to the next round when the rather tacky plastic sword (the type which has the blade that disappears into the handle) got stuck in the chicken's gullet.

Watford's very own Jean Michel Jarre provided us with an electric light show synchronised with music. The whole operation was well thought out and contained within a sort of kiosk, rather like the cigarette and newspaper kiosks that were a feature of London's West End in those days. Seated inside the kiosk the performer pedalled a bicycle without wheels. At a certain speed the motion would activate the music and electricity, which were coordinated to produce a display of coloured lights going on and off in sequence to the beat of the music. The idea was based on the human generator principle. All went well until the explosion and subsequent fire, fortunately was quickly put out by an extinguisher wielding stagehand.

"I told him his wiring was faulty when I helped him to set up the kiosk," said the stagehand

The artiste collected the remains of his set and departed for Watford via the back stairs.

Another memorable competitor who went right through to the semi-finals by default, was a sixty-year-old Scottish gentleman living in Slough. He had an amusing line of patter and sang old Scottish shanty's while playing the banjo. In the heats he gained considerable audience appreciation on completion of his first number singing and playing the banjo assisted by the Blazers orchestra.

"Thank you Ladies and Gentlemen" he gushed, acknowledging the applause. He then went into some patter and cracked the old gag – 'How do you torture a Scotsman? Answer, nail his feet to the floor and play a Jimmy Shand record'. This got a good laugh and I thought the audience were being particularly sympathetic to him because of his age. Having completed his second number, he told the audience he would 'leave them momentarily to effect a change of clothing'. Geoff Walker my orchestra leader went into 'Bye Bye Blackbird' and the Scot disappeared backstage.

I should explain that because Blazers was a top floor venue its dressing rooms gave on to the back stair well. Sometimes this caused slight confusion but usually a visiting performer would sort out the levels prior to going on stage.

However, to an ageing Scottish performer rushing to his dressing room for a speedy change into highland garb of kilt, sporran, black patent shoes and tweedy socks carrying a shepherd's crook, the stair well became a labyrinth. Losing his bearings altogether he descended past the stage level entrance and carried on down and out through the ground floor exit into William Street. The self-closing door shut behind him and left him stranded. Meanwhile the auditorium bubbled with excitement as the minutes ticked away. Geoff Walker gesticulated to his musicians to 'go round again' with Bye Bye Blackbird. Fifteen or twenty minutes passed and a major search failed to locate our performer. The orchestra played Bye Bye Blackbird for the umpteenth time and the audience were in hysterics. The internal phone rang; it was Chris my ground floor doorman.

"Sorry to trouble you Mr Savva" said Chris "but I've got a chap down here who wants to come in. I keep sending him away but he keeps coming back says he's something to do with the show. He's not even dressed properly," Chris continued. "He's wearing a skirt and carrying a stick, which, by the way I've confiscated. I think he's a Scot," he concluded.

"Send him up in the lift Chris, straight away" I said rather desperately. A few seconds later, the lift doors opened and there stood the artiste in full Scottish regalia.

"Err, I'm sorry about that," he murmured as we rushed him to the stage. He came back on to thunderous applause and before going into his final song – The Banks of Loch Lommond – he uttered the immortal line he had rehearsed and therefore had to be said –

"That Ladies and Gentlemen, is what we people in showbiz call a quick change".

The audience collapsed in laughter and he won a place in the Semi's, the clap-ommeter saw to that.

Les Dawson, Des O'Connor and Andy Williams featured prominently in our spring programme. It was very pleasant to suffer little interference from the Chairman, who let me run the club more or less as I saw fit. I continually strived to involve Pat in the social side of showbiz and as often as I could would introduce him to an artiste or a star in the hope of developing a friendship between the owner of Blazers and show business in general. Pat retained a mistrust of what he called the plastic, unreal world of entertainers, branding most of them greedy, disloyal and self-opinionated people, who were not altogether honest.

"They could not lie straight in bed" Pat used to say; but when the opportunity arose to introduce Les Dawson to Pat I did not hesitate.

Les was at my house for afternoon tea during his week's cabaret appearance at Blazers. Pat often popped around for tea rather than flog all the way home to Ascot and so the two men met. Pat was charming as always, displaying perfect manners. Originally from Hull, but without the trace of a Northern accent, he immediately struck up a warm and friendly relationship with Les who was also a Northerner and during that afternoon became like two lost Northern brothers. Pat said he hoped Les could join him and his party in his box at Royal Ascot, the great racing occasion being only a month or so away. Les readily agreed and as he had never been to Royal Ascot, he vowed that wherever he was during Ascot Week he'd make it to the box. "I'll walk over broken glass to get there." He promised Pat.

Des O'Connor made another of his regular appearances and once again strode through an excellent week at the club. Des was often underrated as a cabaret performer and like Bob Monkhouse carried the cross of appearing slightly false and smarmy on TV. But Des, like Bob, was a great entertainer and first time visitors to his shows were soon won over and joined the ever-growing legion of fans.

Des of course met Pat long before I did and being something of a horse race punter soon struck up a friendship with him. Indeed at one stage Pat and Des jointly owned a racehorse. Whilst Des was with us he officially opened Molly Cowan's antique emporium in Peascod Street, Windsor.

"Great to see you again George" said Des.

We had known each other for a long time.

"I had no idea you knew my boss so well" I said.

"Oh yes" replied Des. "As a matter of fact when your name came up as the possible Manager of his new club I told him look no further."

I thanked him for that and at the same time commented on how well he was working.

"Your act is really excellent Des," I said. "You've developed into a quality star performer". I really meant what I said.

I remembered Des in the Cesars Palace early days as part of a double act with Jack Douglas and I was delighted with the way he had crossed the barrier to become a star entertainer, despite his TV image, or being the butt of so many comedians' jokes. Eric and Ernie spent a decade ridiculing Des, and Bernard Manning and other comedians got great laughs from their Des O'Connor material. An example of this was the gag about a thief who stole a Des O'Connor album from outside a record shop display rack; the thief returned it the following day and gave himself up to the Police. Many such gags although degrading Des as a singer and performer were done with the best of intentions by his friends and actually helped Des in his career.

Andy Williams came to the U.K. to watch the tennis at Wimbledon. His connections suggested he linked a visit to Britain with a tour of one nighter's at venues in and around the London area. Andy agreed and the tour was put together. Blazers was offered a date and although a rather expensive package, Pat he went for it. He felt that a heavyweight of that calibre would be in keeping with Blazers image. I agreed.

The date was only a couple of weeks away when a gentleman representing the Andy Williams tour called in. 'Send him over to my office,' I instructed my receptionist. Minutes later there was a tap on the door and in walked none other than Tennyson Flowers, Andy's tour manager. It had been approximately eight years since I'd played Andy at Cesars; eight years since I had last seen Flowers, and eight years since we had to be pulled apart.

"Hi I'm Tennyson Flowers from the Andy Williams office. I hope I'm not disturbing you but I'm in Britain ahead of Andy to check out the venues for rigging, logistics, that sort of thing. Mind if I look around?"

He did not recognise me, not a glimmer of recognition. It had been eight years after all and I'd put on six stones in weight since our last somewhat tempestuous encounter.

"I don't mind at all Mr Flowers. Let me show you around" I replied gracefully. "I'm George," I added as we shook hands.

During our tour of the auditorium, he advised of the considerable amount of equipment that Andy carried with him from gig to gig. Tell me about it I thought. Cesars palace, built in the early sixties, could not have possibly imagined the revolution in lighting and sound to come and had had no reason to make provision for it during construction and design. Blazers on the other hand was built in the late seventies, slap bang in the middle of the technical revolution and as well as possessing its own top of the range sound and lighting, the architects provided storage, lift and specific areas to cope with the extra equipment of visiting stars. I took Flowers through these areas pointing out the very advanced facilities on offer.

Flowers purred, "This is just wonderful. You seem to have everything we need".

"I am sure this area will be perfect for your sound desk and this for your lighting consul" I suggested.

"Yes, yes," said the enthusiastic Flowers. "This is perfect and you seem to know just what we need. That's really what's so refreshing". If only you knew I thought.

After the walk about, over coffee, we finalised the minute items, stagehand food, Andy's dressing room requirements, merchandising etc.

"Well I guess that about wraps it up George" said Flowers. "It has been a real pleasure".

"Likewise" I replied. "But tell me, I've seen the list of venues you are playing and I'm surprised Cesars Palace at Luton is not on the list. After all I recall Andy has played there some years ago" I prodded.

"Yes, we did play it, but never again. The Manager there is a lunatic; caused me no end of grief. We will never play there again".

"Maybe the management has changed," I said. "What was his name?"

"I don't remember," said Flowers. "I only remember him as a tall slim guy with an attitude problem".

The Andy Williams evening was a great occasion, very much a Royal Windsor show. The fairly heavy ticket price, necessary to cover costs, was easily affordable to the local Berkshire society who turned out in droves, making the evening very successful. Tennyson Flowers departed singing the praises of both the club and its Manager.

"Thanks a lot old buddy, it's been great". Another warm handshake and fond farewell. The scene was set for that favour mentioned earlier. The wheel would turn full circle and Tennyson Flowers would oblige on the other side of the world.

Looking back at various situations can often justify one's belief in fate. The reader will be well aware that I was a subscriber. To me, fate is at the core of everything I had achieved in my career so far and now fate was once again about to take a hand in shaping my progress and future successes. Through the booking of a hitherto unknown Welsh female vocalist, I was inadvertently to achieve the unachievable.

13

I'M VERY BIG IN GATEAU

GIRLS WILL BE GIRLS

CARMEN MIRANDA – A SECOND COMING

GLORIA GAYNOR – I SURVIVE

IRIS AT THE TALK

MY NAME IS EDDIE JARRETT

THE CHARING CROSS ROAD AGREEMENT

ME AND MY SHADOWS

SIMON GIVES BLOOD

FREDDIE STARR'S FIVE WEEKS

TINA TURNER

JIM CLIVE AND GEORGE

Throughout my career I've often had to deal with awkward situations and difficult people. Customers could be very demanding, in fact downright objectionable at times, but on the basis of 'he that pays the piper calls the tune' each demanding occasion had to be met and dealt with delicately and as diplomatically as possible. There were of course times when no amount of pacification could calm an aggrieved punter. Like the person who raged at me for not being able to see the stage clearly because they been seated behind a pillar. I assured the customer that at the time of the evening there was precious little to see, but at show time the dance floor would hydraulically lift eight feet into the air, offering an elevated stage for the show.

"I suppose the pillar obstructing my view folds away into the ceiling at the same time" replied the customer, sarcastically, before storming off.

Take for example the case of Mr Hare and his party of eight, who were the very last to arrive for their night out and therefore got the worst seats in the house. They were taken to the back tier, known to the staff as the ledger or mantelshelf, but which I preferred to call my Neapolitan veranda. After showing the redoubtable Mr. Hare and his party to the spot which offered a view of practically nothing, unless one was a contortionist, I beat a speedy retreat. Back at my lectern I turned to find Mr. Hare was still with me.

"I'm not accepting that table" he said, "you've got to be joking" etc etc.

I explained that the seating was offered on a first come first served basis. "You and your party were the last to arrive so you have the last available table" I explained. He was not at all amused and complained bitterly for a considerable time. I offered free wine, a return visit even, as unbelievable as it may seem I considered a refund but the idea soon passed.

"If I could have moved you to a better seat even this late in the evening I would" I offered. "But there just is no other available space as you can see".

Mr. Hare would not be placated. "You don't seem to realise who I am".

"You're Mr. Hare" I answered gently. "Yes yes, but I am also very big in Gateau".

On hearing this from Mr. Hare I found it almost impossible to contain an urge to plunge into hysterical laughter. However I managed to control the urge. Mr. Hare went on to explain that he owned Elizabethan Bakeries, specialists in magnificent and exotic gateaux. I offered a few other gestures of goodwill.

"Perhaps the ladies in your group would accept a cuddly Gandhi each; I know Jim would be delighted to personally autograph the loin cloths for you". Jim Davidson was headlining our show that night.

All was to no avail. If anything the situation seemed worse than ever. Mr. Hare was more irate than when I had started. At this point I cracked, no longer prepared to take further abuse I looked menacingly at him I said,

"Mr. Hare here is one final offer. I will roll up my sleeves, slash my wrists and bleed to death before your very eyes".

The statement came out of my mouth with a fair amount of sarcasm and a huge leering grin.

"That's the best suggestion you've made all night" Mr. Hare replied. Which to be fair was totally appropriate.

Pam, having been informed of the problem, came to my rescue and I retired to my office hearing her say,

"What seems to be the problem Mr. Hare" as I walked away.

Incredibly she managed to pacify him within minutes. I asked her how she did it.

"Simple" she said. "I told him to sit down and stop moaning or go home".

There was no other option that late in the evening so he opted for the first suggestion and sat down with his party. I used to jokingly say that Pam, when under pressure, went into her centurion tank mode ready to crush anyone that got in her way; our complaining customers were no match for my missus!

Despite these examples, difficult or obnoxious customers were mercifully few and far between. Having already mentioned the old adage, he that pays the piper calls the tune; it is sad to have to say that this did not necessarily apply as far as artistes were concerned. Many stars were a law unto themselves. I was known as a person who understood them and was held in high regard within the business. Nevertheless there were times when artistes forgot who was paying their wages and made additional demands or became objectionable over trivia.

To do what they do – entertain – takes an extrovert personality, therefore, it seems fair to assume that they sometimes react differently to situations than another worker might. Also, the most likely source of backstage aggravation would be from a female, not male, artiste. Over the years I had met and presented a whole number of female performers. Earlier I highlighted the Lita Rosa and Shirley Bassey appearances as examples of female temperament and there were other instances of feminine behaviour which were, to say the least odd, and not in keeping with the best traditions of the business.

I remember vividly the night that compere Del Derrick was left standing on stage clutching a basket of red roses; a present for Dionne Warwick on her closing night. After taking her bow she left the stage, completely ignoring Del and the flowers. At first I thought she may not have seen Del because of the glare of the stage lights, but she returned to take another bow and could not have failed to spot him and the enormous basket. Obviously Miss Warwick had had a bad day at the office!

Martha Reeves and The Vandelas played Blazers for a much-publicised one nighter and although the show seemed to be going extremely well, Martha and her backing singers suddenly walked off the stage, after only thirty-two minutes. I rushed backstage to establish why she had walked off to be told that God had called her to prayer.

"Could you ask him to call back later?" I said. "You are in breach of contract". The argument went on for a while but to no avail. The lady was not for turning and did not reappear. She received no fee.

I'm sorry to appear so chauvinistic, I could relate several occasions when the behaviour of male artistes left a lot to be desired, but on balance, if we were going to have a problem, the women seemed to have a greater talent for rocking the boat than there male counterparts. However, whatever minor problems I may have had over the years there were many great ladies who provided a talented and glamorous background to my career. Lena Martell, Tammy Jones, Vicky Carr, Selina Jones, Madeline Bell, Tessie O'Shea, Olivia Newton John, Pet Clark, Three degrees, The Beverley Sisters, Sister Sledge, Shirley Bassey and Dionne Warwick are just a few of the girl greats that played the club and swept all before them.

Pat Cowan preferred to play female stars at Blazer's and occasionally he became quite excited when a new girl took the charts by storm. I remember one such occasion vividly,

"She has a most unusual voice" he said "but that's what makes her unique. I think the girl is going places,"

"What's her name and where is she from Sir" I asked.

"I think she's Welsh and I think her name is Williams," answered Pat.

That tells me a lot I thought. Most Welsh people can sing and most are named Williams, Jones or Rees.

"I'll find out what I can and try and secure her for the club" I said.

"Be sure you do Georgie" said Pat. "I know this girl will be a star".

I rang Jimmy Smith who knew of the girl and the record, the chart bound sound was attracting major interest with the industry.

"Iris Williams" said Jimmy. "By all accounts a good performer".

"But surely you can't mean that Jimmy" I questioned. "After all one good song does not make an act".

"Agreed" replied Jimmy. "But she's been working a lot of the social clubs for some years now, particularly in Wales, and you have to be a pretty accomplished performer to work those places. They can really be tough".

The song 'He Was Beautiful' or 'Cavatina' from the film The Deer Hunter was fast becoming a hit. It seemed that every widow bought the single in memory to a lost loved one, young girls who had just fallen in love bought it and even those who had just lost a love. The lyrics meant different things to different people. It was a song with a meaning. I managed to book a week of Iris for Blazers and reported to Pat who was delighted. I must say I was less than enthusiastic for the obvious reasons. Number one I was booking blind again, although since the Wayne Dobson saga I was less anxious on that score. Number two yet another female vocalist, perhaps another glamorous pain in the ass. Number three, jimmy had warned me to be wary of the lady's fiancé and manager Mr. Clive Brandy. He apparently could be very difficult and demanding.

As far as the bookings were concerned, Iris filled the club to capacity all seven nights, yet I remained slightly apprehensive as opening night approached. To ensure partial cover in the event Miss Williams failed to entertain for an hour or so, I booked Lawrence Xavier and his ducks as the supporting act. Xavier, a Belgian, had appeared at Blazers on two previous occasions and was a very popular performer with a comedy skill and show that was both unique and entertaining. His comedy and magic was sensational, and his performing ducks a revelation. He could work a fifteen or twenty minute cameo or full forty-five minute slot as required.

The moment came for me to meet the lady. Arriving back stage I tapped on her dressing room door and went in.

"I'm what is laughingly called the manager of this establishment," I said frivolously, in an effort to take any tension out of the first time meeting. The introduction brought a chuckle from Clive Brandy, Iris' manager and fiancé; he was the first person I met on entering.

"I'm Clive," said the affable gentleman.

"I'm George" I replied and we shook hands. Iris Williams emerged from the inner en-suite make-up room sporting, what appeared to be, a bowl of fruit on top of her head and wearing a long beaded gown.

"Oh my word" I exclaimed. "Carmen Miranda I believe".

"No, Iris Williams doing Carmen Miranda" answered Iris with a giggle.

Tall, slim, Iris Williams made me welcome and thanked me for booking her at 'This great club'. Any pre-opening night tension was soon thoroughly dissipated and Iris, speaking with her rolling Welsh accent, was most charming and friendly. After chatting with them both for a short while, I took my leave so that Iris could continue to prepare for the show. On my way from backstage, I called on Xavier. Keeping my voice low, so as not to be overheard, I proceeded to relay my anxiety over the top of the bill.

"You mean Monsieur Savva, the lady is yet another – how do you say – pain in the ass fem Voc".

"No, not at all Xavier" I answered. "Quite the opposite, she's too nice to be a star, she's incredibly charming, and that's why I suspect her show is flawed". Xavier looked at me strangely, obviously struggling to understandably my reasoning. The ducks, in various cages about the room, were becoming restless.

"All I'm saying Xavier is be prepared to come back on if Miss Williams falls flat on her face. I'll get Del to take her off and bring you back on to get me off the hook. Remember, if you hear them chanting 'bring back the duck' be ready to come on with your 'B' show".

Following Xavier's excellent twenty-minute cameo spot, Iris took the stage and with power, grace and style took Blazers by storm. Her repertoire was well thought out and exciting and her tribute to 'the Ladies' (which included Carmen Miranda) was rounded off by a stunning rendition of Edith Piaf's 'No Regrets'.

From that first meeting at Blazers, grew a close friendship that exists to this day. Iris and Clive took a house in nearby Sunningdale and my newly acquired friends became neighbours.

Clive far from being a tyrant was a kind and generous man, although I have to say over generous most of the time. He indulged in a millionaire lifestyle without actually having the million to go with it. For example, I remember that his bill at Blazers for champagne consumed during the Iris Williams week, even with discount, almost amounted to the total of Iris' fee. As far as his temperament, I can only say that for sure he did not suffer fools lightly and he was quite definite about his requirements, for Iris, from the world of show business. But above all, he was a fun loving and incredibly humorous man with a string of tales and exploits from around the globe.

Before Iris, Clive had managed David Whitfield and was also closely associated with the Dallas Boys, one of whom became a close personal friend of his and therefore, inevitably, mine – Leon Fisk. Clive also had a very close friendship with Jim Davidson and rightly, in my opinion, thought him a comic genius.

Pat's enthusiasm for female vocalists continued unabated. Indeed fired up by his Iris Williams success he 'got the hots' as he put it for Gloria Gaynor, the black American star who's hit, 'I will survive', catapulted her into the U.K. charts. Pat not only wanted to fly her in to play a week at Blazers, but also fancied presenting her in concert in the centre of London. He argued that by flying her in we would have an exclusivity that would work, financially, in our favour.

Once again I found myself counselling caution on what I considered to be a somewhat risky venture, but my advice was to no avail, Pat was to have his way. Despite pointing out that G.G. was somewhat off the boil – her hit being behind her by now - negotiations went ahead and I found myself waiting patiently with work permits and other necessary paperwork to welcome Miss Gaynor off the early morning flight from the United States.

A luxury limo was laid on for her use during her entire stay in the U.K., together with a security guard to ensure protection for her, particularly when she was out and about. This she insisted upon as part of her contract. As well as a week at Blazers she was also contracted, by us, to perform two concerts at the Dominion Theatre, Tottenham Court Road in Central London, thus setting in motion the first 'Blazers Adengrove Production' star name mini tour. It would be foolish of me to dwell on which of two disasters was the worse; the cabaret at Windsor or the concerts in London, my fears were realised on both fronts. The public were not remotely interested in seeing G.G. at either venue so box office receipts hit an all time low for that calibre of star. Gloria's show was good, but at that time with only 'I Will Survive' to hang her hat on she simply did not possess the credentials to maximise box office takings.

As well as her fee and airfares for her and her entourage, we were also burdened with the cost of hotel accommodation, the hire of the Dominion, the limo and security guard. Gloria really believed she was a mega-star in the U.K. and although she never admitted it, I believe she was as shocked as the rest of us at the lack of recognition she received during her visit. The security guard told me that before a shopping visit to Harrods, the famous London store, she had warned him to be particularly vigilant as she anticipated being mobbed by admirers. No one recognised her and in an effort to gain attention, a disappointed Gloria Gaynor finally resorted to calling out to various sales personnel that she was Gloria Gaynor and could she try this cosmetic or sample that perfume etc. etc.

"She got louder as the store visit continued," said the security guard, but still no one gave a glimmer of recognition.

They say every dark cloud has a silver lining and during the Gloria Gaynor disaster fate once again took my hand. Approximately half way through the G.G. week at Blazers I received a call from Clive Brandy reminding me that Iris was at the Talk of The Town and inviting me to join his table of V.I.P.'s that evening.

"I would be delighted." I said, "Anything to get out of here for an evening".

"I've heard G.G. was not doing it for you" said Clive sympathetically.

"That's the understatement of the year" I retorted. "There are so few in that I toyed with the idea of moving the show to local phone box".

"Pat must have been off his head booking her," said Clive. "It would be like Iris playing L.A. You need more than one hit and you need a fair amount of TV exposure".

I arrived at the Talk of The Town and joined Clive's table, taking a seat alongside Eddie Jarratt. Eddie, a Welshman, was obviously delighted at Iris' progress.

"What did you think of her George? I believe you played her at Blazers".

"Brilliant Eddie" I replied.

"You see we Welsh can certainly sing" he chuckled.

"Don't you dare" I replied.

To any club operator, Eddie Jarratt was the most desired dinner companion one could wish to be seated with. As head of the Saville Artiste Agency he represented The Shadows and Cliff Richard. Over the years I'd had many conversations with Eddie but was always left with words 'they will not work clubs' or 'they are strictly concert artistes only'. The reply, although disappointing, was never a Derrick Block type of rude brush-off, but quite the opposite. Eddie was politeness itself and always explained that perhaps one day the artistes in his stable could be persuaded to do a club or two. Time would tell.

Eddie, like me had a fondness for a tot of whiskey, and Clive, the extra generous host as always, placed a bottle of Bells on the table prior to departing backstage to prepare Iris for her performance. Eddie and I indulged ourselves, unashamedly, soaking up the atmosphere at the Talk's full house and soaking up most of the contents of the bells bottle during Iris' excellent performance. At the end of the show Clive guided Eddie and I backstage to take champagne with the star and so by the time we took our leave of our host and his lady we were both, happy, high and slightly inebriated. Standing on the pavement, waiting for a cab, I again broached the subject of Eddie's superstars and a possible date at Blazers.

"You've been asking me that question for years," said Eddie "and I must say I rate you the best club operator in the business. I also hear that Blazers is much more than a club; by all accounts it's quite spectacular".

"Come and see for yourself Eddie" I replied. "Anytime; I'm sure you will be impressed".

Eddie turned to me "I'll say one thing for you George; you've not become a pest like some other club people I could mention. You ask once a year and that is that. So I'll tell you what I'll do. I'll ask the Shadows to do it.

If they like it then most likely you will get cliff. Ring my office tomorrow with available dates and we will take it from there".

The following day I rang to provide Eddie with Blazers availability and about a week later Eddie called me.

"My name is Eddie Jarratt," he said. He always started his phone calls in this manner, even if you knew him for a thousand years. "I have your Shadows week," he continued. Within minutes the deal was done and the fee agreed. There was never a contract between us only a verbal agreement. The sort of understanding only experienced between honourable friends, the conclusion to a commitment made outside the 'Talk' one night while waiting for a cab that became known as the Charing Cross Road agreement.

I was to make an enormous impact on the cabaret scene, quite literally because of that Charing Cross Road agreement and what it came to represent. The agreement was made only ten yards from 'The Prime Cut', where my career had begun all those years ago, where I met and then worked for a man called Gelineau who ultimately introduced me to showbiz and who, by taking me to Cesars Palace at Luton, changed my life forever.

The Shadows week not only sold out quickly but brought to Blazers Shadows fans from all over the United Kingdom. Luckily my card had been marked, so to speak, when I was advised early on that the Shadows official fan club should be notified before opening the dates to the general public. I took this advice and once the news had circulated the fan club branches our credit card hot line became extra hot as fans phoned from every part of the country.

I was determined to ensure that the Shadows were comfortable with all arrangements whilst at Blazers. I installed a set four-course menu for speedier service and for the first time sold pre-arranged seats to ensure that everyone knew where they were to sit prior to their arrival in order to negate any possible arguments with late arrivals. I held an executive staff meeting prior to their arrival to stress the importance of quick, efficient service of food and drink so that meals were completed and cleared away prior to the Shadows entrance. We also had to ensure that everyone was well supplied with drinks as there would be no bar service while the boys were on stage.

Brian Goode their Manager introduced me to Hank Marvin and the rest of the group and I found them all to be great professionals and easy to work with. The cabaret dates were as much of a departure from their normal concert work as they were for me presenting a top international concert act on my cabaret stage. They were not at all apprehensive. They were sensational.

Brian Goode and I hit it off from day one and became good friends, another plus. The week ended as it began on the highest of notes and I bade a fond farewell to a very happy group. The fans were also ecstatic and made it their business to tell me so. Seeing their idols in the intimate setting of the club was much better than the concert halls they had become accustomed to.

"I do hope you will have them back" was a unanimous request.

"I certainly will try" I replied.

Deep down I hoped I'd done enough to make a return date irresistible. A happy group plus several thousand very happy fans, it now remained to be seen whether that would be enough to tempt the number one man himself. Cliff Richard. To play him had become a major ambition and by playing the Shadows I hoped I had managed to unlock the door and that he might walk through it. People in the business knew I had taken a step nearer but, in the words of Derick Wright a Midlands club operator and friend; 'I'd more chance of finding the Holy Grail than playing Cliff Richard in cabaret'.

Simon Ward was not a professional; he was an amateur vocalist, not particularly good, but with the claim to fame of a two week contract supporting two major stars at Blazers. Simon was not a talent competition winner and did not come through the rigours of a showcase. He came to our attention by appearing at Blazers one Sunday lunch time as part of our academy of 'New for You' talent.

The Blazers academy was an exercise operated as a permanent doorway for new talent to access the big stage. The Blazers memberships became the source of a seemingly unlimited supply of performers when they were invited to nominate any person or group that they felt had potential. They responded magnificently. The candidates were vetted usually by Del the compere in batches of six or eight and each successful nominee had an opportunity to perform before an audience at a Sunday lunchtime show.

Thus the 'New for You' spot was created and was very successful; it gave Blazers an image boost as a venue that cared for local talent and gave budding amateurs a chance to flower. It also helped fill out the Sunday lunch time bill at no extra cost and attracted added attendance from members of families and other supporters of nominees. This was how Simon Ward found himself supporting Rod Hull and Emu at a Sunday lunchtime special. Simon, a twenty-seven year old motor mechanic, put great effort and spared no expense in preparing himself for the experience. He emerged from his dressing room sporting a beautiful new white suit (3 piece) with matching white patent shoes, a lemon shirt, silk tie and kerchief; and took the stage.

Now; the stage design at Blazers featured a classic semi-oval proscenium and protruding floor riser. At the two end points where the raised section met the permanently fixed proscenium, there was a sharp and fairly deep gully that dropped several feet to dance floor level. It was easily spotted and even easier to negotiate by people coming on and going off stage. Whether it was euphoria or nerves, the amateur about to take his first steps upon our famous stage, Simon, making his grand entrance, fell into the gully.

Simon was only missing from view for a few seconds before climbing unceremoniously back onto the stage and, as if nothing had happened, continued his performance. Halfway through his offering of 'Love on the Rocks', the first of his two number allocation, I was horrified not at the song or to do be more precise the rendition of it, but by the sight of his white right trouser leg and the right sleeve of his jacket changing colour from brilliant white to soggy crimson. The young man was clearly bleeding from wounds to his arm and leg following his unfortunate entrance.

The audience too were obviously anxious with respect to the boy's injuries, but he soldiered on, determined not to let it obstruct his attempt at stardom. Finishing on 'My Way' he took a well-deserved bow from a relieved audience and before leaving the stage he thanked he thanked them.

"I hope you enjoyed my little spot," he told them. "At least I can honestly say that Simon Ward bled for his audience," he concluded with a grin.

Gary Hunt my Assistant manager was first to reach me.

"What did you think Mr. Savva?" he said.

"I'm going to give him at least a fortnight's work" I replied.

"I'm surprised," said Gary.

"I thought he was O.K. but not that good," he said truthfully.

"I agree," I said. "However I'm hoping to avoid a law suit".

Simon appeared with Tommy Cooper and hale and Pace. He gave a set of reasonable performances and avoided the physical scares of his earlier Blazers debut.

By this time my neighbour Freddie Starr was fast approaching the peak of his career. He was in great demand all over club land with his unpredictable and very visual style of comedy and a successful TV series kept Freddie in the entertainment limelight week after week. I resisted playing him for a period of close on a year. I was saving Freddy for the big one; the Blazers Christmas season.

I launched him on a five-week season that took him right across the month of December and into the first week in January. It was the first ever five-week season of a major star in a British nightclub. My reasons for playing the five-week spectacular were quite simple. Any cabaret club manager unable to organise a successful Christmas season would be unable to organise a piss up in the proverbial. Most clubs turned away customers at this time of year as they were sold out months in advance. On the other hand the first week in January was a complete waste of time for a variety of reasons. Many people needed to recover from festive over indulgence and those who may have wished to continue the celebrations could not be tempted to attend a scaled down version of a star studded Christmas extravaganza.

This being the case you may wonder why club operators not opt for a major star to kick-start the January programme. The short answer is there is a total lack of star availability at that time of the year. The heavyweights of the business were either tied to a major pantomime production, or, having completed their tough autumn/winter cabaret and TV commitments, disappeared to the Caribbean for a well-earned winter break.

For Freddie a home date at Christmas was very desirable and for the sake of the extra week in January well worth playing and so the deal was done. Some of my colleagues were sceptical and admittedly I did run the risk of losing much of the profits of a highly successful Christmas season if the fifth week failed. Thankfully it worked, and the success of the fifth week was due largely to the overflow from the Christmas season and a record breaking five weeks was achieved. A very happy George and Pam Savva went for a welcome break to Martinique. Freddie and wife Sandy bolted to Barbados.

My friend Bob Wheatley, one of the club land sceptics, returned to his almost empty Circus Tavern, a one thousand seater at Purfleet in Essex after visiting the Freddie Starr show sitting among a Blazer mid week audience of over a thousand people on a cold night in the first week of January.

*   *   *   *   *   *   *

Ike and Tina Turner were, as most people will undoubtedly recall, a very successful American husband and wife act. After an acrimonious split from her husband, Tina Turner went on to become one of a very select few who became an even bigger star in her own right. When, shortly after the split, I was offered a couple of dates for Tina, I took the dates on the basis that there was still enough interest in the Turners' previous work to give her an audience and in addition, she had been in the public eye because of her marriage problems.

However, as my dates approached, it became clear that I had made an error of judgement. I had received only eight reservations for one of the nights and not one booking for the other; in short we were in for a real hammering. I called Alan Field who was presenting the tour and was a close friend of mine and asked if I could have my two Tina dates pulled out.

"Not a chance I'm afraid," said Alan. "The fact is the whole tour is in trouble. I've had call after call from operators wanting to get out of their dates, but the Americans will not play ball. They insist on play and pay".

This came as bad news to me and everyone else but there it was, with contracts signed and exchanged we were well and truly lumbered. Having already suffered a loss with Gloria Gaynor all I needed was another disaster with another female American black vocalist. Alan called me the following day to give me the semi good news that due to the disinterest in the upcoming tour, the American management had decided to put the tour back two months, but that was their last word on the subject. Everyone holding a contract would be expected to Pay and Play.

"Well at least it's a gesture of good will I suppose Alan" I said "but frankly they are only postponing the inevitable. What makes them think the situation is going to be any different in two months from now".

"That was precisely my point," replied Allan with a sigh. "But it seems a couple of records are about to be released. They think it will help".

"I've heard it all before Allan, but we live in hope" I said. "Having postponed under pressure they may be persuaded to cancel altogether if the new dates don't fill. After all what artiste wants to work to empty houses".

I bit the bullet and decided to do no more for the time being. About two weeks before the play dates, I'd open up a barrage of advertising in an effort to cut our losses. Why worry and be depressed for two months when I only needed to worry and be depressed for a fortnight before the dates of doom.

Closing my mind to the problem I got on with other matters and quite forgot about the T.T. situation, until one day I was disturbed from my afternoon siesta by my secretary Shirley who asked if I could I organise some help for her. Both Shirley and my day receptionist Lizzie were being snowed under with reservations for Tina Turner.

"Most of the callers want to pay by credit card which all takes time" gasped Shirley.

"Just a minute Shirley" I interrupted. "I thought for a moment you said Tina Turner reservations".

"I did," said Shirley. "I know it is unbelievable but it seems a radio D.J. has just played two of her new releases which are roaring up the charts. Apparently he reckoned that she'd have two in the top five at the same time. Help please Help".

I decided to go to Blazers and help rather than call one of my staff and as I drove to the club I still thought it was some kind of a joke. On arrival I soon realised it was just as Shirley had said. We were sold out within forty-eight hours and turned down bookings by the dozen. Her launch as a solo artiste was nothing short of an onslaught on the U.K. market and her meteoric rise to super stardom meant that this set of club dates would be the last ones she would ever work. On her return to our shores she would play the Palladium or The Albert Hall or various stadiums. As a club operator, I was privileged to be in on a great artiste's solo beginning, I would always be able to say I played Tina Turner in a cabaret club at Windsor.

As she took our stage by storm and rocked Blazers to its very foundations, it was hard to believe that a few weeks before I was hoping that she'd fall victim to something awful enough to prevent her from fulfilling her obligation to us. I felt slightly ashamed. There is no business like show business that's for sure.

Jim Davidson continued to pop into Blazers quite often, professionally and socially on his way home to Wentworth from a gig. During this period we became close friends and whether working for us on stage or just grabbing a nightcap it was always a great pleasure to see him

My friendship with Iris Williams and her fiancé / manager Clive also became very strong through this period. It transpired that Clive had known Jim Davidson long before Jim's rise to fame and stories of their exploits together were legendary. Clive, Jim and I became almost inseparable and when we got together there were always copious amounts of champagne and great amounts of laughter and merriment. Jim and I loved Clive's devil may care attitude to life and his wonderful stories of the ups and downs of a show business manager. Clive and I loved the fast cockney humour of Jim who at that time had perfectly portrayed the 'cheeky boy next door' style, which was both hilarious and refreshingly new. Jim and Clive loved my tales of the pitfalls and situations in running what to all intents and purposes was a thousand seater restaurant and both howled with laughter at some of the real life stories that actually happened during dinner and before show time.

I suppose it was because we all had input of our own, made possible by our different experiences, that the three of us were drawn together as close friends. During the next few years that friendship became even more involved than I had ever imagined. There were many happy times ahead.

Around that time I received a phone call that made me very happy. Eddie Jarratt called to tell me that Cliff Richard had spoken to Hank Marvin following the Shadows dates at Blazers. Hank apparently gave the club a great recommendation and suggested to Cliff that he ought to play it.

"It is a perfect room, large yet intimate and after dinner they (the management) seem able to create concert conditions," said Hank. "It's a concert with food" he summed up.

"My name is Eddie Jarratt; I'm pleased to tell you that Cliff has agreed to play Blazers. Lets fix a fee and a date," said Eddie.

DAN THROWS ANOTHER PARTY

MANHATTAN TRANSFER AND TV

THE UNBELIEVABLE JIM DAVIDSON

JOE LONGTHORNE RECOMMENDED

MY GREATEST SHOW

JIM AND I CLASH

A DONKEY FOR ME

DUCKS FOR JIM

GOATS FOR PAT

By the mid eighties Danny la Rue quite apart from being the toast of London's West End was an immense national star, the Mr Show Business of the British musical and variety stage. As friends Pam and I invariably received invitations to the fabulous parties he held at Walton Hall, his stately home near Stratford in Warwickshire. It was part home and part hotel and he hoped that the hotel side would become a successful business particularly with his name attached, but early results seemed disappointing. The difficulty was that neither the busy star nor his close associates were sufficiently familiar with the hotel trade, particularly a secluded one, which needed a major, professional marketing campaign.

Pam and I were delighted, as always, to receive an invitation to attend the relaunch of the hotel and pleased to hear that Dan had made a deal with a couple of Canadian business men in connection with it. A glittering Banquet and Ball was to be held to highlight the hotel and its plans for the future.

The party turned out to be one of the biggest and best I have ever attended. The guest list was a who's who of showbiz society plus a large number of local business people who could be useful to the hotel's future. In all, there were over three thousand guests, but despite the huge numbers Dan was his usual self, the perfect host of the party of the year. The party itself took place in a huge marquee attached to the main building. Dancing was to a twenty-seven-piece orchestra. It was the greatest party I'd ever had the good fortune to attend. Sadly the Canadians would become a problem for Dan a few years later.

Meanwhile, back at Blazers, Thames Television had chosen the Windsor club for an outside broadcast. The programme was to feature a typical night out at a cabaret club and would attempt to capture the unique atmosphere of our dinning, dancing and cabaret operation.

Pat Cowan became quite excited at the prospect of a 'Live from Blazers' TV Broadcast. He realised that a prime time show from the club would result in excellent publicity for us. Once again he would not settle for good home grown talent for the special evening, but wanted to import something really unique for the occasion.

"I fancy flying in an American group," suggested Pat.

"Like the Four Tops Sir" I replied.

"No. No; we've already played them at the club. What we need is a group that has not previously appeared at Blazers; a group that is not even touring the U.K. We need to import a group especially for this TV show".

Having set out his stall, Pat sat back. Here we go again I thought, but why not, after all this was a big moment for the club.

"Let me think" I said finally. "Who could we bring over to headline the special?" After considerable thought Pat suddenly responded. "Manhattan Transfer" he proclaimed. "I spotted them some time ago in an American show and they were sensational. They would be perfect. Go get 'em Georgie and don't take no for an answer".

Through Jimmy Smith I found out that Manhattan Transfer were available to do the show and the fee was quickly agreed. The contracts were being drawn up when we hit a major problem. The act required full payment, in advance, before undertaking the engagement. They would not leave the U.S.A. before payment was received. The money was not a problem but Pat abhorred the 'money up front' scenario.

"It questions my integrity," he said. "Don't they know who I am?"

"Well Sir" I said hesitantly, "I don't think they do. If you don't mind me saying so you are not all that big in the U.S.A."

Pat laughed at this then insisted that I go back and demand they fly to the U.K., he would pay them at Heathrow Airport prior to them arriving in Windsor to do the gig.

"They won't play ball," said Jimmy glumly. "I've just had their Manager on the phone with his usual American intransigence. I'm afraid its money up front or they won't come".

The row dragged on and time began to run out. The TV Company needed confirmation to meet the deadline for their programme publications but Pat dug his heels in and I began to look for an alternative last minute replacement from Britain; something home-grown with less aggro. An act that would die for a prime time TV slot. I was called to the office just one week before the TV event to give an up to dated report to Pat. Pat was not in a good mood, he looked more uncompromising than ever. I explained that the situation had not really changed. Manhattan Transfer still insisted on money up front and, as yet, I had not succeeded in securing a replacement.

"I did not ask you to look for a replacement," said Pat.

"I know that Sir" I answered. "But I felt I was duty bound to do so, rather than stand idly by and allow the whole proposal for a Blazers TV special to disintegrate before my very eyes". Pat grunted.

"Quite so" he uttered. As he paused for a moment I interrupted his train of thought.

"After all Sir, time is of the essence".

"What do you mean?" he asked.

"Well Manhattan Transfer's management gave us forty-eight hours to pay up or forget it; that was forty-nine hours ago".

Pat seldom displayed any emotion when it came to business dealings. He sat in contemplative silence for a while and then issued a set of instruction that he felt went more than half way to resolving the problem. I was to advise the Americans that payment of the fee could be made, in full, to any nominated lawyer or bank in America, to be held in escrow for the act and released to them on completion of their appearance at Blazers. The American agent phoned Jimmy to confirm acceptance and asked that the clause be added to the unsigned contract still in our possession.

It would have been comparatively easy to despatch the completed and signed documents to Los Angeles but Pat decided to despatch someone to L.A. with the signed contract, obtain Manhattan Transfer's signature and return to the U.K. with our copy. My wife Pam was asked to carry out the chore and she agreed, taking a flight to Los Angeles, a cab to an office on Sunset Boulevard, a cab back to L.A. International Airport and the same plane and crew returning to London. The aircrew were so amazed to welcome her back on board that they invited her to dine with them on the upper deck during the flight. After all said the captain, it's seldom we fly a passenger all the way to L.A. and back on the same day.

The TV show itself was very well done and I vividly recall how large and luxurious Blazers looked on camera. Manhattan Transfer were very good but I personally was not over impressed and wondered if they were really worth all the aggravation and effort.

Jim Davidson featured on that TV show and many others from Blazers. That Jim and I were good friends is well documented but laying that to one side, Jim was a very sought after star, and although fair to say that Blazers played Jim more than any other venue, I think it equally fair to state that Jim preferred to play the Windsor venue above most other clubs as he knew he would be amongst friends and Blazers was so near to his home it was his local venue.

The British love affair with Jim began when he popped up on New Faces and was voted the overwhelming winner. Danny La Rue was one of the panellists and gave him top marks of twelve out of twelve. Wally Dent was Jim's early agent but it was not long before Jim was taken over by International Artistes, a major London agency. Laurie Mansfield was the chief of the agency and became Jim's personal manager.

To try and record all the ups and downs of our sixteen-year friendship would be impossible. Therefore, I have selected just a few situations that are vivid memories to me. Pam and I went on a fabulous holiday to Acapulco, Mexico where, on recommendation, we had stayed at a really great five star hotel called Las Brisas. The hotel, its facilities and surroundings was the nearest thing to paradise anyone could encounter this side of a funeral. On our return we went to one of Jim's wedding receptions (yes he has had a few weddings).

"You two look terrific," he said. "Where have you been?" We told him and gave him all the details.

"I'll have to take the new wife away and I think I'll take her there".

The wedding reception was in full swing and his new bride Julie looked stunning. As promised I wrote down on a wedding serviette all the details so that Jim could make the arrangements for himself and Julie the following day.

I pointed out that to get there one had to fly to Texas and catch a connecting flight to Acapulco. Like Barbados, Acapulco also experienced a daily shower of rain, quite a common occurrence in that part of the world, which, like the Caribbean, was quite tropical. Finally I reminded him that a driving licence was essential to secure the free jeep on arrival at the hotel. A few days after the wedding, Jim called to tell me that he and Julie were just setting off to 'paradise' in Mexico!

A week later, Jim rang again. "My word Jim" I exclaimed "isn't modern communication wonderful, all the way from Acapulco yet you sound as if you are just around the corner".

"I am just around the corner thanks to you," he said.

"What do you mean?" I asked.

"Well we got to Texas, but unfortunately we arrived late and missed our connecting flight. We did not mind, we even had a laugh, particularly at the awful overnight hotel where the airline put us. Next day we continued our journey and finally arrived in Acapulco; it was raining; one of those tropical showers you mentioned. At the hotel Julia discovered she'd forgotten our driving licences so we could not have our jeep. Another minor setback we thought, but we still managed to laugh about it. By the way it was still raining. The casita was very nice but we were stranded without wheels. Taking a walk was not on – still raining! You warned us, and so did various pamphlets, that we should not drink the water but Julie put ice in her drinks and caught what I can only describe as Montezuma's revenge and retired to the loo. Day two, three and four were pretty much the same as day one. The rain kept falling and Julie stayed in the loo. I finished the book I was reading and considered calling a cab to take me back to civilisation to buy another paperback, but didn't want to leave Julie on her own; in the loo".

"Oh dear, oh dear Jim" I said. "What a disaster – was it then that you decided to return home".

"No George" he answered. "It was the earthquake that did it,"

I gasped with disbelief. "You're kidding,"

"Nope, I kid you not. I ventured out on to my balcony to see if the rain had eased but no; it was still pissing down – then I noticed that everything was shaking. Our casita was gradually moving down the mountainside. I shouted to Julie, in the loo. We're off and that was that. I'm just ringing to tell you that next time you return from a vacation to keep your recommendations to yourself. Hello, hello George are you there?"

I could not answer. I was on the floor in hysterics.

Jim, like most people, liked music and had his own personal favourites. I remember he particularly enjoyed Emerson Lake and Palmer and I also remember being introduced to them at one of his parties at Sunningdale. Some of the music and its performers got under his skin and for a while Jim fancied himself as a bit of a pop entertainer, so after some thought and careful planning,

Jim hit the road on a nine week tour as a music and comedy spectacular. The idea was a good one and Jim spared no expense in surrounding himself with the very best high tech lighting and sound equipment. In fact I suspect that at the end of the nine-week tour and despite receiving top fees, he probably lost money. The cost of his 'road show' must have been astronomical.

His arrival at Blazers with the new show took us all by complete surprise. Two forty foot articulated lorry's arrived loaded with equipment. Clive Brandy (Iris Williams' manager) popped in during the afternoon. He had spotted the huge transporters outside the club and was well aware of Jim's new idea. Meeting me in the foyer he uttered the immoral word. "I see the comic has arrived". The remark summed up the situation perfectly.

The fact that Jim could walk on with only a microphone and entertain for an hour or two with brilliant comedy made the inclusion of so much equipment superfluous. Jim was attempting to move away from the old concept of stand-up comedy and broaden his appeal using music and song but his legion of fans did not want this. His rapid delivery and ability to portray every day situations through the medium of comedy was the basis of his appeal; his fans did not want a singing Jim.

During his week at Blazers Jim and his tour manager Rick Price sent word that they needed to see me backstage. Jim's entire week was a sell out and as usual I pushing was in extra tables wherever possible. I had acquired the nick-name 'Pack Em In Savva' throughout the industry and was the recipient of countless jibes about overcrowding. I went back stage just prior to the show and was asked the whereabouts' of one of Jim's flight cases. "I've used it as a table for some extra unexpected and unreserved customers" I said. Because of the mass of extra equipment Jim had brought there were plenty of cases around and it seemed a good idea to put them to use.

"But the one that's missing is not an empty one" said Jim. "It contains the pyro's for the end of show visual".

Pyro's are a Roman candle type of firework that the pop industry often uses for effect during or at the end of a production. Jim cracked up with hysterical laughter, but soon as the laughter subsided explained.

"I hope the punters sitting around the flight case table don't smoke, because it they set those pyro's off they'll be blown into the middle of next week".

I quickly made my way to the table and exchanged it for another flight case – a much nicer one, new, silver and shiny but above all empty.

"You really should keep the full ones or the ones you need out the back," I explained. "After all how is a man supposed to know which to use and which not to use" I concluded. Rick Price and Jim's road crew thought I was quite mad.

The following evening again, just before show time, the internal phone rang in the kitchen and Chef advised me that I was needed at reception. He was relieved to see me go as I had spent the last twenty minutes hectoring him and his staff about lack of presentation. As I left the kitchen I again stressed, 'remember preparation and presentation is everything. Please try and focus on that'.

I arrived at reception to find Pam, Pauline and Liz standing at the lift. The girls told me that a very important person had arrived and would be coming up any moment. They had apparently received a call from Chris the doorman on the ground floor. The lift doors opened there sat Jim Davidson and Rick Price at a table for two, completely clothed and laid ready for dinner.

"Are you sure this is the best you can do Mr Stavros" said Rick.

"What a way to run an establishment" added Jim. Hoots of laughter all round, especially when the doors of the lift closed again, taking the occupants back down to the ground floor.

Apart from setting fire to the Blazers velvet stage pelmet with one of his lasers during band call, the rest of the week passed off without incident.

The friendship between Clive, Jim and me was best illustrated when it was decided that we would buy a greyhound. I had often related stories arising from my greyhound racing days, which amused Jim and Clive so much that they decided they would like to enter the greyhound racing fraternity. Clive knew a fairly prominent trainer with kennels at Sunninghill near Ascot and we decided that the three of us would go along one evening to see the trainer and discuss the matter. We must have looked a touch shady to the trainer as he opened his door on that dark winter's evening; a cockney comedy star, a nightclub boss and the bulky frame of Clive.

"What can I do for you gentlemen?" said the trainer.

"We want to become the gangsters of the dog world," said Jim amusingly.

The trainer smiled and ushered us into his lounge where I elaborated on Jim's opening remarks. "What we are looking for is a potential open racer that we can enter for the big classic races and hopefully the Greyhound Derby itself, and we want you to train it for us".

"Gentlemen, I'd be delighted to do the job for you" answered the trainer. "My advice is to buy an untrained dog from Ireland – a trailer with good times to his credit and potential for improvement". The trainer was duly despatched to Ireland and, paying a third each, we eventually became the owners of a young dog called Academy Lad which became the symbol of our friendship.

The dog soon began racing at various London tracks which we attended as we were available and Clive and Jim began to feel the buzz of owning their own runner; the look in their eyes as the dogs paraded was very familiar to me. As far as betting was concerned Clive and I were quite conservative our resources were limited and we just wanted to have an additional interest in the outcome of the race. On the other hand, Jim was a highly paid star and a fairly serious punter. Sadly, Academy Lad never quite made it across the line in first place.

The other problem we continually ran into was bad advice. I told my colleagues about the many times that my trainer had marked my card, as often as not resulting in me losing nearly all my money before it got to my dog's race. Or; my dog was often a cert but in fact finished down the field further draining my limited resources. I told them of the night at Henlow Grange when my dog, Sir Andrew, was entered in a fairly major race. I went to support my runner only to be told by the trainer that Sir Andrew had no chance of winning that night. However, he went on, here are some tips for the other races on the card. His information was flawed in two parts. None of his tips won and my dog Sir Andrew won its race at odds of ten to one.

The cost of buying, feeding, training and betting mounted and we reached breaking point at an evening meeting in Slough. Jim was in cabaret at the Night Out in Birmingham, and I was unable to leave blazers due to the weight of business for Frankie Valli and the Four Seasons, this meant that Clive had to go to Slough alone. None of us were inclined to bet on 'Academy' as the trainer had told us on the phone that morning that the dog was up against a very powerful field and unlikely to win.

I was in the reception area of Blazers at about eleven p.m. when the lift doors opened and there stood an a dripping wet Clive clutching a small, cheap, plastic trophy, valued at no more than about four pounds and fifty pence and a cheque for twenty-two pounds, the winner's prize money. As you will have guessed Academy Lad won his race and none of us were 'on him'. The trainer had marked Clive's card with at least half a dozen certs; all of which lost and stripped Clive of even his cab fare back to Blazers. As the sorry story was related to me I suffered more that a touch of de ja vous.

"What did the trainer have to say about all this?" I asked.

"I couldn't find him" said Clive – "and believe me I looked, 'cause I wanted to strangle the bastard".

Jim phoned at half past midnight and was given the news. "Let's sell the bloody thing" said he before hanging up.

The trainer found an interested potential buyer, an Irishman. A three-dog trial was set at Wembley and Clive was again given the task of representing us at the sale. He rang me later that morning. "I have good news and bad news," he reported. "The good news is Academy has won his trial by half the track in an excellent time. The bad news is that while the Irishman was gently patting him (the dog) and discussing a price, Academy Lad dropped dead at his feet. It was a heart attack apparently," concluded Clive.

"I'm not surprised," said Jim philosophically on hearing the news. "We were jinxed from day on".

"In fairness" interrupted Clive "George did warn us about the possible pitfalls. The only thing was we did not expect the possible to become the probable and then reality all at once".

"This whole disastrous episode reminds me of the story of Mick and John and their greyhound," said Jim. "On their way home one night from another bad evening at a dog track, where the dog had failed yet. Mick turned to John and said. 'Let's get rid of him, the dog has to go or it will lead us to financial ruin'.

'I must admit," replied John the dog is much too slow to win races'.

'Too slow' shouted Mick, 'the bloody thing is positively lethargic'.

They both gazed down at their animal as it walked gently along at their side. 'I mean, look at him,' continued Mick. 'He looks barely able to stroll let alone run. We should never have bought him' .

Clive and I sat patiently listening to Jim's story unfold. He was an amazing raconteur. "'Anyway, Mick and John were walking by a canal. 'Let's throw the bloody dog in the canal' said Mick.

'Certainly not' replied his co-owner, 'that would be cruel and may result in a slow horrible death by drowning'.

'OK' said Mick, somewhat exasperated by now. 'Let's cut its throat, at least it will be over nice and quick'.

'I can't believe what you are saying,' cried John. 'This is mega cruelty; I won't have any of it'.

The two men and their mutt walked on in silence for a while, until suddenly John piped up.

'I know how to get rid of him,' said John triumphantly.

'How' said Mick sceptically?

'We will just run away from him,' answered John. 'After all we are both faster than the sodding dog'".

Clive and I collapsed in hysterical laughter at a tale well told by a great pro.

Very few stars would go out of their way to praise another artiste. Even less would bother to recommend another artiste. Great stars like Bob Monkhouse, Matt Munroe and Tommy Cooper were all performers I knew well and worked with on many occasions. They were genuine folk who would never hesitate to recommend an artiste who in their opinion was impressive enough to warrant advancement.

Jim Davidson was also a person who endorsed and assisted fellow artistes to stardom, probably more so than any other I have known. During yet another week of cabaret at blazers, he told me of two highly talented artistes. One, a Cornish comic called Jethro was apparently an extremely funny man with an unusual style all his own. He was more of a storyteller than a gag-cracking comic and his stories were so hilarious, and Jim so impressed, that he invited him on to his TV show for a guest appearance. I promised I would catch the show and see for myself. Jim also took me to one side at band call before his opening night to tell me he had worked with an artiste the night before and that if I should ever play him at Blazers, as a supporting act to himself for example, he would want to go on first.

"George I would never wish to follow him" he said.

Jim felt he was sensational, an impressionist singer with a dash of comedy named Joe Longthorne.

"Joe who" I queried.

"Joe Longthorne" replied Jim. "Just think of Longhorne then replace horne with thorne – Joe Longthorne".

The greatest accolade any artiste could receive from a big star would be the statement that they would not wish to follow that artiste. Jim gave Joe that accolade. Such is the generosity of Jim Davidson the star, ever ready with a helping hand.

I took Jim's recommendation and played both Jethro and Joe Longthorne, both with great success. Jethro and Joe went on to become major stars, thanks largely to Jim, whose star status could open so many doors, not just in club land but in TV as well. Jethro, Joe and many other artistes owe a lot to Jim. In some cases much more than they would ever know, or care to admit.

Jethro's debut on one of Jim's TV shows was a success and he was soon in great demand by club land nationwide. However, Joe Longthorne was still climbing the proverbial ladder when I played him at Blazers, shortly after Jim's endorsement, as a support act to the Chilites, an American band touring the U.K. at that time. I remember vividly Joe bursting on to the stage, his powerful voice enchanted the audience and his impressions of some of our greatest stars were sensational. He did the best Tom Jones and Shirley Bassey impressions in the business and finished his performance with a Bassey Jones duet, taking off both voices superbly. It was clear to me he was destined for the top.

*   *   *   *   *   *   *

H.R.H. Princess Anne is rightly known as a hard working royal and I had catered for her on numerous occasions at Blazers charity events and fund raising dinner dances. She was touring Australia around this time and, apparently, on arriving at Sydney was disappointed to learn that she had, once again, missed the show of master raconteur Victor Borge who had just completed his Australian tour. Before departing for home however, he was able to accept a dinner invitation from Princess Anne. During dinner H.R.H. told him of her frustration at once again missing his show. "You are my favourite artiste and yet I invariably arrive at a destination, only to learn that you had just finished your tour. It's uncanny really, it has happened on numerous occasions".

Victor thanked her for her flattering remarks and indicated that he too was sorry she had missed his show yet again. "I believe your Royal Highness is at the moment very active for the charity Children in Need," said Victor. "May I make a proposal?" he continued. "I will fly to the U.K. at my own expense and do a show for your Children in Need charity, at a venue of your choice, for no fee. You could attend as Patron and guest of honour, thus catching my show and raising funds for your very worthy charity at the same time".

The Princess was delighted and gratefully accepted the marvellous offer. The first I knew of the matter was when Victor's Manager, Tito Burns called me; he told me of the agreement and asked for Blazers cooperation. I readily agreed and a date was set.

"So it seems H.R.H loves Blazers and has had some happy times there," said Tito. "I am more than happy to stage the show there," he concluded.

I was aware that Victor Borge in company with our Royal guest of honour was going to bring the very best of society through our doors that night. One thousand pounds per table of ten was the fee that set the standard for the event. Companies were invited to sponsor tables and even at a 'grand' per table queued to buy. To support Victor Borge, I chose Iris Williams and Joe Longthorne, artistes I felt would further add to the class of the occasion and make for a perfect balance for Victor's show. I was blissfully unaware that

I had added ingredients to this show which was going to produce the greatest night of entertainment that I'd ever put together.

Joe Longthorne took the best of his act for his twelve-minute slot and this little known performer tore the well-heeled, jewel-bedecked audience apart. At the end of his spot he received a standing ovation and screams for an encore, which unfortunately time would not permit. A good friend of mine, Steve Rutland, who owned the Cromwell Mint Casino in London, and who was one of my major table sponsors, came up to me with the words,

"Where did you find that great guy" – but not pausing for my answer continued "I tell you George, Iris Williams will never follow Joe – what's – his – name".

Iris had an eighteen-minute slot and she too took the best of her work and presented it with class and style as her unusual voice portrayed some of the great songs of Europe and the Americas. She finished with her hit 'He Was Beautiful'. Iris still received plenty of air play daily and was still very much in the public ear. She also brought the house down. Another standing ovation with some people even standing on their chairs.

Steve Rutland found me again. "I would not have believed it if I had not seen it with my own eyes" he said. "I really could not see how Iris could follow the first act; but she did, and how. She was incredible". He ended rather philosophically by saying, "I'm a lifetime fan of Victor Borge but he'll have to pull out all the stops to follow those two".

Victor Borge was allocated one hour. Having played him once before at Cesars palace, I knew he was capable of entertaining an audience for twice as long as the spot given, but when presenting a royal evening time was of the essence. One was given a royal arrival and departure time and you simply had to stick to it. Victor finished exactly on time, a sixty-minute spot of absolute brilliance and took a well-deserved standing ovation. H.R.H. Princess Anne, the Princess Royal, was one of the first to stand and by doing so led the ovation. Victor stood, smiling and bowing, but all the time the applause became more and more intense and the cheering louder.

He looked across at the princess, and then his watch, and again at the Princess who clearly gave him the nod to continue. He went on to perform a further thirty-five minutes, with the audience hanging on every word and enjoying every enthralling moment. After the show I guided the sponsors to the private reception room to meet H.R.H. and was once again approached by Steve Rutland and his charming wife Ruth.

"That's the most fantastic show I have ever seen from start to finish" he exclaimed, and I must say I had to agree.

I had put on many shows at this point in my career and officiated or organised many spectacular occasions as was my job, but this particular evening was on its own. A show that built and built from the moment Joe Longthorne walked on until the moment Victor Borge took his final bow.

At the after show reception I introduced the artistes to the Princess one by one, although no introduction was really needed. Thanking each of them and enthusing at the quality of the show, H.R.H. reached Victor Borge.

"My dear Mr. Borge, your performance was brilliant. I am so very grateful to you," she said.

Victor thanked the Princess. "However Ma'am I'm afraid I have somewhat delayed you by overrunning" said he apologetically.

"Mr. Borge, being entertained by you was so very enjoyable I could have stayed all night", a quick reply from a delighted Royal.

This was the best and most entertaining variety show I'd ever produced and remained so until the end of my showbiz career.

Jim, Clive and I remained almost inseparable and enjoyed each other's company at various parties and gatherings. Life was good for all of us, Jim's career was at its peak and he seemed destined to stay at the top of his profession for many years to come. Iris' career too was going well and it was at this time that Clive and Iris married. For me, Blazers was truly established as the Number One U.K. club and apart from the success of the business I managed to win the Propriety Club of the year award once again. Halcyon days indeed.

Clive and Iris bought a pub, 'The Cottage' at Winkfield Row, Ascot which Clive promptly renamed the Pheasant Plucker. In my opinion Clive was no more a publican than I was head of the C.I.A., but he was determined to have a go and as close friends Jim and I with others gave the venture our full support. It was at the Pheasant Plucker one dark and dreary evening that Jim and I had the most horrific row.

On my night off from the club I had taken Pam to the Pheasant Plucker for a meal. After dinner, which included a substantial amount of wine, we settled down for drinks and conversation with Clive. Some time later Jim dropped in. He did not seem best pleased with himself, clearly a bad day at the office I thought. Well all of us have a bad day from time to time.

Jim joined us, which seemed to cheer him up a little and an hour of serious drinking went by, during which time light conversation, jokes and general banter took place. Jim had had a drink or two before arriving at the pub and by now became quite inebriated; and so was I after consuming wine with dinner followed by numerous brandies. The upshot of the whole thing was that in our somewhat intoxicated state, we managed to get involved in a political discussion. I don't recall how it started but I believe it was Jim's mention of Margaret Thatcher the then Prime Minister that lit the fuse. I detested Thatcher and all she stood for. Jim on the other hand revered her to the point where he felt she should be canonised. My immediate reaction was one of joy. The thought of filling a cannon full of Thatcher and firing her into the middle of next week had great appeal to me, but alas I was to discover that Jim was referring to Mrs. Thatcher becoming a saint.

Alcohol has a habit of prompting a person or persons to speak their minds out loud. Indeed very loud and it usually enables its imbibers to argue irrationally and to the point of no return. The conversation between Jim and I became heated then overheated.

"Your right wing views are nothing short of Fascism" I accused.

"If you don't like it why don't you go back to Russia" came his uncompromising reply etc. etc.

The argument got completely out of hand and despite an attempt by Clive to intervene with conciliatory words and gestures; nothing could stop the two run away trains roaring down the track from the left and the right; a collision was inevitable.

The meeting broke up in disarray as we hurled abuse at each other. Clive was mortified. I stormed out of the pub taking Pam with me while Clive pursued us across the car park trying to calm the situation, to no avail.

Jim called from the pub entrance. "I'll never work for you again Savva".

"You're quite right. You won't!" was my terse reply.

Many months went by before Jim and I rekindled our friendship. Clive told Jim how much I regretted the incident and then told Jim the same story. It was inevitable that our friendship would be renewed and Clive was instrumental in bringing that about. After our reconciliation I decided to push the boat out to celebrate my birthday with an organised birthday bash at Blazers. I invited a number of close friends, including Jim Davidson, Clive Brandy and others. The staff of Blazers was also invited.

Our special cabaret was the Great Durrant, a sound impressionist. Technically Tony Durrant's sound impressions were very good; it was only when all were strung together for a stage show that the act became dreadful. He was renowned for his bird impressions; his hawk, bluefinch, crow, blackbirds and various tits were excellent. Apparently he recorded the seagull sounds for Fantasy Island, the TV series. The problem with Tony was that he would insist on mixing his bird songs with the sounds of the African jungle or with Concorde landing and taking off, or the sound of high-speed trains and the London Underground.

Audiences found it amusing to be whisked from a walk down an English country lane (birds), to a platform at Paddington station, to a safari in deepest Congo, or being catapulted from a stroll through a monastery garden (more birds) to rush hour on the London Underground. In short, his act was so bad it was hilarious. Tony was totally serious and as dedicated as a monk but his seriousness was lost on the audience. They rolled in the aisles with laughter. I will always remember the evening that Tony came off to tumultuous laughter and later told me that in view of his current audience reaction, he was considering injecting comedy into his performance. He was certainly the right choice for my birthday bash, which after all, was very much an audience of Pro's.

The great Durrant was a great success. However, the highlight of the evening was the arrival of Clive with a fully-grown mule, brought into the club by way of the goods service lift. The mule is the most unusual birthday gift I have ever received. Slightly bewildered, I took charge of the creature, which had a blue bow about its belly and a straw hat on its head. The gift was the result of collusion between Jim and Clive. Instantly named Blaze; it was tethered to the bar and instructed not to piss or shit on the club carpet and that the famous B.Z. letters woven into the carpet would should not be construed as an invitation.

It was a great party, but it was only when the last guest had said goodbye that I realised I was stuck on the top floor of a building in the centre of Windsor with a mule.
Blaze looked at me with huge mournful eyes and licked her lips; perhaps as a signal to tell me she was hungry. Once I'd got her down to street level, locked up and handed the premises to the night security officer, Blaze and I set out at a steady pace down Vansitart Road towards the maidenhead Road and my home.

Our combined six legged jaunt took about thirty minutes to reach my house, a semi-detached at Bradshaw Close. After Some deliberation, Pam and I decided Blaze would be best left in the front garden rather than attempt bringing her through the rather restricted access to the back of the house. Pam, who had arrived ahead of me in the car, was mindful of the predicament, and it was after all four o'clock in the morning.

The following day I arranged a farmer' field for Blaze, paying a monthly fee for her board and lodge. One day whilst on my way to Blazers I took the long route in order to visit my four-legged birthday present. Blaze stood by the five bar gate staring at the road and passing traffic. She seemed a touch lonely and I found myself pleased that I had taken the decision to visit her, although she seemed indifferent to my presence. I told her a couple of gags to cheer her up but to no avail. My timing was always suspect:

"I know you must feel a bit miffed having to come out here" I said. "I know you preferred my front garden but you have to understand, one cannot keep a mule in a front garden in a Close at Royal Windsor. It's just not done. Even I, a well-known non-conformist know that. It's simply no good you thinking you were the centre of attention and enjoying every moment of it. Those four neighbours were most insistent you had to move on, and the policeman was not very helpful either". Blaze gazed at me and back to the passing traffic and although she looked well she seemed sad.

"I know what I'll do; I'll find you a new home with other animals of your own kind. What do you think about that?" I asked. Blaze never even batted an eyelid but then maybe she did not understand, she may not have even understood English for all I knew. On the hand she may have decided not to engage in any discourse with a Night Club Manager who was obviously quite mad. After all who other than a nutcase would drive into the countryside to have a conversation with a mule?

A few days later I managed to fix Blaze a place at the famous Woking Donkey Sanctuary. On checking a month or two later I discovered she had settled in really well and was very happy.

It turned out that my birthday gift was the mere tip of the iceberg and in its way ushered in the silly season in birthday presents. Jim Davidson was next to celebrate his birthday. He was working a week at the Lakeside Country Club at nearby Camberley and the opportunity for Clive and I to hatch a plot to surprise Jim was obvious. With Bob Potter's permission we could pop over to lakeside while Jim was on stage and leave our calling card in his dressing room to surprise him when he came off stage.

Clive suggested a crocodile but then Clive would. I was totally opposed to the croc proposal. Firstly the problem of acquiring the beast, secondly, handling the bloody thing, and thirdly it might get over excited and bite our comedian friend, perhaps even severing an arm or leg. Clive felt that Jim would still see the funny side of it, but I could not imagine, even Jim, laughing at the loss of a limb.

After much discussion we settled for a pair of fully-grown ducks. We arranged to take delivery of the ducks from a local farmer on the night of Jim's birthday and took them to lakeside where, by arrangement, we were admitted to the back stage area and to the star dressing room. Once inside we released the ducks into the shower room and leaving a card with our best wishes Clive and I scarpered back to Windsor.

"You bastards" Jim screamed down the phone about an hour or so later. "I went to take a shower when I came off and find two bloody ducks, I don't mind sharing a shower but they shit everywhere".

Clive's birthday was a long way off, outside the silly season, but there was one other birthday celebration in the immediate future. Pat Cowan, the owner of Blazers and my boss. There was one thing I'll say of Pat, he was always game for a laugh and so we had no hesitation in ordering a herd of goats. Pat's celebration took the form of a fancy dress party at the Hinds Head at Bray, Pam went as a St. Trinian pupil and I went as Alexander the Great. There were approximately forty guests in all, everyone having gone to immense trouble in dressing up in the most elaborate costumes with great attention paid to make up. In fact it was difficult to recognise most of the guests, with the exception of Cinderella's Ugly Sisters; two of Pat's business friends who were very easily recognisable because of their natural everyday ugliness. Jim was working in the North so it was left to Clive and I to represent our joint interests.

Clive arrived, wearing a sort of Wurzel Gummidge outfit, which was supposed to depict a shepherd, driving before him a small herd of goats. He entered the Hinds Head where Pat, along with the rest of the guests, seemed totally bemused and certainly very surprised to see the goats approaching.

"Mr. Cowan" said Clive. "I've been informed that you are often overheard uttering the words 'silly old goat', when chastising someone. You apparently tend to use the term on people who either disagree with your point of view or when you are unable to get your own way. Well the goats have complained at having their good name taken in vain and have seen fit to send this delegation to reside with you as a constant reminder not to use this term again" Clive concluding his little speech earned a great round of applause from the guests and hoots of laughter.

Pat raised his glass, apologised to the goats and promised he would change his remarks and organised the Chef and second Assistant to usher the goats to an enclosed pasture, owned by Pat, opposite the Hinds Head.

I have taken up some space and time to record some of the many amusing tales that arose during the period when Jim Davidson went from being a cheeky support comic to a major national star and at the same time became a lifelong and much respected friend. Following the phone call from Eddie Jarrett, telling me of Cliff's agreement to play Blazers, the time came to announce that tickets were going on sale. What happened next was remarkable.

15

THE INCREDIBLE CLIFF RICHARD
PERSONAL PRIDE AND ANGUISH
ROBERT HERBERT AND CO.
DUNCAN NORVELLE AND FRIENDS
THE HOLLYWOOD PALLADIUM
PAT'S PERSONAL TRAGEDY

From the moment tickets went on sale for the six night appearance of Cliff Richard and his backing group, I realised that I was entering a new era and that my conception of the entertainment business would never be the same again. Up to then I had presented almost every kind of artiste from the totally unknown to superstars, but I was about to present a living legend.

I was asked by Cliff's management not to release news of Cliff's impending dates at Blazers until they had an opportunity to send word of the arranged club dates' via their regular newsletter, to the fan club branches. European fan clubs were also advised and I became aware of the army of followers Cliff enjoyed all over Europe. Mindful of the response to the Shadows when their tickets had gone on sale, I made sure that I had plenty of staff on hand to answer the telephones as well as deal with customers who came to buy tickets directly over the counter.

The day for ticket sales arrived. I took morning coffee with my staff and the opportunity to again outline the modus operandi for the sale of the tickets. "We shall organise the event along the same lines as we did for the Shadows," I explained yet again. "Each customer booking a table will pay for it in full and will receive a receipt as their ticket. This will incorporate a copy of the table-plan showing the location of their seats and a miniature copy of the set menu" The staff were familiar with the menu and well versed in dealing with 'how to find us' questions.

Ten o'clock came and went, and eleven; perhaps I had been given wrong information. But could this be? After all Cliff's office was so precise and efficient. In any case I'd agreed to break the news to Blazers membership three days after the fan clubs had had their fill. My membership mail shot was ready and standing by. At eleven thirty the bubble burst and all the phones began ringing. For the next twenty-four hours, even through the night, the fans rang with their reservations - from all over the country. Despite my mini lecture in which I had reminded and advised of the potential Shadows type rush for tickets, Cliff's box office was far beyond anything I'd ever experienced. The immense following this man had took me by surprise, I was well aware of his super star status, but even knowing this did not prepare me for the avalanche of bookings that followed the news that he was to play Blazers.

Three days later when Blazers members were advised, yet another hectic day ensued, as members from all over the Home Counties clamoured for tickets. Our phone lines were constantly busy throughout this period, and our front reception desk too was bombarded by people who had decided to visit Blazers in person to secure their tickets. One gentleman asked to see me and entered my office carrying a black brief case; he then requested three thousand tickets which represented half our total capacity for the six nights.

"Five hundred seats per night" he explained "and I don't mind where they are located".

I pointed out that the fully inclusive dinner and show tickets were not cheap and therefore his request for such a large amount of tickets would be very costly.

"That is not a problem" he replied and placing the brief case on my desk in front of me, he released the catch.

The lid sprung open to reveal the contents, bundles upon bundles of bank notes neatly displayed in two layers.

"Payment in full" he said with a grin. I gulped at the sight of the loot but I turned down his
request.

"I'm sorry" I said, "but I have a policy of limiting the number of tickets per person and therefore cannot oblige you".

The man, obviously a ticket tout, was very peeved at being unable to secure his objective. After some argument as to the rights and wrongs of my policy and even an offer of a management bribe to change my mind, he slammed his brief case closed and left. To say I was not tempted to make the sale would be a lie, but I had a responsibility to the customers who visited week after week as well as a responsibility to Cliff's fans. The fact that his office took the matter of the inclusion of his fans as central to all sales, I felt could only mean that Cliff and his management cared very deeply about his fans and therefore, I ensured both sets of supporters were accommodated at least until we had sold out completely.

It took under a week to sell out and for the next five weeks up to the start of the six evening special, we had to refuse many many people, but at least we had the satisfaction of knowing that the ticket sales had been spread fairly and evenly; no one was going to be ripped off by touts.

During the run up to the opening, some of Cliff's lighting and sound crew had paid fact finding visits to Blazers. Cliff's Personal Manager David Bryce had also visited and walked the course with me in order to report back to Cliff on other logistical matters. The Cliff Richard operation was extremely thorough and each member of the team was an expert in his own field.

Cliff's entourage arrived very early in the morning to set up. Steve Rawlins, my Stage Manager, along with Garry Hunt and yours truly, were all on hand to assist with the 'get in' and offer any information that might prove helpful. I went home to lunch but instead of resting in the afternoon I returned to Blazers to find rehearsals in full swing. There on stage was the great man himself; the greatest name I was to ever play.

I met David Bryce standing at my lectern watching the rehearsal. David was a charming man with an ability to put people at their ease who organised Cliff's requirements without fuss or bother. In short an excellent person to deal with. David was also the brother of the late Dickie Bryce, better known as Dickie Valentine, who had been hugely successful for me at a time when I was establishing myself as a nightclub operator. His untimely death, in a car crash in Wales, was a great loss to the entertainment world. David signalled to Cliff and the rehearsal stopped as he led me down to the stage to introduce me.

"I'm very pleased to meet you George"

"And me you Cliff" I answered. "In fact I may never wash this hand again".

There was some laughter at this remark and then Cliff continued.

"Eddie has told me a lot about you and your club, which I must say is beautiful; it has a lovely feel about it".

I thanked him. "I hope you have a happy week with us" I said.

"I'm sure I shall. Hank and the Shads did. By the way George I've had some fan mail and I want to thank you and your staff for the way you've looked after the fans. Some of them have written to tell me of the courtesy and helpfulness they have received when phoning to book. I'm really very grateful".

"Cliff it's been a pleasure" I answered.

He returned to his rehearsing. I returned to the back of the auditorium with David.

"You know George, he meant every word he said. Cliff is very concerned that his fans are looked after".

"Funnily enough David, I sensed that from very early on," I said. "I am so honoured to have been offered the opportunity to play the great man that I would not tolerate any thing that could disrupt what I believe will be an historic week". Cliff's and David's remarks simply underlined to me what I had anticipated, and justified my attitude, and that of my staff, of treating every individual, no matter who they were or where they were from, equally; as friends.

The Cliff Richard show was absolutely superb. The audience comprised both regulars of Blazers and strangers from all over the U.K. and Europe, very appreciative of their idol and his music especially in a cabaret atmosphere, and as one fan club member told me, "I have seen Cliff hundreds of times and attended concerts all over the U.K. but I have never been so close to the stage as here at Blazers. Indeed even to sit at the back of your auditorium would put one closer to the show than the front row in most huge concert halls".

The setting, the audience and the show complimented each other for six wonderful evenings; I felt that this had been the highlight of my career to date. Cliff was charming throughout the engagement and really enjoyed working at the club. He also enjoyed being able to present a show near to his home. For most artistes traveling long distances before and after a show was a nightmare.

Cliff was also amazed that the whole business of preparing, cooking, serving and clearing away meals was completed before curtain up.

"A thousand people wined and dined before I go on" he used to say "and yet hardly an item of debris. I don't know how you do it George".

Laughter usually followed my answer, "I think I've got it right now. It's only taken me twenty years Cliff".

During this first encounter with Cliff, a respect grew between us. Perhaps it was because we were both professionals. Rod Hull once said to me; 'performers can feel the mood of an audience and if the audience have had a good evening - had been welcomed and looked after, received good food and good service, then their contentment and enjoyment could be felt on stage. Their response to the show would be much stronger and instantaneous; in short, if the job out front is performed correctly then the performance on stage becomes easier and infinitely more agreeable'.

Cliff's week was a triumph; six thousand happy people and a very happy star. I knew that some of my rivals in the business were hoping that I might fall on my face. For instance, one in particular offered Eddie Jarrett double the fee I was paying to get Cliff to appear at his club. I neither fell on my face nor did the financial inducement shake the integrity and friendship of Eddie, and an added bonus was the friendship which grew between Cliff and myself over future years.

*   *   *   *   *   *   *

Following another hugely successful year we again decided to enjoy an end of year Caribbean holiday. Iris Williams was starring on the Q.E.2 and, after a short break, was rejoining the ship at its stopover in Barbados. This provided us with an opportunity to invite Clive and Iris to join us so that at least for once Pam and I could play host to them and reciprocate for the many time we had enjoyed hospitality at their home.

I was delighted to see that Iris was so busy at this but this of course meant that Clive was more demanding and, sometimes, more unreasonable than ever. They flew in a day before the arrival of the Q.E.2 and we whisked them from the airport to our hotel, where we had arranged a suite for them, and dinner at Reid's; a superb restaurant.

However; all was not well. Clive had a disagreement with the hotel manager upon their arrival, which had, apparently, led to an ugly scene. I was asked to call to see the Manager, which I did, to be told that Mr. Brandy was an unwelcome guest and that to have such an obnoxious friend was beyond his comprehension. I made some feeble excuse about Clive being an eccentric millionaire egg farmer from Hampshire and that his bark was worse than his bite. The Hotel Manager was not impressed and asked me to refrain from booking any other friends into his hotel in future. The following day, Clive and Iris were required to vacate their suite by midday; as was normal. Clive, who was furious that the hotel Manager had called me in to complain about the booking, dragged his feet and by 1.00 p.m. the suite had still not been vacated although Pam and I, Iris and Clive had agreed to go out for the afternoon and end the day with dinner on the QE2 with the Captain.

When Pam and I met Clive and Iris in the foyer as arranged there was a hell of a row going on between Clive and the hotel officials probably sparked off by Clive's late departure from the suite. Mercifully the row was just ending as Pam and I entered the foyer.

"You will please ensure that you do not request a suite at this hotel at any time in the future" bellowed the Reception Manager. Almost on cue, Clive pointed out to sea. The Reception windows of the foyer offered an excellent view of St. James bay.

"There's my suite my man, just coming round the corner. Who needs you and your hotel" boomed Clive.

The QE2 was passing the headland on its way to dock at Bridgetown and looked magnificent as she glided by. That evening we made our way to the docks to take Clive and Iris on board and dine with the Captain. As my little hire car turned into the port area we caught sight of the mighty ship, all lit up and looking even more majestic.

"Oh" I said. "That is beautiful".

"Well George it's not much, but its home" joked Iris with one of her famous quips.

"Thank God it's not our home," grunted Clive "someone left all the bloody lights on"!

Dinner at the Captain's table was a splendid affair, Iris was the star guest at the table, which apart from the Captain, Pam and I, Iris and Clive also included an English MP and his Wife and a Lord and Lady somebody. Following an excellent dinner and an entertaining and interesting after dinner discussion, Pam and I bade our goodbyes and took our leave. We didn't want the liner to depart with us still on board , did we? (Or did we?)

I feel that I can describe my feelings on life at this time as great contentment. I was at the peak of my profession and enjoyed great pride in my achievements. I enjoyed excellent health, a happy and stable home life and worked for an excellent company whose chairman, Pat Cowan, was both a marvelous boss and close friend. My previous marriages to Roberta Heron and Joanne Gabillet had both ended in divorce and had left me sceptical of marriage, but I was very lucky to have met Pam Robinson and find the happiness of a home life that I thought I may never have. We lived together for almost eleven years before marrying at the Maidenhead Registry Office on a bright sunny day in November 1984. Our reception was at the Hinds Head at Bray, a gift from Pat and his Wife Molly. I had packed over forty guests into a room that barely seated thirty, and the marvelous relationship between my three children and Pam's three children was a real blessing. All six attended and seemed to get along with each other just fine.

Pam and I acquired a lease to an apartment in Monte Carlo and set up a holiday home there. The little studio flat on the Avenue Princess Grace belonged to Susan and Allan Blackburn and when the Blackburn's announced their intention to move to a larger apartment there was a race to buy the lease between Pam and I and Petula Clarke and Claude Wolfe, and they were favorites. I arranged the finance through Lombard North Central so that when the phone rang one afternoon and Allan told us that Pet and Claude had decided to by a boat instead of an apartment we were able to complete the deal in record time.

Following our wedding at Maidenhead, I arranged a second bash in Monte Carlo a week later, which included a Wedding Blessing at the church there and a reception at the Hotel Beach Plaza. The guests included Vince and Ann Hill, Clive and Iris Williams, Jim Smith and Jackie his Wife, Steve Rutland and Ruth, Susan and Allan Blackburn, Molly and Emma Cowan, Rod Johnson and Joan, Chick Murphy and Tracey Terry and Janet Mabey and Elizabeth Ferguson and Pedro. After dinner we adjourned to the Monte Carlo Casino where Clive had an amazing piece of good luck. He placed a substantial amount of money on number fourteen on a roulette table and it came up, paying him thirty-five to one. He won enough money to pay for the christening of their son Blake and a party afterwards. Pam and I, Sue and Allan and Ruth and Steve officiated as Godparents.

At Blazers one successful year followed another and Pam and I took a fortnight in the Caribbean each January following the end of the busy Christmas season. Coupled with our summer break in Monte Carlo life was very sweet indeed. During the second half of my term at Blazers, having established the club and with it my credentials, I became a leading light in the entertainment industry celebrated and admired wherever I went.

As active members of the Variety Club, the world-renowned children's charity, we attended lavish banquets and balls. Members of the Variety Club are called Barkers and membership of this great organisation meant, amongst other things, supporting as many of the organisations fund raising events as possible. Pam and I supported most such events, often taking parties of friends. The annual Royal Variety Performance and historic film premieres of E.T., Gandhi and many others were all part of our social diary. We never missed Royal Ascot week and our annual attendance at Epsom for Derby Day was guaranteed. We moved with ease in the high society of those days but I never forgot where I came from or my obligation to work and my customers who, ultimately, made my interesting and exciting lifestyle possible.

Having now done the right thing, as they say, and tied the knot, I decided to make our first wedding anniversary very special by taking Pam to New York and Atlantic City. It was to be a 'there and back' scenario because of pressure of work at the club, which was booming at this time. I discussed my plans with Pat who thought it a great idea but was not overjoyed to hear of my intention to cross the Atlantic and return within a few days. I explained to Pat the reasons for being unable to extend my Stateside visit, and as owner of the club he understood more than anyone why I could only take a short break. He asked me to call by the office the following day and I did as requested whereupon he thrust two Concorde tickets into my hand. "I've spoken to your travel agent Lou Berlin and changed your flight arrangements Georgie," said Pat. "If you must fly the Atlantic and return within three or four days at least do it with style and a certain amount of speed". After a short pause he concluded by saying "Oh and by the way the flights are on me - an anniversary present".

I was gob smacked at Pat's generosity and I let him know in no uncertain terms. My love of flying was well known. As well as having flown in almost every sort of plane ever made, I had also taken a trip in a hot air balloon and a glider flight above the Dunstable Downs. But to fly Concorde, this comparatively new supersonic airliner - the pride of Britain and France - must be the ultimate; and it was.

The thrill of soaring away at supersonic speed, the oddity of arriving in the U.S. before leaving the U.K. and the sheer luxury of the whole flight are fond memories we shall treasure forever, We stayed at the Waldorf Astoria and had an anniversary dinner at Emsley Palace. The following day I hired a Cadillac and drove Pam to Atlantic City the Las Vegas of the Eastern seaboard. We wined and dined in the very best restaurants that Atlantic City had to offer where our accommodation at Caesars Palace was a sumptuous suite. So many wonderful occasions; so many wonderful memories. The Blazers years saw the fruition of my career from the seeds sown many years ago at Cesars of Luton, where my show business journey had begun.

During the Blazers decade there were inevitably sad events too, as well as joy and satisfaction. I had my share of sadness and anguish. My much loved Stepfather, Fred, passed away and my beloved Mother a short time afterwards. Their passing filled my Stepbrother Albert and I with grief but I could take comfort in the knowledge that they had lived to see both of us 'set up and settled' as Mum would say.

Another tragedy during these Blazers years was the death from cancer of Jean Stanley, Mother of my Son James. He joined Pam, her daughter Jayne and me at Windsor. I was further saddened by the loss of dear friends Ronnie Dukes, Rickie Lee and Tommy Cooper. Ronnie Dukes died while working a summer season in the Channel isles. All of us that knew Ronnie well knew that unless he learnt to slow down he was sure to harm himself by the way he worked on stage. He was a stout man, but during his high-powered show he would sing dance and generally leap about the stage like a teenager. He put everything into his show and paid the ultimate price. Rickie Lee, his adorable wife, died very soon after of a broken heart.

Tommy died of a heart attack on stage at Her Majesty's Theatre London, performing his part of the weekly T.V. production 'Live at Her Majesty's'. I recorded the show; I recorded all of Tommy's appearances as he was the only comic that could make me laugh uncontrollably. Tommy took me aside one day. "I hear you video my T.V. shows," he said. "Listen" he continued, drawing me a little closer and dropping his voice to a whisper. "If you ever see me get a laugh phone me". Such was Tommy's wonderfully silly humour.

As I watched the last show, Tommy began his ladder, sledgehammer and other monstrous items from the handbag routine. Suddenly he sank to his knees and I knew that this was the end of a comic giant; a great artiste and a very dear friend.

Another wonderful friend, Susan Blackburn, also had a brush with death. An had an ache in her arm, which virtually prevented her from using it, she reported the ailment to Pam who took her to a specialist. A tumour was discovered, very close to a major heart organ, to close to enable an operation on it. Chemotherapy was administered but without much enthusiasm or anticipation of success. Thankfully all was not lost. No one had allowed for the fighting spirit and determination of a very ill but incredibly strong willed lady called Susan Blackburn.

Just when her case seemed like a lost cause, Susan got out of bed saying, "I refuse to die. I enjoy life far too much and I'm nowhere near ready to go. So there". She battled her way back to health, a battle she won convincingly to our great relief.

Towards the end of my term at Cesars I found myself flattered by offers of employment by many of our competitors, which as recorded led me firstly to Wales and later to Windsor and Blazers. Now at the pinnacle of my career one would have thought that similar offers would have been received, but this was not the case. Perhaps headhunters assumed that the cost of dislodging me would be too great, or perhaps Blazers Windsor and I were regarded as inseparable. I suspect however the real reason was the early signs of a decline within our industry. The signs were hard to detect, but they were there. The loss of casino revenues because of the 1970 Gaming Act which previously did much to subsidise entertainment had been one factor. The rising costs of operating in a fairly labour intensive industry was another, and of course the rising cost of artiste fees, driven up by a system of 'dutch auctioning' by club owners, where the artiste played for the highest bidder was another. The club scene had shrunk considerably by the late 1980's and some of the remaining traders trimmed costs by reducing the number of evenings the clubs opened. Offers from other would be employers were therefore not forthcoming and indeed not sought. Suggestions of a different nature were made from time to time, even though I felt at home and happy with my situation.

Throughout this period, people who had known me for many years often asked me whether I'd ever considered owning my own club. Invariably my reply was to dismiss the possibility because of my contentment at Blazers and lack of finance. Friends and colleagues often pointed out that a person with the experience contacts and credentials that I had, could easily raise the necessary finance. But I still resisted the temptation.

I am a person who has always preferred the comfort of my own home and would only go visiting when invited or for a specific occasion. Chic Murphy my neighbour called me one afternoon and asked me to visit his house before going to the club as he had prepared contracts for both the Three Degrees and the Platters for signature. I had negotiated and agreed to play both acts as part of our forthcoming entertainment programme.

Wintergarden House was a hive of activity with the usual comings and goings of various people. Our business was quickly concluded in Chic's office, which apart from anything else, had a great view of the River Thames. The grounds of his home gently sloped away to the edge of the river and a medium sized motor cruiser called "Tres-Chic" bobbed gently at his mooring. Chick had made considerable improvements to the property since moving there from West Drayton and I took the opportunity to congratulate him.

"I'm still not happy," he said. "The fact is my gardener is no good - he's a bit like the six million dollar man; barely alive".

"Why don't you use my man Patrick Ryan?" I suggested. "He's a hard working Irishman with vast experience, drives his own van and has all his own equipment".

"Next time you see him send him to see me" said Chick obviously pleased with the recommendation. Just then the office door opened and in walked Robert Herbert Chic's Accountant. Chic introduced me to him.

"I'm very pleased to meet you," said the Accountant. "Chic has told me a lot about you".

Bob Herbert was a charming man of about my age and unlike any accountant I'd ever met, nothing like the usual perception of a 'grey man'. In fairness I can't think why I most people have this opinion. Ivor Bending, Victor Silverstone and Russell de Fries, all accountants that I had come to know over the years, were far from dull and boring. However it must be said that the large accountancy firms, many of which were customers of mine at organized parties, really did fit the unflattering description to a tee.

Bob's stylish dress and easy going manner gave the impression of a well-educated salesman rather than a man of figures. After a conversation including jokes and banter I left, but not before inviting Bob to visit Blazers for one of our shows.

That chance meeting was to have a major influence on my future. Bob and his wife Anne visited Blazers shortly afterwards and quickly became firm friends of my wife and myself and, along with Chic and his wife Tracy, we spent many happy hours in restaurants such as La Taverna, The Thatched Inn and Jade Fountain. I also included Bob and Anne in most of the Royal Command performance evenings and other West End showbiz gatherings. Bob took to show business and to show people like a duck to water and was clearly fascinated by it all. As well as looking after Chic's showbiz accounts, he also became accountant to Iris Williams. To his credit, he never tried to sell himself to the show people he met. None of us realised, but he had higher goals and he was going to achieve them.

Meanwhile I told Patrick Ryan, my gardener, that Wintergarden House was seeking a gardener. I told him that the owner was the Manager of both the Three Degrees and the Platters knowing that Patrick would not be able to resist the opportunity of gardening for him. I used to give Patrick an occasional free invitation to Blazers - he loved it and became totally star struck. I once introduced him to Irish star Brendan Shine and he nearly swooned. I also on another occasion introduced him to Frank Carson and he did swoon.

I forgot about the gardening introduction until Chic called to thank me for the recommendation. "He's excellent," he said with satisfaction. Driving past the studios at Bray a few days later I spotted Patrick's van outside a large house. As I drew closer, I caught sight of a large green notice board that leaned against the gatepost. I must say I really laughed because there in bold white letters were the words 'Patrick Ryan Esquire, gardener to the stars'.

Another three Royal nights at the club included the annual Princess Royal evening on behalf of the Windsor Horse Trials and Riding for the Disabled. A Princess Alexandra night for one of the many special charities of which she was patron and a Prince Phillip evening on behalf of the Horse Drawn Carriages Fund. The closed circuit big screen showing of the Hagler v Hem Boxing Championship from Las Vegas by satellite was a real feather in our cap. The event began with dinner, followed by cabaret, followed by the boxing, shown on three massive screens which offered an unrestricted view from all parts of the club. The evening was a complete sell-out. My mate Geoff

Petts was building a very successful business in the satellite field in those days, when the whole concept was in its infancy.

Also about this time Arlene Phillips presented an act called 'Hot Gossip'. The group of scantily clad and very sexy dancers hit our T.V. screens via the Kenny Everett show and their erotic dancing fired the imagination of the nation. The summer was always a bad time for clubs. To begin with the big box office attractions were away in summer seasons and at Holiday Camps. Also we suffered from an audience triple whammy e.g.:

(a) People were feverishly saving up to go on holiday or

(b) They were already on holiday or

(c) They had returned from holiday broke

Either way June, July and August were usually a bad time for our industry. I asked Jimmy to get me a week of Hot Gossip and sold out all seven nights. This sell out week was unlike any other in that it attracted a young audience of eighteen to thirty years old. They were not diners as such, but were happy to purchase admission only tickets and once inside around thirty per cent would eat one-course snack meals. All were happy to watch the show, drink and dance until the small hours of the morning. It had not escaped my attention that these youngsters were not part of the great holiday tradition. Many spent their leave from college, university or work meeting up with pals for days and nights out in their localities. So I went after the youth market and arranged through Jimmy Smith to play a whole summer season of attractions that included Sister Sledge, Sad Cafe, Womack and Womack, Imagination and many others. I topped this off with a four week run of Hot Gossip. This gave me one of the best summer seasons I ever had.

Another triumph was the twenty-fifth anniversary celebration tour of The Shadows. I took a three-week, twenty-one-night season. The Shadows Silver Tour, as it became known, was a total success, but none more so than the Blazers date. The fans were fully familiar with the closeness and intimacy of seeing their idols at the club as opposed to huge concert centers. In three weeks we catered for twenty-one thousand people, the fans came from all over Europe, some of them attended the show twenty-one times.

The Stylistics, David Essex, a sixties show comprising Dave Berry and the Cruisers, Dave Dee and Marmalade and The Searchers and a parade of comics, all made for a comprehensive programme of summer entertainment. One matter that gave me cause for concern was the lack of new stars coming through. True there was no shortage of talent, our New for You entertainment academy proved that, but without the break of a T.V. slot, the unknown remained unknown outside our locality. Opportunity Knocks had long gone and there was no other a creditable vehicle to launch new talent on the road to stardom.

Lew Lewis, Mick Miller, Tony Dowling, Charlie Smithers, Mike Terry, Johnny Hachet, David Copperfield and an unending list of others were all sensational comedians, guaranteed to brighten up any dull day and all did well. But that big T.V. break was not forthcoming.

There was however, one exception. A young good-looking comedian called Duncan Norvelle. Duncan had a style all of his own and his 'chase me chase me' routine in which he assumed the attitude of a gay and chased various male customers around the room was hilarious. He got a break by appearing on a 'Live at Her Majesty's' T.V. show and his style and presentation were an instant hit. In addition he had a T.V. face, a term I use to explain why some people on T.V. come over that much better than others.

I saw in Duncan a new star in the making. His show relied on a great deal of audience participation which I saw as perfect for a Christmas season when the audience was made up almost entirely of party bookings. Taking the bull by the horns, I signed Duncan for a three week Christmas run and although I arranged the dates in the February of that year some ten months prior to Christmas, I felt that Duncan would become better known as we went through that year. I was somewhat wrong footed however, as Duncan climbed the ladder to stardom with amazing speed and I held a contract for the three-week season for a phenomenally low fee.

What I was to pay per week for Duncan he was already earning per night. I was concerned that because the difference in fees was so great, he might baulk at the prospect and decline to play the dates, even though a contract had been signed. In similar circumstances, artistes had been known to 'go ill' or find a way out of honouring an obligation under contract. I suggested to Pat that it would be worth our while arranging a short holiday for Duncan and his girl friend Tina in Monte Carlo. Pam and I had planned our usual mid summer break and we could take them with us. Pat agreed, and that Summer the four of us descended on Monte for what turned out to be an enjoyable vacation which brought us closer together and, at the end of it, I knew that Duncan would not let us down at Christmas. I was proved to be correct.

Suggestions that I ought to set up a club of my own continued to be made by various people. Roy and Mavis Marsh used to visit me almost every Sunday evening. They had a very successful Fish and Chip business in Newbury, Berkshire, and since they closed every Sunday and Monday they arranged a Sunday night out at Blazers most weeks. They had been customers of mine for almost twenty years and become good friends. I often joined them for a chat at the end of their evening and Ray often mentioned that although a business of my own was long overdue, he erred on the side of caution.

"Things ain't what they used to be out there," Roy would say. "Running a business these days can be tough. It's important to choose the right business, pay the right price for it and choose the right location".

I remained unimpressed with the proposition of owning my own club, despite continuous urging by friends and colleagues.

The nearest I got to actually setting up a business which would at least be partly my own, came when I became involved in a secret proposal put to me by Allan Blackburn. For some time Alan had been thinking of putting together a major operation in Los Angeles. London had its Talk of the Town, Paris its Lido or Moulin Rouge, but Los Angeles had no major show room and Allan, quite rightly in my view, felt that there was a definite need for such an operation.

Allan found premises through a contact of his, a Mr. Nick Vanhoff, who was part owner of Columbia Studios. They had premises on a parking lot on Sunset Boulevard that turned out to be a three thousand seater called the Hollywood Palladium. They bought the site for the parking lot and some adjacent facilities for the construction of a hotel but had no interest in retaining the Palladium and sought to dispose of it.

I was invited to do a feasibility study as part of a plan which would be put forward to a party of private investors who would finance the purchase and refurbishment of the premises, then Allan and I would go in as a partnership, Allan organising the show side of the business and me the marketing and catering. The prospect of organising a three thousand-seater dining room fired my imagination. It was a challenging prospect which I viewed with relish. Meanwhile, under the guise of a stateside holiday, Pam and I flew to L.A. and met up with the Blackburns. I presented the feasibility study to Allan, who seemed quite pleased with its findings.

Allan had managed to assemble a number of interested investors and it seemed that the venture was certain to go ahead. We met with Nick Vanhoff and visited the Hollywood Palladium, which although in some need of repair and refurbishment was still very impressive. The magnificent two tier room offered an unrestricted view of the stage and proscenium. The configuration was perfect and since the building stood on a large parking lot, parking was obviously not a problem. Our visit to the Palladium, followed by drinks at Nick's Beverley Hills home and then dinner at a Hollywood Restaurant, seemed to set the seal on a deal. Allan negotiated throughout, using his vast experience and knowledge of both the business and the American location. The finance was almost in place. So sure were we that the proposition would go ahead that Pam and I started to look at accommodation prospects should we have to sell up and move from Windsor to L.A.

The whole plan remained secret for obvious reasons but on our return to England I was so convinced that the move to the United States was imminent that I began to practice my resignation speech. Breaking the news to Pat was certainly not going to be easy. However two major set backs were to occur which sank the proposal. The investors were all English based with the exception of one American based in Los Angeles. At the eleventh hour, the Los Angeles investor changed his mind and it seemed his contribution was pivotal as far as the other investors were concerned. Once he became a non-starter the others dropped out one by one.

The second disastrous event, which took me totally by surprise, was to see Pat Cowan totally devastated by the break up of his marriage. I was unaware that there was even a problem between him and his wife Molly, but she had found another guy and had decided to leave Pat.

To say Pat loved Molly would be an understatement. He adored her. So strong were his feelings for her that the break up almost totally destroyed him and I feared that he might do something serious. In a way I was glad that the L.A. deal had fallen through as it was to me that Pat turned for help. It was my shoulder he cried on and I could never have gone ahead with my resignation and would have had to let Allan and everyone else down. I could not have let down the man who built Blazers and gave me the chance to run it; a man who treated me and my family as his own and given us such staunch support. No; now he needed us and we would not fail him.

However, molly's departure was a turning point in my life as well as Pats and two years of turmoil were about to begin.

16

DEMIS ROUSSOS REVISITED

FREDDIE STARR'S BIRTHDAY PARTY

LEO SAYER AND ROY ORBISON

PAT'S FAMILY CRISIS BEGINS TO TAKE ITS TOLL

THE BIG YIN AND THE BOUNCING CHEQUE

A ROYAL NIGHT WITH PRINCE PHILLIP

ENTER BOB HERBERT WITH GLOSS

GLOSS BECOMES BROSS

I BECOME ANXIOUS ABOUT THE FUTURE

JOHN MILLS TELEPHONES

As if the aggravation of Pat's marriage and family crisis was not enough to cope with, while at the same time running the business for him, my stress levels were further increased by the arrival of Demis Roussos for a couple of dates as part of my Autumn line up. I remember when Jimmy Smith offered him to me remarking how reasonable his fee was. It had hardly increased since the days of his success at Cesars of Luton.

"I think it's because he uses less musicians these days" said Jimmy.

Jimmy was wrong; Demis Roussos did not use any musicians. He arrived with three men who pretended to play while he sang to recorded music through an elaborate sound system complete with a sound engineer. While I understood that this kind of presentation was quite acceptable in certain parts of the world, it was definitely not acceptable in England. I knew that unless an event advertised with the words 'backing by recorded music', an English audience would feel cheated and would let us know their feelings in no uncertain terms.

This is all I needed I thought, as my eyes viewed the high tech music centre installed at the back of the auditorium. I immediately confronted Demis regarding the whole unacceptable situation pointing out that had I had been informed when the deal to bring him to Blazers was struck, I could at least have made sure that our advertising reflected the fact that the musical backing was recorded rather than live. Privately I thought that had I known at the time of discussing the deal I would not have booked him. With the audience due to arrive in an hour or so, a strategy had to be worked out to get Blazers and me off the hook. No one was going to blame the fat Greek; it would be me that would bear the displeasure of the unhappy audience.

Maybe it was my Greek background that persuaded Demis to listen to my suggestions, some Hellenic affinity that obliged him to take on board my advice. I will never know, but he saved the situation, and got me off the hook in the process.

"After your first number, take time out to thank the audience for buying your records and giving you your success in the U.K."I told him. Demis listened carefully. "Point out" I continued, "That to recreate the sound of your records requires forty musicians and that this would make the show far too expensive and set ticket prices at unaffordable levels. Tell them that in order to recreate the sounds that they have come to love and enjoy, tonight you will use the assistance of tapes for your show etc. etc". I concluded by telling him that without this statement early in the proceedings we could be in for a heap of trouble.

Demis came on singing one of his well known numbers and it soon dawned on the audience that the trio behind the singer was not creating that huge orchestral backing. Little did they know that the trio was not providing any backing at all? At the end of his first number, Demis standing at the microphone in his colourful kaftan, gushed forth pretty well word for word the agreed statement, adding the extra cosmetic dressing of telling the audience of his love of Britain and the British people and so on. A round of applause and the situation saved.

Well we had got away with it; but I realised just how very lucky we were. It was not only that our star turn up with backing tapes, but the execution of his performance to recorded music was so badly done. The singer and his engineer were hardly ever 'in sinc' with each other and there were a number of false starts and numerous other errors in the performance. I was never so relieved to get to the end of a show. For me the Singing Frock became the Singing Schmuck.

For some unknown reason Roussos did not use the patter we had so carefully worked out when appearing at Cesars of Luton a short time later. The lack of an explanation resulted in a customer riot and a considerable amount of refunding.

The revisit of Demis Roussos was closely followed by a revisit of my dear friend Rod Hull with his famous Emu for another of my famous Sunday Lunch shows. During a conversation with Rod he called my attention to a comedy version of the Twelve Days of Christmas, a send up of the traditional version. This took the shape of a series of letters purportedly written by one Agnes Fullbody to her lover each time she received a gift from him. The language was bawdy and the swearing intense, but it was one of the funniest pieces of send up comedy I'd ever read. Rod told me that a fellow Australian had given him the ode, which he also found very amusing.

"I'm glad you like it too. I thought you would," he said.

"Like it, I bloody love it" I replied. "In fact Rod, I'd love to take a copy of it".

"Of course you can" he said and passed the written piece to me.

I cherished that photocopy and decided to 'dirty it up' by adding more outrageous words and making it even more filthy. Little did I know it was going to come in handy at an upcoming birthday party?

Leon Fisk, formerly of the Dallas Boys and now Freddie Starr's Manager, told me of a birthday party he was organising for Freddie at the Centurion Restaurant at Windlesham. He invited Pam and I but insisted that admittance to the bash was by 'party piece' only. Leon had ensured that a bevy of Pro's (artistes) who had a tale to tell or a song to sing were invited and I pondered as to what I could do for my party piece when the time came. Surely as a mere night club manager I could not be expected to contribute anything of artistic value in such illustrious company. Fate once again came to my aid.

The Twelve Days of Christmas lay on my dressing table, having undergone a literary refurbishment since being given to me by Rod Hull. I picked up the document and read it through again. It made me laugh; and I had read it several times. This might just work I thought. The night of Freddie's birthday party arrived. It was a late affair, an after show bash to allow working artistes to get to the Centurion after work. I arrived with Pam at about midnight and Leon was the first to welcome us.

"I hope you've brought your party piece" said he. I made no reply and simply smiled, but deep down I knew he meant it. No one not even a night club manager was exempt.

I decided my best course of action, in order to avoid having to perform when my turn came, was to get quite drunk and be judged incapable of making any kind of coherent contribution to the proceedings. We all consumed copious amounts of food and wine and the party really got under way, fun packed from the very beginning as the Pro's queued up to do their party pieces, all of which were very entertaining. Del Derrick, my compere, sang a ditty and Clive Brandy recited a poem. Both ditty and poem were of the X rated variety and hilarious. Leon's very own 'Lad in a betting shop doorway' was a classic and received with raucous laughter and so the night roiled on.

The amount of wine I consumed made me pleasantly inebriated, but in doing so had the opposite effect on me to what I had intended. Instead of making me incapable of performing, the alcoholic gave me Dutch courage and I looked forward to being called upon. At last Leon got up and called me to perform my party piece to hoots and jeers from the gathered company. I am sure Leon, and for that matter Freddie and the others, all expected me to get to my feet and make some feeble apology and at best make a wise crack before sitting down again. To everyone's astonishment I rose and said OK and began making my way to the end of the room in order to have a view of all.

The restaurant was dimly lit and I decided that the only way I could possibly read anything was to stand on a chair underneath a wall light. This I did, and once in position I took my spectacles from my pocket and gazed down upon my audience, who by now had fallen into a silence of anticipation.

"I will now perform for you the Twelve Days of Christmas" I boomed "A new version" I added.

I withdrew the script from my pocket and began to read from it, slowly unfolding the very naughty story. Because I was quite drunk, I took my time lest I should lose my way, the result was that I accidentally found perfect timing and was able to emphasise the key parts of the story to achieve maximum impact. Every pornographic point was greeted with raucous laughter. I had them rolling in the proverbial aisles and, on finishing, received a standing ovation. Leon stood and as soon as he'd restored order addressed the partygoers.

"Ladies and Gentlemen" he began. "We have been treated to a piece of comedy genius and I don't think there is one of us here that would care to follow that". The remark was greeted by nods of agreement.

"George" he concluded, "you have truly stopped the show". Guest after guest came over to congratulate me and my contribution was the topic of conversation for the rest of the party.

Chubby Oats, a wonderfully funny comedian from the North of England and a long time friend of Freddie, asked me if he could use the Twelve Days in his stage act.

"Of course you can" said I. "I'm not a Pro. I have no use for it".

"You could have fooled me" he replied.

Blazers continued to present the very best in entertainment for its legions of customers. Through my good friend Allan Field I managed to secure the services of Leo Sayer for a first time appearance at the club; a booking that proved very popular indeed. Roy Orbison made a very welcome return to the U.K. and played a week at Blazers to capacity audiences. Roy was now managed by his brother, who incidentally, was a dead ringer for Roy; in fact they could almost pass for twins. Unfortunately this date would be the last that Roy would play for me and the last time I would see him alive. His untimely death was a shock to us all.

Chas and Dave, The Grumbleweeds, Mike Reid, Hale and Pace, Jim Davidson, Des O'Connor and many other top stars continued to sparkle at Blazers. Yet while they did so, unknown to them, the crisis of Pat Cowan's marriage collapse and its effect on him continued to be a source of continuing worry to me.

The effect it was having on Pat manifested itself in many ways. His reasoning, thinking and work were undermined. His love for Molly was such that the split was an impossible situation for Pat, one with which he could not cope. It became clear to me that unless he could overcome the trauma he felt, his empire would crash around him as it eroded his grip on business. I could see this clearly and desperately tried talking to him about it. Of all his executive employees it was me he continued to turn to for advice and consolation. A bond of mutual respect and trust had grown between us over the years, but despite long nights and days of discussion nothing I could say or do seemed to console him.

Because Pat was a fairly private person, almost a recluse, very few people knew of his anguish. The showbiz fraternity was certainly the last to know. As far as the stars, their agents and managers were concerned, Blazers was as solid as a rock. Blazers had become a showbiz institution. Soon however, the rock was to turn to sand.

Through Jimmy Smith and Mel Bush I secured a week of Billy Connolly known to many as the Big Yin. This was another Blazers first and was going to be a big date, a very big date. I will always remember it as the date that marked the beginning of the end of my association with Pat and Blazers of Windsor.

People who experience personal tragedy react in different ways. Some have been known to turn to drink or drugs; others have turned to gambling or even ended their lives. Pat Cowan found peace and solace in the Casino society of London and his business interests declined because of a lack of personal supervision. Only Blazers stood as the one business that he could rely on, the only business that continued to prosper.

Having had a watching brief at Cesars Luton Casino, I was well aware that if Pat continued with his newly acquired habit, he would wind up broke. He began to telephone the club to ask me to bring him the cash element of that evening's takings, saying be would reimburse with his personal cheque the following morning. Despite his assurances, the opposite was taking place. We were only banking credit card receipts and cheque's while more and more cash was being used by the boss to fund his habit. I tried to discuss the matter with him but usually received the sharp edge of his tongue for my trouble except for one time when he at least gave me a reason for his habit.

One morning at around two we were having breakfast at the Casanova. I had been summoned to bring more cash from Windsor and tried again to broach the subject of his gambling.

"If you don't mind me saying so Sir" I began, "I really do think that it may be a good idea to start easing up on the gambling".

"What do you mean" came the stiff reply.

"Well Sir the fact is I'm worried about the knock on effect on your businesses and although I know better than anyone what you've been through this is not the answer".

I waited for the blast. "Georgie" said Pat sharply, "what I do with my money is of no concern to anyone".

Fair enough Sir" I answered hurriedly, my bottle gone completely. "I hope you didn't mind me mentioning my concern,"

I thought that was the end of the conversation when suddenly Pat, after a short silence said,

"Look Georgie, I know you mean well but you must try and understand. I can't sleep, I can't find peace. I can't live a normal life. I am continually lonely all day and all night; except in the casino. It's the only place I find any sort of companionship, a friendship between fellow punters. A sort of camaraderie of winners and losers that takes my mind off things for a while.

I found his explanation sad but I understood what he was trying say. I also realised at that moment that there was going to be no way back for Pat; we had lost him. Roughly a week after Billy Connelly's appearance at the club I received a phone call from Jimmy Smith telling me that the Mel Bush office were unhappy at having to represent Billy's cheque. It had 'bounced'.

"Is everything alright at Blazers?" enquired Jimmy.

"Oh yes" I replied. "Pat has probably bought another building and as usual has forgotten to replace the cash by transfer".

Jimmy was well aware that Pat used to buy and sell property and make a great deal of money by doing so. The story was accepted by Jimmy, who presumably, would pass the information to Mel Bush.

As soon as I finished my telephone conversation with Jimmy I phoned our accountant Victor Silverstone for an explanation.

"I knew there were insufficient funds there" said Victor, "but the Boss told me he was arranging a transfer from the property company the same day as I had issued the cheque".

My first reaction to this information was to realise that my excuse to Jimmy was not all that far removed from the truth. Victor went on to tell me that the cheque would not be met on representation because the funds were still not there and there appeared to be precious little money in the property account.

"It seems our man" said Victor "has been taking money out in fairly large quantities, over and above the cash he's taking from the club."

He confirmed what deep down I already knew. Pat was on the slide and bills were not being paid. Victor had only just spotted the problem. My worst suspicions were confirmed. It would not be long before alarm bells would start to ring throughout the showbiz world. It was imperative that Victor and I met secretly to discuss the crisis. We did, that very afternoon at my home.

On comparing notes, Victor and I discovered that Pat's finances were far from good. It seemed that as well as hijacking the club's nightly takings, he was also drawing money on his other companies. Obviously he still had major assets, but his drift towards the total addiction of gambling had to be halted or he could go on to lose everything. I told Victor of my efforts to pull him back from the edge and my failure to do so. Our meeting ended on a rather gloomy note.

Bob Herbert, the accountant who had become my close friend, heard on the grapevine that I had taken a short term loan from Chic Murphy to make sure the Billy Connelly cheque was honored. (Such was Pats distraction that I borrowed and repaid loan without his knowledge). He suggested that with the build up of recent problems it really was time for me to move on and acquire my own premises.

"I really could not afford my own club Bob," I reiterated. "I don't have that kind of money".

"Money should not be a problem," replied Bob. "You have a house, therefore you have collateral, and with a combination of brewery finance and Bank assistance I'm sure I could cobble together sufficient funds to put you into your own premises" he insisted.

I have to say that the idea of leaving Blazers to run my own operation was beginning to appeal to me. Every day new problems reared their ugly heads. Rumbles of discontent from suppliers were becoming quite common; the gambling continued and I received word from Victor that assets were being sold or mortgaged.

The next major event at the club was a Royal Gala Night at which His Royal Highness the Duke of Edinburgh would be guest of honour. We offered a guarantee of £20,000 for Prince Phillip's charity fund and although the date was some way off I was becoming apprehensive as to whether we would be able to come up with the money for H.R.H. The night was a sell out and already the sponsors of tables were paying large sums of money in advance but it was being hijacked. I decided to mount a covert operation to secure our charity donation without my boss finding out.

In Blazers foyer stood two fruit machines and I was the only person that had keys to them. I never set a regular day for emptying them; sometimes I left them for two weeks before opening them and banking the takings. They averaged approximately two hundred and fifty pounds per week between them. I decided to empty them at fairly regular intervals and changed the coins into notes, placing them in a dated envelope back in the machine drawer, instead of my banking bag. This was the start of my Prince Phillip fund and although this covert operation stretched over several months, no one at head office detected the absence of the fruit machine takings during this period.

The night was a great success, a prestige event for the club, which by now had acquired the sobriquet 'the place that entertained Royalty'. The following morning I opened the fruit machines and extracted the envelopes from each machine. I had managed to save an incredible £14,000. I added the raffle proceeds from the royal night itself, a further £4000 and £2000 from the takings. I then arranged for a Banker's draft to be drawn for £20,000 and dispatched it to Windsor Castle without delay. I arranged to meet Pat at the office that afternoon knowing that I had to face him and explain my covert activities and the results. He looked tired and unkempt. Inwardly I cursed his ex-wife for what she had done to him. "How was it last night?" he asked. He seldom attended any functions at the club these days.

"It was excellent," I answered. "In fact a triumph for the club I'd say".

I proceeded to give Pat a run down of events that had taken place during the evening, but while trying to show real interest I felt he was far removed from our conversation. It was as if he or at least his mind was elsewhere. Suddenly he asked,

"How much did we guarantee Prince Phillip?"

"£20, 000" I replied.

"Well I think he may have to wait a while" Pat retorted a touch disparagingly.

"I've already sent the amount in full to his office" I said and waited for the reaction.

"What do you mean you've paid the sum in full - how could you" asked Pat, who now seemed to have mentally returned to the conversation and had a look of real interest on his face. Whilst I was obviously pleased at Pat's reaction to the covert money raising exercise, I was nevertheless astounded that he the Boss was not in the least embarrassed by the fact that one of his employees, had had to make such a provision. Even more importantly, surely he must have known the reason I felt compelled to do it and yet it did not seem to bother him at all.

I still admired the man, whom I had faithfully served for ten years. I was still grateful for his wonderful support and generosity over the period of time and above all I respected him then as I do now and always will. But it was time to move on.

Meanwhile, as a side issue, Bob Herbert's growing love affair with showbiz had reached a point which found him promoting and rehearsing a group of three lads he was convinced had the potential to make it big in the pop world. He set up a company called Hart Management specifically to handle his fledgling show business interests and told me of his intentions to enter the pop music scene and make a substantial impact upon it.

At my invitation he brought the boys to Blazers on a number of occasions and I made sure that Del my compere gave them recognition from the stage.

"Ladies and Gentlemen" he would say, "We are pleased to welcome to Blazers this evening, the up and coming pop group Gloss, who will shortly be in the charts with their first single".

The boys, Matt, Luke and Craig would stand and take a bow, loving every minute of the exercise in showbiz minihype. The boys certainly had the ingredients for stardom including stunning good looks and smart designer gear; they looked a million dollars. Gloss were every bit a Bob Herbert product and despite a huge workload with his accountancy and financial services businesses, he gave unlimited time and energy to the group. Despite their ages, they were all under eighteen; they had good and intelligent conversation and appreciated everything that Bob was doing for them. Assisted by his son Christopher, Bob embarked on a punishing schedule of working and rehearsing Gloss and notched up endless miles doing the rounds of the record companies in an effort to land them a recording contract which might set them on the road to stardom.

At last the day came when all his hard work was about to pay off. Bob excitedly told me over dinner at the Jade Fountain Chinese Restaurant in Sunninghill, that there was now a definite interest in Gloss which would almost certainly result in a record deal. I warned him to ensure his management of the boys was watertight. I had seen so much poaching in the business by one management from another at all levels. Bob assured me that contracts binding the boys to the Hart Management Company were already being drawn up for signature. He thanked me for my concern.

"Think nothing of it," said I." That's what friends are for. Always remember Bob there is seldom a hit without a writ in the pop business. Or so the saying goes".

A short while later an understandably annoyed Bob Herbert called me to tell me that Gloss had been lost to other management. Apparently, since the boys were all under eighteen, the management contracts that had been prepared were taken to the parents for signature and the parents refused to sign saying that they were signing with another management company that they felt had more to offer than Hart Management. The man who had done all the hard work was out. I had seen this happen many times.

There followed a complete change of image and style. The golden curls went in favour of short-cropped hair and the more casual designer gear of the eighties replaced the smart dress suits and their name was changed from Gloss to Bross. The rest is history. Luke and Matt were brothers and their surname was Goss, so I guess that Bross is a derivative of the Brothers Goss.

Once Bob got over the disappointment and shock of his first taste of the callousness that purveyed the pop world, he became philosophical about the exercise. A lesser person would have called time on the showbiz involvement, but not Bob.

"I'm going to find another group, but this time they will be eighteen years old or more" he said determinedly. "I'll get there George. I'll make my mark you'll see,"

As I have already said, it was time to move on. The club continued to limp along despite Pats distractions and looting, playing such stars as Frank Valli and the Four Seasons, The Drifters, The Supremes and Lenny Henry headed another star-studded line up of entertainment at Blazers. Saucy, if not blue comedians were coming into fashion. Also what was termed alternative comedy was very evident at this time. From 1985 onwards our programme included Bernard Manning, Roger De Courcey and Jimmy Jones as well as Rick Mayall, Hale and Pace and of course a now much bluer Jim Davidson. Phil Cool also joined our line up. The reader may feel that by making plans to move on I was showing disloyalty to a man that had given me such opportunity and support, so I will attempt to explain my feelings at this time.

Showbiz, unlike any other business I know, rarely recognised the true heroes of the industry, the owners, the guys that took the risk and put their money down to create the clubs. It was guys like me who came along to manage the clubs that collected the kudos and the recognition. To most artistes or stars working any showroom the Manager was the number one man. As an example, Blazers had become George Savva's place e.g. 'Where did you work last week'. 'Oh I went to Windsor and did a week for George at Blazers'.

The club gave me great prestige and a superb reputation, but if things started to go wrong, it would be the Manager and <u>his </u>reputation that would be on the line, not the owners. To the artistes who worked Blazers, the owner was seldom seen. There was only one Guv'nor and that was me.

I knew that Pat's continuing gambling would destroy the club and undo all the good things we had done. And I knew that if the club crashed I would crash with it. Pat would not listen to reason when I broached the subject of his gambling and therefore I was left with precious little alternative.

Out of the blue John Mills, the South West of England agent, called me from his Bristol office. It was just after Christmas and he was trying to place the remaining couple of weeks of his adult pantomimes. He also had some availability of the excellent 'That'll Be the Day, Rock and Roll Laughter Show'. I took a date on the latter but could not find an available date for the Panto.

With business done we swiftly moved on to the gossip of the day as was usual It seemed most showbiz deals having been completed would usually end with a by the way have you heard' type of conversation. During our chat he mentioned that Eddie Heyward was looking to sell The Stardust at Usk.

"Eddie" I said, "I didn't know he owned it".

"Oh yes he's had the club for quite a while" replied John. "The James's required some financial assistance from Eddie and when they defaulted Eddie acquired the premises. He had a charge on it".

I was surprised at the news of the premises being on the market, the club would suit me very well. I fell in love with the place when I did a year of management there for the James gang. I knew my way around it and during my time there I had made many friends. Could this be fate taking a hand in my future again?

John had no idea what price Eddie was asking for it, and was surprised by my interest in it. I let John into my secret; my intention to leave Blazers, and my desire to buy my own premises, and I made him promise not to tell a living soul other than Eddie Heyward. I asked John to make representations to Eddie on my behalf; to ascertain the asking price and to secure permission for me to view the club. John took no time at all in fulfilling my requests and got back to me within a couple of hours.

John told me the asking price and that I was welcome to visit any time I wished. I thanked him and told him I'd keep in touch. Then I called Bob Herbert to fill him in with the details. To say I was excited at the prospects of owning the Stardust would be an understatement.

"The finance is certainly achievable" advised Bob "and in any case we can knock a few grand off the price without making it a deal buster" he said.

On my next day off from Blazers and by arrangement with Ken Trott the resident Manager of the Stardust, I took the drive down to Wales to inspect the club at Usk. As I drove over the Severn Bridge I began to recall the interesting year I had spent at Usk managing the club for the James's. Despite the highs and lows of that year, and the experiences that went with it, I had enjoyed the club and the warmth of the Welsh people.

As I neared Usk, I looked across and could clearly see the club on the other side of the valley. I could see the tower above the entrance, which was something of a landmark, I could see the roof of the cabaret room, and to the left of the main building I could see the eight double-bedded chalets. The visit to Usk was purely academic. I was determined to have the club before I'd even reached the outskirts of Usk. I went through the motion of inspection and found it perfect for my purpose. Little had changed.

So many memories came flooding back as I 'walked the course' with Ken Trott. Once the inspection was completed I thanked Ken and returned to

Windsor. I had always believed in the potential of the club and I still felt that way as I drove up the M4 towards home. To me the place was ready for me to go to work. I knew that if I could acquire it I could turn it into the centre of club entertainment in Wales.

Bob began organising the finance. We made Eddie an offer well below his asking price and after some negotiation, in which both of us moved positions, we agreed a price. The sale of my Windsor home, together with my brother Nick's contribution, (he wanted a piece of the action) a loan from The Ushers Brewery Company and an accommodation from Lloyds Bank of Woking, meant that Bob had organized sufficient funds to enable me to buy the club and have an operating float. Bob introduced me to a Lloyds Bank Executive named Edward Merritt and a solicitor named Ivor Turk who dealt with the necessary legal work. Following a meeting between me, Eddie, Bob, Ivor and Eddie's legal eagle at the Crest Hotel, Swindon in the late spring of 1987 an agreement was reached.

The completion date for the takeover was set. It was to be on my Birthday, September the 15th. All that remained was the inevitable meeting with Pat, my boss of the last ten years, to discuss my resignation from Adengrove Productions, the controlling company for Blazers. I did not relish telling Pat of my intention to quit. Quite apart from working for him for such a long time, we had become very close friends and as Pat was blissfully unaware of the unease amongst his executives at this time it made leaving him even more difficult. We met in the Tangtze Chinese Restaurant opposite the Castle at Windsor, we often dined there.

"I've worked for you for ten years now Sir" I began "and despite our occasional ups and downs I can honestly say I've enjoyed every moment; but times change, and situations change, and to be absolutely frank its time to move on".

Pat suddenly began to take notice and for the first time looked up from his plate of food.

"You're not leaving Georgie surely" he interrupted, throwing me off balance completely.

"Well yes Sir" I stumbled. "That is; I wish to give you three months notice"

"But why" he asked with an air of disbelief.

"Well it's like this Sir" I replied. "I have been tinkering with the idea of owning my own cabaret club for some time now, and you remember the little Stardust Club in Wales? Well it's up for sale and I'm in the process of buying it".

"But how did you raise the money" he asked, with a tone of even greater disbelief than before.

I explained to him the financial package put together by Bob Herbert and he listened avidly, looking to the heavens as he often did when making a calculation, he thought for a moment and then spoke positively and with authority.

"Well bearing in mind what you are paying for this place, and what you are borrowing to make the purchase possible, I think you are under funded and will be up against it from day one".

I listened carefully and would like to have told him there and then my real reason for wishing to get out of the organisation. Inwardly I wanted to tell the truth. I wanted nothing more than to stay at Windsor, secure in the knowledge that we could continue to prosper, but he had prevented that happening. He had set us on a course for disaster. Instead I opted for the soft option and lied.

"I know that I have a bit of an uphill battle Sir" I said "but the club is trading and I am sure I can do well. After all, apart from the Double Diamond at Caerphilly, there's little competition."

I thought to myself, the risk I take at Usk is far less than the risk I would take by staying at Blazers. After further discussion, Pat finally accepted that my mind was made up and reluctantly accepted my notice.

The stage was set. The move was on; and although remaining in the cabaret business a whole new ball game awaited me at Usk. My self-confidence was at a peak, my contacts worldwide and the Dragon was ready to breathe fire in Wales.

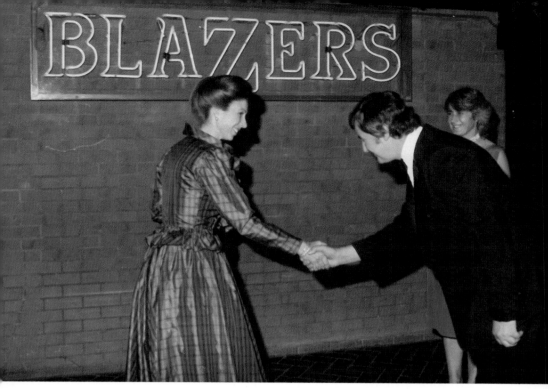

HRH Princess Anne at another Royal gala

The man himself, Sir Cliff Richard

Frankie Vaughan, a truly international artist.

Iris Williams and me.

'Club of the year' award with Joe Longthorne.

All eyes and teeth for the camera.

Another Gala evening, this time with Joe Longthorne.

And yet another gala evening, this time with HRH Princess Alexandra

Bobby Ball behind bars at 'Savvas' in Usk

A few words of Wisdom from the star himself.

Tom Jones - what a man. What a voice.

17

GOODBYE WINDSOR

HELLO USK

SAVVAS IS BORN

THE HEALTH INSPECTOR IS A NAZI

WEATHER FROM HELL

THERES A TREE IN MY SOUP

DANNY LA RUE ARRIVES

THE FIRE OFFICER

MRS CROW TAKES FLIGHT

CLIFF DROPS IN

CLIVE BRANDY AND IRIS

The summer of 1987 was a strange time for me. I was approaching my departure from Windsor and could hardly lumber my successor with a winter programme not of his own choosing although I had already some secured artistes for the period up to and including Christmas of that year. Equally I could not get involved in the cabaret line up for my new venture until after the sale completion date.

Graham White, the former general manager of Baileys accepted the offer to take over from me and I allayed his concern with regard to Pat Cowan's reputation for eccentricity by saying to him.

"I can assure you Graham you will find him a darling to work for" I said "and although he often takes time to get to know people, once he does and he likes them he is the nicest person in the world".

In a sense my comments were truthful, although I put them across with tongue in cheek. Pat after all was a great guy, but I dare not fill Graham in on the current situation.

I decided to keep my leaving a very low key affair as I had no wish to disturb the settled business pattern of an established business. The staff on the other hand had their own ideas and gave me a wonderful send off. They threw a great party for me and presented me with gifts suitably inscribed which would be a constant reminder of the happy decade I had spent at Windsor. I knew I'd miss Windsor. I knew I'd miss Berkshire. It was full of so many happy memories and the scene of some great triumphs. Due to some hitches, the September 15th deadline for the move to Usk was delayed until October the 6th.

The day began with Pam and I overseeing the loading of our furniture onto a removal truck bound for Usk and, once loaded, Pam and I set off in our car for the same destination. It is hard to describe my feelings as I drove to the new beginning; an inner joy that at last I was master of my own destiny combined with a happiness and confidence to go forward with the Usk club wrapped in a feeling of relief that I had broken free from the gathering gloom and problems at Blazers.

As I drove west I began to focus on the task in hand. John Mills had filled me in on the line up of artistes already booked for the run up to Christmas. Basically, the club operated a four nights a week policy, each Wednesday it featured an under fourteen Disco evening and on Friday's another Disco evening for eighteen year olds and over. Every Saturday was cabaret night and a name or semi name artiste would provide the entertainment. Sunday evenings were reserved for the Stardust's very own Divorced, Single and Separated club, a disco for lonely hearts.

I remember asking John about a cabaret artiste called Dave Jade who was featured as a Thursday night special on the Stardust programme. The evening was billed as a Ladies Only evening.

"Ah yes" said John. "He's a male stripper".

"You are kidding" was my heistant reply.

"I can assure you I'm not," insisted John. "Hen nights and Stag nights are part of the scene in this part of the world".

"Well I'm not having any of that in my club" I protested. "It will lower the tone of the place".

"George" said John. "I can assure you the show is very tastefully done. Dave Jade sings and gags throughout and thoroughly entertains and it is only at the end of his show, a spot he calls 'Winkle Time' that he becomes totally naked, apart from a cloak that is, which he uses with great precision".

"You mean totally naked," I asked in disbelief. "He actually gets it out".

"Yes" said John.

I could not believe what I was hearing; John went on to tell me that after some circulating amongst the audience, when he allowed various ladies to stick their heads in his cloak, he dropped his private part in a lady's drink. "This really does bring the house down," said John.

"I am not having him on my stage" I said again "and that's final".

"That's a real shame because he is sold out again - he always does sell out," John said mournfully.

"How much is he anyway," I asked.

"£125" said John.

"And he's sold out you say".

"Oh yes, totally, all five hundred and fifty seats are gone" stated John with some satisfaction. "In fact Eddie reckoned he made Three Grand clear profit each time he played Dave Jade".

I paused for a moment and then said, "Perhaps I'm being a little hasty John. Leave him on the programme". Dave Jade became a regular visitor to my programme, along with the Flaming Helmet, Big John, Brett the Magnificent Adonis and a whole number of other ladies evening attractions.

We arrived at the Stardust during the early evening and Eddie's sister Valerie made us very welcome, she was a charming lady and seemed quite pivotal to the Usk operation. She took us through the inevitable paperwork which went with the takeover of the business. Artiste contracts, signed bookings and reservations, deposits and other up front booking payments were all outlined and discussed as Val gave us an up to date picture for the takeover. Also listed were staff levels and a who's who from kitchen to stage and she was able to fill us in on suppliers and local officialdom for good measure. All in all, by the time she took her leave of us, we felt totally comfortable and informed in all aspects of the club's activities and personnel.

Pam and I decided to take one of our eight chalets for that night as our furniture was not due to arrive until the following day, something to do with driving regulations; We were lucky as the other seven were let. Upstairs over the club, was a four-roomed apartment, spacious and ideal for our needs; when the furniture arrived. The windows offered a spectacular view of the beautiful Vale of Usk. Tomorrow, we thought, we will be settled once and for all. At about 8.30.p.m. a gentleman called in and asked the price of a chalet with breakfast.

"£15" I told him "and I've only one left".

"I'll take it," said he.

He parted with his cash and I parted with the key. Pam looked dumbstruck. "What are we to do now?"

"We'll manage" I replied. "In any case it's not all bad. Here is our first fifteen quid in readies and we have only just arrived".

I passed Pam the money and we went off in search of something to use as covering for our night on the floor of our apartment. After assembling various overcoats and jumble found on the premises, we settled down on the hard floor of one of our apartment rooms and did our best to keep warm in the cold surroundings of our home above the dark empty club. "What did you call the club when you first told me about it?" Pam said.

"A veritable oasis; a positive Shangri La'" she continued, refreshing my memory. "If this is it, I'd rather settle for a pub in Vietnam," she concluded.

We drifted off to sleep and dream of the exciting challenges to come. I awoke early in the morning racked with aches and pains. "Are you sure Delfont started like this?" I asked myself.

The resident D.J. and Compere was a man called Clive Anthony. The Chef, a part timer, was a local brewery chef, who attended on occasions when meals were required. The Manager, Ken Trott, and his family, who had been associated with the club for an age, now had to move on as I intended to manage the place myself. He joined Eddie Hayward at his plant hire firm at nearby Chepstow.

The first evening we held the under fourteen disco that ran from 7 till 11p.m. No alcohol was sold, only soft drinks and very few staff were required, just one or two bar staff and a D.J. The kids that attended, even at that tender age, were horrendous and got into all kinds of mischief. After every Wednesday evening we found wanton vandalism in various parts of the premises. No amount of income in the world could warrant the continuation of this Wednesday evening activity and there was little financial gain from the exercise anyway. I determined to kill off the under 14 club and did so after three weeks despite furious complaints from parents. I felt that if they, the parents, could not control their children I had no chance and it was not my vocation to keep children off the streets.

Ladies night was, as John had predicted, superb, with huge sales of food and drink; a raucous occasion from start to finish and a very, very profitable evening. The Friday night disco was quite another matter. It was profitable in so far as the amount paid out in staff, D.J. and security officers was minuscule, against an excellent admission and bar take. The problem was the crowd, the bulk of which came by coach from all over the valleys. For a nominal charge buses would pick up people from various points and bring them to the club.

The system was highly organised and the network of transportation in place was a remarkable achievement. The only flaw in this was the lack of selectivity as to who would be permitted on to the premises and who ought to be refused admission for reasons of security. When the public makes their own way to a disco or club, the club has a right to refuse admission to anyone they deem to be a known troublemaker or found to be intoxicated on arrival or very badly dressed. If the youngsters are bussed in they have no means of returning home until the end of the evening at one a.m. when the bus returns to the valleys. Our dilemma was having to admit five hundred unvetted young people; the 'Good the Bad and the Ugly' as my bouncers used to call them. There was never a Friday night without trouble of one sort or another. Friday night fights were commonplace because we had no on the door selection policy at our disposal. The club was trapped by its own promotion.

The non-event of the week was undoubtedly the 'Sunday Singles Night'. It brought together one of the strangest groups of people it has been my misfortune to cater for. If becoming a member of the club and attending its weekly gathering became compulsory, I am sure divorce or separation would become a thing of the past. I'm confident that people would prefer to stick with their marriage, however unsatisfactory, than to split and have to suffer the S.D. and S club. Boy meets girl is one thing, but jilted woman meets wronged male is quite another. So I axed the Sunday night exercise early on because

(a) It earned hardly any money for us and

(b) It would have turned me into a manic-depressive.

Needless to say the cancellation of the S.D. and S club was also greeted with cries of outrage but nothing compared to the furore that met my decision to end the Friday disco and dust-up night. As well the pain of losing a ready-made profit, I also had to suffer grief from customers and coach companies. But I remained adamant that the way forward was along a totally different path and style of operation.

The reader will no doubt have noticed that before this chapter I hardly used the word Disco throughout my showbiz career, but since my arrival at Usk I have already mentioned the word Disco at least a dozen times. In Wales the club operators caught on to the new Discothèque craze ahead of the rest of Britain. Maybe it was on purely economic grounds, or maybe they were visionaries, whichever it was the disco trend that had swept across the Atlantic, swept across Wales first.

Live music, the love of my life, was becoming a thing of the past and like an idiot I couldn't see it. I installed a resident band led by Eric Bennett an excellent musician from Gloucester, and a local trio to provide the after cabaret dance music. Customers were soon protesting at the lack of after show Disco music, which I found extraordinary. Even Steve Austwick my restaurant manager took me to task over the matter.

"They love disco music in this part of the world," he said. For the life of me I could not understand how D.J's got away with it; playing records for people to dance to and charging them for the privilege. "Surely people could play and dance to records in their own home. Why go out and pay for the same thing" I used to argue.

Having cancelled three of my weekly activities and axed my D.J., I was not exactly making many friends. Clive's departure was due partly to my dislike of disco music and partly because we did not hit it off. I felt his influence had grown out of all proportion prior to my arrival at Usk and we clashed from the outset and parted company as a result. I approached Bryn Yemm to become resident compere, remembering the excellent work he did when I was at Usk ten years previously. However, Bryn and I could not agree terms as since the Seventies, he had become a local personality and commanded a fee far in excess of what I could afford to pay him.

So I sought, and successfully signed, Bristolian Roddy Miles, an excellent linkman and who jumped at the chance of regular work and was proved right to do so, especially as the club progressed. After a while, and under increasing pressure all sides I decided to replace the house trio with a D.J to play the after show music for dancing. Although a much less expensive option than paying three musicians, I still mourned the loss of my all live music policy. After a while and the arrival and departure of a number of D.J's, I signed Kevin King, as resident D.J. an old friend and another guy that did well at the Stardust a decade ago. I also engaged a part time secretary, a young married lady with two children, able to drop the kids at school and collect them on the way home from work. Marilyn Strangemore was the perfect secretary and worked with me for many many years. Lots of people thought of her at times as something of a dragon but this was because she was fiercely loyal and protective as a good secretary should be.

My team now complete I felt ready to proceed with the tried and tested policy that had served me so well over two decades. I wanted to stamp my authority on the entertainment scene in Wales which I viewed as mediocre at that time. Therefore, to complete the reorganisation I renamed the club. 'Savvas' was born.

'Savvas Club at Usk; where the stars come out at night'. Our slogan screamed across the local press 'Entertainment at its best'. 'Savvas for a great night out'. We trotted out all the usual hyperbole that usually accompanies a programme of entertainment but in the early days it was heavy going. We were going to have to work very hard to reestablish the club with its new policy. I remember my friend Johnny Hackett, one of the first artistes to play as a replacement for the Friday night Disco, only thirty-two people turned up, including a drunken female heckler.

I remember vividly Johnny standing on a dimly lit stage one cold night in November and working the near empty auditorium. I had not yet begun the refurbishment and this made the scene even more shabby and dim.

"I don't want you to think show business is always as glamorous as this," said Johnny to the audience.

The Rockinberries, the Grumbleweeds, the Baron Knights, Duncan Norvelle, Joe Longthorne and David Essex were all part of a line up that appeared at the club, along with the Supremes, The Platters, Lenny Henry and Jim Davidson. All these names appeared on the Savvas Club entertainment programme to take us through the spring and summer 1988.

At the same time I embarked on a refurbishment programme that greatly enhanced the facilities throughout, including new lighting and sound equipment.

Kitchen, bars and toilets were all renewed. Partly because they badly needed refurbishment and partly due to pressure from the local Health Inspector who gave me no peace. "Would you strangle my baby at birth" I said to him, pointing out that as income came to hand so reinvestment could continue to take place. The Inspector was not prepared to wait and pressed ahead with a prosecution against the club. We had no alternative but to bring the whole refurbishment programme forward and pay for it from our meagre reserves.

I don't remember the Health Inspector's name because he was such a nonentity, as so many local officials are. I do however remember that he was a small man with a pointed nose and narrow grey eyes that peered through glasses the thickness of jam jars and I remember thinking that he looked like Martin Borman the German Nazi who disappeared after the war. To any readers from any organisation seeking him please note that Borman is not in Rio he is in Cwmbran, or was in 1987/88.

The star studded line up, the refurbished premises, the class, and ambience of Savvas Club soon began to draw the crowds and a very different sort of coach party attended the cabaret nights which were Dinner, Dance and Cabaret packages sold by agents and coach operators, as well as privately organised. We began to attract people from a wide area and enjoyed support from Swindon and Bristol, Gloucester, Hereford and Cheltenham and from Newport, Cardiff and the valleys. The finest advertising is by word of mouth and our reputation for a top class, night out was rapidly established.

I had only been at Usk a short while when I received a phone call from Graham White, Blazers General Manager.

"When are you going to Buckingham Palace?" asked Graham.

"What do you mean Graham?" I answered.

"Well to receive your award, your medal" he said. "You know for working with Cowan for ten years. I only lasted ten days".

"Oh no" I sighed. "What went wrong"?

"Nothing went wrong George, as such. I just could not get on with the man. He did not like me from the start. That was obvious. In fact he phoned the club on numerous occasions and talked to everyone except me. I got sent to Coventry. When I did eventually catch up with him, his manner and his approach to matters needing decisions were those of an escaped lunatic. Eccentric is one thing. That guy is a nut case. How you did ten years with him I don't know"

I must say I had a feeling that the new Manager's early exit could be on the cards, given Pat's personal problems at that time.

Throughout 1988 and 1989 we operated seven nights a week and occasional Sunday lunch times as well. Our little club, our Palladium in the sticks, as a Times newspaper reporter put it, was the envy of club land nationwide and we won the Club of the Year award. It was truly the centre of entertainment for Wales and the West. Out of the way as we were, we had none of the problems with neighbours, noise or parking which are often experienced by other clubs.

The one problem that must be recorded however was that of the weather. When the weather was bad, it was very very bad, but when it was good, it was still bad. When we arrived in Wales it rained almost continuously for seven weeks; forty-nine consecutive nights and days without a break. High winds were a further feature, a howling almost hurricane wind would blow up the Usk valley. Often, when showing friends over our apartment, would make a point of stopping at one of our large windows in order to point out the stunning view (weather permitting of course). "Twenty thousand Roman soldiers were encamped there" I used to say, impressing my audience with my new found local knowledge.

I remember Frank Carson retorting "Christ I'm surprised they didn't get bloody blown away or drowned. Who needs Bodecia with weather like this?"

To cap it all, the auditorium roof leaked in many places and despite a lot of patching, problems persisted. My fear was that the leaks would damage the new carpet and other refurbished items. Had I had the time and the finance to plan the job properly I would of course have started by repairing the roof, but because of the intervention of 'Martin Borman', I was forced to put the cart before the horse. A series of pots and pans were situated above the false ceiling to catch the water from known leaks.

Gary Hunt, who had joined me from Windsor, was my chief lighting and soundman and pots and pans controller. Armed with a stepladder and almost on a daily basis he would remove the various receptacles from the loft empty them and put them back in position. None of our ever-increasing followers and customers knew what was above their heads beyond the ceiling tiles.

The inclement weather did once do me a favour and lets face it a favour or a stroke of luck was long overdue. In the middle of an excellent Frankie Vaughan week, a particularly vicious wind blew up. The audiences were safely in their seats and the music and audience chatter blotted out the howling wind outside. In fact there was a kind of cosiness in the clubroom. The table lamps blended with the newly fitted own lighters to give a wonderful atmosphere to the whole layout.

Steve Austwick hurried up to me out of breath.

"Table seven is complaining about his soup" he gasped.

"Well what's wrong with it" I asked impatiently.

"There is a tree in it" replied Austwick and ran back to his duties.

Intrigued, I made my way to table seven, a table for two situated by a large window covered by a rather smart velvet curtain. Two people sat quite motionless opposite each other and between them lying across the table and protruding through the velvet curtain was the fully-grown branch of a tree.

"It seems" said the customer, "something of a storm is blowing outside.

"We were just sitting quietly, minding our minestrone," quipped the other customer.

"I hope you are both O.K."I said.

"Oh yes we are fine. The glass from the window shattered behind the heavy curtain and fell down inside but did not trouble us. The curtain however, could not sustain the weight of the tree. The only thing is we are getting rather cold from the wind blowing beneath what remains of your curtain."

I moved the couple to another spare table, provided them with fresh soup and a bottle of wine for being so damn nice about it. We managed to saw off the offending branch and sealed up the broken window as best we could.

Also on that night, some friends of mine had decided to pay me a visit from London. I had called by their table occasionally and they seemed to be having a great time. Meanwhile Vince Kenningale, my security officer come bouncer, donned his coat and went outside to inspect the damage. On returning he reported that apart from the broken window there was little evidence of any other damage. Although he did report that we had lost and were continuing to lose some fragments of our rather old and leaky roof. "Oh and one other thing Mr. Savva" said Vince, "there is a car crushed under the tree".

That's all I need I thought. I asked for the car's registration number. "Not possible to see" said Vince. Apparently it took the full force of one of our huge trees as it came down and the car was completely buried beneath the branches and foliage of the tree.

I decided there was nothing we could do until the evening had ended. Only then, as people began making their way to their vehicles would the owner of the crushed car appear. The evening ended and I sat chatting with my London friends, completely forgetting the crushed car in the car park. Eventually my friends took their leave; they were the last to depart. Seconds later they reappeared, you guessed it. Of all the five hundred plus customers in the club that night, it had to be their car that had got crushed.

Following a call to my insurance company the next morning an assessor duly arrived and, after seeing the substantial damage to my roof caused by the storm, instructed me to carry out the necessary repairs. It was indeed an ill wind that blew some good that night. A new roof and the leaks became a thing of the past.

After only eighteen months at Usk, I was already beginning to feel the need to expand. I knew that by removing two pillars and a bar from the middle of the room I could gain an incredible one hundred and fifty extra seats. Also, by removing the cloakroom at the back of the room, I could replace it with a bar, thus retaining my bar service area. The cloakroom could be moved to a new foyer area which could easily be added. Anwell Williams the builder who had carried out the reroofing of the club called by at my invitation and the matter was discussed in detail. He assured me that the alterations could be carried out as planned and although I was not quite ready to go ahead, we decided to apply for the necessary planning permission, to be ready when the time came to proceed. With this increased capacity, I could go after even bigger attractions. The extra seating would at least ensure that the playing of such stars would be viable.

Talking of big names, I noticed that Cliff was about to play the Newport Leisure Centre on his U.K. concert tour. The Leisure Centre was a huge auditorium and had no problem playing the truly mega stars. I contacted Cliff's office and invited him to visit Savvas and then have dinner with me the Three Salmons Hotel at Usk. I remembered mentioning to Cliff my intention of taking my own club; he had seemed really interested and insisted he would help by playing it. I received a positive response from his office.

"Cliff would be pleased to visit Usk after his Newport concert, have a look at the club and join you for dinner at The Salmons" I was told.

Bob Monkhouse was appearing at Savvas that week. Concerts 'come down' at around 10.30.p.m. whilst club entertainment 'goes up' at 11p.m. so Cliff arrived at the back of our auditorium while Bob was on stage. We kept Cliff's visit a closely guarded secret. Only Pam and I knew, and of course Marilyn my secretary, an avid Cliff fan long before she joined our organisation. She elected to do a stint on the reception desk in order to catch a glimpse of her idol. Undisturbed, he was able to take in the whole layout and the atmosphere. He really seemed impressed with what he saw.

We went on to the Three Salmons Hotel, leaving Bob and his audience unaware of their distinguished visitor although Bob had an invitation to join us for dinner after the show. Ramond Gomez, the Salmons Maitre D Hotel welcomed us and showed us into the private oak panelled dining room on the first floor; a really impressive setting for a private dinner party. Cliff's entourage included his personal manager David Bryce, Roger Bruce and one or two other colleagues. Pam and I were joined by Bob Monkhouse and the scene was set for an excellent late night dinner. Bob was the life and soul of the proceedings, relating amusing stories and experiences. Bob was very generous in his remarks about Savvas Club, and emphasised the closeness of the audience, something essential for cabaret. Cliff said how much he liked the feel of the place. After a superb meal and some more light hearted conversation, Cliff thanked me for my hospitality and mentioned the fact that he was preparing a show for Australia. Part of that preparation is rehearsing and running through the whole show in a studio behind closed doors.

"Once we have put it together and thoroughly rehearsed it, I would really like to run it through in a live setting, so I can make sure it works and I can gauge audience reaction" he said. "To tell you the truth, I've never really cared for the studio scenario. Perhaps we could bring the show to Usk for a week".

"I would be delighted" I replied "and honoured to have you play my little club".

We said our goodbyes and Cliff promised he'd 'be in touch". I knew he would because he is absolutely sincere in everything he says.

Meanwhile Jethro, Michael Barrymore and Little and Large put more than just a smile on the face of Usk. Their comedy had audiences rolling in the aisles. The club was reaching more and more people, its reputation going before it. So that when the news broke of the mighty La Rue's booking to play the club, the phones went wild and reservations went through the ceiling. Danny did seven evening performances and five lunchtime shows, a total of twelve shows in one week. In an interview for BBC Radio Wales he was generous with his remarks, complimenting me and my club. The wealth of media publicity from Dan's visit to Wales was quite remarkable.

Marilyn my secretary alerted me that a fire prevention officer had made a reservation for one of Danny's evening performances. The lady was not our local officer but from outside our area and while making the reservation asked to be considered for a good table as she was a big La Rue fan, she then dropped into the conversation, that she was a fire prevention officer.   I have never been sure whether her desire for us to know her occupation was pure intimidation or she felt that as an employee of the state she should have special treatment. Whichever it was it worked. They say a leopard never changes its spots. I was the same old 'pack em in Savva' unable to say no or turn anyone away.

Although the woman was not our friendly neighbourhood fire inspector, I decided she must not be trusted. She may know the local F.O. and could certainly use a telephone. I was by this time into my 'overcrowding mode' most nights of the week. "I really must get a bigger room" I sighed.

I placed the alien fire officer's table right in front of the centre of the stage, in that little town of Usk, she had the greatest table in the world. In addition, Dan agreed to meet her, her husband and her two guests after the show. She was after all a fan and both Dan and I aimed to please!!

Steve Austwick called by my office after setting up the room ready for the evening performance.

"Christ that's quite a table for four you've placed on the front. The fire officer must be coming in" he said.

"What makes you think that" I asked sourly.

"Well the way you've positioned the table, the only people the occupants are likely to see are Danny La Rue and his company. The other hundreds of people will all be sitting behind them. I figure you don't want a certain party counting numbers" Austwick concluded with a wry smile.

"Well for your information, it is not <u>the</u> fire officer it's <u>a</u> fire officer - and by the way no one likes a clever dick," I said.

My seating and Dan's charm sent our lady visitor into a seventh heaven and in due course I received a most charming and complementary letter. She appeared to love everything, the show, the food, the service, the cleanliness of the toilets, the brilliant organisation, even the colour of the wallpaper in Dan's dressing.

Another rather interesting incident took place during the Danny La Rue week which brought home to me for the very first time, how old people view death differently to younger people. It was a midweek O.A.P. lunchtime show and like all the others that week, Danny had sold out completely. Armed with my table plan of all the various expected parties, I prepared myself for the arrival of the coaches, mini buses and cars, bringing our senior citizen audience.

Roddy Miles offered to help me with the seating so I gave him the list of parties and sizes and asked him to get the name and number of each party so that I could take them to their allocated seating as per my table plan. It was not long before we were both in full swing.

"Mrs. Rees for twenty-four" boomed Roddy.

"This way Mrs. Rees" I shouted back, taking her and her party to seating for twenty-four people.

"Sam Beech for thirty-eight" cried Roddy.

"This way" came my swift reply.

"Mrs. Bevan for sixty" called Roddy.

"This way Mrs. Bevan" I responded and so it went on.

"Mrs. Crow for fifty-two" shouted Roddy.

"This way Mrs. Crow" said I.

"No" Came the lady's reply, "I'm not Mrs. Crow, I'm Mrs. Jones. Mrs. Crow passed away yesterday".

"Oh I'm so sorry Mrs. Jones. I had no idea," I said apologetically.

"Oh that's alright," replied Mrs. Jones. "As a matter of fact, Mrs. Crow's death was a stroke of luck really. You see Mrs. Evans wanted a ticket but we could not fit her in. The booking was full and so was the coach, but with Mrs. Crow up and dying like that, it meant that Mrs. Evans could have her ticket and come with us to see Danny La Rue. So alls well that ends well" she concluded.

I sat the party and returned to the entrance, where Roddy who had also heard the story of the unfortunate Mrs. Crow was doubled up in hysterics. Gasping for breath he said,

"Mrs. Crow is probably still warm and Mrs. Jones is saying alls well that ends well. That has got to tbe the funniest truism I've heard" he said and laughing still more he blurted out "not forgetting the fortunate Mrs. Evans who got her dead friend's seat - how lucky can you get".

A sensational week of Tommy Steel completed a triumphant season. The most wonderful memory I have of the establishment of the club at Usk is the support of family, friends and loyal customers. Ray and Mavis Marsh, my friends from Newbury visited the club every Sunday evening. Other weekly visitors included Del and Graham Dee and family, Sam and Linda Jones and Sylvia and Haydn Cook.

Pam's Daughter Jayne and Granddaughter Chloe lived with us at Savvas club, as did my Son James. Our other children Christopher, Steven, George and Andrew all paid regular visits. Customers of many years and family, all marvelled at the growth and popularity of the club. The icing was about to be put upon the cake as they say, when I received a phone call from David Bryce confirming that Cliff wanted to go ahead with a half dozen shows as a pre-run for his forthcoming Australian tour. Dates were agreed and everything organized to bring about the greatest club date ever seen in Wales.

Once again I launched ticket sales in the direction of the fans in the first instance, before releasing them to members of the public. Cliff's followers were already aware of the special setting of seeing Cliff in a club; the closeness of the artiste to the audience and the intimate atmosphere, already experienced at Cliff's club dates at Blazers. Just wait and see I thought, Cliff on stage at the much smaller Savvas club would be closeness with a capital 'C'.

With Cliff's lighting and sound equipment rigged and in place the great man arrived to begin an unforgettable week of pure magic. Umpteen newspapers, TV and radio interviews, presented Savvas club with publicity that money could never buy and throughout, Cliff complemented the club and its organisation. When asked by an interviewer if Savvas was the only club he was playing in the U.K. at this time Cliff replied "It is the only club I am playing in the world".

It was just after this joyous time that Pam and I were devastated to receive the news of Clive and Iris' marriage breakup. Clive, who phoned us with the news, was absolutely gutted and we were totally shocked. Pam and I had no idea that the marriage had become strained let alone had collapsed. Clive's larger than life image and Iris' witty sense of humour seemed to sit so well together. It was a very tearful Clive that visited us at Usk and stayed for a while. Without taking sides in the dispute, Pam and I offered comfort and friendship as best we could to both Clive and Iris as two of out most treasured friends.

I learned that our mutual pal Jim Davidson was appearing at Torquey in the summer season and since the seaside resort was a fairly simple drive from Usk, Pam, Clive and I decided to pay J.D. a visit, catch his show and perhaps dine with him afterwards. I felt that seeing Jim again would help Clive still further by lifting him from his somewhat melancholy outlook on life. I was certainly proved right, Jim was bloody marvelous with Clive and soon had him laughing, joking and being his old self again. After dinner we ended the evening on board Jim's boat that was moored at the local marina.

Clive readily accepted Jim's invitation to stay on the boat and remain in Torquey a while. Jim came to see Pam and I off on our journey back to Usk. "Clive will be alright now," he whispered. "I'm really glad you fetched him down here. I've slipped him a couple of grand so he need not want for anything, it is one thing to loose your missus, it's another to be skint as well". This was J.D. at his best – in his own caring way.

18

Anwell Williams and his team began work on Savvas Club in the spring of 1990; the removal of the two huge pillars that held up the entire cabaret room roof was an amazing feat of engineering. To take the load, two huge metal girders were put in place that stretched the entire length of the auditorium. The girders were held in place by two stacks of reinforced concrete at either end of the room instead of the middle as before. The transference of the bar to the rear of the room and moving the cloakroom completed an amazing transformation. Two Grecian columns supporting a triangular shaped backdrop were built at the front and a 'SAVVAS' sign was installed. I made full use of the palindrome by having the S at either end of the name larger than the other letters. The alterations to the building not only gave a new smart look to the place and more comfort for the punters but added a hundred and fifty extra seats bringing our official capacity to seven hundred. Unofficially of course the sky was the limit. 'Pack em in Savva rides again'.

Throughout the week of Cliff's appearance at the club he praised it, told me how much he enjoyed playing there and said he hoped to come back. Cliff seldom, if ever, said anything he did not mean, so I was not surprised to hear from David Bryce that Cliff was hoping to make another trip to Usk, with a totally different show, the following year.

As the evening entertainment menu was operating satisfactorily, I began promoting more daytime shows and expanded my Sunday lunchtime program from occasional to regular Sunday shows. John Mills was the source of many of my supporting artistes, but Jimmy Smith remained my principal booker and with the assistance of both I built a solid Sunday business. Jimmy delivered such box office attractions as The Ninja Turtles, Rainbow, Grotbags the Witch, Mr. Blobby, Keith Chegwin and the P.G. Tips Chimps. My dear friend Rod Hull, with Emu, made many visits, as well as my long time friend and colleague Poz and his world of magic and a whole host of other family attractions.

John Mills began marketing a pantomime with two scripts; the first for a family audience and the second an X-rated version for late night adult cabaret. Cinderella was a revelation, but I turned it down.

"George you've just got to get with it" said John. "Comedy, even sit-com, is getting more risqué by the minute. Take it from me filth sells".

He was proven to be right of course and in the fullness of time I succumbed like everyone else.

The other direction I took in my quest for daytime traffic was the presenting of a large number of Senior Citizen lunches with cabaret. Both Jimmy and John kept me well supplied with a constant stream of yesterday's stars as well as up to date singers and comedians that appealed to senior audiences. Sam Beech and his wife Marjorie kept me supplied with coach loads of OAPs. Despite living at Beaufort near Ebbw Vale, Sam had contacts throughout the Welsh valleys and was our most successful agent as far as senior citizens were concerned.

During these halcyon days I welcomed many of my mates to the club; Iris Williams, Des O'Connor, Bob Monkhouse, Vince Hill and of course Jim Davidson made early visits. On one occasion Jim Davidson's support act was an up and coming artiste called Brian Connolly. While Jim, whose cabaret performance had got considerably bluer, was on stage one evening, Roddy Miles and I took the moment of calm to discuss matters of forthcoming attractions etc. We were standing near the foyer bar, which was deserted at the time, save for the supporting artiste Brian who now arrived from backstage having 'done his bit'.

"Cor" said Brian. "This bar's a bit quiet".

"That's the sign of a great artiste at work" said I. "Jim's on so the bar is empty" I added.

"I never thought of it like that," said Brian. After a moment's reflection he asked. "How was the bar when I was on?"

"Absolutely bloody packed" I replied without hesitation. My remark was followed by fits of laughter from Brian and Roddy.

The Big Yin, Billy Connolly arrived to perform at the club as one of the bigger and more expensive stars that I could afford because of the increased capacity. The Celtic connection between the Scots and the Welsh was reflected in the large numbers of punters that booked to see the great Scot. Billy was a big box office attraction all over the U.K. but was particularly popular in Wales. During his week at Usk, Billy inquired about fishing in one of the local rivers. I assured him there would not be a problem and that I would organise something for him. Through local contacts I arranged some salmon fishing for Billy at a spot on the River Usk upstream from the club and gave him a lift to the spot, returning to pick him up about five in the evening.

"Did you have a good day? How was the fishing"? I asked as we drove away.

"Lets put it this way," answered Billy. "The fish did not disturb the peace and tranquility of the day. Not one of the bastards".

Hale and Pace had a TV series achieving top ratings week after week so it was no surprise that they proved to be a popular attraction when they arrived Usk. Most visiting stars opted to stay at one of the leading hotels in the area such as The Salmons or Cwrt Bleddyn, but one of the boys, I don't recall whether it was Gareth or Norman decided to rent a cottage at Little Mill, just outside Usk, and hire some horses to ride during their week at Savvas. They invited my daughter Jayne, an accomplished rider, to join them for a spell of trekking through Wentwood Forest nearby. Jayne returned after a very full day 'on the range' and told me one of the boys would be unable to perform that evening due to a riding accident.

"Oh no" I said. "What happened"?

"I don't know exactly," replied Jayne. "I think he hit a branch of a tree and fell off his horse onto his coccyx".

"What"? I yelled beginning to panic.

"His coccyx Dad - you know his ass," explained Jayne.

"That's great and what am I supposed to do with a full house and no act", I asked lifting my face to the heavens.

"No problem Dad, one of the boys will be in and has told me to tell you to be prepared. He reckons you've seen them work so many times that you can easily fill in for the missing one. So tonight it will be Savva and Pace," she said with a mischievous giggle. It was a wind up. I smiled, but went white with fright.

Billy Pearce was another excellent comedian that regularly graced the boards at Savvas Club. His arrival at this time, hot on the heels of Jim Davidson, Brian Connelly, Billy Connelly and Hale and Pace, presented me with an opportunity to feature another angle on comedy for my public. Billy Pearce had a very funny act, which was essentially clean family comedy. Instead of the use of four letter based words, Billy Pearce invented, or perhaps brought with him from the North of England the word Chuffin. With Billy it was chuffin this and chuffin that all the way through his performance. Passed over by TV, his box office appeal was less than others, but so was his fee and he did well and was excellent value for money. Another great Northern comic to appear in the same season was Stan Boardman. Stan was not a blue comic either and like Billy had not hit the really big time, but each time he came to Usk we enjoyed a good week although not necessarily a sell out. However, this changed after Stan made an appearance on the Des O'Connor show.

Des had a very popular weekly talk show which went out live. Stan's appearance created something of a sensation because when asked by Des about the anti Nazi jibes for which Stan was famous, he could not resist the temptation to tell his Fokker story. Old clubbers like me had heard the story many times but as far as TV was concerned, Stan was about to have a first. Stan, sitting comfortably on Des's sofa began:

"On a show not unlike this Des, a talk show, the interviewer introduced his guest as Mr. Shinken of the Polish Free Air Force, who fought alongside the RAF during the Second World War. Flying alone one day in his Spitfire aircraft, Mr.Shinken related in his broken English his experience. 'I understand you had a frightening time,' stated the interviewer. 'Yes, zis is correct. I was flying along when suddenly I spot zis Fokker on ze left hand side of my plane. Oh dear I thought, when zuddenly I spot another Fokker on ze right hand side of ze plane. I don't like the look of these Fokkers I said to myself, just before glancing into the rear view mirror when I spot four more Fokkers. I began to panic. After all I'm surrounded by all zees Fokkers'. At that moment the interviewer interrupted.

'For the sake of those viewers back home and to avoid any misunderstanding of the word Fokker, Mr. Shinken is obviously referring to the German Fokkerwolf aircraft. Is that not so Herr Shinken'?

'Yes zis is so, but these Fokkers were Messerschmitt' ".

When Stan had finished, Des, together with the TV studio audience was rocked with hysterical laughter. There was something of a rumpus the following day with virtually every newspaper carrying the story.

Should he, or should he not was the debate but, as far as the general public was concerned, Stan was a hero. The controversy did him a lot of good. Suddenly a little known comic became a household name. The box office sales for his visit to Savvas a couple of weeks later shot through the roof.

I suppose this was another indication that comedy was becoming more risqué or blue. Jim, Billy Connelly and Hale and Pace were all fairly blue in their performances. They were relating to every day life and were enormously popular. Stan told one suggestive story on TV and his box office soared as a consequence. Singing artistes, male and female, by dress and suggestion enhanced their musical performances by being raunchy and displaying as much sex appeal as was possible.

The promise made to Pam and I by Danny La Rue during one of our visits to his Stratford home that the portraits of the clowns that adorned the wails of the 'Clowns' bar at Walton Hall would one day be mine came true in amazing circumstances. Dan was in pantomime in Bath, not far from Usk. Playing pantomime meant that Dan had Sunday's free so we made an agreement to present a Noon and Night show on one of our Sundays in January. However, the Welsh weather had other ideas!

The incessant January rain decided to fail as snow and the original date had to be postponed. Indeed the blizzard effectively cut the club off from the outside world for a couple of days. I remember the Brother Lee's comedy trio, who were booked for a four night stint during the first week of January being trapped at Usk with no hope of an audience getting to see them. As I sat with them at dinner on one of the evenings in a totally empty club, I remember turning to them and saying

"Well boys here we are, trapped at a night club in South Wales with no sign of rescue and with only enough food and drink to last us about eighteen months"!!

The white wilderness had vanished as quickly as it had arrived -washed away by the monsoon like rain that once again fell from the heavens and Dan's date was re-booked. On a cold wet Sunday morning Dan arrived and immediately sent his driver to the rear of the car. From the boot he took six magnificent paintings, the clowns from his bar at Walton Hall. "I said one day they would be yours and today is that day," said Dan.

While at Blazers I became accustomed to an annual visit to Royal Ascot where Pat Cowan had his own box and each year threw the most fabulous party, to which Pam and I were always invited. My friends Victor and Betty Baldwin, customers and supporters of mine for many years, also had a box at the famous racecourse and Pam and I were also invited to spend a day with them. Occasionally the brewery that supplied all our drink requirements held a day at the Royal meeting and Pam and I received an invitation. All in all, during the five days of the Royal meeting, we would go to Ascot at least twice and on occasions three times.

I have never been a gambler as such, perhaps I might call myself a flutterer, but I did enjoy Royal Ascot as a spectacle. After moving to Usk I decided I was not going to cut myself off from things that I had enjoyed at Windsor, or in and around the London area, so it was not unusual for Pam and me to drive to Windsor or London for dinner with friends. Susan and Allan Blackburn who lived at Chobham not far from Windsor, seemed to be spending more and more time in Monte Carlo, but we kept in touch and met up each time we holidayed in our apartment there.

Iris Williams and Clive had the Pheasant Plucker at Winkfield Row, the pub once called the Cottage. We would often spend a day and an evening off by driving from South Wales to the sleepy Berkshire village to spend some time with them. So, since I continued to maintain a strong presence in my former stomping ground I decided I would hire my own box at Royal Ascot and throw a Gala Lunch and Race Party on the opening day of the Royal meeting.

It was an excellent promotion for the club, but surprising how many people, well heeled people that is, that had never sampled the delights of a day at the Royal meeting in a box.

I went ahead and hired the box and I proceeded to invite my very best customers and friends. The list included:-

Eddie and Sandra Heywood,
Ken and Ginette Parslow,
Allan and Tracy Darlow
Sam and Linda Jones
Victor and Betty Baldwin
Ray and Mavis Marsh

Chic and Tracy Murphy
Ken and Linda Jenner
Del and Graham Dee
John and Diane Mill
Bob and Anne Herbert.

All were customers who had become friends. All had helped me since my arrival at Usk by giving me huge support thus enabling me to establish a successful club.

The Ascot boxes are designed for a dozen people in comfort or perhaps sixteen to twenty people less comfortably, but on one particular occasion I had a total of thirty-eight in the box. 'Pack em in Savva' was at it again. Every one enjoyed the superb food drink and ambience, despite somewhat cramped conditions and it was a day to remember. Many of my guests had companies of their own and engaged in similar public relations exercises so it was no surprise that many asked me for details of box hire and catering arrangements, as one said; "I take my best customers to the Monaco Grand Prix each year and frankly I don't think half of them enjoy it. Here at Ascot on the other hand, there is so much more to see and do and the atmosphere is all so exciting".

I decided to continue another activity I had grown accustomed to while at Windsor. Each year Pam and I took a January break and flew to the Caribbean for some winter sunshine and a rest after the hectic Christmas season. I decided that on this occasion, because of the success of the Usk operation, we would take a two-week holiday in Barbados. But this time I intended to fly there in style.

Kuoni, a travel company, were offering Concorde flights to Barbados and I managed to acquire two tickets for one of these special flights.

"It's rather expensive" complained my Wife Pam, but when I explained that we would gain another five hours of sunshine by flying on Concorde, she warmed to the idea.

The flight was sensational, and as promised we arrived in the Caribbean and checked into our hotel almost five earlier than by flying by a standard airline. Unfortunately it was raining. Like all tropical islands, Barbados has a shower, on average, once a day. It soon comes and goes, but not this one. Had the Welsh rain followed us?

I changed into my swimming trunks and readied myself for the beach; Pam asked what I was doing.

"I've not paid all that money to come here on Concorde and not enjoy an extra four and a half hours on the beach, rain or no rain. I suggest you get ready too"

Ten minutes later we made our way to the beach and, sitting on two sun beds under an umbrella, we viewed the downpour from our vantage point on the deserted beach.

"This is the life," I said. "Just think, right now the grockles will be still out over the Atlantic somewhere, chugging along in their battered old British Airways Jumbo, while here we are ahead of them, sitting in - in -in the pissing rain". We looked at each other and burst out laughing.

The rain eventually came to an end some four and a half hours later. Just in time to welcome the grockels to the island in brilliant sunshine.

"Do you think it's the sun shining on the righteous" asked Pam.

"No it's the devil looking after his own" I replied sullenly.

Barbados is an island that receives daily visits from cruise liners as one of the main stopping places along the Caribbean routes. Allan and Susan Blackburn arranged to meet us and spend a day with us as the liner on which they were cruising, quite by coincidence, visited Barbados while we were there. Allan was the head of a very large booking agency and show organiser for many of the major cruise companies and so often found himself having to go on a cruise to acquaint himself with the logistics of a particular ship's requirements, as far as entertainment was concerned.

We met Susan and Allan and took them to the Royal Pavilion for lunch. Afterwards we settled for a quiet afternoon on the beach. Allan wanted to know all about the club at Usk and Susan wanted to catch up on all the local gossip. Allan and Susan had not yet had an opportunity to visit the club and during the course of the afternoon I attempted to paint a verbal picture of the club, and life in general at Usk. Both of them were fascinated to learn of the possibility of Cliff returning to the club for another week.

"He obviously enjoyed working the venue," said Allan.

"Oh immensely" I confirmed. "You see" I continued, "from the very beginning back at Blazers, I recognised Cliff as a perfectionist, as I am; and so each time we work together our joint professional approach makes the date really special".

I did not wish to sound too grand, but I honestly believed that Cliff, who after all could pick and choose his dates, felt comfortable with our organisation and ability to present the very top stars like him in a club setting that made the date both acceptable and enjoyable.

"Any plans to bring Royalty to Usk" asked Allan. He was well aware of my history of countless Royal Gala's at Blazers.

I told him there was a possibility of Princess Anne attending a charity evening on behalf of the 'Riding for the Disabled' organisation. I had had discussions with Davinia Cannon, one of the Princess Royal's chief aides and Davinia, who I knew well, had visited Usk, liked what she saw and would report back to the Princess.

Susan and Pam engrossed themselves in family discussions, the kids, their wives or sweethearts and all that, while Allan and I continued to talk shop.

"Any gaps in your spring and summer programme" asked Allan.

"One or two" I replied.

"Well I've got a very good male vocalist who will be free to do a week or so because he will be between ships" explained Allan. "His name is David Christian and he's a Sinatra type singer, with a great personality who always goes down well with the audience. He is not well enough known to 'top', but perhaps he could support one of your stars" Allan concluded.

I went through my list of forthcoming attractions from memory to see where I could fit the artiste.

"The Barron Knights or the Rockinberries might be a possibility, as their respective shows have a large comedy content" I speculated. "On the other hand, I have two great comedians in Jethro and Les Dawson coming to the club during the period and a male or female vocalist would be perfect to support one of these".

Allan was delighted at the prospect of David Christian working with either of the two star comics. I continued to run down the list in my mind and after exhausting the rest of the programme I could remember without the aid of my date sheet, I realised it had to be Les Dawson.

"The only other stars that need support yet to be arranged are Gene Pitney, Frankie Lain and Billy Eckstein. I need comedy or a magician to support them," I said.

"What about Jethro" Allan reminded me." You mentioned him as well as Les earlier on".

"No, I've remembered that Jethro is introducing his own support, also from Cornwall. Jethro reckons they're absolutely fantastic. Called, believe it or not, 'The Mechanical Horse Trough'. I told Jethro to go ahead and bring them with him"

"You've got some real heavy weights in that line up," observed Allan.

"I hope I've not pushed the boat out too far" I replied. "After all, having established the club, I'm going for the jugular so to speak. Let's hope the advance bookings justify the fees".

I was not unduly worried about my spring and summer program. The advance bookings were above average on most of the dates, even at this early stage, but Gene Pitney and Billy Eckstein's bookings were not yet coming up to expectations.

It was a shame that cruise liners only stopped at the various Caribbean islands for one day because the day with our friends came too rapidly to an end. We escorted them back to the cruise liner and bade them a fond farewell. The following day we decided to have one of those wonderful lazy by the sea. I was not to know that it would turn out to be one of the most amazing afternoons of my life.

At about two pm, immediately after lunch, I was called by a hotel beach attendant to take a phone call deemed urgent enough to bring me off the beach. Marilyn my secretary apologised for disturbing me and in a voice quivering with excitement told me that Cliff had confirmed his dates for a return to lJsk. I related this good news to Pam and settled back to reflect on the wonderful news. Shortly afterwards, I was interrupted a second time and once again came from the beach to take a call. It was Marilyn again.

"I'm sorry to disturb you again, but I've just received more good news. Davinia Cannon has just rung to say that HRH the Princess Royal has agreed to attend a Gala Charity night at Usk. And," continued Marilyn, "I don't know if you are aware but Gene Pitney is flying up the charts".

"You're joking" I interrupted.

"No" said Marilyn. "He's released a remake of 'Something's got a hold of my heart' in collaboration with the singer Marc Almond and its racing up the charts."

"Well I never" I replied. "Well, let us hope it does something for the bookings".

Marilyn was quick to respond. "Oh it has already. The phone bookings are coming in thick and fast.

I returned to Pam on the beach with the good news. Cliff and Princess Anne confirmed and Pitney heading for a sell-out. I could scarcely believe my luck and, deciding a celebration was in order, immediately ordered a bottle of champagne. While waiting for the bottle to arrive we decided to have a dip in the blue waters of the Caribbean. I suddenly heard a voice call my name. Standing on the beach was our waiter with the champagne and two glasses.

"Your champagne Sir" he said.

"Well" I replied mischievously "fetch it in".

The wonderful thing about this story is that the waiter did not even hesitate.

"Certainly Sir" he said and walked straight into the sea and out to the spot where we were standing. The water was at stomach height. I held the tray and glasses whilst he popped the cork and poured.

"Will there be anything else Sir," asked the waiter.

"Not at the moment thank you" and he departed, placing the remainder of the champagne and the bucket on our sun bed table before returning to the hotel his very smart, but dripping wet uniform.

Pam and I clinked glasses and toasted our good news day in style; belly deep in the Caribbean. It was only then that I noticed a fairly large number of fellow tourists were eying us with looks of amazement. An American, who could contain his curiosity no longer, called across.

"Hi there, I saw that. You know the waiter walking in the sea and all that. Something of a celebration?" he suggested.

"Yes" I said.

"Wedding anniversary I'd guess" He speculated.

"You've got it in one" I replied.

On returning to the UK there was much to do. Gene Pitney was sold out. I prepared the launch of the Cliff Richard week and began to put in place the promotion of our Royal Gala Charity night. Bob Herbert my friend and accountant to the club rang me to discuss the interim figures.

"The bottom line" he concluded after a long and, at times, dreary report. "You have done very well indeed. In fact you are worth in cash and assets a million pounds".

Bob was a cautious man and warned me of over exuberance. Be prepared for every eventuality he would say; consolidate for a rainy day. Needless to say I took no notice of Bob's warnings. Instead I rejoiced on having made my mark at Usk. I had proved that if the product was right one could make a successful business, even way out in the sticks

The clearest memory I have of the late eighties is the incredible increase in property values. My property at Usk was at one point increasing in value at an astonishing £50,000 per annum and it was for that reason I decided to buy a riverside property at Windsor as an investment for the future. Although Bob my accountant had his doubts as to the wisdom of my actions, I could see no end to the good times and felt it would prove a shrewd move in the long run.

Jethro, the hilarious Cornish comedian made a welcome return to Savvas. He had progressed enormously since being discovered by Jim Davidson a few years earlier and was now a household name. With his Cornish accent and drawl presentation he portrayed a unique brand of comedy that was enormously popular nationwide. I had played Jethro on numerous occasions since Jim brought him to my attention and I suppose I felt extra empathy towards him because of my eleven years in Cornwall as a boy.

During Jethro's week at Usk he told me he had bought a club in Cornwall. I'd heard that he'd bought a club and that it was doing very well but he explained to me that although it was doing good business, the operation had a number of flaws that worried Jethro. In particular the billing side of the business had a touch of hit and miss about it.

"I've noticed George that your operation of meals and particularly the payment is very efficient," said Jethro. "Whereas I have a hell of a job separating those that have prepaid from those that haven't, and I have a feeling that I am wide open to fiddling by the staff. I'm not saying it is happening for sure, it's just that I don't know, and not knowing is just as bad as the abuse itself. The truth is I need a system like yours".

I assured Jethro that he should not panic, after all he had only recently become a club owner, whereas I'd been in the catering game most of my life and I was sure we could pass on our experience and our systems to him.

Jethro jumped at this offer and asked if he could send one or two senior members of his staff to spend a little time at Savvas in order to gain knowledge of our catering and billing systems. I agreed and he duly dispatched two of his staff, who after a short time at Savvas soon grasped the workings of our billing system. I know Jethro was grateful and had no further problems.

The Jethro story reminds me of a similar problem I experienced at Jack King's club, called 'Kings of East Bourne'. I went there to support his Royal night along with a number of 'Club land Celebs'. In those days club operators would turn out to support a colleague. Prince Charles was guest of honour and The Three Degrees provided the entertainment. The night was to become famous as the night that Sheila Ferguson of the Three Degrees got Prince Charles out of the audience to dance with the act on stage, which of course brought the house down. Incidentally, ever since that night, the Three Degrees are described as Prince Charles's favourite group. The publicist that put that story out must have been a genius and I hope was knighted for his brilliant, but dubious story.

On the night of my visit to Jack's place his manager who was obviously under intense pressure with a Royal guest and so many VIP's to look after. Nevertheless, he found time to seek me out and ask if he could call me with regard to a certain problem with his catering. A few days later he called and told me his problem. It seemed that although his room dined about six hundred people, he found it a real struggle to get the food out of the kitchen and onto the table quickly enough. "I've noticed when visiting you George, that you are able to cater for twice as many as us with half the staff. Perhaps you could pop down some time, have a look at our set up and tell us where we are going wrong".

I agreed to visit Kings in an effort to help the beleaguered manager. Standing in a kitchen at Eastbourne is not my idea of a perfect night off, but I went and watched the service of food on a fairly busy night at Kings.

After fifteen minutes I came out to see the manager. "I think I've spotted your problem," I said.

"Already" he replied, rather sceptically I thought.

"Oh yes" I continued. "You see very often a problem is caused, created or exasperated by something very simple and at Kings this is the case. Your problem" I said, "is that your serving staff are taking only two or three plates of food out at a time, so that a waitress, for example serving a party of twelve, will have to go to and fro at least six times. This results in the service being slow and the waitress unable to serve large numbers of people, which means twice the staff, making the whole operation slow and labour intensive".

"But my staff cannot carry more than two or three plates at a time" said the manager somewhat impatiently.

I decided to hit him with the solution, and I must admit to becoming somewhat authoritarian. "Your plate's dear boy.".

"Plates" he replied with a bewildered look on his face.

"Yes plates, they are the wrong shape. They may well be lovely plates, but they are huge ovals instead of round and because they are not round they cannot be stacked on rings like mine".

The manager was amazed. "Of course" he muttered, "I remember now your staff carting a dozen or even more each time from the kitchen, in stacks on rings".

"Precisely" I interrupted. "It's as simple as that. Get rid of the ovals. Get standard round plates and some catering rings and you will find that not only will the staff soon learn to carry twelve, sixteen or even eighteen at a time, but also you will serve with half the staff you employ at present".

Genuinely impressed, my host thanked me profusely for the advice, which I know he had taken on board for I recall bumping into Jack himself sometime later and he told me they had taken my advice and it was just as I had predicted.

I often smile at the thought of Kings, plate revolution or Jethro's booking and billing systems and reflect on those early days of food riots at Cesars. Now I had set myself up as a kind of father figure of our industry. I guess I always knew I would go a long way in life - how far is it from Cornwall to Usk?

19

WATER WATER EVERYWHERE
CLIFF REVISITS - I COMPERE
PRINCESS ANNE AT USK
I NOTCH UP A LOSS OR TWO
VANISHING CLUBLAND
THE WIND OF RECESSION
ROY CHUBBY BROWN
THE CHIPPENDALES

Despite the fact that I was married to an Aquarian and had homes in Monte Carlo, Windsor and Usk, all with a close proximity to water, I am not a great fan of the element because throughout my life I have had a number of narrow escapes while attempting to enjoy it. For example, my brother in law John had a boat called Hang Ten which he moored at a place called Rock in Cornwall. He invited us and other members of the family to join him for a weekend soiree. When we arrived at the small seaside town I was surprised to find that John's boat was much smaller than I had expected.

"Hang Ten is not very big," I observed as John busied himself untying her for a brief voyage.

"What did you expect" said John with a laugh "the bloody Q.E.2.".

"No" I said "of course not, but there are rather a lot of us for such a small boat".

"Nonsense" John assured me. "The old girl will handle our lot, no problem".

We eventually got under way with he 'old girl' creaking under the strain of carrying John and Jenny, Pam and I, as well as John's two kids and our Jayne, a total of seven of us in all. As we began to clear the jetty John opened up the throttle and Hang Ten flew over the water at quite a speed. Although, with speed, she seemed higher out of the water I still felt very unsafe and told our host. "I can't swim John you know," I said.

"What" bellowed John, the noise of the engine partially blocking my comment? I repeated it louder this time.

"No need to worry, you're perfectly safe on here" he said.

We passed down the inlet with Rock on one side and Padstow on the other and headed out of the mouth of the estuary and into the open sea. As we left the calm of the inlet we ran into some hideous waves and I still remember the feeling of incredible terror that enveloped me. I am sure I was as near to a heart attack as I will ever get as the boat was thrown about from side to side. Pam was conscious of my extreme anxiety and asked John to take the boat back into Rock; which he did.

"I'll drop you all off and tie up near the beach," said John

"I'm all for that" I said. "May I help you with anything"? I was trying to put aside my harrowing experience in the knowledge that I would be soon getting off the confounded thing.

"Well as a matter of fact you could," said John, taking me up on my offer. "You see those metal rings there by the rocks to the side of the beach, I'll tie up there, could you just pop over the side with the line and do the necessary for me".

"I'll be glad to" I responded. Frankly I could not wait to get off.

The boat was only a few yards from the beach and the mooring rings, but what I did not realise and what John failed to tell me was that even in close this was not a gently sloping shallow bay but one with a notoriously steep incline. With the line in my hand I popped over the side and went straight to the bottom. Completely out of my depth, with a piece of string in my hand and to all intents and purposes drowning, I remembered that when I stepped into the water I was facing the beach a few feet away, so, with as much composure as possible I walked up the slope and on to the beach, gulping a much-needed intake of air as my head emerged above the water.

"You O.K." shouted the irrepressible John.

"Oh yes; fine" I said I tied up the boat and asked to be excused to go and phone my office which I did every day when away. On my return to the beach I made my apologies and said we could not stay any longer as my top of the bill had gone ill and I had to get back. I collected Pam and Jayne and we departed.

"Poor Frankie Vaughan" said Pam. "What is it, flu"? She asked.

"What are you on about"

"Well Frankie is topping the bill, so he must be the one who has gone ill" she concluded.

"Don't be daft," I said. "I lied. Frank is fine, and now thank God so am I. I've got away from that place and I'm still alive. To run the risk of drowning once is enough, but twice in a morning, that's really pushing the boat out". Oops!! A bad pun.

I will not bore you with all the details of my sail boat fiasco. Having been persuaded by Chic Murphy, (against my better judgement), to hire a small sail boat while holidaying together in Martinique, we had to be rescued from disaster as the sail boat, out of control in my inexperienced hands, sailed under a huge catamaran moored just outside the entrance to the bay. Passing helplessly underneath her belly and between her two huge floats was a most frightening experience, but the crack that followed as the small sail broke off was terrifying.

Imagine the panic that followed as we emerged sailess from the other side of the 'Cat'. Without our sail we were helpless as we were pulled out to sea by the strong current. Mercifully, after much waving and shouting, we were towed us back to the safety of the hotel marina by the lifeguards, under the watchful eye of a throng of assorted tourists including Pam Savva and Tracy Murphy.

On another occasion, during a summer holiday break in Monte Carlo, I allowed the temptation to take to the water get the better of me once again. It was a hot sunny day without a breeze and the water was as still as glass with hundreds of water lovers taking advantage of the idyllic conditions. I spotted a pedalo resting at the waters edge; the others were all in use. These vehicles were for the use of the patrons of the Miami Plage beach resort, Monte Carlo so as customers ourselves we made our way to the pedalo and launched it into the calm water.

"Are you sure you want to do this" said Pam sceptically, knowing my fear of water and drowning in it.

"Nothing can go wrong" I insisted. "It's a perfect day, look how many people are in the water. Besides, pedalos are almost unsinkable".

We took off, carefully pedalling our way through the crowded inshore water and gradually made our way out into the bay. As we pedalled along we chatted about this and that, when suddenly I noticed that Pam's side of the vehicle was gradually lifting out of the water, while my side was slowly sinking. "We seem to be tilting over" I said with some concern.

"Oh you're right" Pam replied and after a pause said, "you know, I think your float is taking in water. It must have a hole in it somewhere; I think we'd better pedal back to the beach".

The tilt was getting more pronounced by the minute and it was obvious to me that eventually the whole machine would flip over, drowning me whilst Pam (who could swim quite well) swam back to the shore. "Pedal for your life" I rasped absolutely filled with panic. Reflecting on the incident now, I'm sure that if someone had monitored the time it took us to pedal from that point in the bay to the beach, it would have shown a new pedalling record. By the time we reached the beach Pam's side of the pedalo was clear of the water; we arrived back in an almost horizontal position.

I furiously reproached the beach attendant for allowing a faulty piece of equipment to be left unattended on the beach for the use of patrons.

"Monsieur Savva I did not see you take it" flapped the embarrassed Gerrard. "I was on my break when you took to the water" he continued. "Otherwise I would have told you not to use the pedalo because there is a hole in one of the floats".

"With respect Garrard" I bellowed. "You should have removed the bloody thing from the beach or hung a notice on it warning potential users".

"I understand your anger" said the beleaguered Gerrard "but surely if you have a problem you simply leave the craft and swim back to the beach".

There followed a brief pause and then I showed my hand. "I can't swim," I said. "I've never learnt and that is why it is important to me that water craft must be safe at all times". "You don't swim," repeated Gerrard parrot fashion, with an air of total surprise. "Then Monsieur Savva you must learn, or do not go into the water at all. Anything can happen while you are out there. If you cannot swim then sooner or later you will probably drown". Charming I thought.

I will not relate the near end of my existence when crossing the English Channel in a hovercraft, neither will I tell the tale of my escape when a massive twenty foot tidal wave tried to crush me in Northern Hawaii. The incident that proved to me that, somehow, I had offended a supernatural being with oceanic responsibilities, happened to me on my way from Cobblers Cove to the Royal Pavilion Hotel, a lunch time excursion during a Barbados holiday.

As we set off by boat for the lunch I took no chances. As I sat in the small modern motorboat I wore a life jacket and clutched a rubber safety ring for good measure. I felt fairly secure. The trip to Cobblers Creek was lovely. After a great lunch, during which I consumed a bottle of white wine, we returned to the jetty and our waiting boat. I was quite merry and certainly relaxed about the trip back. I declined our boatman's invitation to don the life jacket again and did not bother with the large rubber ring; Dutch courage had taken over. Incidentally, we had affectionately named our boatman Black Adder, after the well-known TV series of the same name.

As we climbed on board Black Adder approached me and asked if he might take another passenger for the trip back. "My cousin is one of the chefs here, and if you don't mind he would like a lift home - he lives near your hotel,"

"Of course dear boy" I said merrily.

Black Adder's cousin turned out to be a twenty-two stone heavyweight, who thanked me profusely as he joined me in the back of the craft. Pam moved to the front to make room for him. As we motored away from the jetty it became clear to anyone with a modicum of sense, that we had become overloaded. On the other hand with the boat being thrust along by the powerful outboard motor we had little anxiety. That is until it was discovered that we were taking on water, then, as if this was not enough, a few minutes later the outboard motor stopped.

Black Adder apologised but assured us that he had 'gassed her up' before making the trip but in any event produced a can of petrol and after asking me to hold a funnel attempted to fill the outboard motor on the bobbing stationary boat. The tank was indeed at least three quarters full and took very little extra petrol from his can. Most of the contents spilled over me, the chef and the back of the boat. As this activity was taking place water continued to rise in the back of the boat, adding to the combined overweight of the chef and I.

"I think I must have an engine blockage" said the Adder.

"No, I think the problem is here," said his cousin, holding up a disconnected fuel line. I realised we were going to sink. At last the sea had got me I thought. Our situation had an understandably sobering effect on me and Pam was quick to spot my anxiety.

"Enough of this messing about" she said. "Get us to the shore and drop us off".

Black Adder explained that without a working engine it was going to be difficult getting to the shore.

"You know my husband cannot swim. You know how he fears the water. So get us to that shore. Roll up your sleeves gentlemen and we'll row the boat with our hands."

This we did and as soon as we reached the shallows we popped over the side and waded ashore leaving Black Adder and his cousin to their boat repairs and bailing.

"That's it," said I. "We are walking home".

"You're bloody right we are," replied Pam.

As we strode out along the beach I reached into my breast pocket for my cigarettes and lighter.

"What are you doing Say" asked Pam.

"I'm just going to have a fag," I answered.

"Are you off your head? You're soaked in petrol remember?" she said. "If you light up now you'll probably burn for a week". Some years later I learnt to swim and as an added bonus gave up fags as well.

Cliff Richard's return visit to Usk was another milestone in in my career as I was invited by the star to present the show personally. Cliff's date was specially arranged by him and he put together a show just for Savvas at Usk. I am sure that following his previous visit to the club, he was taken by the unique atmosphere of the room and decided to turn that to his advantage, by playing a sort of one-man show. The usual backing band were missing, as were the dancers that often accompanied his productions. Cliff arrived with only his excellent keyboard player Paul Mossul, and apart from Cliff playing acoustic guitar, this was the only musical accompaniment for the show. The show was a two hour presentation of 'Cliff, the Man and his Music' and the show was appropriately named 'Just Cliff'.

The invitation to present him from stage came directly from Cliff.

"Cliff feels that since Savvas is the only club date that he has undertaken and since the show 'Just Cliff' is put together especially for your club, he thought it would be nice for you to personally introduce him each evening" said his Manager David Bryce. I was more than happy, and very honoured to oblige.

"Ladies and Gentlemen" I began, "I know many of you have travelled many miles to be here tonight, and I know it's because you have come to see not only a Star but a living legend. For me it is an honour not only to present a great star, but also a very special friend. Ladies and Gentlemen, please welcome 'Just Cliff' ".

A handshake as Cliff arrived on stage to loud applause and I departed, followed by a magical two-hour performance from Cliff using his guitar and keyboard accompaniment as well as between songs chat that was both amusing and often profound, but above all interesting, Cliff performed a broad selection of numbers that had propelled him to super stardom and the audience thrilled to hear hit after hit from Cliff's immense repertoire.

The show ran for a week, was a huge success and received rave notices from the local media.

"The Artiste was described by Savva as a living legend, I thought was a touch over the top" said one commentator. "But I have to say that I quickly changed my mind and attitude. Watching Cliff weave his special magic on a spellbound audience of 800 people, I have to agree with the billing."

Princess Anne's visit to the club was another feather in our cap. I'd catered for Her Royal Highness on many previous occasions and was becoming a dab hand at what was required of me. Her Royal Highness was the guest of honour at our special charity occasion, which included the Welsh branch of Riding for the Disabled.

A particular new element sticks in my memory which made it different from the other Princess Anne royal nights I had previously organised and this was the extraordinary security that surrounded her visit. Royalty had never been as popular in Wales as in England nevertheless; Princess Anne was one of the most popular royals and was seen as a hard worker for various charities. The security screen thrown around the club had more to do with a possible terrorist attack than anything else as the early nineties saw an increase in the activities of the I.R.A.

Just prior to and during the Royal visit, gun toting officers in plain clothes, photocopied lists of ticket carrying punters, uniformed police, complete with sniffer dogs, constantly checked the grounds, the roof, the basement and even the drains of the club. The day before the Gala night, the security was so tight simply coming and going from the premises a real hassle. Almost everyone within a mile of Savvas was stopped and searched. I still smile as I recall a security officer carefully scrutinising our delivery of fruit and vegetables. Mr. Reynolds, our fruit and veg man, patiently stood by his van as security personnel swarmed all over it.

"You take the tomatoes and the lettuce," said one uniform to another "I'll get the fruit and Bill can take care of the cucumbers and the other items". Diligently they went about their work, examining each item prior to releasing it to the kitchen. I don't remember anyone checking the strawberries.

We had undertaken to raise enough cash to buy a Sunshine Coach through our organisation The Variety Club of Great Britain and present it to a local children's home or school. The fund raising, spearheaded by Pam, had reached the target of Fourteen Thousand Pounds, the cost of the coach, which stood gleaming and new in our car park ready for presentation. H.R.H. agreed to make the presentation upon her arrival at the club and duly performed the function, presenting the keys to the principals of an orphanage and school from nearby Chepstow.

The Princess Royal was always willing to contribute to an evening's proceedings in any possible way and she will always have my utmost admiration as the charity evenings organised around her presence were a joy because she lent a hand wherever possible to make the event a happy and memorable one.

As usual, she shook hands, met and chatted to the endless line of sponsors, thanking them for their support before sitting down to dinner and then shook hands and chatted to yet another long line of artistes and staff, before departing. The show comprised Jimmy Tarbuck, Kenny Lynch and Joe Longthorne and was hosted and compered by Danny La Rue. During the intermission, H.R.H. joined me on stage to draw numbers and present the raffle prizes. The first two tickets she drew from the drum were colleagues of the Princess and were her top table guests. The unusual coincidence brought hoots of laughter from the audience. Smiling, H.R.H. turned to me and asked, "Do you think they (the audience) will think it is a fix?"

"I'm sure not Ma'am" I replied," but if they do don't worry, I have a back way out of here".

"Thank heavens for that Mr. Savva" she chuckled. "You think of everything".

Another amusing incident comes to mind which occurred during the sales run up to the Royal night. While on reception duty one evening I took a call from a lady who asking for four tickets for the Princess Anne Gala.

"I'm sorry madam," said I "I'm afraid we're fully booked".

"Fully booked" answered the lady. "What all week?"

"Oh No Madam" I replied. "The Princess Royal is only here for one night".

"Only one night" echoed the lady. "Well why isn't she doing seven nights like everybody else that you have at the club," she complained before hanging up.

Ever since the day Bob Herbert told me I was worth a million pounds a curse seemed to have settled upon our business. At first a few cracks appeared such as disappointing sales for a few dates where we expected better, but clubs up and down the country were experiencing similar difficulties; attendances were definitely dwindling. Autumn and Christmas came and went and the seasonal box office was fairly successful, but even so I viewed the New Year with some concern. The lack of enthusiasm for some of our forthcoming attractions reflected in an overall drop in sales. It was obvious that the country was heading into recession.

Like many club proprietors, while worried about the possibility of recession, I was not running scared. After all we had been through recessions before. In fact I opened Blazers in the middle of one. As we turned into the New Year a meeting of the Cabaret Clubs Federation was called to discuss current problems involving our industry. Artiste fees, Performing Rights Society rates, Licensing and other club related matters were on the agenda. But overriding all of this was the genuine anxiety expressed by many members to the general state of our industry and the gathering economic gloom.

To underline the decline of our industry, clubs like Batley Variety Club, The Wakefield Theatre Club, The Talk of the Midlands at Derby, The Webbington at Weston, Blazers at Windsor and many many more were sold off or went bankrupt during this period.

The biggest club in the country, Jollees at Stoke on Trent and the Fiesta at Sheffield, one of the most beautiful clubs in Britain, were the next two to close and a rumour that the Forte Group intended to dispose of their cabaret interests proved to be factual. They sold their Midlands operation the Night Out at Birmingham and their Golden Garter at Manchester to a group called First Leisure. First Leisure were specialists in the Disco field and lost no time in converting the previously famous cabaret operations into giant, magnificently refurbished, high tec discos. The Forte flagship cabaret showroom in London's West End, the famous Talk of the Town was taken over by Peter Stringfellow and became Stringfellows Disco Night Club.

Bob Wheatly, well known entrepreneur, and head of the Wheatly Taverns added to his empire the Kings Club at Leicester and the Queens Club at Westcliff on Sea, both of which failed to do business for him. Later he took over Cesars Palace at Luton, acquiring the lease from Ladbrokes, who after struggling with the operation had given up on it. Sadly Cesars was the straw that broke Bob's business back. I received news of his bankruptcy with sadness. Cesars Palace later became yet another disco.

Saddest of all was Pat Cowan's demise at Windsor. After battling bravely for a couple of years following my departure, Pat's empire collapsed around him. The personal problems which had led to his gambling addiction finally brought about his downfall. I surveyed these business failures happenings, but I was still not convinced that the industry as I knew it was dying. I must have been blind or stupid or both.

In fairness I was out on my own at Usk, there was no opposition or competition for miles. The Club Double Diamond, The Webbington, The Showboat and the White Wheat at Maesteg, had all either ceased to trade or converted into a part time cabaret and disco. In addition, because of my long association with the cabaret business, I was able to continue to bring to Wales some of the great names that might otherwise have been reluctant to play a club in the sticks. Notable successes with Tommy Steele, Dame Edna Everidge and alas Smith and Jones, all helped to cushion me against some of the problems facing other clubs and the almost annual appearance of Cliff Richard must not be underestimated in helping the operation at Savvas to remain in operation well beyond its sell by date.

Despite the successes with the great stars, I too recorded a number of loss making weeks and this was a shock to the system for me. Many of my hard hit colleagues blamed the banks for their demise in calling in their loans. These were the same managers of the same banks that had encouraged us to borrow like hell during the mid eighties.

Old Ted Merritt, my Bank Manager, had retired and been replaced by a dynamic creature called Mr. Bird. I thought from the outset that his name was appropriate in that he was something of a high flier. When I first met him I was left with the impression that this humourless grey individual probably got his kicks out of attending funerals, or perhaps he got his laughs from open graves or burning churches. One thing's for certain, had he been around a couple of thousand years earlier he would have been right there at Christ's crucifixion, seated in the front row.

Having notched up a loss or two, repayments of our bank loan became somewhat erratic. The Bird was quick to spot this and called in the loan in its entirety. Undoubtedly, problems were beginning to surface but the biggest problem was the bank's intransigence. Unlike days of old, banks would no longer stand by clients during a recessionary period, but instead withdrew their support in its entirety. It seemed the Black Horse, (Lloyd's famous logo), had bolted.

At this time I changed breweries. I had been approached several times by brewers asking me to change and offering lucrative terms to do so. Having made up my mind to make the change, I secured a new supplier and negotiated a new loan. This enabled me to repay the loan of the outgoing brewery and pay off the outstanding balance of the bank loan to the Bird (vulture?) at Lloyds of Woking. Looking back, it seems strange that at a time when the banks were 'drying up' the brewing industry was still prepared to weigh in with a substantial financial commitment. However, it is more understandable when their willingness to loan and thereby secure our account, is set against the fact that the level of trade at Savvas was equal to fifteen pubs in weekly consumption.

        Still confident that the recent set backs in trade were nothing but a blip due to a recession that would soon end, I continued to plan my programme of entertainment and activities well into the future and produced the first ever year long programme which ran from January 1991 until December of the same year. I was making a promise to our customers that we would continue to produce major entertainment at Usk. Although I did make the decision to tread more carefully, dispensing with regular seven night trading in favour of five night presentations for many of our forthcoming attractions as Mondays to Wednesdays became almost impossible to sell at this time unless presenting the biggest stars.

Mick Millar, Johnny Hackett, Frank Carson and Paul Melba were just a few of the comedians that graced our boards at this time, comedians of great stature and great value for money. The emphasis was very much on comedy as I felt that people would still welcome an opportunity to laugh in these difficult times. Comedy heavyweights, Barrymore, Dawson, Davidson, Starr and others, were also part of the programme, as were comedy groups such as the Barron Knights, Grumbleweeds, Rockinberries and Black Onyx.

        Despite the twelve month programme and the mass distribution of it throughout towns and cities within a fifty mile radius, we still suffered the occasional loss regardless of the fact that everything we had put together was the very best and represented the ultimate in entertainment and in value.

        Around this time a Newport publican approached me one evening just after the show.

        "Jimmy Jones was great George, a great comedian". He said

        "He sure is," I agreed. "Do you know that years ago I would not play Jimmy because he was too blue, now I play him on a regular basis?"

        The publican thought for a moment and then made the following observation.

        "Blue or not blue, comedy has got to reflect every day life. I'm surprised you've not played Roy Chubby Brown yet. He's really blue but everybody loves him and he fills everywhere he goes. You have heard of him haven't you?"

        "Oh yes," I lied. "I'm sure he will be at Savvas Club before long."

        "Well I'll tell you now" replied the publican excitedly. "If you book him I will personally require five hundred tickets". He left his card and strode off into the night.

        I'm bound to say I'd never heard of Roy Chubby Brown up to that moment and had lied to the publican because how could a foremost entrepreneur, Wales's leading entertainment guru, the mighty Savva etc etc, not have heard of any entertainer, let alone one that fills venues wherever he goes. I must get on the phone to Jimmy Smith I thought.

"Roy Chubby Brown" said Jimmy parrot fashion at the other end of the line the following morning. "Yes a Northern comedian, very blue" he continued. "I believe he is doing big business wherever he goes."

"Well I had never heard of him" I replied "and I certainly have never been offered him as I recall".

"I've never given it a thought to tell you the truth," said Jimmy. "To be fair, I've never really seen Chubby Brown as a Savvas Club type act. After all Say, you've tended to draw the line at Jimmy Jones and Bernard Manning up to now".

I told Jimmy about my conversation with the Newport publican and asked him to try for a set of four or five days as a try out for Chubby Brown at Usk. Roy was managed by George Foster, a Northern agent who by the end of that day agreed to a set of dates for Chubby at Savvas Club. It was the start of a long and pleasant relationship between Roy, George and me.

Having advised the publican of the upcoming dates, he duly obliged by buying five hundred tickets for opening night, as he had said he would. In fact he came back for more. In a short time I was sold out completely and delighted at my good fortune particularly as the venture had taken off as it were, with the minimum of advertising. Word of mouth had sold the dates and, bearing in mind that Chubby's previous previous work in Wales amounted to no more than an appearance at the Barry Memorial Hall, it made the sell out even more remarkable. Chubby had obviously attained cult status.

I remember my first meeting with Chubby on the morning of his Usk debut. He was Chubby by name and chubby by nature and wore a straw hat that partially covered a round gentle face. Sitting in my office drinking tea, he looked for all the world like one of those monks you often see in films tending vegetables in the fields. One would never imagine that this vicar like, very pleasant gentleman, could be the same guy who would go on stage with by far the filthiest act ever performed on a British stage.

He asked me what time he was on stage and I told him that top of the bill time was normally at eleven p.m. and that the supporting artiste would be on stage at ten p.m. for a forty-five minute spot, allowing a fifteen-minute interval between support and top.

"Two mistakes" said Chubby immediately. "I should go on at nine thirty p.m. and you don't need any supporting artiste".

This advice took me by complete surprise. I pointed out that at Savvas Club, like any other similar venue, we always worked to the times specified.

"Maybe, maybe" insisted Chubby. "But you've never played me or my type of act and therefore never experienced my type of audience. I will bring in an audience of animals compared to your normal club crowd."

His description of his 'following' was unexpected to say the least. Even though he went further in explaining that his following were wild, rough and intimidating, I still saw no reason to change my modus operandi and stuck with tradition, spurning all attempts by Chubby to get me to alter them.

"Well don't say I didn't warn you George," he said. "If you want a club tomorrow, then you ought to do what I say tonight" he said emphatically. "Oh and by the way, have plenty of beer on hand, my crowd are drinkers; and plenty of bouncers."

Chubby was right about everything. His opening night at Usk was almost a catastrophe; and without doubt the wildest and most frightening of my life. The timing of the show was wrong, as was the inclusion of a support act. The length of the evening was also a terrible mistake. After that first night I was very lucky to have survived with the club intact. My three bouncers, assisted by Chubby's own security officer, were adequate in so far as no number of bouncers would have been able to quell an outbreak of trouble. An audience of seven hundred for Chubby would have needed six hundred bouncers to ensure complete security because nearly every customer was a pissed time bomb.

The punters turned up between 7.00.p.m. and 7.45.p.m. and once allocated their seating began to drink; very little food was ordered. If there was a silver lining to the cloud of that night it was that the bar takings hit an all time record. Figures of two thousand pounds an hour were achieved and I found myself rushing from cash register to cash register in an effort to empty them before they overflowed. Chubby, in his dressing room back stage, was more than a little peeved at my refusal to alter the timings on his advice, and expressed his disquiet in no uncertain terms as the audience became more and more raucous. I gave a sigh of relief at 10p.m. when the support act came on stage.

Clive Webb, a zany comedy magician, had the dubious task of warming the crowd for the top of the bill but, anticipating Chubby coming on stage, the audience greeted Roddy's introduction of Clive Webb with a round of booing and abuse. Despite this and the chanting of 'We want Chubby, we want Chubby' over and over again. Clive a very experienced old trouper could not make himself heard above the din. Failing to quell the noise of the audience, who were now shouting 'off off'', Clive reached into his armoury of props and went straight to his firing of the gun routine.

Normally, following the gun's loud report, Clive would follow up with the line "Come on now; own up, how many of you shit yourselves?". This almost guaranteed a laugh, but not this night. There were attempts by a few punters to grab Clive and pull him off the stage, but all attempts were stopped by my security staff, assisted by 'Banger' Chubby's aptly named personal bouncer.

I sent a message back stage to Roddy telling him to get Clive off as the situation was getting totally out of hand. Clive by this time had decided to have a confrontation with the entire audience, on a sort of, one to seven hundred basis. I beat a hasty retreat to the foyer, away from the intimidating crowd and did not see Clive dip into his props and emerge with his axe.

Most magicians sawed people in half, but Clive chopped heads off, an excellent illusion that usually ensured rapturous applause. But tonight Clive made no attempt at executing the illusion, if you will pardon the pun, but rushed about the stage waving the axe Red Indian style, hooting, hollering and hurling abuse to all and sundry.

"I think he's been driven off his head," said Roddy, who also arrived at reception.

"What are you doing here Roddy?" I asked. "Why aren't you back stage bringing matters under control like I asked you".

"George" replied Roddy firmly. "I tried to do what you asked but Clive would not come off. The audience has told me to fuck off, all seven hundred of them. The support act has told me to fuck off; the top of the bill has told me to fuck off. Therefore, I am complying with instructions."

Clive Webb eventually left the stage to the sound of his own feet and the abuse and obscenities of an audience baying for blood.

"Do you think they liked me?" asked Clive, as he went through the back door to his car. A remark that we laughed at many times in the future when working together under totally different circumstances. The fifteen-minute intermission between Clive's departure and Chubby's arrival on stage gave the volatile punters a chance to visit both the toilets and the bar. Both areas came under extreme and sustained pressure.

The lights dimmed, the intro music, the theme from Rocky, filled the auditorium and on stage came Chubby Brown. The cheers were deafening as he stood there in a brightly coloured two-piece suit and a Biggles flying hat and goggles. He silenced the audience as he pumped out gag after gag each met with huge laughter and copious applause. The content of the material stunned me. I was aware that he was the bluest of comedians, but this was filth, outrageous and unbelievable. The sort of material that comedians in earlier times would have been locked up for, along with the club manager and anyone else associated with the presentation.

Chubby Brown brought the house down. At the end of a 90-minute performance he left the stage to a tumultuous standing ovation, shrieks and yells of satisfaction and cries for more. No sooner had he departed to the sanctity of his dressing room for a well-earned cup of tea than the legion of drunken louts and loutesses, yobs and yobesses decided it was time to fight. Skirmishes broke out in every part of the club. Only stopping the music, bringing up the house lights and announcing the early closing of the club avoided a blood bath. Chubby's advice was absolutely correct and I knew I had to rearrange things for any future appearances at the club. I reorganised the times to open at 7.30.p.m. Showtime at 9.30.p.m. close at 11.30.p.m. Chubby became a regular visitor to Usk and the club profited handsomely each time he appeared.

Past experience has taught club operators that over exposure of an act could cause a diminished following for that particular act. This however did not seem to apply in Chubby's case. In fact quite the opposite occurred. Instead of his following diminishing it increased. His popularity spread as the public simply could not get enough of him. I must also say that once the new timings were put in place I had no further trouble. In fact I looked forward to Chubby's visits as it meant a guaranteed sell out every time and a short night at which record bar takings were achieved.

Chubby Brown represented the dramatic change that was taking place within the entertainment industry. Tastes were changing as the new generation looked for a totally different entertainment scenario and John Mills comment of 'filth sells' some years earlier, echoed in my ears. How right he was proved to be, but his 'Ladies only' evenings with Dave Jade and his 'Winkle time' or Jimmy Smith's 'gentlemen only' evenings with Bernard Manning and three strippers were the thin end of the wedge. Club operators, struggling with a recession, were quick to see the profit from this new demand and I was no exception.

Jimmy Smith, to his eternal credit, acquired a video and promotion pack of an American all male dance group called the Chippendales and immediately saw a potentially rewarding act for the club. The Chippendales were a specially chosen group of good looking American hunks that already had female hearts fluttering across the U.S.A. The act comprised of a series of dance routines in which the boys came on dressed as Sailors, Soldiers or Slaves etc. During their dance routines they would gradually disrobe, revealing the body beautiful to the exited female audience. They never revealed all, but at the same time left little to the imagination. As far as audiences go they were to transform the art of striptease from a previously male dominated entertainment, to a female entertainment that quickly became hugely popular.

The Chippendales introduction into the U.K. was a surprise appearance at a Royal Charity Gala in London. The Piccadilly Theatre was packed to the gunnels with a totally female audience, including most Fleet Street reporters, and they gave the boys a rapturous reception and reports on the show appeared in most newspapers the following day. Jimmy Smith, on behalf of Savvas Club, stepped in and secured a date for the club immediately following the end of their Piccadilly run. The news of their impending arrival at Savvas, gripped the South Wales media's imagination and their date at the club quickly sold out. Such was the demand for tickets for this, the first ever appearance of the Chippendales in a British Cabaret Club, that it seemed as if every female wanted to catch their act.

Their show was outrageously suggestive and yet tastefully presented and utterly professional. Savvas Club was way out in front in playing the Chippendales several times before the remainder of club land woke up to the hot box office property that had crossed the Atlantic.

With Chubby Brown and The Chippendales appearing on our programme with increasing regularity, I turned my entertainment direction towards a growing list of sleazy artistes in order to satisfy the seemingly unquenchable thirst of my customers. Kevin Bloody Wilson, a very blue Australian comic, was followed by a Northern comedian who arrived on stage totally naked and told very blue gags while getting dressed, were just two of other blue comedians that were booked to appear at the club at this time. In addition, new, all male dance troupes that were springing up everywhere were also contracted to appear, these included Adonis, Men of Hollywood, The Dreamboys, Knights of Fantasy and the Centurions. I had become South Wales's King of Sleaze and Jimmy Smith my procurer!!

The fact was that business was getting tough as the recession began to bite. Against this background club operators seized on any new form of entertainment with box office appeal, ditching any preconceived ideas in the process. However, there are fifty-two weeks in every year and therefore our programme had to reflect the old as well as the new. Lennie Peters, David Essex, The Hollies, Renato, Duncan Norvelle and Little and Large were proudly presented, sharing our programme with the likes of the 'Chips', the 'Chops' and the 'Chaps', if you'll pardon the abbreviated expression. It was strange to see the club programme with such a wide range of entertainment; to see the bluest of comedians or the most suggestive attractions interspersed with solid traditional family entertainment. But we did feature both on the same list of forthcoming attractions and the one did not in any way damage or interfere with the other. Customers simply chose the acts they wanted to see.

I viewed the early nineties with a sense of foreboding; No one could escape the realities of rising unemployment, disappearing audiences and disappearing clubs. From being confident that once again I could ride out yet another recession, I began to wonder whether this one was going to be the mother of them all.

As an entertainment operator my job was to take people on a journey away from their daily problems into a world of fun, fantasy and make believe. For a few hours per evening to offer a glamorous escape. To that end I dedicated my efforts and had made a good living in the process, my beaming face meeting and greeting customers, a task I genuinely enjoyed, always.

Little did the public - my public, my friends and supporters realise that behind that greeting, that smile and those friendly words there was often anxiety or pain because of business problems or concern for friends or colleagues, perhaps family grief or tragedy. I remember my colleague Gerry Brooke, compere at Cesars Palace on one particular occasion uttering those immortal words 'The show must go on'. This after his usual performance of fun, laughter and introduction of the show, which he carried out that night, even after receiving word of the death of one of his beloved twins just before he went on.

Like those totally professional troupers on stage, we operators too often had to close our minds to our troubles. For us also the show had to go on even as we wrestled with our problems and moved further into the worst recession ever known in our industry.

20

THE FAMILY
LENNIE PETERS AND RODDY
DAVID ESSEX AND ME
CLIFF RICHARD IN AUSTRALIA
H.R.H. PRINCE PHILLIP VISITS USK
BARRY AND MIKE PICK UP A ROYAL
THE PROBLEMS MOUNT
JOHN MAJOR WINS
THE COUNTRY LOSES

When asked about family I have always replied that my wife and I have six children; I do this for two main reasons. Firstly, it is far easier than a complicated explanation of multiple marriages and relationships and secondly, to my Greek Cypriot half, it sounds far more macho! For the record I have three sons, George, Andrew and James, and my wife has three children from a previous marriage, Steven, Andrew and Jayne.

Steven completed an apprenticeship and is a fully qualified carpenter and joiner, George has an Honor's Degree from University and has moved into the world of computers, and Christopher, who as a young lad always wanted to drive a train, succeeded in his ambition by joining British Rail and becoming a driver of Intercity 125's. After leaving school Andrew and James, our youngest two lads, headed for the London area where Andrew sought a career in catering, whilst James settled into a position with the Royal Mail at Twickenham.

Our Daughter Jayne, not only a very pretty girl, but also with an extremely good head on her shoulders, seemed to have secured a bright future with Honeywell Computers in West London but her marriage to Keith Warner and subsequent pregnancy changed her situation forcing her to leave the world of computers and become a housewife. However, Jayne's marriage did not last and she returned home bringing with her our beautiful Granddaughter Khloe. When Pam and I moved to Usk, Jayne and James came with us. James finished his schooling at Caerleon before departing for Twickenham.

Steven and Christopher married. Steven and Julie have two children Alana and Lloyd, but Christopher and Allison's marriage has remained childless while they both pay attention to their careers. Andrew has fathered a son, a lovely little lad called Kane, but prefers to live with, rather than marry his girlfriend. Finally James, he feels he is too young to form any meaningful relationship and enjoys the bright lights of London's West End, easily accessible from his base at Twickenham.

Pam and I saw to it that the children got support within the family but they knew that once they started working they were expected to stand on their own feet, and in fairness to them all they have done so. I am very proud of the way each of them has built a future for themselves by their own endeavour. All our children were to Pam and I our family. There were no 'steps' in our house; ever.

The success I had achieved in the club business down the years owed much to my decision to move into the corporate and party booking market. As far back as Cesars Palace in the sixties, I had engaged a person to market cabaret entertainment as a product like any other and this had proved one of my great strengths as corporate business became eighty per cent of our trade at Usk.

Among such corporate clients were Big Batteries of Cwmbran, Ken Parslow's Isotemp also from Cwmbran, Eddie Heywood's Chepstow Plant Hire, Scandinavian Designs, Monsanto Chemicals of Newport and some great colliery parties from the Welsh valleys. All of these large corporate bookings involved parties of between two hundred and four hundred customers per visit.

One evening I spotted at the bar a man who had begun to use the club regularly. I decided to speak to him in order to let him know that the management of the club recognised him as a valued customer, just a customer relation exercise that invariably paid dividends. That was never more true than now. His name was David Lewis and he owned a Civil Engineering Company and having visited the club quite frequently of late he decided it might be suitable for his annual staff outing – a party of approximately two hundred and forty people. I promptly bought him a drink, gave him a few brief details and popped a programme into his hand. He promised to get back to me.

At the end of the evening, on talking to Pam about the brief meeting, she surprised me by knowing more about Mr. Lewis than I did. "Yes" she said.

"I know who you mean. He has been coming to the club quite regularly. I think he's taken a shine to our Jayne."

"Oh so you think the talk of a large party booking was a blinder" I replied sadly.

"Not necessarily" said Pam. "He certainly does own a large company and by all accounts has a bob or two." For some reason my sadness immediately evaporated.

A couple of nights later he was in again and on spotting me bought me a drink. He told me he had decided to bring his party to the club and that he would instruct his secretary to phone me with the numbers and other details. I thanked him and promised to personally look after his employees. He thanked me and added, "I want them to have a good time. Give them anything they want - a free bar all night and plenty of wine with the meal. I'll leave it to you" he said. This was like music to my ears.

Sure enough the very next day, his secretary rang and agreed the most suitable date and the numbers involved for the bash. "By the way Pam" I said. "That David Lewis booked his company in with us".

"I thought he would," she said. "He was chatting to me for ages last night at the desk, probably before he spoke to you about the booking. He definitely wants to take our Jayne out, although he has not said so in so many words; but I can tell; a mother usually can".

"Well maybe she should meet him, perhaps have a drink with him. There's no harm in that after all, he's turning out to be a bloody good punter. Call it customer relations or P.R. if you like" I declared.

"Well she won't" stated her Mum. "She says he's not her type".

"Since when is a wealthy young man, who owns his own company, not her type? He's everybody's type" I said.

"Well she won't meet him and that's that," said Pam. "Anyway you can't force her to do things against her will".

"I only would like her to say hello and have a drink with him for God's sake" I said. "She doesn't have to sleep with the guy".

The David Lewis party came and went and all had a good evening. David Lewis spared no expense in entertaining his employees and their partners. I presented the bill to Mr. Lewis who stuffed it into his pocket said "Thank you for an excellent night. Everyone had a great time. I'll pop in and pay you tomorrow night".

"Y'yes Mr. Lewis of course" I said and with that he was gone.

"That was some bill," commented Pam at the end of business that evening.

"Yes" I said. "It sure was" hoping she would not ask me about the payment of it.

"So how did he pay?" she asked. "Cheque or credit card".

"Er, neither" I mumbled.

"What do you mean neither" she said slightly aggravated.

"He's popping in to pay me tomorrow." I said and waited for the blast.

It came in the shape of the usual cliché ridden verbal barrage about how do we know he'll pay, we may never see him again, after all we hardly know him etc etc, The wonderful thing about wives is they come on strongly with the rights and wrongs of their husband's decision, but would do exactly the same if they were confronted with the same situation. To my wife the answer would be 'he seemed like a nice boy'. In any event, the next morning David Lewis came and settled up, added a substantial gratuity for the staff and told me how much he had enjoyed the show.

"I am delighted Mr. Lewis. Please feel free to visit us at any time" I gushed adding. "You will always be most welcome."

I did not have to wait too long, he was back the same evening and on spotting him I tripped over two punters in my rush to buy him a drink. A little later in the evening Jayne came downstairs to the club, but on hearing that D.L. was at the bar decided to go back upstairs.

"Don't be silly" remonstrated her Mum. "He may not be your type, but he seems like a nice boy and he is a good customer. Your Father is right. It is good P.R. to have a drink with him if invited to do so".

"Oh O.K. Mother" replied Jayne sarcastically and headed into the clubroom. I knew nothing of the conversation between Mother and Daughter so you can imagine how stunned I was to spot Jayne standing at the back bar having a drink with D.L.

The following day Jayne stuck her head around my office door to tell me she would not be available for work that evening as she was going out to dinner with guess who - D.L. The following morning the biggest bouquet of roses I have ever seen arrived for Jayne, so big was the bouquet I could scarcely carry it up the stairs. The rest of course is history. David swept her off her feet and a relationship developed between them that has stood the test of time. Jayne Warner, dite Savva, eventually became Mrs. Lewis the second. David brought with him four children, three boys and a girl; Wesley, Darren, Stacey and Carly, and Jayne brought Khloe. Like the linking of Pam's family and mine, David and Jayne cared for all their children and they all got on with each other just fine.

I still recall an incident which makes me smile and which happened not long after Jayne and David's relationship had started. At the end of most evenings I would catch an hour or two of television before turning in. Pam would go straight to bed; she sensibly felt sleep more important than a late night movie after a night's work. One night Jayne had invited David to stay and they had retired before our arrival upstairs. I was sitting alone, thoroughly enjoying the film Guns of Navarone when the door burst open and in came David Lewis wearing nothing but a smile. I smiled and said 'wrong door'. He retreated, somewhat embarrassed. The next day he apologised for his naked intrusion. "Oh don't worry about that Dave," I said. "I'm in show business you know."

The visit of Lennie Peters, formerly of Peters and Lee but now working alone again, was an enjoyable week. Apart from the fact that he still did quite well at the box office and gave us a break-even result, his arrival at Usk brought back happy memories, particularly at Cesars of Luton and the memorable golden treble.

During his week at Usk a major faux pas occurred. I had taken a large booking of two hundred people for a night out at the Lennie Peters show, organised by a locally based organisation for the deaf. Being midweek and therefore an off peak booking, I was able to offer the oorganisation a special deal which meant they were able to bring such a larger number of people than usual.

The support act for the show that week was a ventriloquist John Bouchier, one of the foremost vents in the world. The evening in question seemed to be going well and everyone appeared to be having a good time; everyone that is, except Roddy Miles our compere. He arrived at reception looking a little aggrieved after introducing Lennie and proceeded to tell me why the evening, in his view, was an ill thought out mess.

"I have had no communication from back stage telling me that a party of deaf people were in and occupying most of the front of stage. So when I came on to warm the audience up and to introduce John the Vent all I can see through the glare of the spotlights is someone standing up near the front waving his arms about. I had no idea the man was an official from the party, who was relating my every word, by sign language, even the lyrics from my song to his party. I thought he was some drunk."

"Oh Roddy" I said. "Didn't Gareth the Stage Manager or Eric Bennett the band leader, tell you that this unusual party were in?"

"Only after I'd put John on," he replied.

"I had to put them in the front so they could lip read" I qualified. "The man carrying out the sign language is an additional aid for those who perhaps cannot lip read too well or cannot see the lips too clearly".

"Be that as it may" continued Roddy. "If you don't mind me saying so George, the selection of this show for this kind of party of people was ill conceived to say the least".

"What do you mean" I interrupted. "I fail to see your point".

"Well look what we have" replied Roddy. "We have one of the best vents in the world to open the show and a blind singer topping the bill. In a nutshell that audience can't read John's lips as his lips never move and they can't hear Lennie Peters singing and Lennie can't see them. Having a blind top of the bill and a ventriloquist support for a largely deaf audience I would say constitutes a major faux pas" concluded Roddy.

"Oh dear I see what you mean" I said very embarrassed.

To this day I can't think why I did not advise the deaf organisation to choose a different show, the thought never occurred to me. Roddy piped up again as these thoughts were going through my mind.

"I mean" he began. "Spotting the guy standing and waving his arms about and assuming he was a drunk I did the usual lines of 'sit down we've seen the suit' and 'sober up now its school in the morning'. You know the usual one liner and I should have sussed then because I was not getting laughs, in fact my comments became faux pas number two."

At the end of the evening, we were heartily thanked by the organisers. They recognised there were a few problems but all in all it was a wonderful night out and all the party had enjoyed themselves.

The story of the mishap eventually filtered back stage and both our support and top of the bill found the incident somewhat amusing. John Bouchier the vent, in particular was pleased, indeed proud of the fact that he was so good at his craft, it rendered the ability of lip reading what he was saying an impossibility

I am reminded of a joke that sums up an artiste's attitude to certain situations and underlines his belief that the performance is paramount and above all other considerations. The story goes that an out of work vent phones his agent in desperation asking why he is not getting any work. The agent is apologetic, but informs his client that there is no longer enough work to go round because of the glut of speciality acts and particularly vents. Pointing to his desperate situation, the vent asks his agent for advice on what was to be done to relieve his poverty.

"Why don't you try a bit of spiritualism?" suggests the agent. "You have the ability of throwing your voice without moving your lips; why not set yourself up as a medium, its big business nowadays". The vent hesitated and then replied.

"I'm not sure I'm cut out for that sort of thing."

"Well it's either that or starve," said the agent and went on to say how much money there was to be made by becoming a medium. The vent still hesitated.

"I'm not sure I can go through with it," he said eventually.

The agent, sensing that his client was tottering on the brink of a decision, suggested he arrange one visit of a potential customer so that the vent could give the idea a try.

"If you find you can cope with it and that you actually enjoy the experience, then the sky is the limit," he continued.

The vent reluctantly agreed to the suggestion and it wasn't long before the agent phoned back and advised that the first customer would visit the vent in two days time.

The day arrived and at 2p.m. precisely Mrs. Ethel Green arrived.

"I'm anxious to contact my late husband Harold," she told the ventriloquist. "He passed away a couple of years ago". The vent led Ethel into a darkened parlour and after sitting Ethel opposite him, began to call Harold.

"Are you there Harold?" he cried. "Ethel is here to speak to you. Harold are you there?" he chanted over and over again. Eventually, having created a suitable atmosphere, he threw his voice without moving his lips.

"I am here," said Harold.

"Oh" said Ethel slightly startled. "Harold is that really you? How are you dear? I've missed you, but I want you to know I am OK". The information and questions poured out at such a rate that Harold could hardly get a word in.

At last Ethel calmed down sufficiently as to permit the vent to throw his voice and Harold answered the questions fired at him by his wife. A substantial conversation took place and after a while Harold took his leave of Ethel. Throwing his voice the vent said. "I have to go now Ethel. It's been great talking to you. Bye for now. Bye - bye -bye" and gently the voice faded away.

"I cannot thank you enough" said the grateful Mrs. Green,' drawing the agreed £10 note from her purse. "It was absolutely wonderful. In fact if I may, I'd like to make an appointment for next week, same day, same time if possible?"

"Certainly" replied the vent. "But next week I shall have to charge you twenty pounds."

"Why?" queried Mrs. Green

"Well next week I shall bring Harold back whilst drinking a glass of water" was the vent's immediate reply.

David Essex continued to be a great favourite with audiences all over the UK and Usk was no exception; whenever we had an opportunity to play him we did well. A combination of Mel Bush's skilful management and David's programme of old and new material, kept him at the top of his profession. Even in these difficult times of disappearing audiences, David could still pull a good crowd.

The South Wales branch of The Variety Club organised a fund raising lunch and the date coincided with David's engagement at Usk. As a member of The Variety Club for over twenty years and having personally organised at least eighteen Christmas parties for needy children, I was happy to ask David to put in an appearance at the event as I new he would be pleased to help.

"Is there anything you want me to do while I'm there?" asked David.

"Perhaps you would be good enough to give out the raffle prizes and maybe help with the auction," I suggested.

"Of course I will" replied David without hesitation and after pausing for a moment added "I'll donate one of my silver discs, and autograph it, if you think it will raise a few bob."

I was thrilled with his generous offer. "Raise a few bob," I echoed. "It'll be the star auction"

As I had agreed to provide transport for his journey to Cardiff, I decided to collect him myself. I had a couple of staff work on my Merc the day before the luncheon, cleaning and valeting the vehicle and transforming it from a mobile ashtray and dog kennel to a gleaming limo fit for a star. After calling at the Newport Hilton to collect my V.I.P. and his burly minder, who incidentally turned out to be a Greek Cypriot, we travelled towards Cardiff.

"Now, when we arrive at the entrance to the function rooms" I began, "you'll find we shall probably encounter a large gathering of females who on spotting us will probably rush towards us". Pausing to take a peek in my rear view mirror I spotted the minder listening intently to my every word. "Now when this happens" I continued, addressing my remarks to the minder, "you will probably leap forward to protect David as is your job, but there will be no need for you to do this, because the girls will be attempting to mob me". David began to laugh and the minder amused by my story said,

"So you want me to protect you".

"No, no" came my swift reply. "Let them come for Christ's sake, it'll give me a lift, even though I'm the oldest toy boy in town". This brought great bursts of laughter.

"You may well laugh David Essex," I continued, "you may be big around the country, but I'm very big in Cardiff".

"I'm sure you are George," said the star still laughing "and if you don't stop putting on weight, you will probably be big all over the country as well; in fact huge"

The lunch was a huge success and the presence of David Essex lit the whole proceedings. A great deal of money was raised. The largest amount was the four thousand pounds paid by Allan Darlow, the estate agent, for David's silver disc. Because of this magnificent gesture, David and Allan formed a friendship and the two families remain close friends to the present day.

Guests on my table included Eddie and Sandra Hayward. I invited the Hayward's to join us at various showbiz functions because not only did Pam and I really enjoy their company but Eddie was, and still is, one of the most generous and hard working charity contributors in Wales. Other guests at our table included friends Bob and Anne Herbert and Sam and Lynda Jones. Since our move to South Wales we were unable to see our friends Bob and Anne Herbert quite as much but although geographically there was a distance between us, our friendship remained as strong as ever and we got together as often as possible. Bob had taken on a new boy band, which he called 'Blue' and was attempting to make progress with them. Work with the band, with his financial services and his accountancy business kept Bob very busy.

In Wales, I was kept busy as the economic situation deteriorated requiring extra efforts to find new customers. Unemployment was a constant fear in Wales and as the figures steadily increased the idea of an expensive evening wining and dinning receded, as did the spending on most non-essential items. Most industries were feeling the effects of the recession as in these difficult times, not only were banks not forthcoming with support, but were busy withdrawing any support they had given, (by mistake?)

We were privileged to be invited to the weddings of two of the three daughters of Eddie and Sandra Heywood and were invited to join them for dinner on numerous occasions. Pam and I reciprocated by ensuring that Eddie and Sandra were our guests at various show biz occasions as well as our annual Royal Ascot day and our Cliff Richard private dinner parties. Eddie's wife Sandra was always keen on Cliff's music and seeing him live in the intimate atmosphere of the club and then dining with him as our guests soon confirmed

Sandra as a devoted fan. My secretary Marilyn Strangemore, my wife and my best friend's Wife were all dedicated fans. It seemed I had become surrounded by the aura of the mighty Cliff.

Our friendship with Eddie and Sandra was underlined by our joint trip to Australia. Eddie and I organised a ten day winter break to the other side of the world and the adventure is worth recalling because of a gag I pulled on Cliff while I was there. Cliff was on tour in Australia at the time and had half a dozen concerts in Melbourne, after secret discussions with David Bryce I established where Cliff was staying and where he intended to dine on a particular evening. Unknown to Cliff, the four of us arrived and checked into the same hotel.

Cliff and his entourage were dining at an Indian Restaurant that night so Eddie, Sandra, Pam and I headed for the eatery ahead of Cliff's party and once there, I dressed up as an Indian waiter, and the other three hid behind a rather large pillar. In the fullness of time Cliff and his party arrived, a gaggle of fourteen people, all of whom seemed to be talking at once about the ups and downs of the performance.

Still chattering they took their seats, which was a signal for me and the other Indian waiters to arrive at the table clutching menus. I proceeded to give Cliff the menu, which he took from me without looking up and without breaking his conversation with the dinner guest sitting next to him. I waited for a short while and then in the best Indian accent I could muster I said, "What may I get you this evening Mr. Richard". I think I was over the top with the accent and I sounded like an outboard motor.

"I'm not quite ready to order yet," replied Cliff, again without looking up.

"I really do need to take your order Sir" chugged the outboard motor. Cliff looked up, a touch annoyed with the interruption, and I think he was about to tell me to go away when he suddenly he recognised who was standing over him. There followed the ultimate double take. "G-George!" he exclaimed. "What are you doing here?"

"Well the job pays well and its readies," I answered to much laughter.

Cliff got to his feet and greeted Pam and I and our guests with hugs and kisses.

"It really is a wonderful surprise," he said. "I'm so thrilled to see you".

We Joined Cliff for dinner that night and enjoyed being part of his entourage for the rest of our stay in Melbourne. We also took in Cliff's remaining concerts which were absolutely sensational. Cliff wasted no time in thanking Eddie for the use of his rods while appearing at Usk and Eddie threw a dinner party for Cliff at our hotel; booking a private room and ordering the finest wines and champagne. The evening must have cost Eddie a small fortune but such was his generosity, Eddie has always stuck by his principle of only accepting generosity, in this case Cliff's, on condition that he was permitted to reciprocate. This he did with style.

Our show with H.R.H. Prince Phillip as guest of honour went without a hitch. Having catered for him at both Cesars and Blazers, I must confess I had become confident at presenting Royal occasions. Again security was very tight, but again the Club took great Kudos from the staging of the event.

Two friends of mine, who operated a beautiful club at Bardon near Leicester, called to say they were still having difficulty in establishing their new eight hundred seater venue. Since they had opened the Stardust at Bardon we had spoken on many occasions about a number of issues relating to business at the club but Barry Young and Michael Morris were becoming more and more concerned about difficulties in publicising their club. The boys often came to Windsor and stayed over for a night or two and we used to dine together and chat about everything to do with the club

"You ought to put on a Royal show," I suggested on one occasion. "You know, a Charity Night with a Royal Guest of Honour. There's nothing like a Royal night for publicity".

"How would we go about it?" asked Barry.

"Well I could make the initial contact for you and I'm sure that with my connections and track record at these sort of things, added to the fact that you have a very impressive Club, a Royal visit could be arranged" I said confidently.

"Do you think you could?" asked Barry.

"I think so. Would you like me to try"?

"Yes please" they said. "That would be fantastic".

Having received a clear mandate, I decided to try and tempt H.R.H. the Princess Royal to do the honours as I felt my credentials were probably strongest in her camp. I got in touch with Davinia Cannon who was wonderful from the word go. She was interested in the idea of a Midlands Gala and would visit the Stardust to see the facilities for herself and, if suitable, present the proposal to H.R.H. Time passed by until one afternoon Marilyn, my secretary, gave me the good news that the Princess Royal had agreed to host a Royal Gala Charity at the Stardust. "The boys will be pleased," I said.

Marilyn went back to her typing and I went about my daily chores. I laid the fax to one side and decided to call the boys later with the good news; the fax lay on my desk for almost a week. Barry and Mike rang me for a chat on Friday of that week and after catching up with the showbiz gossip Barry said in passing.

"I don't suppose you've heard from Princess Anne's people yet Sav?"

"Ah yes, I knew there was something I had to tell you" I answered. "It's all on and the date is agreed."

"Are you sure?" said Barry.

"Yes" I answered.

"Hang on Sav" replied Barry as he passed the phone to Mike. "Would you say again Sav?"

I repeated the facts to Mike, adding that I had received a fax several days ago.

"So can we go ahead and announce the event?" asked Mike.

"Yes" I said. "Go ahead".

Both the boys thanked me profusely for my assistance and were clearly over the moon with excitement, a few minutes later the phone rang again.

"Sav" said Barry, "Er if you wouldn't mind, could you fax us a copy of the confirmation."

"Of course I will, right away" I replied.

I remember turning to Marilyn as I faxed the confirmation to them, and saying. "I don't think the boys really believe me."

"Of course they do" she replied. "But what you fail to realise is, this is a big first time Royal event for them whereas you've done so many of them you've become totally blasé".

Marilyn was right! To me the arrangements of a Royal Gala at Bardon with H.R.H. Princess Anne was all part of a days work, but to Barry and Mike it was a first, the icing on the cake and they were incredibly exited. They were also so grateful for my help that at their press conference to announce the Royal date they gave me star billing as the friend and colleague who was responsible for the grand occasion. They also insisted that Pam and I sit at the top table on the big night with the Royal guest.

To be fair they gave me too much credit. They had beautiful premises which were ideal for such an occasion and I knew the boys well enough to know that they would produce both catering and cabaret with class and style. I was certain that their presentation would suit their Royal visitor therefore my job of selling the idea to Princess Anne's representative was extremely easy.

During the remainder of 1991 and into the spring of 1992 the economic situation became even worse, four million people were unemployed; bankruptcy and repossession of property was rife. Margaret Thatcher had been ousted by her own party and replaced by John Major but it soon became evident that the policies pursued by Thatcher remained. Nothing had really changed. The failure of the 1991 Christmas season and the poor start to 1992 meant my back was against the wall and, rightly or wrongly, I blamed many of my ills on bad government. The change of leadership had meant nothing; the policies had remained the same. I am reminded of the gag about the man who became shipwrecked and was picked up by the Titanic. He'd no sooner had his hot drink and hot shower and settled into his cabin when down he went again.

Audiences were melting away as corporate business became almost non-existent. By the end of March 1992 I found myself under extreme financial pressure. I simply could not make ends meet. I adopted various money saving measures in an effort to stay afloat, such as reducing my number of nights of trading still further from five nights per week to four or even three which meant that I also had to lay off some of the excellent staff that had been with me for many years. By robbing Peter to pay Paul I managed to continue trading; but only just.

The ninth of April was the date set for a General Election. I was under no illusions that a change of government would put matters right, but like many people I felt a change might bring back a feel good factor and confidence might be restored. I sensed a mood for change and became increasingly confident that the future was again golden and forged ahead with an autumn programme of giants. From October to Christmas, a seven night per week star studded extravaganza of the countries finest. Jim Davidson, Lennie Henry, Joe Longthorne, The Drifters, The Chippendales, Michael Barrymore, Jimmy Jones, The Hollies, Hale and Pace, Little and Large, Adonis, Brian Conley, The Rockinberries, The Barron Knights and a whole gaggle of sixties bands, all headed for Usk. The line up was the talk of Wales and the West; I was convinced that on April the ninth there would be a change of government and that Mr. Kinnock and Labour would replace Major and the Tories. Whether good bad or indifferent, the first thing that would surely happen would be a rise in confidence and, I assumed that in this euphoria customers would start searching for enjoyment and entertainment. The feel good factor would return.

I took the ninth of April off from work and Pam and I drove to our home at Windsor. There is an old saying: One will always remember one's location when receiving news of a disaster.

I was sitting in my lounge at Windsor; in front of me was a low coffee table on which was placed a champagne bucket containing a bottle of very fine Rene Lalou champagne. I settled down to watch the all night election programme intending to crack open the champagne when Peter Snow and colleagues confirmed a change in power had taken place and that the old order had been swept away.

As the night wore on and as Snow rushed around his studio like a demon, from his ever swinging pendulum to his little blue, red and yellow men sitting in rows in an imaginary chamber, I began to feel a touch pessimistic about the outcome of the poll. In the early hours of the morning I viewed with disbelief the swing from reds to blues. I was in a state of shock by the time I realised that Major had won and Kinnock had conceded. I retired to bed, informing Pam who had given up on the TV before the result.

"I don't believe it," she said.

"You'd better believe it" I replied.

For the first time in a very long while I became extremely emotional. I felt, perhaps wrongly, that Kinnock's loss was the countries and that my effort to lift my business that coming autumn with such a glittering line up of stars took on a very different meaning.

Decisions had to be made. Either I pressed ahead with my plans or tried to unravel all my contractual obligations and closed down. I had survived when so many of my colleagues had failed, but I knew I had reached a crossroads. A decision had to be made; tomorrow.

A VISIT FROM COOPERS AND LYBRAND

ACT ONE: THE AUTUMN OF 1992

ACT TWO: NEW YEARS EVE

THE FINALE

OR

FALSE TABS

FRIENDS

DISCOTEQUES: MY BAPTISM

By the summer of 1992 I was in real financial difficulties. The business was operating on only a couple of evenings each week, and even then not to full houses and could not pay its way. The unpaid bills were beginning to mount and it was clear to anyone, apart from me, that disaster was just around the corner. I remained defiantly optimistic, still believing that the longest and deepest recession since the 1930's had to end soon and that our industry would come out of the doldrums. I took the decision to carry on, despite John Major's victory, and part of that decision was to leave the programme intact, my amazing line up of top stars for the autumn stood; all I had to do was hold things together through the summer.

To that end I put together a programme of entertainment to suit everyone. Female vocalist Rosemarie and the storyteller with guitar, Richard Digence, were two artistes with an excellent following that set the pace for a line up that included a Jazz Festival with Acker Bil and Kenny Ball. A Country and Western show featuring a gaggle of local artistes and a superb Welsh weekend that featured Iris Williams, Bryn Yemm, Max Boyce and of course a male voice choir. I also presented an Irish festival starring Brendan Shine and his band and featuring amazing Irish dance routines performed by members of the Bristol Irish Music Society School of Dancing. This unique form of Irish dance was later to become world famous when Riverdance burst on to the stage of a Eurovision Song Contest as a 'filler' and literally stole the show. All these great shows were reasonably well supported but it is impossible to pay the overheads of a business designed to trade seven nights per week if you are only open for two and our debts rose rapidly.

Comedy had become frighteningly bluer, to a point where it seemed that the more filthy the material, the greater the support. Nevertheless, I attempted to buck the trend and go for the more traditional type of comedy. During the autumn a first class line up of comics and comic support acts gave some light relief to an otherwise gloomy period. As my problems worsened I could at least enjoy the humour of some of our finest comedians including the visual comedy of Sonny Hays and Co, the cranky but very humorous Tony Brutus 'strongman extraordinaire' and of course the evergreen Victor Burnett and June, all gave performances of excellence; as always.

Comedians Terry Denton, Stan Boardman, Duncan Norvelle, Frank Carson and Johnny Hackett had them rolling in the aisles, but above all I have a lasting memory of Bob Monkhouse. Bob was the first comic I played at Cesars Palace twenty-seven years earlier, and was making yet another appearance for me. Still as funny, if not funnier than ever and amazingly up to date - a comic genius who had the ability to grab a story from an evening newspaper on his way to a gig and make a gag or two from it for that evening's show.

As a caterer all my working life, I appreciated more than most the hilarious catering related gags told by various comedians of the day. These jokes are regarded as corny now, but for me they represented an era of good and clean comedy. For instance;

"Waiter there is a fly in my soup".

"Don't worry madam, the spider on your bread will get him".

"But the fly is swimming in my soup".

"Swimming madam, it should be paddling. You obviously have too much soup".

Or "Here is your lobster Sir".

"Hang on it only has one claw".

"Well it's been in a fight".

"Then take it back and bring me the winner".

Banter of a very different kind, from a different time,

As business got worse and my excuses began to wear thin my main supplier, Whitbread Ltd, became more involved in my problems. With such a large investment in the club they were obviously worried and asked the accountants,

Coopers and Lybrand, to carry out a survey of the clubs finances and prospects. I welcomed the representative from Coopers and Lybrand and after a day of intensive discussions, during which I produced up to date figures and projections, he assured me that his report to Whitbread would be optimistic and that in his view there was every possibility of working our way out of our current difficulties. Then two things happened that made me feel even more confident in my future.

Cliff Richard confirmed a date for the last week in August and the Allied Irish Bank, who looked after my illustrious Son-in-law's very lucrative business, agreed a small overdraft facility in exchange for my banking business. The date of Cliff's appearance was like a beacon as it was just a week prior to the opening of my 'Grand Autumn Season' - a kick-start into the Savvas Club Entertainment Bonanza. Had I managed to get through the recession I asked myself? Perhaps our house at Windsor and our flat in Monaco would now sell; they had both been on the market for some time.

I remember strolling across the fields of the Vale of Usk with my faithful golden retriever Gazza, as I did every day. This day was different from others of late in that the good news from two different sources had relieved my recent worries over the business. I felt upbeat and alive; vindicated in my decision to hang on for better times. I have never been a religious man, but on that peaceful evening in those beautiful surroundings I stopped for a moment and looking up to the sky I thanked God!!

On receipt of the Coopers and Lybrand report the brewery gave me the green light to continue. In a nutshell, Coopers reported that, although the club was in serious difficulties, it had no more problems than other businesses were experiencing, but had one distinct advantage, and that was that it had an excellent winter programme on offer which should generate sufficient profit to enable the operation to trade out of its present difficulties.

However, as the summer wore on and the financial crises worsened The Allied Irish Bank withdrew its support and demanded the repayment of its facility with even more speed than it was given. I am sure people in higher positions at the bank, had, on seeing poor return on their investment, put pressure on Liam the local Manager to pursue the return of the loan, which in their view should not have been given in the first place. It seemed my thanks to the Almighty some months earlier were a touch premature.

To repay the Bank, who had set a deadline, and to clear the other debts I knew I had to secure a large loan to get through to the autumn when the problems should ease. With reluctance I turned to a very different and dubious source for a short-term loan repayable with interest at a rate of twenty-five per cent. Taking this route may, with hindsight, have been foolhardy perhaps even dangerous, nevertheless I owe my ability to get through this period to those faceless people who, with no questions asked, came up with the money within hours, enabling me to repulse the VAT collectors and other threatening debtors and avoid foreclosure. Although I paid a high price for this dark money, I remain grateful for the assistance I received.

With the exception of clubs owned by large corporations able to subsidise there operations the cabaret club scene no longer existed and the survival of my little club at Usk stood out as something of a miracle. Little did any outsider know that I relied on loan sharks to keep the appearance of a solid business, an appearance vital if I wanted to retain the support of any members of the public who could still afford a night out.

At last the autumn season arrived, Cliff Richard's week a total sell out which should set the scene for a blistering run up to Christmas. This was to be the defining period for the club. It was make or break time.

I had been in the business long enough to know the signs of a good or bad season and I knew very early on that the signs were not good. By mid September the month of December should have been be pretty well sold out, and October and November should be heavily booked. Two thirds of our total box office capacity for those two months should have been taken up by this time. The reality was very different. It did not take a genius to work out that our much trumpeted season of the country's leading stars was heading towards the greatest non-event of my career.

With alarm bells ringing from every direction and with suppliers pressing for payment on all sides, I entered the most stressful period of my life. My dear friend Bob Herbert, who had given me such good advice about consolidation and making provision for a rainy day, which I spurned at the time, admitted that even he could not have predicted such a protracted recession. Bob did everything possible to help me through this period by rescheduling loans and payments and even arranging for some of his own clients to help by investing in the operation at Usk, but it was to no avail. I was fighting a losing battle. I arrived at New Year's Eve 1992, my twenty-seventh New Years Eve in show business; the first that had not sold out.

The cabaret of the evening was the Drifters who were completing their two-week short season for me. They had received some payments from me as they progressed through their dates, but were obviously anxious to secure the remainder of their fee before performing for that special and final evening. The brewery had pulled the plug as far as any further deliveries were concerned so on the afternoon of the biggest celebration of the year, I sat in my office wondering how to cope with a New Year's Eve and the prospects of no drinks behind the bar and no top of the bill.

In depths of despair I called my son in law, David Lewis and explained my situation; within thirty minutes he had joined me at my office. In the meantime I had negotiated an accommodation with the Drifters management which meant that at least the show would go on. David provided me with sufficient funds to acquire drinks from a local wholesaler and I sent Carl Corbett my security officer and right hand man to pick up the drinks order and bring it to the club.

Eddie Heyward joined us in the office and we began a soul-searching conversation between me, David and Eddie as to the future of the club. Speaking first, David advised me that it was time to call it a day.

"You can't go on like this George" he insisted. "You have known for some time that the writing has been on the wall. You have done your best, but to try and continue would be futile".

Eddie Heyward agreed. "Not only is it futile, but in trying to keep going you will simply make matters worse and in the end will make yourself ill into the bargain".

My head was spinning and I realised that I was on the verge of becoming totally overwhelmed by the constant stress and strain of trying to cope with my problems. I was used to a telephone ringing constantly as customers demanded tickets for a sold out concert, but the sound of a ringing phone now meant creditors demanding payment and seemed to have a different tone. I had no choice but to bow to the inevitable.

"I - I know you are both right" I stuttered. "I could not face another day like today or another week or month like those that have just gone before; but how do I handle this closure- this ending?"

"You don't" said David. "You have taken enough. There is no shame in closing down. Quite frankly you have done more than anyone I know to keep going. What you must do" he continued "is to see tonight through and then leave. Go to Windsor and leave everything to me. I will deal with creditors, press and staff and keep everyone off your back. Enough is enough. Just go and leave the rest to me".

Eddie nodded with approval. "You must get right away from all this" he concurred. "Wouldn't you like to wake up and face a day of peace, a day without pressure?" He asked.

"Oh Eddie" I replied. "I long for that, more than anything else. Just to be able to sleep would be heaven for me and Pam".

That evening looking spick and span in my dinner suit, I took up my position out front and welcomed the customers into the premises and into their seats. The fully decorated room looked magnificent as befitted a New Years Eve. The whole evening was delivered with our usual style and panache. No one failed to have a good time and on the stroke of midnight the hearty cheers went up as the balloons came down and the audience burst into the usual rendition of Auld Lang Syne, ably led by a Scottish piper in full highland regalia. Trumpets and hooters sounded, party poppers popped and streamers filled the air. I stood at the back of the room and surveying the scene and suddenly realised that once before on a New Years Eve twenty-seven years earlier, my destiny had changed. Billy Cotton and his Band Show came on and rounded off a superb and successful evening; my first triumph since arriving at the new Cesars Palace at Luton, twenty-seven wonderful years coming to end with another New Years Eve party.

On January 1st 1993 Pam and I left Usk and headed for Windsor. David and Eddie, as promised, took care of everything. They would see the members of staff and put them in the picture and there was enough in takings from the night before to take care of wages. Pam was very tearful, as she had been for the last few months and I was gutted that my creation at Usk had come to an end. My shattered pride was going to be hard to bear but I vowed that I would do my utmost to get back on my feet. I vowed too that I never wanted to see Pam cry again.

The first day of our stay at Windsor passed peacefully. Our neighbor and friend Chic came over to see us and was pleased that I had called 'time at Usk'.

"For the last three months you've been flogging a dead horse," said Chic. "In fact for the last twelve months really" he added.

"I know," I answered. "But I really thought that the recession would have ended by now and things would be picking up."

"It's not just the recession George" said Chic. "It's the whole cabaret scene. It's finished. The younger generation doesn't want to know. They want discos, drugs and sex."

His conclusions had a ring of truth about them and he wasn't alone in his opinion. The cabaret scene as we knew it was a dinosaur in its death throes. During the final days at Usk I had taken the time to visit two very dear friends of mine who operated the Newmarket Cabaret Club and had managed to pull back from the brink, by revamping their premises and turning into a modern disco. I had a look over it and I must say I was impressed. Slowly and surely their business prospects turned around and they were on a winner. Yet despite that visit to Newmarket, I did nothing to alter my operation. Discothèques were alien to me. I was the dinosaur.

Chic was very kind and pressed five hundred pounds in my hand. "A gift from Tracy and me" he said, the gift was very welcome as I left Usk with a plastic bucket containing £33 in change. Eddie had kindly pushed five hundred pounds into Pam's purse.

"When you get to Windsor, get some shopping in and take a break for a while" he said. "I've been through a business failure myself some years ago and I know what its like believe me. But at the end of the day you will both recover from this and that weight pressing down on you day in and day out over the last few months will be lifted off your shoulders".   The kindness of Eddie, Chic and David had enabled Pam and I to take a much needed breather and to take stock of our lives.

Waking up the next morning after a wonderful sleep, I can say that for the very first time in many months I did not have a depressive fear of what the day ahead may have in store. It was as if a huge burden had been lifted from my shoulders. Jayne and David phoned to check that we were well and to tell me that the news of my demise had gone around show business like wildfire and that messages of support were being received from all over the country.

Barry and Michael were the first to visit us. Like the true friends they were, they rushed down from Leicester to offer support and a shoulder to cry on if needed, as I had offered them only a year or so earlier when Barry had suffered the same fate at the Stardust.

"Like me" Barry advised, "you have to pick up the pieces and start over again. This is not the finale. Its false tabs Sav."

Cliff Richard, Jim Davidson, Lennie Henry, Stan Boardman, Danny La Rue, Roy Chubby Brown and many other stars were very supportive throughout this period. But sadly the Drifters management, or in particular Fay Treadwell their Manager, behaved very aggressively. I understood that I owed them the balance of their fee and that their chances of ever receiving it were extremely remote, but faced with the choice of a New Years Eve with a cancelled cabaret or going ahead with the final week aware of the possibility of being unable to pay them, was just part of the pressure I was under in those final days at Usk. Fay Treadwell knew that I was in difficulties and had demanded and received a number of payments for her artistes as their Christmas fortnight progressed. It was the final balance plus the VAT that I was unable to pay. I had played the Drifters for a quarter of a century, two or three times a year and although they owed me nothing for the many dates and the thousands of pounds I had paid them over the years, I believe their Manager could have been less vitriolic towards me in my hour of despair.

At first it saddened me, but when some months later it was Fay Treadwell who called in the Receiver to close my company I became very angry that, apart from her, every one of my creditors seemed prepared to wait in the hope that someone might buy the club thus providing funds to pay a large portion of the club's debts, Fay was not prepared to wait. She ended any hope of an eventual sale. The brewery, the Tax and VAT agencies, could now move in and do their worst in 'forced sale' conditions.

Talking to Jimmy Smith one day I said that when Fay died I would dance on her grave.

"I don't think that's a good idea," replied Jim. "I hear she is getting buried at sea".

Jimmy rang me often relaying the many messages of support and best wishes from people in showbiz and kept me amused by feeding me the odd gag, as fed to him by his friend and neighbour, Northampton comic Lew Lewis. I got word from Jimmy that Peter Rue and Paul Aaron Stone at the Circus Tavern, wanted to organise a benefit night for me and Chubby Brown also weighed in with an offer to present four shows, the proceeds of which going to me to assist with disbursements. Stan Boardman, The Rockinberries and the Barron Knights, all wanted to do something on my behalf. I wanted to accept help from these wonderful people but my pride would not allow it. I was deeply hurt by what had happened and could not face meeting so many friends at a charity night; for my benefit.

I lay low for most of January, mulling over our future and reflecting on the past. I gradually got my head together and without the stress I could see clearly how foolish I had been to keep going as I had. The recession continued unabated, with reports of thousands of bankruptcies and repossessions daily. For the very first time, I realised at last that the industry as we knew it was dead and buried.

I had been blessed with the ability to shake a million hands, kiss a million cheeks, and gush a million hellos', I had turned the business of meeting and greeting into an art form. The ability to welcome a thousand punters into a room and make each and everyone of them feel special by virtue of that greeting is a gift. I was lucky to have this ability and deep down, although still licking my wounds, I knew that with a little luck, this ability and my preparedness to work would ensure that I could rise again. My heart was always where I hung my coat, rolled up my sleeves and got on with my craft.

Barry and Michael arranged a visit to Cyprus for us and towards the end of January; we all took off to spend a week on my favourite island. The break was a real tonic for Pam and I, we were able to set our troubles to one side and enjoy a truly memorable holiday. Show business people always have a story to tell and Pam and I and Barry and Michael were no exception. The week together was enhanced by an immense amount of banter and laughter and I shall always be grateful to the boy's thoughtfulness and generosity towards Pam and myself at this difficult time.

On returning to Windsor I felt rejuvenated and ready to take on the world. I seemed to have regained my spirit and was itching to go to work. Bob and Anne Herbert paid us a visit; it was such a pleasure to see them.

"You look well George," observed Bob.

"Thank God I've never felt better Bob" I replied. "My only concern is finding a job."

"You'll have no problem there" assured Bob. "You've always been a grafter."

Bob's statement may have been reassuring but I knew that I faced a dilemma common to a lot of unemployed people. I had no experience in how to go about looking for a job and the skills I had were wedded to an industry that hardly existed any more. Still, I could always go to the West End and do a little bit of waitering or washing dishes or some thing. I am a proud person, proud enough to do any job rather than rely on handouts, I am also a realist who knows that one occasionally has to take a step back before taking two forward. However, following a surprise phone call from Dougie Flood I found myself heading for Stockport, to discuss with him the position of General Manager for his Quaffers night spot, a major establishment in the town.

I had known Dougie for many years and had the utmost respect for him as a charming and astute businessman. At one time Dougie and his partner, Gerry Slinger, had big cabaret interests in and around the Manchester area; their flagship room was Blightys, a huge cabaret venue at Farnsworth. Since the parting of the ways between the two partners I had lost track of Dougie mainly because of my problems over the last couple of years, but I guess everyone was immersed in the fight to retain their businesses.

Dougie, shrewdly, had foreseen the end of the full time cabaret club when so many of us hadn't and was quick off the mark in establishing a multi purpose nightspot, which he named Quaffers, fairly close to the centre of Stockport. Quaffers was a large discothèque with the facilities to feature an occasional cabaret evening if required. The beautiful room was also perfect for conferences and exhibitions; in fact its design incorporated the features necessary to present any number of different activities at any time.

Dougie, who ran Quaffers as well as a Hotel he owned close by, was intending to take life a little easier and because of that was looking for a General Manager to run things for him. "I was sorry to hear of your closure," he said, as we chatted in his office at the club. "But the writing had been on the wall for a long time. Cabaret clubs were becoming less supported and not viable. I genuinely felt that with a lack of new talent coming through, falling audiences and rising operating costs, the industry as we knew it could not survive". I listened and nodded my agreement.

"I'm afraid I went a cabaret too far" I replied.

Although I not over excited about the thought of living in Stockport, the offer was a good one and I knew Dougie well enough to know he was a good man and would be good to work for. We agreed that I would spend the evening at the club, look at everything, go wherever I pleased, ask any questions of the staff and he would contact me at Windsor after the weekend.

My evening at Quaffers was an education. I was one of the longest and most experienced Managers in club land but I was totally unprepared for my night at Quaffers.

The evening started quietly as staff arrived and began setting up bars and tables. The tables were obviously being set for drinks only, not dinner as this after all was a Disco. There were numerous bars on each of the several levels and a top level at the furthermost point from the huge dance floor where hot snacks could be purchased from a buffet operation. Eight o'clock came and went as did nine, but still there had been no admissions to speak of. I asked the chief doorman if it would be a quiet night.

"No Sir" he answered politely. "It's early yet".

Early I thought. This is indeed a strange business. I was advised that the entrance fee of five pounds was available until ten p.m. after which time it would double. At that point, everything started to happen. At a cabaret club nine thirty p.m. would signify the end of dinner and the start of a thirty-minute dance spot before the show. Here at Quaffers at nine thirty we were still awaiting an audience; but not for long.

At about nine forty young people, hundreds of them, started to arrive. They came by bus, coach, car, taxi, some even walked, all with the intention of entering the premises by Ten p.m. Smartly dressed young people came from everywhere, suddenly, thronging the entrance, paying their money and gaining admission for a night of dancing to a D.J., the club was heaving at the seams as the click meter passed the Thirteen hundred mark. Six and a half thousand pounds on the door I thought, to listen to and dance to a D.J. and his records.

I wandered about the club as best I could through throngs of people and noted that at each bar large numbers of young customers, ten deep in places, patiently waited to get their drinks. What an operation I reflected; high turnover, low expenses. I went back to the entrance to see at least another one hundred or so stragglers arrive between Ten and midnight each paying a tenner for the privilege of what was left of a night out at Quaffers.

As I drove back to Windsor, I was still slightly bemused with what I had seen. At last I realised just how out of date I was. Dougie Flood had got it right. The boys at Newmarket who had had the foresight to convert their place of live entertainment to a disco had gone from strength to strength, and I had been a fool. I had blamed falling audiences and lack of business on other factors. Certainly the prevailing economic situation had not helped, but I now realised that overriding all this was the shift from one form of entertainment to another; the rise of a new generation with new tastes.

As I turned into my drive at Windsor I had decided to accept Dougie's offer and go to Southport. I was still not enthusiastic about the move and I knew I'd have to sell the idea to my wife but at the end of the day we had little choice. Stockport was where the money was and I needed to be earning again if we were to get back on our feet. The wrench of moving house was not a consideration in our present circumstances as it was in danger of being repossessed, as had already happened to the flat in Monte Carlo. (The for sale sign had almost taken root in the garden as 'desirable' riverside properties for sale were plentiful, but prospective buyers were non existent).

"I have to let Dougie know by Monday Pam" I said,

"Well the offer is certainly very good," she agreed. "But I don't fancy Stockport, do you?"

"Needs must" I replied.

"I guess you're right Sav" she conceded. After a pause she asked. "Well what is Stockport like as a town?"

"How should I know, I spent most of my day and evening, within the four walls of the club. I didn't get to see the town". After a moment of silence I added. "Anyway it can't be bad, I believe it's twinned with Cannes" I lied.

"Oh well in that case we'll go," said Pam. "Twinned with Cannes eh" she continued. "That's funny, I never even knew it was beside the sea," she concluded.

That settled it. We were off to Cannes lock stock and barrel. I mean Stockport, or we were until a few hours later, the phone rang again, changing our lives for the next twelve months quite dramatically.

"Hello, my name is John Blower," said the voice on the other end of the line.

CESARS OF LUTON AGAIN
THE CYPRUS EXPERIMENT
THE MAES MANOR HOTEL

F reddie Starr's Manager, Leon Fisk, had told Chic Murphy of a possible
vacancy at Cesars. Chic in turn came across to tell me, on what turned
out to be, an eventful Sunday morning. Apparently a man called John
Blower had become the owner of Cesars Palace but was having difficulty
obtaining a drinks license. Leon and others had mentioned my name to John
as someone who might be able help with the problem, hence the phone call.

"You don't know me" began the friendly voice, "but I've come to know
you or at least your name quite well. I'm the new owner of Cesars Palace at
Luton. I won't bore you with the details, but I am having difficulty getting
a drinks License. Every time I go before the local Magistrates, I get knocked
back and everyone tells me that the only man who could get the old place
licensed is George Savva".

Since I left, the club had given the powers that be a lot of problems;
fights became commonplace and its reputation had degenerated as it became a
victim of the bad management of one unsuccessful owner after another. John
Blower therefore, had two main concerns:

1. Did I think I could get a license for the club?
2. Was I interested in doing so?

My answer to both questions was yes and he asked for a meeting at the earliest
possible opportunity.

That evening I telephoned Ron Clayton, the Clerk to the Magistrates
at Luton, and asked if he could put me in the picture as far as Cesars Licensing
applications were concerned. Ron, whom I had known for many years, was
helpful and quickly filled me in on the problems they had had with the club and
it's previous owners. "Mr. Blower, the present owner had put forward, people

who quite frankly had backgrounds that made his nominees inappropriate to become Liquor License holders."

It seemed that John Blower himself was a nice enough sort of chap, but he kept some peculiar company said Ron, choosing his words carefully. I told Ron that I might return to Luton to manage Cesars Palace for Mr. Blower.

"How would I stand in acquiring a Licence?"

"You are an experienced club operator and Licensee for thirty years or so with a proven track record in Luton. I'm sure you would have no problem" he assured me.

Ron went on to advise me that it might be possible to convene a hearing for the application on Thursday of the coming week, five days hence and before ending the conversation he said how pleased everyone would be if I returned to Cesars; in my present circumstances that made me feel very good.

As arranged, I met John Blower the following day at the Halfway House, a pub-restaurant a stones throw from Cesars Palace. John was tall and lean and had the assurance of a self made man; we hit it off immediately and once lunch was ordered I sat back and let John do the talking. He told me he knew of my recent problems and offered his commiserations then told me of his own problems. John Blower was a money lender who had lent a substantial amount of money to a Welshman named Clive Rees, the previous owner of Cesars, who like me, had run into financial difficulties and defaulted on the loan. The club had been the security for the loan and John was attempting to recoup his loses.

"I never wanted the bloody place George," said John. "But what was I to do. I have to try and get my money back somehow. I'm not a club operator, but I'm sure that given time I could get back what I put in. I know the state of the cabaret business, but two days a week with a huge capacity like Cesars should be enough to make a profit."

Apparently, during the time Bob Wheatly owned of the club, substantial renovation and refurbishment had taken place and the club's seating capacity had been extended yet again. The club seated One thousand three hundred (unofficially more) nowadays.

"So I need a Licence in to trade and the Bench hasn't seen fit to give my last couple of nominees the time of day let alone a Licence to sell alcohol."

It was no surprise that John had run into difficulties with the local Magistrates given the recent history of the place and the fact that his nominees were people with criminal conviction.

"Anyway" continued John. "Everyone tells me you are the only man likely to get a license for Cesars. Do you think you can do it?"

"Yes, I'm sure I could," I replied "and quite quickly too. I can go before the Magistrates by this coming Thursday."

"As soon as that?" said John, obviously impressed.

"As soon as that!" I replied; somewhat smugly.

"So what do you want in order to do this for me" asked John.

I thought for a moment or two and wrestled with the knowledge that I only had to pick up the phone and a job at Quaffers was mine. I also knew, from bitter experience, that the cabaret scene could be s short term proposition; but at least I would not have to move to Stockport, I could commute from Windsor.

"Well John I will be perfectly frank. Because of our recent problems, yours and mine, maybe it was fate as well as Leon Fisk and Chic Murphy that has thrown us together. It seems to me we need each other."

John nodded his agreement.

"You need a Licence and I need a job, it's as simple as that".

"That is absolutely correct," said John.

I continued by adding the fact that as Licensee I would have to be on the premises anyway and John assured me that a General Manager was needed in any case. We agreed terms and although my salary was above the going rate for a club G.M. I knew that both my employer and I needed to make a fast buck. He wanted to retrieve his money and I wanted to get back on my feet. We shook hands and the deal was done. I went before the Magistrates the following Thursday and secured the Licence and returned to Cesars Palace to take up the management of the magnificent cabaret club. The wheel had turned a complete circle. I was back.

I called Dougie Flood at Stockport, told him of my decision and thanked him for his offer. I knew that Quaffers not Cesars should have been my destination as it offered a more long term solution to my problems, but the upheaval of moving North and the fact that despite my acceptance that Disco had replaced live cabaret, I still found it difficult to contemplate a career in Discothèques. It was just not my scene.

Everyone expected me to take Cesars back to its former glory but it would have been a mammoth task, (for a dinosaur), I just felt I could get her up and running and make money for a year or two. As I walked through the auditorium memories echoed from the walls in welcome; if the walls could talk they would tell a tale or two of triumphs and disasters. However, before the nostalgia comes the hard work.

As General Manager I was given carte blanche to reorganise the club and it did not take me long to realise that there were far too many people drawing wages but making little contribution. The club was after all only a two night operation as far as performances were concerned and seven days and evenings of reception duties for bookings, ticket sales and reservations. I worked closely with John's associate, Bobby Ball and made sure he agreed. I was able to carry him with me and in so doing gained John's approval for my restructuring plans.

The pruning of staff made massive savings on our overheads which now had to contend with the added weight of my (huge) salary. I booked the artistes, mainly through Jimmy Smith, and I manned the phones six evenings a week and promoted the business most days. I felt obliged to justify my salary and immersed myself in every aspect of running the club.

The best way to describe my entertainment programme is probably, 'Old ones, new ones, loved ones and neglected ones'. Cannon and Ball, Duncan Norvelle, The Platters, Mary Wilson's Supremes, Lennie Peters and Mike Reid were just a few of the artistes lined up to appear at the new Cesars. I scored notable successes with the Irish group The Commitments and a great success with Billy Connelly. That'll be the Day the Rock and Roll Laughter show, Hale and Pace and various Tribute shows, look-alike, sound alike combinations also did very well.

The sounds of the sixties show also featured regularly on our programme, the evergreen music from that era was always guaranteed to pull a crowd. I also used 'Blue', Bob Herbert's new boy band; Blue were ultra modern and performed their own material. I shared the audience's view that they lacked star quality; I felt they were going nowhere.

This programme of entertainment helped reestablish the club, as local support had been alienated by desperately bad management and the reputation of Cesars had reached rock bottom. My arrival helped the revival and many thanks must go to my old pal Eric Harris, who wrote for the Herald and Post, the local newspaper and who gave me some great coverage at this time.

I discovered that John Blower had an amazing connection with Ritz records through its owner Mick Clerkin. John and Mick were very close friends, but more importantly, Mick's record company controlled some of the biggest names in Irish music, including Daniel O'Donnell. Daniel had a huge following throughout the U.K. On my return to Cesars I discovered that a six-night appearance had been arranged for Daniel, this was great news and very important as, handled correctly, I knew that six nights full of satisfied punters could do the club nothing but good. Between 7000 and 8000 people could be walking, talking adverts for our renewed operation. Word of mouth was still the best advert of any successful business and Daniel's appearance offered a great opportunity to lift the club's reputation a notch or two.

The Daniel O'Donnell week did indeed kick start a very good year in which I renewed contact with many of the artistes and stars I had associated with for such a long time. Without exception everybody seemed genuinely pleased to see me back in the business. Usually trading just two days a week we often enjoyed near capacity audiences for our offerings and John seemed more than pleased with the performance of the business. I was under no illusions however, that nothing had changed and that beneath the surface the continuing problems of recession and unemployment still represented a threat to what was left of our industry.

Cesars was a leasehold property with the freehold owned by Ladbrokes and I have to say that I never felt secure back at the Palace. Yes, we enjoyed a honeymoon period, but even trading well there was no way John was going to be able to cope with the overheads and running costs long term. I was also well aware that if John recovered his original investment i.e. the Clive Rees loan, he would probably walk away. Nevertheless, the year at Cesars was good for me. Financially, it enabled me to get back on my feet, and it helped restore my self-confidence and my self-respect, both of which had taken a hammering.

My mortgage repayments had fallen so badly behind that there was no possibility of keeping our home at Windsor; nor did we wish to. The house had become a burden and frankly, luxuries had given way to essentials. An added problem was that the housing market had remained flat and there were no takers, in fact not even viewers at that time. Failure to sell resulted in the eventual repossession of our home by the Halifax and the last piece of a glorious era disappeared. Pam and I rented a basement flat in Dunstable. The apartment was very small. In fact I'd seen cardboard boxes larger than our lounge.

"Compact and Bijou is the word you're looking for." stated Roddy Miles, my stand in compere at Cesars.

I was describing our accommodation in a 'how the mighty hath fallen' type conversation.

"It's so small Roddy, that in the bedroom, you can turn off the light and be in bed before it gets dark. I was watching the film Zulu the other afternoon" I continued "and because the lounge is so small I was so near the action I nearly got shot twice".

Roddy still lived in South Wales but stayed in a small boarding house at Dunstable when working at Cesars. He smiled at my description of our accommodation, thought for a moment and then replied.

"If you think your place is bad, you should see where I stay. I found a dead flea in my bed last week".

"A dead flea can do you no harm" I interrupted.

"I know that" he said. "But 20,000 other fleas came to the funeral".

During this year of revival, I was able to take stock of my situation and be on the lookout for alternative employment for when the present one came to an end, as I knew it would. Bob Wheatly rang me at the club one day, quite out of the blue. He had also crashed out of the business and lost everything.

"I was pleased to hear you are back at Cesars" he said "and I wondered of there was any employment for me there"

"Well not at the moment" I said surprised by the enquiry. "I run a very tight ship here Bob, most of the staff do double duties, its the only way to survive in these difficult times, as you know."

"I understand George" replied Bob, "but if anything does come up keep me in mind, I'll clean toilets or do anything".

On hearing this I severely rebuked him. "I never ever want to hear you say that again, remember who you are. You just don't lower yourself to clean toilets.

"You were quoted as saying, 'if push comes to shove, you'd go to the West End and wash dishes for a living' " Bob pointed out.

"That's true" I replied. "But anonymously. I would do anything to make a living, but only in the West End where no one would know who I was or where I came from. That way I'd keep my dignity and self respect".

"I see what you mean," said Bob reflectively.

"There is nothing wrong in cleaning toilets if you have to, but do it somewhere and for someone who does not know who Bob Wheatly is" I concluded.

We had dinner together shortly after that conversation and I underlined the points already made. I went on to point out that a man of his knowledge and experience would surely find a niche. I am pleased to say Bob did land a very good position with a company in the entertainment business and rang me to tell me. The last I heard he was comfortable and doing well. Meantime my friends Barry and Michael from Leicester, who had also suffered something of a battering, but were up and running at the Stardust again via another company were looking for an opportunity to try their luck elsewhere.

Like many in our industry, they had given up on being able to earn a decent living in the U.K and felt that a business abroad might be the answer. They were both impressed with Cyprus when we visited it back in January 1993 and had been back to the Island on a number of occasions. The three of us discussed the idea of a showroom in Cyprus that would cater for tourists and Cypriots alike. For obvious reasons I was unable to contribute to the financing of the Cypriot project, but my experience and knowledge of the language was deemed an asset. Barry was able to raise sufficient funds to rent premises which could be redesigned and refurbished as an international showroom.

I had been managing Cesars for about a year and despite one or two notable successes and a reasonable Christmas season the signs of decline began to reappear. Our programme had begun to be repetitive and with the continuing recession it was clear that audiences were becoming more and more difficult to come by. After discussing matters with John, who was aware of the Cyprus project, I departed, having fulfilled my twelve-month contract. I left my former Savvas' club assistant, Steve Austwick to manage the club and agreed to return to Luton from time to time to arrange the entertainment and attend to any other matters on behalf of John Blower. This loose relationship also came to an end a few months later as Steve Austwick proved quite capable of booking the cabaret and carrying out all other duties required to run a major cabaret club.

John Blower visited Cyprus with his wife Sandra for a short stay and our friendship continues to this day. Cesars Palace was eventually bought out and its cabaret mode immediately dropped. I don't know if John managed to get his investment back in its entirety and probably never will; it's none of my business. I only know that our year together was a good one and that working for him was a joy. Also to his eternal credit, if a department needed assistance, his jacket came off, his sleeves were rolled up and he got stuck in with the rest of us.

After renting accommodation on Cyprus, Pam and I became resident and Barry, Michael and I set about putting the finishing touches to the premises Barry had rented at Amathus, just outside Limassol. The seven hundred-seater auditorium came with ample parking and a house in which Barry and Michael set up their Cyprus home.

After completing the refurbishment a show was produced which included half a dozen dancers, Antonio Zambardi a specialty act and comedian and a very good male vocalist named Andy Paul, a Greek Cypriot who came fourth when representing Cyprus in the Eurovision Song Contest.

In addition, a group of musicians were engaged to provide music for both the early tourist dinner show and Bazouki music for the late night Greek cocktail show.

We opened in August but it soon became clear that there would not be enough business to sustain it. Cyprus had its own problems with recession due to a shrinking tourist market as holidaymakers from other countries in recession could not afford to visit. Barry's brilliant idea never got off the ground and to cut further losses the operation closed. Barry and Michael returned to Leicester. Pam and I remained in Cyprus.

I suppose it would be fair to say that we had reached rock bottom. To be broke anywhere would have been bad enough, but to be broke two thousand miles from home was infinitely worse. However, this period of time in Cyprus became one of the happiest periods of our life, Pam and I, free of the pressures of business, enjoyed a time of peace and tranquility. We may have had little, but we had our home, our memories and each other. We still look back to that brief period and recall how content we were.

I took a job as a waiter for a while; this paid the princely sum of £10 per session plus a share of the gratuities. The only problem was that both the wages and tips were paid on a monthly basis and it was beneath my dignity to ask for a sub. Towards the end of the first month we were down to our last few cents. I recall a moment one particular day when we had to make a decision of great importance; should we buy an ice cream or a newspaper, we could not afford both. At the end of the month I got paid and we knew that with careful budgeting, we could live, frugally but reasonably comfortably. I knew however, that I had to continue to be on the lookout for any opportunity to better my position.

One particularly hot afternoon, I was walking the dog prior to my departure for the restaurant for another daily installment of Savva the waiter. As I walked along the dusty unmade road which ran near our home, I reflected on my life so far. A shamal breeze fanned the white dust sending little swirls ahead of me as I walked. The shamal is the wind that flows across the Mediterranean from the deserts of North Africa. I must have cut a lonely figure that hot afternoon, a man who had walked with the Stars walking alone. I wondered whether fate, which had held my hand so many times over the years, had finally given up on me. I remembered reading that in olden times, before Christ; prophets and holy men were sent into the wilderness by God to be cleansed. When they had learnt that it could be more painful to live than to die they were deemed ready to carry out their Master's work. I can report that I encountered no burning bush and received no heavenly sign. However, having returned home from my lengthy safari with my dog, the phone rang.

David Lewis, my Son in Law from Wales, seemed to have been monitoring our situation for some time and knew that I had slipped into my 1956 waitering mode; I suppose it did not take a genius to work out that things were not altogether good. The end of the tourist season loomed and in another month or possibly two, the Island would close down for the winter. David's timing was as good as Monkhouse, Dawson or Cooper.

"How's things then" he asked.

"Oh OK" I replied. "I'm working at the moment, although the season is drawing to an end".

"How's the season been, has it been a good one, or has the recession had an effect on it; it affected Spain you know"

"And Cyprus" was my immediate reply. "Numbers were well down on previous years, but there was enough to get a living"

Following some additional chat about this and that, mainly family matters, he suddenly came to the point of his phone call. Catching me totally by surprise he said.

"Have you ever heard of the Maes Manor Hotel?"

"Yes I have" I said. "I think it's in the Valleys somewhere."

"That's right," said David. "In fact it's at Blackwood in Gwent".

David went on to tell me how like many Hotels and Inns, the Maes Manor had suffered the effects of the recession and was barely hanging on financially.

"I've looked at it as a possible new home for Jayne and me but to be honest it's too big. I can however buy it and I think if a few quid is spent on it and with the right person in charge, it could turn out to be a good business". He paused and then asked, "How do you fancy running it."

Before I had a chance to answer he went on to say that he would only buy the Maes if I'd come and run it. I answered without hesitation that I would be delighted to manage the Hotel and I agreed to fly to Wales and take a look at it, and if I felt that it was worth having a go, Dave would close the deal on it. I arrived back in the UK on a cold but sunny October morning and was driven straight to the Maes Manor to make my assessment. Dave's view was that with Christmas only a couple of month's away, if the deal was to be done, the sooner the better.

"I'm sure with your experience we can get some mileage out of the place over the festive season" he suggested. "So it's up to you."

I am still unaware how much Dave knew of my situation or that his offer was a lifeline to me. As we traveled down the M4 to Wales, my mind raced; in my present situation, there was no way I could pass up this opportunity. I had already made up my mind that even if the Maes turned out to be a broken down cowshed with a one legged doorman, a barman who watered down the drinks and stole the takings and a chef whose basic training was done in the soup kitchens of Cambodia, I would give the Hotel the thumbs up and praise its amazing potential.

The impressive tree lined drive of the Maes and the beautiful old Manor House itself, was an incredible sight. I was astounded that such a magnificent place existed in a major coal mining area; it must have been surrounded by collieries. The coal industry in Wales was all but gone now and with its departure the valley had been returned to its original beauty. Gone were the black slag heaps that were once such a feature of this area. On all sides now are green and pleasant mountains, cool clear streams and forests of lofty pines and in the middle of all this, the magnificent Maes Manor Hotel.

Needless to say, the deal was done before much more water had passed under the bridge and I was installed as General Manager with a brief to revive the flagging business. David set about refurbishing the Hotel and carried out renovations with devastating speed. On my advice, the hotel ballroom was the first area to be renovated and by using his own men and resources he completely transformed the two hundred seater room almost overnight. I saw massive potential in extending our dinner dance capacity, especially during the Christmas season, which loomed high on the horizon.

There were of people who were sceptical of our chances of success. Comments like, 'It's been a white elephant for years' or 'you will never make it pay' were plentiful and I vividly remember my first day in charge. We were not lucky enough to have a guest staying that day, the restaurant did not serve a meal and I managed to serve one drink all day to a gentleman who was lost and had dropped in to ask his way to somewhere. Being new to the area I was unable to help. Resigned to his fate, the gent bought a drink. This meant that our gross takings for that day were £1.50.

Dave phoned that evening and I reported the day's activities and concluded with the financial report.

"Oh well" he replied on hearing the news, "at least there is only one-way to go and that's up".

I surprised even myself with the effort I put in to the launch of the business and of making a success of the Hotel. Calling on all my reserves I worked night and day, transforming the operation into a stylish but affordable place to go and be seen at. I set about making the Maes the centre for all occasions large and small.

I surrounded myself with tried and tested people who had worked with me before, at Usk. Gareth Hunt became my assistant and Marilyn Strangemore my personal secretary and receptionist. Pam featured in the equation, making the comfort of guests a top priority from arrival to departure and together with Jayne our daughter, she carefully selected furnishings and colour coded, room by room as David continued the renovations.

Just before Christmas I received a surprise visit from Ramon Gomez, arguably the finest Maitre'D in Wales. Ramon worked at the Three Salmons Hotel in Usk and had done so for at least twenty years, but the hotel group of which the Salmons was a part had gone into receivership and the Official Receiver broke up the group of hotels, to sell them off. The Salmons sold to a man called Burke, who had made a fortune in Rubber!! The upshot was that Ramon and Mr. Burke did not hit it off and Ramon wanted out and on hearing of my arrival at the Maes he hot footed it up to Blackwood and offered me his services as Maitre D Hotel. We agreed terms, shook hands and Ramon joined my team.

Known throughout the length and breadth of the Principality because of my years at Usk, I turned my attention to ensuring that everyone knew I was back and ready to offer quality, style, ambience and above all value for money in a first class hotel. To this end the local media were very obliging and using the best traditions of my show biz past, I made an entrance one more time; the stage was set and the players in place.

The Hotel had always enjoyed a good wedding trade; in fact it was the large number of wedding functions that had kept the previous owners in business. I managed to increase the number of functions still further as weddings, dinner dances, exhibitions and conferences, all seemed to enjoy my hands on style and the renewed facilities. As in the past, I moved quickly to secure as much corporate business as possible and once again success followed. Our twenty-eight rooms reached maximum occupancy; my previous experience of getting 'bums on seats' stood me in good stead by getting 'heads on pillows'.

I could not contemplate our beautifully refurbished ballroom standing empty or unused on any Friday or Saturday evening so on rare occasions when a private function was not forthcoming, I created my own by staging a cabaret evening. This was to be the icing on the cake as it were. Evenings of Disco with our resident D.J. Steve Alderson and a local band were a major hit, but in addition, a full blown Dinner Dance and Cabaret evening also received great support. After all such nights were hard to come by since the collapse of Club land and I was experienced enough to know that an occasional cabaret evening could still command great support. The key was not to overdo them.

I began playing great family favourites such as The Barron Knights, The Rockinberries, Dave Berry and the Cruisers and a whole bevy of look-alike artistes. This type of cabaret had become very popular. I guess it meant that punters could see star favourites without having to cough up exorbitant ticket prices. At the Maes; Dinner, Dancing and Tina Turner for £17.50 was excellent value for money.

Fraser Lawson provided my resident band and became my booking agent. He helped put together some excellent nights on behalf of the Hotel; Jimmy Smith continued to book some of our star cabaret attractions when required.

Other notable triumphs included appearances by Iris Williams, Joe Pasquale, Danny La Rue, Vince Hill and The Beverley Sisters. My confidence restored, my dignity renewed, I once again felt like a panjandrum of my profession. I found time for everyone and succeeded in providing the very best for our public. My fame went before me and I felt proud to be back and in charge of my destiny once more.

To my friends: Eddie and Sandra Heywood, Clive and Iris Williams, Jim Davidson. Jimmy and Jackie Smith and Ken and Ginette Parslow, I offer my grateful thanks for their support that never wavered through the period from 1992 to 1994 and of course my very special thanks to Chic and Tracy Murphy and Bob and Anne Herbert. I had known Chic and Bob over a long and important time in my life and could truly count on them when situations arose that needed the best possible advice to resolve them. At all times they were there for me and in my corner.

I was delighted when I received the news that Chic and Bob had collaborated in putting together another band. Bob's band 'Blue' had not delivered and Chic no longer managed the Three Degrees. I suspect that both the guys had good reasons to cast their nets in fresh waters. An advert in the Stage and a series of auditions produced a five-girl band.

There are differing versions of what happened next, but the five girl band, as yet unnamed, suddenly left the fold, opting to sign up with Simon Fuller. Simon named them the Spice Girls and the rest is history. The jinx had struck and Bob was sidelined once again.

To David Lewis I owe a huge debt of gratitude for throwing me the lifeline that enabled me to climb back to a decent life. I was delighted to have repaid some that debt by providing him with success at the Maes. As the Maes Manor passed the One Million mark annual turnover I thought, where are the 'Doubting Thomas's' that said the Maes would never work.

I feel very, very lucky to have done the things that I have done and to have met so many great personalities and to have grown up in the world of show business along side many of today's stars. My thirty or so years in showbiz were the most wonderful years of my life and despite the setbacks I feel privileged to have travelled such a star-studded road. Although the era has passed I feel honoured to have been part of the cabaret scene of the 60's, 70's and 80's; undoubtedly the best years of the business.

Paul Anka wrote 'My Way' and the song became a massive hit worldwide for Frank Sinatra. It was so popular when it first topped the charts, that for months, in fact a couple of years, it seemed that every vocalist male and female alike, ended their show with their rendition of it. The show ending number was performed week after week at the end of show after show throughout club land until inevitably; the much-performed number became the basis of a classic gag.

The story goes: Frank Sinatra was engaged to appear at Batley Variety Club in the north of England as a date on his European tour. On the night in question he arrived at the club from Berlin, but his orchestra, flying in separately, was unavoidably delayed by a sudden bout of fog.

"I can't go on," said Frank to Jimmy Corrigan, Batley's owner. "I don't have my orchestra".

"But Frank you have to" replied the distraught Corrigan. "I have sixteen hundred people out front that have paid top money to see you. I can't let them down. I'll be lynched".

"How can I perform without an orchestra?" insisted Sinatra.

"Well" said Corrigan with an air of triumph "why not use our in house musicians, Burt and Arthur Batley's very own organ and drums duo".

"I can't believe you are serious" said Sinatra. "You're asking me to go on with a non reading club duo?"

"Why not?" said Corrigan "The show must go on and the boys, who admittedly play by ear, are very experienced".

After a lot of pleading and more than a little soul searching an agreement was reached and Burt and Arthur were asked to join Frank Sinatra in his dressing room for a pre-show 'talk through'.

"Evening Mr. Sinatra" said the two Yorkshire musicians on entering the star's dressing room.

"Hi Guys," replied the sceptical star as he passed to the ageing muso's the running order.

Flicking through the pages, Burt said to Arthur. "Chicago O.K. Arthur?"

"Yes" replied Arthur.

"Lady is a Tramp alright?" asked Arthur. "Yes fine" said Burt.

And so the conversation went on. Number after number, the old guys seemed to recognise them all. Turning to the final sheet, both of them looked at each other, gasped slightly and in unison cried "Oh no, not bloody My Way again".

Why should I be any different to all those that have gone before me. I was there and saw the rise and rise of the classic song! I was part of the rise and decline of the great British Cabaret Club Circuit. So I feel almost entitled to use some of those great lyrics as an ending to my story.

'For what is a man, what has he got, if not himself then he has naught, to say the words he truly feels and not the words of one who kneels, the record shows I took the blows and did it;
My Way'